BURT FRANKLIN: RESEARCH & SOURCE WORKS SERIES 595
American Classics in History & Social Science 157

THE CORRESPONDENCE AND PUBLIC PAPERS

OF

JOHN JAY

VOL. IV

1794–1826

THE CORRESPONDENCE AND PUBLIC PAPERS

OF

JOHN JAY

FIRST CHIEF-JUSTICE OF THE UNITED STATES, MEMBER AND PRESIDENT OF THE
CONTINENTAL CONGRESS, MINISTER TO SPAIN, MEMBER OF COMMISSION
TO NEGOTIATE TREATY OF INDEPENDENCE, ENVOY TO GREAT
BRITAIN, GOVERNOR OF NEW YORK, ETC.

1794-1826

EDITED BY

HENRY P. JOHNSTON, A.M.

VOL. IV

BURT FRANKLIN
NEW YORK

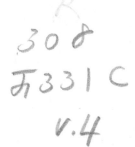

Published by LENOX HILL Pub. & Dist. Co. (Burt Franklin)
235 East 44th St., New York, N.Y. 10017
Originally Published: 1890
Reprinted: 1970
Printed in the U.S.A.

S.B.N.: 8337-18479
Library of Congress Card Catalog No.: 73-140983
Burt Franklin: Research and Source Works Series 595
American Classics in History and Social Science 157

Reprinted from the original edition in the University of Illinois
Library at Urbana.

CONTENTS OF VOLUME IV.

1794.

ADDITIONAL PAPERS.

CORRESPONDENCE AND PUBLIC PAPERS

OF

JOHN JAY.

———

JAY TO DUGALD STEWART.[1]

NEW YORK, 20th March, 1794.

SIR :

Accept my thanks for the ingenious work which you were so obliging as to send me by Mr. Childs. I have read it with pleasure and improvement ; it casts new light on several interesting questions, and I observe in it a degree of perspicuity not always to be found in dissertations on such subjects.

The connection between mind and body, and the operations of the former on and through the latter, continue involved in great obscurity. Persevering attention and inquiry will probably produce further information. The spiritual and material worlds, if I may use the expression, appear to me to be so widely different and opposite, that I am often inclined to suspect the existence of others, intermediate, but of a nature distinct from either.

It is much to be wished that nothing may occur to prevent your finishing the analysis of the intellectual

---

[1] Professor of Moral Philosophy in the University of Edinburgh.

VOL. IV.—1

powers, and extending your speculations to man considered as an active and moral being, and as the member of a political society. There is reason to doubt whether this field of science has, as yet, received the highest cultivation of which it is capable. The republic of letters is under many obligations to your country. May those obligations be increased.

I have the honour to be, with sentiments of respect and esteem, sir,

Your most obedient and very humble servant,

JOHN JAY.

JAY TO MRS. JAY.[1]

PHILADELPHIA, 9th April, 1794.

.   .   .   .

I arrived here on Monday evening; and yesterday dined with the President. The question of war or peace seems to be as much in suspense here as in New York when I left you. I am rather inclined to think that peace will continue, but should not be surprised if war should take place. In the present state of things, it will be best to be ready for the *latter* event in *every* respect.

---

[1] From this point, for about a year, the correspondence chiefly concerns the "Jay Treaty" of 1794. The threatening complications arising from the Revolution in France, and the divided sympathies of the American people, determined Washington to follow up his proclamation of neutrality with a special effort to avert war with Great Britain whose presumption and aggressions had become exasperating. The delicate mission was entrusted to Jay as Envoy Extraordinary, and in the following letters and documents the course of his negotiations may be traced to their successful issue. See Jay's "Life of Jay," vol. i., pp. 301–367, and Pellew's "Jay," pp. 294–317.

10th April, 1794.

.   .   .   .   .

The aspect of the times is such, that prudential arrangements calculated on the prospect of war should not be neglected, nor too long postponed.   Peace or war appears to me a question which cannot be solved. Unless things should take a turn in the meantime, I think it will be best on my return to push our affairs at Bedford briskly.   There is much irritation and agitation in this town, and in Congress.   Great Britain has acted unwisely and unjustly ; and there is some danger of our acting intemperately.

.   .   .   .

JAY TO MRS. JAY.

PHILADELPHIA, 15th April, 1794.

My Dear Sally :

I was this evening favoured with yours of the 14th. It is now between eight and nine o'clock, and I am just returned from court.   I expect, my dear Sally, to see you sooner than we expected.   There is here a serious determination to send me to England, if possible to avert a war.   The object is so interesting to our country, and the combination of circumstances such, that I find myself in a dilemma between personal considerations and public ones.   Nothing can be much more distant from every wish on my own account.   I feel the impulse of duty strongly, and it is probable that if, on the investigation I am now making, my mind should be convinced that it is my duty to go, you will join with me in thinking that, on an occasion so important, I ought to follow its dictates, and commit myself to the care and kindness of that Providence in which we have both the highest reason to repose the most absolute confidence. This is not of my seeking; on the contrary, I regard it as a measure not to be desired, but to be submitted to.

A thousand reflections crowd into my mind, and a thousand emotions into my heart.   I must remember my motto, "*Deo duce perseverandum.*" The knowledge I have of your sentiments on these subjects affords me consolation.

If the nomination should take place, it will be in the course of a few days, and then it will appear in the papers; in the meantime say nothing on the subject, for it is not impossible that the business may take another turn, though I confess I do not expect it will.

My dear, dear Sally, this letter will make you as grave as I am myself; but when we consider how many reasons we have for resignation and acquiescence, I flatter myself that we both shall become composed.

If it should please God to make me instrumental to the continuance of peace, and in preventing the effusion of blood, and other evils and miseries incident to war, we shall both have reason to rejoice. Whatever may be the event, the endeavour will be virtuous, and consequently consolatory.   Let us repose unlimited trust in our Maker; it is our business to adore and to obey. My love to the children.

With very sincere and tender affection,

I am, my dear Sally, ever yours,

JOHN JAY.

P.S.—It is supposed that the object of my mission may be completed in time to return in the fall.

JAY TO MRS. JAY.

PHILADELPHIA, 19th April, 1794.

MY DEAR SALLY :

I refer you to the two last letters which I wrote to you this week. It was expected that the Senate would yesterday have decided on the nomination of an *envoy* to the court of London, but measures re specting the embargo occupied them through the day. To-day *that* business is to be resumed, and you shall have the earliest notice of the result. So far as I am personally concerned, my feelings are very, very far from exciting wishes for its taking place. No appointment ever operated more un- pleasantly upon me ; but the public considerations which were urged, and the manner in which it was pressed, strongly impressed me with a conviction that to refuse it would be to desert my duty for the sake of my ease and domestic concerns and comforts. I .derive some consolation from the prospect that my absence will not be of long continuance, and that the same Providence which has hitherto preserved me will still be pleased to accompany and restore me to you and our dear little family.

The court has unceasingly engrossed my time. We did not adjourn until nine last night. I feel fatigued in body and mind. But reflections of this kind are not to be indulged. I must endeavour to sustain with propriety the part assigned me, and meet with composure and fortitude whatever disagreeable events may occur to counteract my wishes or increase my task. I shall have *rest* in time, and for *that rest* I will not cease to prepare. I am very anxious to be with you ; and the moment the preparatory measures here will permit, I shall set out.

My love to the children ; and believe me to be unalterably and affectionately yours,

JOHN JAY.

PRESIDENT WASHINGTON TO JAY.

To JOHN JAY, GREETING:

Reposing especial trust and confidence in your integrity, prudence, and ability, I have nominated, and, by and with the advice and consent of the Senate, do appoint, you, the said John Jay, Envoy Extraordinary from the United States of America to the Court of His Britannic Majesty, authorizing you hereby to do and perform all such matters and things as to the said place or office doth appertain, or as may be duly given you in charge hereafter, and the said office to hold and exercise during the pleasure of the President of the United States for the time being.

In testimony whereof, I have caused the seal of the United States to be hereunto affixed. Given under my hand, at the city of Philadelphia, the nineteenth day of April in the year of our Lord one thousand seven

L. S. hundred and ninety-four, and of the independence of the United States of America, the eighteenth.

GO. WASHINGTON.

By the President :

EDM. RANDOLPH, Secretary of State.

JAY TO MRS. JAY.

Sunday Evening, 20th April, 1794.

MY DEAR SALLY :

I this moment received yours by General Schuyler. As yet I have not seen him. It found me alone, and not a little pensive. Your own feelings will best suggest an idea of mine. God's will be done ; to him I resign—in him I confide ; do the like. Any other philosophy applicable to this occasion is delusive. Away with it. Your indisposition affects me. Resist despondency ; hope for the best.

Yesterday the Senate approved of the nomination by a great majority. Mr. Burr was among the few who opposed it. I have hopes that our friend, Mr. Trumbull, will consent to go as secretary. To-morrow the preparations for despatching me will begin. When they will be completed, so as to admit of my leaving this place, I cannot yet decide. I am exceedingly impatient to set out for New York.

God bless and preserve you all. Be assured that I shall never cease to be, my dear Sally,

Your very affectionate husband,

JOHN JAY.

MRS. JAY TO JAY.

New York, 22d April, 1794.

My Dear Mr. Jay :

Yesterday I received your two kind letters of Saturday and Sunday. I do indeed judge of your feelings by my own, and for that reason forebore writing while under the first impression of surprise and grief.

Your superiority in fortitude, as well as every other virtue, I am aware of ; yet I know too well your tenderness for your family to doubt the pangs of separation. Your own conflicts are sufficient ; they need not be augmented by the addition of mine. Never was I more sensible of the absolute ascendency you have over my heart. When, almost in despair, I renounced the hope of domestic bliss, your image in my breast seemed to upbraid me with adding to your trials. That idea alone roused me from my despondency. I resumed the charge of my family, and even dare hope that, by your example, I shall be enabled to look up to that Divine Protector from whom we have indeed experienced the most merciful guardianship.

The children continue well. They were exceedingly affected when they received the tidings, and entreated me to endeavour to dissuade you from accepting an appointment that subjects us to so painful a separation.

Farewell, my best beloved.

Your wife till death,

And after that a ministering spirit.

PRESIDENT WASHINGTON TO JAY.

[SECRET AND CONFIDENTIAL.]

Philadelphia, 29 April, 1794.

My Dear Sir :

Receive, I pray you, the suggestion I am going to impart, with the friendship and caution the delicacy of it requires.

You are already informed, that I am under the necessity

of recalling Mr. Gouverneur Morris from France, and you can readily conceive the difficulty which occurs in finding a successor, that would be agreeable to that nation, and who, at the same time, would meet the approbation of the friends of that country in this.

These considerations have induced me to ask you, if it could be made to comport with your inclination, after you shall have finished your business as envoy, and not before, to become the resident minister plenipotentiary at London, that Mr. Pinckney, by that means, might be sent to Paris? I mean no more, than simply to ask the question, not intending, although the measure would remove the above difficulty, to press it in the smallest degree.

If you answer in the affirmative, be so good as to return the enclosed letter to me, and correspondent arrangements shall be made. If in the negative, I pray you to forward it through the penny post, or otherwise, according to circumstances, to the gentleman to whom it is directed without delay; and, in either case, to let the transaction be confined entirely to ourselves.[1] With much truth and regard, I am sincerely and affectionately yours,

Go : WASHINGTON.

JAY TO PRESIDENT WASHINGTON.

NEW YORK, 30th April, 1794.

DEAR SIR :

I was this day honoured with yours of yesterday. There is nothing I more ardently wish for than retirement and leisure to attend to my books and papers; but parental duties not permitting it, I must acquiesce and thank God for the many blessings I enjoy. If the judiciary was on its proper footing,

---

[1] The gentleman referred to was Robert R. Livingston, but neither he nor Jay, as appears in the letter following, accepted the proffered missions, and Monroe was sent to France.—Sparks' "Washington," vol. x., pp. 404–6.

there is not a public station that I should prefer to the one in which you have placed me. It accords with my turn of mind, my education, and my habits.

I expect to sail in the course of a fortnight, and, if my prayers and endeavours avail, my absence will not be of long duration. The gentleman to whom your letter is addressed is not in town. To obviate delay and accidents, I sent it to his brother, who will doubtless forward it immediately, either by a direct conveyance or by the post.

From the confidence you repose in me, I derive the most pleasing emotions, and I thank you for them. Life is uncertain. Whether I take your letter with me, or leave it here, it would, in case of my death, be inspected by others, who, however virtuous, might be indiscreet. After much reflection, I conclude it will be most prudent to commit it to you, without retaining any copy or memorandum, except in my memory, where the numerous proofs of your kind attention to me are carefully preserved.

With perfect respect, esteem, and attachment, I am, dear sir,

>Your obliged and affectionate servant.
>JÓHN JAY.

INSTRUCTIONS TO JAY AS ENVOY EXTRAORDINARY.

PHILADELPHIA, May 6, 1794.

SIR:

The mission upon which you are about to enter, as Envoy Extraordinary to the Court of London, has been dictated by considerations of an interesting and pressing nature.

You will doubtless avail yourself of these to convince Mr. Pinckney, our Minister in Ordinary there, of the necessity of this measure, and will thus prevent any wound to his sensibility. He may be assured that it is the impression, which will naturally accompany this demonstration of the public sentiment, and not the smallest abatement of confidence in him, which has recommended a special appointment ; nor will any of his usual functions be suspended, except so far as they may be embraced in the present commission. It would be unnecessary to add, but for the sake of manifesting this fact, and removing difficulties which may arise in your own breast, that you will communicate with him without reserve.

A full persuasion is entertained that, throughout the whole negotiation, you will make the following its general objects : To keep alive in the mind of the British Minister that opinion which the solemnity of a special mission must naturally inspire, of the strong agitations excited in the people of the United States, by the disturbed condition of things between them and Great Britain ; to repel war, for which we are not disposed, and into which the necessity of vindicating our honor and our property may, but can alone, drive us ; to prevent the British ministry, should they be resolved on war, from carrying with them the British nation ; and, at the same time, to assert, with dignity and firmness, our rights, and our title to reparation for past injuries.

I. One of the causes of your mission being the vexations and spoliations committed on our commerce by the authority of instructions from the British Government, you will receive from the Secretary of State the following documents, viz : the instructions of the 8th of June, 1793, 6th of November, 1793, and 8th of January 1794 ; the Secretary of State's letter to Mr. Pinckney, on September 7th, 1793 ; Mr. Hammond's letter to the Secretary of State, on 12th of

September, 1793; Mr. Pinckney's note and memorial to Lord Grenville; Mr. Hammond's second letter to the Secretary of State, on the 11th of April, 1794; the Secretary of State's answer on the 1st inst.; a list and sketch of the cases upon which complaints have been made to our Government; and the instructions given to N. C. Higginson, who has been lately sent as agent to the British Islands in the West Indies.

These several papers develop the source of our discontent on this head; the representations which have been offered; the answers which have been rendered; and the situation of the business at this moment.

You will perceive that one of the principles, upon which compensation is demanded for the injuries under the instructions of the 8th of June, 1793, is, that provisions, except in the instance of a siege, blockade, or investment, are not to be ranked among contraband. To a country remote as the United States are from Europe and its troubles, it will be of infinite advantage to obtain the establishment of this doctrine.

Upon the instructions of the 6th of November, 1793, Mr. Pinckney has made a representation, and perhaps a memorial, to Lord Grenville; both of which you will procure of Mr. Pinckney. The matter of these instructions fills up the matter of depredation. They were unknown publicly in England until the 26th of December, 1793; there is good reason to suppose that they were communicated to the ships of war, before they were published, and that, in consequence of a private notification of them, a considerable number of new privateers were fitted out; the terms "legal adjudication," in spite of the explanation on the 8th of January, 1794, was most probably intended to be construed away or not, according to events; and many vessels have been condemned under them.

Compensation for all the injuries sustained, and captures,

will be strenuously pressed by you. The documents which the agent in the West Indies is directed to transmit to London will place these matters in the proper legal train, to be heard on appeal. It cannot be doubted that the British ministry will insist that, before we complain to them, their tribunals, in the last resort, must have refused justice. This is true in general; but peculiarities distinguish the present from past cases. Where the error complained of consists solely in the misapplication of the law, it may be corrected by a superior court; but where the error consists in the law itself, it can be corrected only by the law maker, who, in this instance, was the King, or it must be compensated by the Government. The principle, therefore, may be discussed and settled without delay; and, even if you should be told to wait until the result of the appeals shall appear, it may be safely said to be almost certain that some one judgment in the West Indies will be confirmed; and this will be sufficient to bring the principle in question with the British ministry.

Should the principle be adjusted, as we wish and have a right to expect, it may be advisable to employ some person to examine the proper offices in London, for such vessels as may have been originally tried or appealed upon, and finally condemned. You will also reserve an opportunity for new claims, of which we may all be ignorant for some time to come; and if you should be compelled to leave the business in its legal course, you are at liberty to procure professional aid at the expense of the United States.

Whenever matters shall be brought to such a point as that nothing remains for settlement but the items of compensation, this may be entrusted to any skilful and confidential person whom you may appoint.

You will mention, with due stress, the general irritation of the United States at the vexations, spoliations, captures, etc. And being on the field of negotiation you will be more able to judge, than can be prescribed now, how far you may state the difficulty which may occur in restraining the violence of some of our exasperated citizens.

If the British ministry should hint at any supposed predilection in the United States for the French nation, as warranting the whole or any part of these instructions, you will stop the progress of this subject, as being irrelative to the question in hand. It is a circumstance which the British nation have no right to object to us; because we are free in our affections and independent in our government. But it may be safely answered, upon the authority of the correspondence between the Secretary of State and Mr. Hammond, that our neutrality has been scrupulously observed.

II. A second cause of your mission, but not inferior in dignity to the preceding, though subsequent in order, is to draw to a conclusion all points of difference between the United States and Great Britain, concerning the treaty of peace.

You will therefore be furnished with copies of the negotiation upon the inexecution and infractions of that treaty and will resume that business. Except in this negotiation, you have been personally conversant with the whole of the transactions connected with the treaty of peace. You were a minister at its formation, the Secretary of Foreign Affairs when the sentiments of the Congress, under the confederation, were announced through your office ; and as Chief Justice you have been witness to what has passed in our courts, and know the real state of our laws, with respect to British debts. It will be superfluous, therefore, to add more to you, than to express a wish that these debts, and the interest claimed upon them, and all things relating to them, be put outright in a diplomatic discussion, as being certainly of a judicial nature, to be decided by our courts : and if this cannot be accomplished, that you support the doctrines of Government with arguments proper for the occasion, and with that attention to your former public opinions, which self-respect will justify, without relaxing the pretensions which have been hitherto maintained.

In this negotiation as to the treaty of peace, we have been amused by transferring the discussions concerning its inexecution and infractions from one side of the Atlantic to the other. In the meantime, one of the consequences of holding the posts has been much bloodshed on our frontiers by the Indians, and much expense. The British Government having denied their abetting of the Indians, we must of course acquit them. But we have satisfactory proofs, (some of which, however, cannot, as you will discover, be well used in public,) that British agents are guilty of stirring up, and assisting with arms, ammunition, and warlike implements, the different tribes of Indians against us. It is incumbent upon that Government to restrain those agents ; or the forbearance to restrain them cannot be interpretated otherwise than as a determination to countenance them. It is a principle from which the United States will not easily depart, either in their conduct towards other nations, or what they expect from them, that the Indians dwelling within the territories of the one shall not be interfered with by the other.

It may be observed here, as comprehending both of the foregoing points, that the United States testify their sincere love of peace, by being nearly in a state of war, and yet anxious to obviate absolute war by friendly advances ; and if the desire of Great Britain to be in harmony with the United States be equally sincere, she will readily discover what kind of sensations will at length arise when their trade is plundered, their resources wasted in an Indian war, many of their citizens exposed to the cruelties of the savages, their rights by treaty denied, and those of Great Britain enforced in our courts. But you will consider the inexecution and infraction of the treaty as standing on distinct grounds from the vexations and spoliations, so that no adjustment of the former is to be influenced by the latter.

III. It is referred to your discretion whether, in case the two preceding points should be so accommodated as to promise the continuance of tranquillity between the United States and Great Britain, the subject of a commercial treaty may not be listened to by you, or even broken to the British ministry. If it should, let these be the general objects:

1st. Reciprocity in navigation, particularly to the West Indies and even to the East Indies.

2d. The admission of wheat, fish, salt meat, and other great staples, upon the same footing with the admission of the great British staples in our ports.

3d. Free ships to make free goods.

4th. Proper security for the safety of neutral commerce in other respects; and particularly:

By declaring provisions never to be contraband, except in the strongest possible case, as the blockade of a port; or, if attainable, by abolishing contraband altogether;

By defining a blockade, if contraband must continue in some degree, as it is defined in the armed neutrality;

By restricting the opportunities of vexation in visiting vessels; and

By bringing under stricter management privateers; and expediting recoveries against them for misconduct.

5th. Exemption of emigrants, and particularly manufacturers, from restraint.

6th. Free exports of arms and military stores.

7th. The exclusion of the terms "the most favored nation," as being productive of embarrassment.

8th. The convoy of merchant ships by the public ships of war, where it shall be necessary, and they be holding the same course.

British West Indies in our own bottoms generally, or of certain defined burthens, the articles which, by act of Parliament, 28 Geo. III., c. 6, may be carried thither in British bottoms, and of bringing from thence, directly to the United States, in our bottoms, of like description, the articles which, by the same act, may be brought from thence to the United States in British bottoms, this would afford an acceptable basis of a treaty for a term not exceeding fifteen years ; and it would be advisable to conclude a treaty upon that basis. But such a treaty, instead of the usual clause concerning ratification, must contain the following : " This treaty shall be obligatory and conclusive, when the same shall be ratified by his Britannic Majesty of the one part, and by the President of the United States, by and with the advice and consent of the Senate, of the other."

But if a treaty of commerce cannot be formed upon a basis as advantageous as this, you are not to conclude or sign any such, it being conceived that it would not be expedient to do anything more than to digest with the British ministry the articles of such a treaty as they appear willing to accede to, referring them here for consideration and further instruction previous to a formal conclusion.

Some of the other points, which it would be interesting to comprehend in a treaty, may not be attended with difficulty. Among these is the admission of our commodities and manufactures generally into the British European dominions, upon a footing equally good with those of other foreign countries. At present certain enumerated articles only are admitted, and though the enumeration embraces all the articles which it is of present consequence to us to be able to export to those dominions, yet in process of time an extension of the objects may become of moment. The fixing of the privileges which we now enjoy in the British East Indies by toleration of the company's government, if any arrangement can be made with the consent of the company for that purpose, would be also a valuable ingredient.

V. You will have no difficulty in gaining access to the ministers of Russia, Denmark, and Sweden, at the Court of London. The principles of the armed neutrality would abundantly cover our neutral rights. If, therefore, the situation of things with respect to Great Britain should dictate the necessity of taking the precaution of foreign co-operation upon this head; if no prospect of accommodation should be thwarted by the danger of such a measure being known to the British Court; and if an entire view of all our political relations shall, in your judgment, permit the step, you will sound those ministers upon the probability of an alliance with their nations to support those principles.

However, there can be no risk in examining what can be concerted with Denmark and Sweden, or any other Power, against the Algerines. It may be represented to the British ministry how productive of perfect conciliation it might be to the people of the United States if Great Britain would use her influence with the Dey of Algiers for the liberation of the American citizens in captivity, and for a peace upon reasonable terms. It has been communicated from abroad, to be the fixed policy of Great Britain to check our trade in grain to the Mediterranean. This is too doubtful to be assumed, but fit for inquiry.

VI. Such are the outlines of the conduct which the President wishes you to pursue. He is aware that, at this distance, and during the present instability of public events, he cannot undertake to prescribe rules which shall be irrevocable. You will therefore consider the ideas herein expressed as amounting to recommendations only, which in your discretion you may modify as seems most beneficial to the United States, except in the two following cases, which are immutable. 1st. That, as the British ministry will doubtless be solicitous to detach us from France, and may probably make some overture of this kind, you will inform them that the Government of the United States will not derogate from our treaties and engagements with France, and that experience has shown that we can be honest in our duties to the British nation without laying ourselves under any particular restraints as to other nations; and 2d. That no treaty of commerce be concluded or signed contrary to the foregoing prohibition.

Besides the papers and documents mentioned in the former parts of these instructions, you have received your commission as Envoy Extraordinary; letters of credence to the King and Queen of England, the latter of which, being without superscription, you will address as may appear proper, and deliver it or not, as you find to be right on such occasions; four sets of powers, one general, comprehending all the points to be negotiated with Great Britain, the other three special, for each separate point, in order that you may be prepared to exhibit your authority altogether, or by detachment, as may be most convenient; copies of Lord Dorchester's speech to the Indians, the authenticity of which, though not absolutely ascertained, is believed; and of certain affidavits respecting the British interference with our Indians; and a cipher.

You are too well acquainted with the nature of the great functions which you are called to exercise to render it necessary for me to add the earnest wish of the President of the United States that your communications to the Secretary of State should be frequent and full, and that you should correspond with our ministers abroad upon any interesting occasion which may demand it. For the latter of these purposes you will avail yourself of Mr. Pinckney's ciphers.

Your expenses will be paid, together with the allowance of thirteen hundred and fifty dollars per annum for a secretary.

On your return, you will be pleased to deliver into the Secretary of State's office such papers as you may possess of importance sufficient to be filed there ; and will prepare a general report of all your transactions.

Not doubting that you will execute this trust in a manner honourable to yourself and salutary to the United States, I beg leave to offer to you my sincere wishes for your health and safe return.

EDMUND RANDOLPH, Secretary of State.

JAY TO MRS. JAY.

May 12, 1794.

. . . .

I have seen this day's newspapers, and the Philadelphia democratic resolutions published in them.[1] They give me no concern, and I hope they will be equally indifferent to you. The less you say on such subjects, the less you will flatter the importance of those who may not wish us well. We have the prospect of a good voyage, but it would be infinitely less disagreeable if it was towards, instead of being from,

---

[1] This was the date of Jay's sailing from New York for England. A large number of citizens collected at the Battery and cheered and fired a salute as his vessel passed out of the North River. The Tammany Society held its anniversary on the same evening and toasted his mission as well as success to the armies of France. The resolutions referred to in the letter were adopted by one of the many Democratic clubs in the country which grew out of and formed the popular enthusiasm over the French Revolution. The Philadelphia Society denounced the English mission less than it reflected upon the President's appointment of Jay. It was claimed that his office of Chief Justice had been degraded to partisan uses—a step "the most unconstitutional and dangerous in the annals of the United States." Among other criticisms, the resolutions insisted that in case of an impeachment of the Executive the Chief Justice could not act within the spirit and meaning of the Constitution. There was no personal reference to Jay.

you and our children and friends.   I look forward to that pleasure, and sincerely hope and pray that a kind Providence will so order events, that my return be not protracted beyond the time we contemplate. Kiss our little ones for me. Once more farewell :—and that the Author and Giver of all consolation may be and remain with you and them for ever, will not cease to be the prayer of

Your very affectionate husband,

JOHN JAY.

JAY TO LORD GRENVILLE.

FALMOUTH, June 8, 1794.

MY LORD :

I landed here this evening with a commission from the President of the United States, constituting me their envoy to his Majesty.

The state of my health not permitting me to travel rapidly, I transmit the enclosed packet for your Lordship, with one for the Marquis of Buckingham, by the post. They were committed to my care by Sir John Temple ; it appears to me more proper to deny myself the honour of delivering them in person, than, for that purpose, to detain them from your Lordships until my arrival in London.

I have the honour to be with great respect, my Lord, your Lordship's most obedient and most humble servant,

JOHN JAY.

The Right Hon. Lord GRENVILLE,
   One of His Majesty's Principal Secretaries of State, White Hall.

JAY TO LORD GRENVILLE.

PALL-MALL, ROYAL HOTEL,
June 15, 1794.

MY LORD :

You have doubtless received a letter which I had the honour of writing to you from Falmouth. I arrived here this morning. The journey has given me some health and much pleasure, nothing having occurred on the road to induce me to wish it shorter. Col. Trumbull does me the favour of accompanying me as Secretary and I have brought with me a son who I am anxious should form a right estimate of whatever may be interesting to our country. Will you be so obliging, my Lord, as to permit me to present them to you, and to inform me of the time when it will be most agreeable to your Lordship that I should wait upon you and assure you of the respect with which I have the honour to be, my Lord, your Lordship's most obedient and most humble servant,

JOHN JAY.

LORD GRENVILLE TO JAY.

Lord Grenville presents his compliments to Mr. Jay. He had the honor to lay before the King yesterday the copy of Mr. Jay's letter of credence. As Wednesday is the usual day for His Majesty's giving audience to foreign Ministers, and as there will be no levee next Wednesday on account of His Majesty's journey to Portsmouth, His Majesty has fixed Wednesday sev'nnight for receiving Mr. Jay ; but if Mr. Jay, under the circumstances of his Special Commission, should be desirous of having his audience sooner, His Majesty has been graciously pleased to authorize Lord

Grenville to say that His Majesty will permit Lord Grenville to introduce Mr. Jay after the levee to-morrow. In
that case Lord Grenville would wish to see Mr. Jay in the
morning at eleven instead of twelve, as they had before
fixed.

DOWNING STREET,
JOHN JAY, Esq.,   19th June, 1794.
&c., &c., &c.

JAY TO MRS. JAY.

LONDON, PALL-MALL, ROYAL HOTEL,
21st June, 1794.

MY DEAR SALLY :

I wrote you a letter while yet at sea, and on my arrival at Falmouth added to it a few lines. That letter
was left in the care of our consul there, who promised to forward it by the *Active*, Captain Blair, who
expected soon to sail from thence for Philadelphia.

On Sunday morning, the 15th of this month, we
reached this place. Excellent roads, good inns, and
a variety of interesting objects and scenes rendered
the journey agreeable—perhaps the more so from our
having just left the sea. Our way led us through
Glastonbury, famous among other things for a thorn
said to have been introduced by Joseph of Arimathea,
which ancient legends say blossoms at Christmas.
On our arrival at the next town (Wells) we visited
the cathedral, a Gothic structure worth seeing. The
sexton who showed and explained to us its history,
peculiarities, and curiosities, and who seemed an intelligent man, assured us very seriously that there
really was such a thorn at Glastonbury, that some of

the same kind was then growing at Wells, and that he himself had seen it blossom at Christmas. Had it been Christmas, I should have desired him to show it to me.

Peter has carried to Mrs. Low the letters for her that were committed to his care. He was most kindly received by her, and returned much pleased. He called also at Mrs. White's with the letters he had for her. She and her family were all out of town. The two Messrs. Kembles have been so polite as to make me a visit. The Colonel (who was aide-de-camp to General Gage) has left the army. I made inquiries about Mrs. Gage. She is in the city ; her health but delicate. I purpose to make her a visit. Mr. B. Vaughan and his family are out of town. Mr. and Mrs. Church are particularly kind and civil to us, and Peter has much reason to be pleased with the attentions which he has received from them and others of our friends here.

We dined yesterday with Mr. and Mrs. Constable, who made very friendly inquiries about you and the children in the evening. I took tea with Mrs. Low, who looks very well and spoke much of America and her friends in it. Mr. and Mrs. Pinckney seem very amiable and much disposed to do everything that is proper and friendly. As to my political objects, I can as yet say nothing—more time being necessary to acquire information and form a judgment.

This letter will be committed to the care of Mr. Francis, son of Mr. Francis of Philadelphia. He purposes to set out to-morrow for Falmouth, whence he expects immediately to sail for that port. I should have written by the packet, but was afraid that the *Active* would sail before her; it has, however, turned out otherwise. I am this moment informed that a vessel bound for New York will sail on Tuesday next; I shall endeavour to write by her also, but I am so pressed for want of time by business and circumstances which, though not important, consume time that it will not be in my power to write either so many or such long letters as I otherwise should. God bless and preserve you, my dear Sally. My love to the children. Remember me to our friends.

Yours affectionately,

JOHN JAY.

JAY TO PRESIDENT WASHINGTON.

LONDON, 23d June, 1794.

DEAR SIR:

My letter of this date to Mr. Randolph contains an exact account of the present state of the affairs of my mission here. I shall be disappointed if no good should result. As yet, the minister stands entirely uncommitted. From some light circumstances I incline to believe that our mercantile injuries will be redressed; but how or how far I cannot conjecture. My next conference will doubtless place things in more particular and clearer points of view.

Dr. Gordon has information, which he *relies* upon, that the posts will not be surrendered, and he authorizes me to tell you so in confidence. His information does not make so strong an impression upon my mind as it does on his ; it merits attention, but, in my opinion, is not *conclusive.*

The observations I have hitherto made induce me to believe that the war with France is popular, and that a war with us would be unpopular. The word *Jacobin* is here a term of reproach, and used as such among the common people. They who wish the reform of this government do, I apprehend, wish a certain degree of success to the present French cause, not because they like it, but because they think such success would promote their favourite objects. I often hear gentlemen converse on these subjects, but I think it prudent to be reserved ; as to their internal parties and divisions, I make it a rule to remain silent.

Your administration is greatly commended. The idea entertained by some, of applying private debts to compensate public injuries, alarms and disgusts, and impairs credit. I am anxious to have it in my power to communicate something decisive. As yet, I am entirely satisfied with the minister.

I ought to add that Mr. Pinckney's conduct relative to me corresponds with my ideas of delicacy and propriety.

With perfect respect, esteem, and attachment, I am, dear sir, your obliged and obedient servant,

JOHN JAY.

P.S.—The enclosed copies of a note of the 19th inst. from Lord Grenville, and my answer, afford indications of his present temper, that will not escape you. It is always useful to communicate such papers, but seldom useful to publish them. Publication, unnecessarily and. frequently made, must naturally increase reserve and circumspection to such a degree as, in a great measure, to exclude the advantages of confidence and conversation, and to confine negotiation to the slow and wary mode of written communications, written too under the impression and expectation of publication.

Your affectionate servant,
JOHN JAY.

JAY TO EDMUND RANDOLPH.

LONDON, 23d June, 1794.

SIR :

On the 15th I arrived here, and the same day mentioned it by letter to Lord Grenville. He appointed the 18th for my reception, and I then communicated to him my first commission, and left with him a copy of it. This was a visit of ceremony, and nothing passed between us relative to the objects of my mission. The next day I sent him copies of my letter of credence.

On the 20th I had an interview with him by his appointment ; and I communicated to him my general power, of which I have since sent him a copy. Much general conversation took place and the principal topics were touched upon. His Lordship did not commit himself on any point ; he heard me very patiently and politely. He promised to appoint a short day for another conference, and I took my leave impressed with sentiments favorable to his character and manners. If his disposition be hostile, he conceals it admirably. What will be the decision of the court I will not venture even to conjecture. As yet, I have no reason to be dissatisfied, or to consider appearances as being unfavorable. No delays, or arts to procrastinate, have been practised.

It is to be wished that no intelligence of an irritating nature may arrive from America. I do not regard preparations for war as of that nature. They ought not, in my opinion, to be neglected or delayed in the most profound state of peace.

I shall not omit any opportunity of giving you such information as will enable you to see precisely the state of the negotiation, and shall endeavour to avoid deceiving you, or myself, by delusive hopes or groundless fears.

I have the honour to be, with great respect, etc.

JOHN JAY.

JAY TO ALEXANDER HAMILTON.

LONDON, 11th July, 1794.

MY DEAR SIR:

I am still unable to say anything decisive relative to the objects of my mission. Appearances continue to be singularly favourable, but appearances merit only a certain degree of circumspect reliance. The delays occasioned by the new arrangement of the ministry cannot be of long continuance. Circumstances must soon constrain them to form some ultimate system relative to the United States; and although I have much reason to hope that it will be favourable to our wishes, yet I confess I am not without apprehensions that certain points not by us to be yielded will occasion difficulties hard to surmount. Personally I have every reason to be satisfied, and officially I have as yet no reason to complain.

Shortly after my arrival I dined with Lord Grenville. The cabinet ministers were present, but not a single foreigner. On Monday next I am to dine with the Lord Chancellor, and on next Friday with Mr. Pitt. I mention these facts to explain what I mean by favourable appearances. I think it best that they should remain unmentioned for the present, and they make no part of my communications to Mr. Randolph, or others. This is not the season for such communications ; they may be misinterpreted, though not by you.

I fear the posts may labour, but they must not be left. We must not make a delusive settlement ; that would disunite our people, and leave seeds of discord to germinate. I will do everything that prudence and integrity may dictate or permit.

I will endeavour to accommodate rather than dispute ; and if this plan should fail, decent and firm representations must conclude the business of my mission. As yet I do not regret any step I have taken. I wish I may be able to say the same at the conclusion.

Yours affectionately,

JOHN JAY.

5th August.—This letter was inadvertently omitted to be sent when written. Appearances mend—give us a fair chance.

LINDLEY MURRAY TO JAY.

YORK, 15th of 7th mo, 1794.

When I first heard of the commission of my much esteemed friend, John Jay, as envoy extraordinary to the British court, I rejoiced in the prospect which his known abilities, integrity, and benevolence afforded, of a speedy and happy dispersion of those clouds of hostility which have been for some time gathering, and which seemed of late ready to involve the two countries in confusion and distress. I hope I shall be excused when I say that I do not know any other person in America whose appointment to this high office would have given me so much satisfaction, and promised so successful an issue ; and I believe that these sentiments are not merely the effusions of an early admiration of his talents and virtues, but of the most sincere and respectful attachment.

It is the earnest wish of my heart, that thy labours may be happily crowned, and that by them the inestimable blessings of peace and brotherly intercourse may be preserved and established on a permanent foundation.

I trust, too, that the consciousness of this benevolent and Christian work will, amid many other charities of life, frequently rise in grateful and self-approving remembrance, and, if a day of affliction should come, will furnish a cordial of the most sovereign virtue, the recollection of having been the means of preventing the destruction of thousands, and of promoting the harmony and happiness of millions of thy fellow-creatures.

I have but one more wish to express on this subject, which is, that when thou hast been happily instrumental in removing every cause of uneasiness and discord between Great Britain and America, thou mayst find thyself authorized to tender the mediation of America to the present belligerent powers, for stopping the effusion of human blood, and terminating the calamities of a most ferocious and desolating war. To be an instrument in accomplishing a deed so extensively beneficent must, if virtue so exalted needed any accession of happiness, be contemplated and applauded by the wise and good to the latest period of time.

But, whatever may be the issue of thy present negotiation, or however disproportionate may be thy commission to the extent of thy benevolence, thou wilt always have the esteem and regard of one who, though indeed his esteem and regard are of very little consequence, could not withhold this testimony of his respectful remembrance, and who takes the liberty of subscribing himself

Thy affectionately attached friend,
LINDLEY MURRAY.

P.S.—Had it been in my power to travel as far as London, I should have gone with pleasure, on this occasion, to pay my respects to thee in person; but I am in a very feeble state, and unable to go from home more than a few miles each day, for the benefit of exercise; so that I cannot procure myself that satisfaction. I have also for some time been deprived of the usual exertion of my voice, and can converse scarcely above a whisper; but, notwithstanding this, it would be a peculiar gratification if the course of thy travels should include York, to have the favour of seeing thee and enjoying thy company at my house during thy stay in this city. Some years since, I took the liberty of requesting thy acceptance of a small compilation which I had then published, and which I suppose thou received. I have lately revised and enlarged that collection, and, though I think it scarcely worth *thy* attention, yet, as thou hast seen the first edition, I hope it will not be deemed an intrusion to beg thy acceptance of a copy of this last impression.

JAY TO PRESIDENT WASHINGTON.

LONDON, 21st July, 1794.

DEAR SIR :

Among my letters to Mr. Randolph is one stating an agreement between Lord Grenville and myself for preserving things in a pacific and unaltered state between us and the British on the side of Canada and the frontiers ; and Mr. Simcoe will soon receive orders to retire from Miami to his former positions. Some cabinet councils have lately been held, and it is probable the manner of settling their differences with us has been among the subjects of their deliberations. From the silence and circumspection of Lord Grenville, I apprehend that the cabinet has not as yet ultimately concluded on their plan. This delay is unpleasant, but I do not think it unnatural. The opposition members lately come in have so often held a language friendly to America, that it is probable they will find it necessary, in order to be consistent, to adhere to sentiments not agreeable to some of the others. I am led by several little circumstances, not easily detailed or explained, to believe that the late administration looked upon a war with us as inevitable, and I am of opinion that the instructions of the 6th of November were influenced by that idea. I do also believe that Lord Dorchester was instructed to act conformably to that idea, and that Simcoe was governed by it.

I am *certain* that intelligence (which made some impression) was conveyed to the ministry, that our army, if successful against the Indians, had orders to attack and take the posts. There is also room to believe, that the indiscreet reception given to the late French Minister—the unnecessary rejoicings about French successes, and a variety of similar circumstances, did impress the government with strong apprehensions of an unavoidable war with us, and did induce them to entertain a disposition hostile to us.

I have given Lord Grenville positive assurances, that no attack pending the negotiations will be made on the posts held by them at the conclusion of the war; but I also told him that I thought it highly probable that every new advanced post, and particularly the one said to be taken by Mr. Simcoe on the Miami, would be attacked. I must do him the justice to say that hitherto I have found him fair and candid, and apparently free from asperity or irritation.

So far as personal attentions to the envoy may be regarded as symptoms of good-will to his country, my prospect is favourable. These symptoms, however, are never decisive; they justify expectation, but not reliance. I most heartily wish the business over, and myself at home again. But it would not be prudent to urge and press unceasingly, lest ill-humour should result, and ill-humour will mar any negotiation; on the other hand, much forbearance and seeming inactivity invite procrastination and neglect. The line between these extremes is delicate : I will endeavour to find and observe it.

I am, dear sir,

Your obliged and affectionate servant,

JOHN JAY.

JAY TO JOHN ANSTEY.

ROYAL HOTEL, PALL-MALL,
23d July, 1794.

SIR :

Accept my thanks for the friendly congratulations and sentiments expressed in your letter of the 14th of this month.

I regret not knowing that you resided at Bath. We passed from Falmouth through that city in our way to this. It would have given me pleasure to have called upon you, and (to use an Indian expression) have *brightened the chain.*

Many great and unexpected events have taken place since we parted. We live in times that teem with them. A great and wonderful drama is exhibiting on the stage of Europe, perhaps of the world. We are spectators of the first act. What may succeed, or what the catastrophe will be, human prevision cannot discern.

Peace and domestic comforts rise in value as they become precarious ; and individual misery, by abounding, produces national distress ; and yet, even in this age of *reason* and *philosophy*, the passions do not cease to fan the flames of war, and cause them to rage, to spread, and to desolate.

If, during my stay here, you should visit London, I shall be happy to see you, and to assure you of the esteem and regard with which I am

Your obedient and very humble servant,

JOHN JAY.

23d July, 1794.

My Lord :

The cases of captures transmitted to me are numerous, and in some instances voluminous.

My first idea was to make correct statements of these cases and lay them before you. It has since occurred to me that you might prefer receiving these cases in the state they are. Abstracts cannot be so satisfactory. I will communicate them to your Lordship at any time you may be pleased to mention.

It appears to me unfortunate that the vessels lately sailed from hence to America carry with them discontents on account of Americans impressed and detained. Those discontents will naturally add to the impressions made by masters of vessels and others daily returning from the West Indies, and publishing details of the severities which they there experienced. People who suffer will feel ; and their friends and others will also feel for them. With great respect and esteem I have the honour to be, my Lord, your Lordship's most obedient and most humble servant,

JOHN JAY.

JAY TO EDMUND RANDOLPH.

LONDON, 30th July, 1794.

SIR :

The great and, I believe, unexpected events in Flanders, and the unusual number of interesting affairs which constantly demand the attention of the British Cabinet, keep their ministers unceasingly employed, and is, doubtless, one reason why more time has not been allotted to our concerns. We are, nevertheless, beginning to do business apparently in good earnest. The minister is (if I may say so) besieged by our British creditors. The subject of the debts is attended with difficulties. The minister has been informed that the law in Virginia relative to the evidence of book debts has, since the war, been made more *strict* than it was before. If the law has been thus changed, and made to apply to pre-existing transactions, there is room for complaint. I wish to have exact information on this head.

I am to see Lord Grenville to-morrow at 11 o'clock, by appointment, on the business of spoliation and impressments, when I hope he will be prepared to say something decisive. I have laid before him several of the cases you sent me, and also the statement by the captains of vessels taken at Martinique. Of the facts mentioned in the latter, he had never received any information.

I know the impatience that must prevail in our country. At times I find it difficult to repress my own impatience; but for all things there is a season. The importance of moderation and caution in the present moment is obvious, and will, it is to be hoped, continue to operate on the minds and conduct of our fellow-citizens. As yet I do not apprehend that I have committed any mistakes in this business. I wish I may be able to say as much at the conclusion of it.

I have read your thirty odd papers to and from and respecting Mr. Hammond and his complaints. You have, in my opinion, managed that matter well ; continue, by all means, to be temperate, and put him in the wrong. Let us hope for the best and prepare for the worst. I confess I have hopes, but I also perceive circumstances and causes which may render them abortive.

This letter cannot be satisfactory ; it amounts to little more than this : that nothing decisive has yet been done, and that I cannot tell you whether anything, and what, will be done. So is the case ; and such will often be the case pending any negotiation, or any game connected with events not in our power to control. In both, chances frequently defeat skill, and as frequently give to skill unmerited reputation. For these things I must take *my chance.*

I have the honour to be, with great respect, etc.,

JOHN JAY.

JAY TO LORD GRENVILLE.

The undersigned, envoy of the United States of America, has the honour of representing to the Right Honorable Lord Grenville, his Britannic Majesty's Secretary of State for the Department of Foreign Affairs :

That a very considerable number of American vessels have been irregularly captured, and as improperly condemned by certain of his Majesty's officers and judges.

That, in various instances, these captures and condemnations were so conducted, and the captured placed under such unfavourable circumstances, as that, for want of the securities required, and other obstacles, no appeals were made in certain cases, nor any claims in others.

The undersigned presumes that these facts will appear from the documents which he has had the honour of submitting to his Lordship's consideration ; and that it will not be deemed necessary, at *present*, to particularize these cases and their merits, or detail the circumstances which discriminate some from others.

That great and extensive injuries having thus, under colour of his Majesty's authority and commissions, been done to a numerous class of American merchants, the United States can, for reparation, have recourse only to the justice, authority, and interposition of his Majesty.

That the vessels and property taken and condemned have been chiefly sold, and the proceeds divided among a great number of persons, of whom some are dead, some unable to make retribution, and others, from frequent removals and their particular circumstances, not easily reached by civil process.

That as, for these losses and injuries, adequate compensation, by means of judicial proceedings, has become impracticable, and, considering the causes which combined to produce them, the United States confide in his Majesty's justice and magnanimity to cause such compensation to be made to these innocent sufferers as may be consistent with equity ; and the undersigned flatters himself that such principles may, without difficulty, be adopted, as will serve as rules whereby to ascertain the cases and the amount of compensation.

So grievous are the expenses and delays attending litigated suits, to persons whose fortunes have been so materially affected, and so great is the distance of Great Britain from America, that the undersigned thinks he ought to express his anxiety that a mode of proceeding as summary and little expensive may be devised as circumstances and the peculiar hardship of these cases may appear to permit and require.

And as (at least in some of these cases) it may be expedient and necessary, as well as just, that the sentences of the courts of vice-admiralty should be revised and corrected by the Court of Appeals here, the undersigned hopes it will appear reasonable to his Majesty to order that the captured in question (who have not already so done) be there admitted to enter both their *appeals* and their *claims*.

The undersigned also finds it to be his duty to represent that the irregularities before mentioned extended not only to the capture and condemnation of American vessels and property, and to unusual personal severities, but even to the impressment of American citizens to serve on board of armed vessels. He forbears to dwell on the *injuries* done to the unfortunate individuals, or on the *emotions* which they must naturally excite, either in the breast of the nation to whom they belong, or of the just and humane of every country. His reliance on the justice and benevolence of his Majesty leads him to indulge a pleasing expectation that orders will be given that

Americans so circumstanced be immediately liberated, and that persons honoured with his Majesty's commissions do, in future, abstain from similar violences.

It is with cordial satisfaction that the undersigned reflects on the impressions which such equitable and conciliatory measures would make on the minds of the United States, and how naturally they would inspire and cherish those sentiments and dispositions which never fail to preserve, as well as to produce, respect, esteem, and friendship.

JOHN JAY.

LONDON, July 30, 1794.

LORD GRENVILLE TO JAY.

DOWNING ST., August 1, 1794.

The undersigned, Secretary of State, has had the honor to lay before the King, the ministerial note which he has received from Mr. Jay, envoy extraordinary and minister plenipotentiary from the United States of America, respecting the alleged irregularity of the capture and condemnation of several American vessels, and also respecting the circumstances of personal severity by which those proceedings are stated to have been accompanied in some particular instances.

The undersigned is authorized to assure Mr. Jay, that it is His Majesty's wish that the most *complete and impartial justice* should be done to all the citizens of America, who may, in fact, have been injured by any of the proceedings above mentioned. All experience shows that a naval war, extending over the four quarters of the globe, must unavoidably be productive of some inconveniences to the commerce of neutral nations, and that no care can prevent some irregularities in the course of those proceedings, which are universally recognized as resulting from the just rights incident to all belligerent Powers. But the King will always be desirous that these inconveniences and irregularities should be as much limited as the nature of the case will admit, and that the fullest opportunity should be given to all to prefer their complaints, and to obtain redress and compensation where they are due.

In Mr. Jay's note, mention is made of several cases where the parties have hitherto omitted to prefer their claims, and of others where no appeals have been made from the sentences of condemnation pronounced in the first instance.

As to the cases of the *first* description, Lord Grenville apprehends that the regular course of law is still open to the claimants ; and that, by preferring appeals to the commissioners of prize causes here, against the sentence of the courts below, the whole merits of those cases may be brought forward, and the most complete justice obtained.

In the cases of the *second* description the proceedings might, in some instances, be more difficult, from the lapse of time usually allotted for preferring appeals. But His Majesty being anxious that no temporary or local circumstances, such as those to which Mr. Jay refers in his note, should impede the course of substantial justice, has been pleased to refer it to the proper officers to consider of a mode of enlarging the time for receiving the appeals in those cases, in order to admit the claimants to bring their complaints before the regular court appointed for that purpose.

The undersigned has no doubt, that, in this manner, a very *considerable part* of the injuries alleged to have been suffered by the Americans may, if the complaints are well founded, be redressed in the usual course of judicial proceeding, at a very small expense to the parties, and without any other interposition of His Majesty's Government than

is above stated. Until the result and effect of these proceedings shall be known, no definite judgment can be
formed respecting the nature and extent of those cases, (if
any such shall ultimately be found to exist) where it shall
not have been practicable to obtain substantial redress in
this mode. But he does not hesitate to say, beforehand,
that, if cases shall then be found to exist to such an
extent as properly to call for the interposition of Government, where, without the fault of the parties complaining,
they shall be unable, from *whatever circumstances*, to procure such redress, in the ordinary course of law, as the
justice of their cases may entitle them to expect, His
Majesty will be anxious that *justice* should, at *all events*,
be done, and will readily enter into the discussion of the
measures to be adopted, and the *principles* to be established
for that purpose.

With respect to all acts of personal severity and violence,
as the King must entirely disapprove every such transaction,
so His Majesty's courts are always open for the punishment
of offences of this nature ; and for giving redress to the
sufferers in every case, where the fact can be established by
satisfactory proof ; nor does it appear that any case of that
nature can exist where there would be the smallest difficulty
of obtaining, in that mode, substantial and exemplary justice.

On the subject of the *impress*, Lord Grenville has only to
assure Mr. Jay, that if, in any instance, American seamen
have been impressed into the King's service, it has been
contrary to the King's desire ; though such cases may have
occasionally arisen from the difficulty of discriminating
between British and American seamen, especially where
there so often exists an interest and intention to deceive.

Whenever any representation has been made to Lord
Grenville on this subject, he has never failed to receive His
Majesty's command for putting it in a proper course in
order that the facts might be inquired into, and ascertained ;

and to the extent that the persons in question might be released, if the facts appeared to be satisfactorily established.

With respect to the desire expressed by Mr. Jay that new orders might be given with a view to prevent, as far as it is possible, the giving any just ground of complaint on this head, Lord Grenville has no reason to doubt that His Majesty's intentions respecting this point are already sufficiently understood by His Majesty's officers employed on that service; but he has, nevertheless, obtained His Majesty's permission to assure Mr. Jay, that instructions, to the effect desired, will be renewed, in consequence of his application.

The undersigned avails himself, with pleasure, of this opportunity to renew to Mr. Jay his assurances of his sincere esteem and consideration.

GRENVILLE.

JAY TO PRESIDENT WASHINGTON.

LONDON, 5th August, 1794.

DEAR SIR:

I am this moment returned from a long conference with Lord Grenville. Our prospects become more and more promising as we advance in the business. The compensation cases are described in the answer, and the amount of damages will, I have reason to hope, be referred to the decision of commissioners mutually to be appointed by the two governments, and the money paid without delay on their certificate, and the business finished as speedily as may be possible. The question of admitting our vessels into the islands, under certain limitations, is under consideration, and will soon be decided. A treaty of commerce is on the carpet. All other things being agreed, the posts will be included. They contend that the article about the negroes does not extend to those who came in on their proclamation, to whom (being vested with the property in them by the rights of war) they gave freedom ; but only to those who were, *bona fide*, the property of Americans when the war ceased. They will, I think, *insist* that British debts, so far as injured by lawful impediments, should be *repaired* by the United States, by decision of mutual commissioners. These things have passed in conversation, but no commitments on either side— and not to be of any official weight or use whatever.

The king observed to me the other day : " Well, sir, I imagine you begin to see that your mission will probably be successful."—"I am happy, may it please your Majesty, to find that you entertain that idea."— " Well, but don't you perceive that it is like to be so ? " —" There are some recent circumstances (the answer to my representation, etc.) which induce me to flatter myself that it will be so." He nodded with a smile, signifying that it was to those circumstances that he alluded. The conversation then turned to indifferent topics ; this was at the drawing-room.

I have never been more unceasingly employed than I have been for some time past, and still am. I hope for good, but God only knows. The *Wm. Penn* sails in the morning. I write these few lines in haste, to let you see that the business is going on as fast as can reasonably be expected ; and that it is very important that peace and quiet should be preserved for the present. On hearing, last night, that one of our

Indiamen had been carried into Halifax, I mentioned it to Lord Grenville.   He will write immediately by the packet on the subject.   Indeed, I believe that they are endeavouring to restore a proper conduct towards us *everywhere*, but it will take some time before the effect can be visible.   I write all this to you in *confidence*, and for your *private* satisfaction.   I have not time to explain my reasons, but they are cogent.   I could fill some sheets with interesting communications, if I had leisure ; but other matters press, and must not be postponed, for " there is a *tide* in human affairs," of which every moment is precious. Whatever may be the issue, nothing in my power to ensure success shall be neglected or delayed.

With sincere respect, esteem, and attachment, I am, dear sir,

Your obliged and obedient servant,

JOHN JAY.

JAY TO JUDGE HOBART.

LONDON, 12th August, 1794.

MY GOOD FRIEND :

I passed this morning in a visit to Sir John Sinclair, President of the Board of Agriculture, and to Col. Bentham, who is preparing for the establishment of a panopticon, agreeable to the plan delineated in a publication which I once communicated to you.

The Agricultural Society is incorporated with a yearly allowance, by government, of three thousand pounds.   Their plans are extensive ; they have been singularly industrious, and much has been done.   I enclose you the proposed plan of their general report; if executed in the extent and in the manner intended, it will be the most interesting work of the kind, respecting husbandry, which has appeared in any country.

Sir John showed us sheep of different breeds, stuffed and prepared in the highest degree of perfection. Of these, drawings are making; models are collecting of the most useful machines; among them is one for cleaning grain from the straw, which, by the help of two horses and a man and a boy, will do 70 or 80 bushels per day. They begin to be in use among the farmers, which I consider as a proof of their answering the purpose.

Among the sheep, the Teeswater is the largest. Sir John showed me a fleece presented to the Board, which weighed twenty odd pounds. He tells me they frequently weigh sixty pounds a quarter.

From Saxony, he is informed that the Spanish breed had been imported there; that they succeeded well, and did not degenerate. They sent him a sample of the wool. I enclose a lock of it. This fact shows that the fineness of wool depends not less on breed than on management.

Sir John has a farm in Scotland which rented for £300 a year. It was employed in raising store-cattle, which were usually sold into England, and fattened for the London market. He dismissed the cattle, and introduced sheep; it proved profitable, and he is now offered £1,200 a year for it. His flock is 3,000.

The progress of husbandry in this country is astonishing; the king patronizes it, and is himself a great farmer. He has been doing much in that way at Windsor.

Colonel Bentham has invented a number of curious and very useful machines, intended to be introduced into the panopticon. He showed us a model of the building ; it seems admirably calculated for its purposes.

He has a machine for sawing at once from a plank the felloe of a wheel to its form, another contrivance for cutting it to its proper length and angle, another for finishing the spoke, another for boring and mortising the hub, another for driving the spokes. He has one for turning a circular saw for small work, another for making the mouldings, if they may be so called, on the pieces which form sashes ; one for sawing stone, others for working different kinds of saws into many slabs at once, another for polishing them, another for planing boards, and taking a shaving of its full width from one end to the other, etc., etc., etc. He has patents for these machines ; but as yet they cannot be purchased. He has one for cutting corks with incredible expedition.

Governor Hunter, from Norfolk Island, with whom I was last week in company, speaking of its productions, mentioned that among the birds there were swans that were black, having only a few white feathers in the wings. They are plenty. One stuffed and well preserved, I am told, is here. As yet I have not seen it. He also mentioned a wild flax growing on upland to about three feet high, and good. I do not yet learn that any of the seed of it is here.

They who have leisure and a turn for these things, might here acquire much entertaining and some useful information. Want of time represses my curiosity, and will not allow me to pay much attention to objects unconnected with those of my mission.

I am, dear sir,
Your affectionate friend and servant,
JOHN JAY.

JAY TO COLONEL READ.

LONDON, 14th August, 1794.

DEAR SIR :

We have both heard it asserted that a man's character may be discerned from his handwriting. If that be true, you and our friend, Edward Rutledge, must be as enigmatical and unintelligible as Oliver Cromwell, and yet neither of you resemble him more than he did an honest man.

The kindness diffused through your letter of the 19th of June paid me for the trouble of deciphering it. Two or three words, however, proved too hard for me. To judge from the context, I presume they mean something good and friendly, and therefore that I have reason to be pleased with the ideas conveyed by them, although I do not know precisely what they are.

Peace, my dear sir, was formally thought a good sort of thing ; but within these last few years past it seems to have been going fast out of fashion. But; to be serious, there seems to be something more than common at work in, or on, the human mind, and urging it to enterprise, tending to introduce a new state of things. Symptoms of it appear more or less, and in different degrees, in all parts of Europe,—even in Spain, where quiescency in every sense has long been cherished. Geneva is at this moment undergoing another revolution. Where next, no one can tell. Our country may catch the flame. We live in an eventful season. We have nothing to do but our duty, and one part of it is to prepare for every event. Let us preserve peace while it can be done with propriety ; and if in that we fail, let us wage war,— not in newspapers, and impotent sarcasms, but with manly firmness, and unanimous and vigorous efforts.

I have had the pleasure of seeing your brother frequently, and am pleased with him. He is gone to Scotland. He has communicated to me a circumstance that I rejoice in.

Assure Mrs. Read of my best wishes. With real esteem and regard, I am, dear sir,

Your most obedient and humble servant,

JOHN JAY.

JAY TO LINDLEY MURRAY.

ROYAL HOTEL, PALL-MALL,
22d August, 1794.

DEAR SIR :

I thank you very sincerely for the kind letter you were so obliging as to write me on the 15th of last month. The sentiments of esteem and regard which are expressed in it afford additional inducements to my endeavours to deserve them.

To see things as being what they are, to estimate them aright, and to act accordingly, are of all attainments the most important. Circumstanced as we are, it is exceedingly difficult to acquire either of these, and especially the last, in any eminent degree; but in proportion to our progress, so will be our wisdom and our prospect of happiness.

I perceive that we concur in thinking that we must go home to be happy, and that our home is not in this world. Here we have nothing to do but our duty, and by it to regulate our business and our pleasures; for there are innocent as well as vicious pleasures, and travellers through the world (as we all are) may, without scruple, gratefully enjoy the good roads, pleasant scenes, and agreeable accommodations with which Providence may be pleased to render our journey more cheerful and comfortable; but in search of these we are not to deviate from the main road, nor, when they occur, should we permit them to detain or retard us. The theory of prudence is sublime and in many respects simple. The practice is difficult; and it necessarily must be so, or this would cease to be a state of probation.

The sentiments diffused through your book are just, striking, and useful; but, my good friend, our opinions are oftener right than our conduct. Among the strange things of this world, nothing seems more strange than that men pursuing happiness should knowingly quit the right and take a wrong road, and frequently do what their judgments neither approve nor prefer. Yet so is the fact; and this fact points

strongly to the necessity of our being healed, or
restored, or regenerated by a power more energetic
than any of those which properly belong to the
human mind.

We perceive that a great breach has been made in
the moral and physical systems by the introduction
of moral and physical evil; how or why, we know
not; so, however, it is, and it certainly seems proper
that this breach should be closed and order restored.
For this purpose only one adequate plan has ever
appeared in the world, and that is the Christian dispensation.   In this plan I have full faith.   Man, in
his present state, appears to be a degraded creature;
his best gold is mixed with dross, and his best motives
are very far from being pure and free from earth and
impurity.

I mention these things that you may see the state
of my mind relative to these interesting subjects, and
to relieve yours from doubts which your friendship
for me might render disagreeable.

I regret your want of health and the bodily afflictions with which you are visited.   God only knows
what is best.   Many will have reason to rejoice, in
the end, for the days wherein they have seen adversity.   Your mind is in full strength and vigour,
and that is an inestimable blessing.

It really would give me great pleasure to visit you
before I return; but I dare not promise myself that
satisfaction, being so much and so constantly under
the direction of circumstances which I cannot control.

As to the wars now waging, they appear to me to

be of a different description from ordinary ones. They are, in my opinion, as unlike common wars as the great plague in London was unlike common sicknesses. I think we are just entering on the age of revolutions, and that the impurities of our moral *atmosphere* (if if I may use the expression) are about to be purified by a succession of political storms. I sincerely wish for general peace and good-will among men, but I shall be mistaken if (short intervals excepted) the season for those blessings is not at some distance. If any country escapes, I am inclined to think it will be our own ; and I am led to this opinion by general principles and reasonings, and not by particular facts or occurrences, some of which so strongly favour a contrary idea as to produce in my mind much doubt and apprehension.

I am, dear sir,
Your affectionate friend,
JOHN JAY.

JAY TO JAMES MONROE.

LONDON, 28th August, 1794.

SIR :

In July, 1792, Miss Bainstow, a young lady, now of seventeen, and whose family reside near this city, was placed at Boulogne, under the care and in the house of Madame Delseaux, a respectable widow lady there, for the benefit of education.

In September last she was, together with her friend and fellow-pensioner, Miss Hornblow, arrested and confined in a convent.

In the January following they were removed back to Madame Delseaux's house, where they still remain confined in the manner prescribed by the decree.

Miss Bainstow's friends are exceedingly solicitous to interest your kind offices in favour of these young ladies. They entreat me to lay these facts before you, and convey their most earnest requests that you will be so good as to endeavour to obtain permission for them to return home.

When I consider what my feelings would be, had I a daughter of that age so circumstanced, I find it impossible to resist this application. I know by experience that business not connected with the objects of one's mission can seldom be pleasant. The business of humanity, however, seems to be attached to opportunities of doing it. I will not enlarge on this subject; every remark incident to it will occur to you. For my part I am not apprised of any objection to permitting these foreign children to go home to their parents; and should such a general permission be effected by your means, the remembrance of it would be sweet to you for ever.

I remain, sir,

Your most obedient and humble servant,

JOHN JAY.

PRESIDENT WASHINGTON TO JAY.

PHILADELPHIA, August 30, 1794.

MY DEAR SIR:

Your letter of the 23d of June, from London, and duplicate, have both been received; and your safe arrival, after so short a passage, gave sincere pleasure, as well on private as on public account, to all your friends in this country, and to none in a greater degree, I can venture to assure you, than it did to myself.

As you will receive letters from the Secretary of State's office, giving an official account of public occurrences as they have arisen and progressed, it is unnecessary for me to retouch any of them; and yet I cannot restrain myself from making some observations on the most recent of them, the communication of which was received this morning *only*. I mean the protest of the governor of Upper Canada (delivered by Lieut. Sheaffe), against our occupying lands far from any of the posts, which, long ago, they ought to have surrendered, and far within the known, and *until now*, the acknowledged limits of the United States.

On this irregular and high-handed proceeding of Mr. Simcoe, which is no longer *masked*, I would rather hear what the ministry of Great Britain will say, than pronounce my own sentiments thereon. But can that government, or will it attempt, after this *official* act of one of their governors, to hold out ideas of friendly intentions towards the United States, and suffer such conduct to pass with impunity?

This may be considered as the most open and daring act of the British agents in America, though it is not the most hostile or cruel; for there does not remain a doubt, in the mind of any well-informed person in this country (not shut against conviction), that all the difficulties we encounter with the Indians, their hostilities, the murders of helpless women and innocent children along our frontiers, result from the conduct of the agents of Great Britain in this country. In vain, is it, then, for its administration, *in Britain*, to disavow having given orders which will warrant such conduct, while their agents go unpunished, while we have a thousand corroborating circumstances, and indeed almost as many evidences (some of which cannot be brought forward), to prove that they are seducing from our alliances (endeavouring to remove them over the line) tribes that have hitherto been kept in peace and friendship with us, at a heavy expense, and who have no cause of complaint, except pretended ones of their own creating; while they keep in a state of irritation the tribes who are hostile to us, and instigating those who know little of us, or we of them, to unite in the war against us; and while it is an undeniable fact that they are furnishing the whole with arms, ammunition, clothing, and even provisions to carry on the war, I might go further, and if they are not much belied, add men also, in disguise.

Can it be expected, I ask, so long as these things are known in the United States, or at least firmly believed, and suffered with impunity by Great Britain, that there ever will or can be any cordiality between the two countries? I answer, no; and I will undertake, without the gift of prophecy, to predict, that it will be impossible to keep this country in a state of amity with Great Britain long, if the posts are not surrendered. A knowledge of these being my sentiments would have little weight, I am persuaded, with the British administration, nor, perhaps, with the nation, in effecting the measure; but both may rest satisfied that if they want to be in peace with this country, and want to enjoy the benefits of its trade, etc., this is the road to it—withholding them, and the consequences we feel at present continuing—war inevitably.

This letter is written to you in extreme haste, while the papers respecting this subject are copying at the Secretary of State's office, to go by express to New York, for a vessel which we have just heard sails to-morrow; you will readily perceive, therefore, I had no time for digesting and as little for correcting it. I shall only add that you may be assured always of the sincere friendship and affection of

Your obedient humble servant,

GEORGE WASHINGTON.

JAY TO NICHOLAS CRUGER.

Dear Sir :   London, 11 September, 1794.

A gentleman in Holland has been so obliging as to send me a plan to make my fortune, even to the extent of many millions of pounds sterling. It unfortunately happens that more mercantile knowledge is necessary to the execution of this plan than I possess, so that like many others I must go without a fortune for want of knowing how to get one. That, my good friend, is not your case ; having already made one fortune, you certainly know better how to make another than a person who has never made any. You will find this golden plan enclosed. If the extensive concerns in which you are already engaged should render its magnitude inconvenient, might it not be well to let our friends Le Roy and Bayard share in it ? I mention them, because I esteem and like them, and because their acquaintance with the commerce of Holland and their connections in that country would afford facilities to all parties. At any rate, give me credit for good-will. If this plan does not make you more rich it will not make you less merry, and mirth sometimes does a man as much good as money.

Present my best compliments to Mrs. Cruger. With sincere wishes for your and her health and happiness, I am, dear sir,

Your most obedient and humble servant,

John Jay.

P. S.—The address of my correspondent is (in his own words) Mynheer de Heer Dirk Van Beest, op de Voor Straat de Dordrecht.

JAY TO PRESIDENT WASHINGTON.

[Private.]

LONDON, 13 September, 1794.

DEAR SIR :

My letter to Mr. Randolph, which accompanies this, contains very full and accurate information respecting our negotiations here. You will perceive that many points are *under consideration,* and that alterations will probably yet take place in several articles. Although it is uncertain, yet it is not altogether improbable, that Lord Grenville and myself may agree on terms which, in my opinion, should not be rejected. In that case, I shall be strongly induced to conclude, rather than by delays risk a change of views, and measures, and ministers, which unforeseen circumstances might occasion.

The secretary's letter, by Mr. Monroe, and the speech of the latter to the Convention, are printed, and have caused a disagreeable sensation on the public mind here, and probably on that of the government.[1] The one written by you is spoken of as being within the limits of diplomatic forms.

Gentlemen, whether in or out of office, are doubtless free in their affections or predilections for persons or nations ; but as the situation of the United States is neutral, so also should be their language to the

---

[1] While Jay was treating with England, Monroe, American Minister at Paris, was expected to quiet the apprehensions of France and prevent her from taking umbrage at any negotiations the former might conclude. The effort failed and on the heels of the Jay Treaty came increased French spoliations. Upon his recall Monroe issued his "View of the Conduct of the Executive" —a pamphlet to be read in a study of Jay's Mission.

belligerent powers. Neither can it be proper to adopt any mode of pleasing one party that would naturally be offensive to the other ; and more particularly at a time when with that other a negotiation for peace, commerce, and friendship is pending.

To be fair, upright, and prudent is to be politic ; and of the truth of this maxim, your character, and very singular degree of respectability, weight, and reputation, afford the strongest proof.

I learn that Virginia is escheating British property, and I hear of other occurrences which I regret ; but they shall not abate my perseverance in endeavouring to prosecute peace, and bring the negotiation to such a conclusion as will either ensure peace with this country, or produce union among ourselves in prosecuting war against it. Whatever may be the issue, I am determined not to lose the only satisfaction that I can be sure of, viz., the satisfaction resulting from a consciousness of having done my duty.

That attempts will be made in America to frustrate this negotiation, I have not the most distant shadow of a doubt. I brought this belief and opinion with me ; and my dependence then was, and still is, on the wisdom, firmness, and integrity of the government ; on the general good sense of our people ; and on those enlightened and virtuous characters among them who regard the peace, honour, and welfare of their country as *primary* objects. These men regret the differences which subsist between this country and their own, and sincerely desire to see mutual animosities give way to mutual good-will. As to a political connection with any country, I hope it will never be judged necessary, for I very much doubt whether it would ultimately be found useful; it would, in my opinion, introduce foreign influence, which I consider as the worst of political plagues.

With the best wishes for your health and happiness, and with perfect respect, esteem, and attachment,

I am, dear sir,

Your most obedient and obliged servant,

JOHN JAY.

JAY TO EDMUND RANDOLPH.[1]

LONDON, September 13, 1794.

SIR:

Hitherto my letters have communicated to you but little information of much importance, except on one point. Although all the general objects of my mission were opened at once, and were received with every indication of the same candour and disposition to agreement with which they were stated, yet the nature of the business turned the immediate and more particular attention of both parties to the affair of the captures; the result has been communicated to you.

A number of informal conversations on other points then took place, and every difficulty which attended them came into view, and was discussed with great

---

[1] In this communication to his government Jay gives a history of the progress of his negotiations at the British Court and outlines the terms of the treaty agreed upon. The text of the treaty, as finally concluded, with further correspondence, appears in " American State Papers : Foreign Relations," vol. i., p. 520.

fairness and temper; the inquiry naturally led to the
fact, which constituted the first violation of the treaty
of peace? The carrying away of the negroes contrary to the 7th article of the treaty of peace, was
insisted upon as being the *first* aggression. To
this it was answered, in substance, that Great Britain
understood the stipulation contained in that article, in
the obvious sense of the words which expressed it,
viz., as an engagement not to cause any destruction,
nor to carry away *any negroes or other property* of the
American inhabitants; or, in other words, that the
evacuation should be made without depredation; that
no alteration in the actual state of property was
operated or intended by that article, that every slave,
like every horse, which escaped or strayed from within
the American lines, and came into the possession of
the British army, became, by the laws and rights of
war, *British* property; and, therefore, ceasing to be
American property, the exportation thereof was not
inhibited by the stipulation in question; that to extend it to the negroes, who, under the faith of proclamations, had come in to them, of whom they thereby
acquired the property, and to whom, according to promise, liberty had been given, was to give to the article a
greater latitude than the terms of it would warrant,
and was also, *unnecessarily*, to give it a construction
which, being *odious*, could not be supported by the
known and established rules for construing treaties.
To this was replied the several remarks and considerations which are mentioned at large in a report
which I once made to Congress on this subject, and

which, for that reason, it would be useless here to repeat; on this point we could not agree.

I then brought into view another circumstance, as affording us just cause of complaint, antecedent to any of those urged against us, viz., that, from the documents recited and stated in Mr. Jefferson's letter to Mr. Hammond, it appears that the posts were not only not evacuated within the reasonable time stipulated by treaty but also that no orders for the purpose had, at least within that time, if ever, been given.

To this it was answered, that the provisional articles were signed at Paris on the 30th of November, 1782; that those articles were to constitute the treaty of peace proposed to be concluded between Great Britain and the United States, but which treaty was not to be concluded till terms of peace should be agreed upon between Great Britain and France; that the treaty of peace was not concluded until the 3d of September, 1783; that it was not ratified in America until the 14th of January, 1784; and that the ratification was not received in London until the 28th May, 1784, nor exchanged until the end of that month; that, according to the laws of nations, treaties do not oblige the parties to begin to execute the engagements contained in them, until they have received their whole form that is, until after they shall have been ratified by the respective sovereigns that are the parties to them, and until after those ratifications shall have been exchanged; that, therefore, it was not until the end of May, 1784, that Great Britain was bound to give any orders to evacuate the posts; that such orders could not arrive at Quebec, until in July, 1784; and, consequently, that the allegations of a breach of the treaty by the non-execution of the article respecting the posts, grounded on circumstances prior to the 13th July, 1784, are evidently unfounded ; that, in the interval between the arrival and publication in America, of the provisional articles, and the month of July, 1784, by which time, at soonest, orders (issued after the exchange of the ratifications of the treaty of peace, the last of May) could reach Quebec, incontestible violations of the treaty had taken place in the United States ; that reason and the practice of nations warrant, during a suspension of hostilities, *only* such measures as result from a continuance of the *status quo*, until the *final* exchange of ratifications ; that in opposition to this, new legislative acts had, in the interval before mentioned, been passed, which were evidently calculated to be beforehand with the treaty, and to prevent its having its full and fair operation on certain points and objects, when it should be ratified and take effect ; that these acts were the first violations of the treaty, and justified Great Britain in detaining the posts until the injuries caused by their operation should be compensated.

That Great Britain was not bound to evacuate the posts, nor to give any orders for the purpose, until after the exchange of the ratifications, does appear to me to be a proposition that cannot be reasonably disputed.

That certain legislative acts did pass in the United States, in the interval aforesaid, which were inconsistent with the treaty of peace, is equally certain ; but it does not thence necessarily follow that those acts were without justice, even as relative to the treaty, for precedent violations on the part of Great Britain would justify subsequent retaliation on the part of the United States. Here again the affair of the negroes emerged, and was insisted upon, and was answered as before. I confess, however, that his construction of that article has made an impression upon my mind, and induced me to suspect that my former opinion on that head may not be well founded.

Thus it became evident that admissions of infractions of the treaty of peace, and that this or that party committed the *first* aggression, were not to be expected, and that such discussions would never produce a settlement.

It then became advisable to quit those topics, and to try and agree on such a set of reciprocal concessions as (balancing each other) might afford articles for a treaty, so beneficial to both parties as to induce them to bury in it all former questions and disputes. This idea gave occasion to a variety of propositions of different kinds, which it would be tedious and useless to enumerate, and of which you will readily conceive there were some that could not meet with mutual approbation ; among those which were mentioned was one for altering essentially our boundaries in the northwestern corner of the United States ; this I regarded as inadmissible, and hoped would not be persisted in ; one for doing us complete justice respecting captures ; one for partially opening to us a trade with the West India Islands ; one for our paying the damages sustained by British creditors by lawful impediments ; this was strongly insisted on. I did not think it utterly inadmissible in case we received proper justice and privileges under other articles ; for then, in my judgment, it would not be advisable to part and separate on that point, and various reasons convinced me it would be adhered to ; one for putting the ships and merchants of both parties on an equal footing. In short, in order to bring the whole subject comprehensively to view, nothing that occurred was omitted to be mentioned ; these were free conversations, neither of us considering the other as being committed by anything that was said or proposed.

It was necessary then to select points for mutual consideration, and quitting desultory discussions, to fix our attention on certain propositions, each being at liberty to propose what he pleased, and again to retract his proposition, if, on mature reflection, he should be so inclined : with this view, after returning home, I selected the following, and having reduced them to writing, sent them to Lord Grenville for his consideration ; in the mean time employing myself in reflecting, and endeavouring to decide in my own mind, how far, and with what modifications or omissions, it would be proper to adopt them :

August 6th, 1794.

Mr. Jay presents his compliments to Lord Grenville, and encloses some outlines for a convention and treaty of commerce; some of them appear to him questionable. More mature reflection, and the light which usually springs from mutual discussions, may occasion alterations. Many of the *common* articles are omitted, and will be inserted of course. It is very desirable that it may be concluded in season to arrive about the 1st of November.

Right Honorable LORD GRENVILLE, etc., etc.

The paper that was enclosed is in these words, viz

Whereas between His Majesty the King of Great Britain and the United States of America there do exist mutual complaints, and consequent claims, originating as well in certain articles of their treaty of peace as in the law of nations relative to the respective rights of belligerent and neutral nations:

And whereas both the said parties being sincerely desirous to establish permanent peace and friendship, by a convention that may be satisfactory and reciprocally advantageous, have respectfully empowered their undersigned ministers to treat of, and conclude the same:

And whereas the said ministers find it impossible to admit the said mutual complaints and claims of the *first description*, to be well founded in their existing extent; and to the end that the obstacles to concord and agreement, which thence arise, may be done away, they have agreed that all the said complaints and claims shall be forever merged and sunk in the following articles, viz.

The boundaries of the United States, as delineated in the said treaty of peace, and every article in the said treaty contained, are hereby recognized, ratified, and forever confirmed; but, inasmuch as the parties differ as to which is the river intended by the treaty, and therein called the river St. Croix, it is agreed that the said question shall be referred to the final decision of ——— commissioners, to be appointed and empowered as follows, viz.

Whereas it is doubtful whether the river Mississippi extends so far to the northward as to be intersected by the west line from the Lake of the Woods, which is mentioned in the said treaty, it is agreed that the actual extent of the said river to the northward shall be explored and ascertained by commissioners for that purpose, to be appointed and authorized as follows, viz.

It is agreed that if, from the report of said commissioners, it shall appear that the said river does not extend so far to the northward as to be intersected by the west line aforesaid, by reason whereof the boundary lines of the United States in that quarter would not close, then, and forthwith thereupon, such a closing line shall be established as shall be adjudged and determined to be most consistent with the true intent and meaning of the said treaty by ——— commissioners, to be appointed and authorized in the manner prescribed in the article relative to those who are to decide which is the river St. Croix, intended by the said treaty; with these differences only, viz.

It is agreed that His Majesty shall withdraw all his troops and garrisons from every post and place within the limits of the United States, by the 1st of June next, and that all settlers and traders within the precincts or commands of said posts and garrisons shall continue to have and enjoy, unmolested, all their property of every kind, and shall be protected therein; and may either remain and become citizens of the United States, or may sell their land or other property, and remove, with their effects, at any time within two years from the 1st of June next.

It is agreed that His Majesty will cause full and complete satisfaction and compensation to be made for all vessels and property of American citizens which have been, or, during the course of the present war, shall be, illegally captured and condemned, under color of authority and commissions derived from him ; and that in all cases where it shall be apparent full justice and compensation cannot be obtained and actually had, in the ordinary course of judicial proceedings ; and for this purpose —— commissioners shall be appointed and empowered in manner following, viz.

And whereas debts *bona fide* contracted before the peace, and remaining unpaid by American debtors to British creditors, have probably, in some instances, been prejudiced and rendered more precarious by the lawful impediments which, after the peace, did for some time exist, to their being prosecuted and recovered, it is agreed that in all cases where it shall be apparent that the said creditors, by the operation of the said impediments, on the security and value of their debts, have sustained damage, for which adequate reparation cannot now be obtained, and actually had, in the ordinary course of judicial proceedings (it being understood that in these damages, interest shall be included only in cases where, according to equity and good conscience, all things being considered, it ought to be allowed and paid), the United States will make full and complete satisfaction and compensation to the said creditors for the same ; and for this purpose commissioners shall be appointed and authorized in the manner prescribed in the preceding article ; with these differences only, viz.

It is agreed that it shall be and may be lawful for the said United States and their citizens to carry, in their own vessels, of the burthen of one hundred tons, or under, from the said United States, any goods, wares, and merchandises, which British vessels now carry from the United States, to any of His Majesty's islands and ports in the West Indies ; and shall pay in the said islands and ports only such rates of tonnage as British vessels do, or shall be liable to, pay in the United States ; and only such other charges, imposts, and duties, as British vessels and cargoes laden in, and arriving from, the United States, now are, or hereafter shall be, lawfully liable to in the said islands and ports ; and that it shall and may be lawful for the said American vessels to purchase, lade, and carry away, from the said islands and ports, all such of the productions and manufactures of the said islands as they may think proper, and paying only such duties and charges on exportation as such vessels and cargoes, if British, would be liable to ; *Provided always*, That they carry and land the same in the United States, and at no place whatever out of the same ; it being expressly agreed and declared, that West India productions or manufactures shall not be transported in American vessels, either from His Majesty's said islands, or from the United States, to any part of the world except the United States, reasonable sea stores excepted, and excepting, also, rum made in the United States from West India molasses.

It is agreed that all the other ports and territories of His Majesty, whatsoever and wheresoever, (not comprehended within the limits of his chartered trading companies) shall be free and open to the citizens of the United States, and that they, and their vessels and cargoes, shall therein enjoy all the commercial rights, and pay only the same duties and charges, either on importation or exportation, as if they were British merchants' vessels and cargoes, except that they shall pay the same rate of tonnage as may be charged on British vessels in the United States. And, on the other hand, it is agreed that all the ports and territories of the United States, without exception, shall be free and open to British merchants and subjects, and that they and their vessels and cargoes shall therein enjoy all the commercial rights, and pay only the same duties and charges as if they were American merchants' vessels and cargoes ; it being the intention of this article that, in His Majesty's territories (except as before excepted) American merchants and merchant vessels shall be exactly on the same footing with British merchants and merchant vessels, and that British merchants and merchant vessels shall, in all the territories of the United States, be exactly on the same footing with American merchants and merchant vessels, tonnage only excepted.

The trade between the United States and the British West Indies shall be considered as regulated and explained by the preceding article, and therefore as being excluded from the operation of the following articles :

It is agreed that all the productions and manufactures of His Majesty's dominions in any part of the world may freely be imported in British or American vessels into the United States, subject equally and alike to the duties on importation which may there be established ; and that all the productions and manufactures of the United States may be freely imported in American or British vessels into any of the said dominions of His Majesty, subject equally to the duties on importation which may there be established.

And to the end that these duties may be made reciprocal, it is agreed that additional articles for that purpose shall be negotiated and added to this convention as soon as may be conveniently done.

It is agreed that when Great Britain is at war and the United States neutral, no prizes taken from, or by, Great Britain shall be sold in the United States ; and that, when the United States are at war, and Great Britain neutral, no prizes taken from, or by, the United States shall be sold in His Majesty's dominions.

It is agreed that, if it should unfortunately happen that Great Britain and the United States should be at war, there shall be no privateers commissioned by them against each other, and that the merchants and others residing in each other's countries shall be allowed nine months to retire with their effects, and shall not be liable to capture on their way home to their respective countries.

It is agreed that British subjects who now hold lands in the United States, and American citizens who now hold land in His Majesty's dominions, shall continue to hold them according to the nature and tenure of their estates and titles therein, and may grant, and sell, and devise the same, as, and to whom they please, in like manner as if they were natives ; and that neither they, nor their heirs or assigns, shall, so far as may respect the said lands, and the legal remedies incident thereto, be regarded as aliens.

It is agreed that neither debts due from individuals of the one nation to individuals of the other, nor shares or moneys which they may have in the funds, or in the public or private banks, shall ever, in any event of war or national differences be sequestered or confiscated; except that, in case of war, and only during its continuance, payment may be suspended, it being both unjust and impolitic that debts and engagements contracted and made by individuals, having confidence in each other, and in their respective governments, should ever be destroyed or impaired by national authority, on account of national differences and discontents.

From the 6th to the 30th of August nothing of importance occurred.

On the 30th day of August Lord Grenville wrote me a letter, and enclosed two draughts or projets of treaties. The letter is in these words, viz. :

August 30th, 1794.

SIR :

I have now the honor to transmit to you two projets, the one for regulating all points in dispute between His Majesty and the United States, the other for the establishment of commercial regulations. You will perceive that I have proceeded in forming these projets on the foundation of the paper you communicated to me, but that I have occasionally made such variations as seemed to me just and expedient. I have thought that some time might be saved by communicating them to you in this manner. Whenever you have sufficiently considered them to be enabled to converse, either on the whole, or on any distinct branches of so extensive a subject, I shall be very much at your order, having very sincerely at heart the speedy and favorable conclusion of our negotiation.

It would have been more satisfactory to me if I had found it practicable to send you these projets sooner; but you will, I am sure, be sensible of the circumstances which must, at this conjuncture, have interfered with the preparation of an arrangement intended to comprehend so extensive a subject, and to lay the foundation of lasting harmony and friendship between our two countries. Even in the state in which I now send you these papers, I am apprehensive that some verbal corrections may occur as necessary to give full effect to the objects intended to be provided for, supposing those objects to be mutually consented to; and I think there are one or two points, on which we have occasionally touched in our conversations, for which no provision is made in these projets. But I have preferred making the communication in its present shape rather than that any further delay should be created, and I trust, with real confidence, to your candor, respecting such further suggestions as I may occasionally see ground to state to you. I have the honor to be, &c. &c.

GRENVILLE.

The draughts, or projets, are as follows, viz. :

First, the Preamble.

Article 1. It is agreed that His Majesty will withdraw all his troops and garrisons from the posts within the boundary line assigned by the treaty of peace to the United

ry therein described, that question shall be referred to the final decision of commissioners *in London*, to be appointed in the following manner, viz. : That one commissioner shall be named by His Majesty, and one by the United States, and that the said two commissioners shall agree on the choice of a third, or, if they cannot so agree, that they shall each propose one person, and that, of the two names so proposed, one shall be drawn by lot, in the presence of the two original commissioners ; and that the three commissioners so appointed shall be sworn impartially to examine and decide the said question, according to such documents as shall respectively be laid before them, on the part of the British Government, and of the United States.

Secondly.   That whereas it is now understood that the river Mississippi would, at no point thereof, be intersected by such westward line as is described in the said treaty : and, whereas it was stipulated, by the said treaty, that the navigation of the Mississippi should be free to both parties, it is agreed that the boundary line should run in the manner described by the said treaty, from the Lake Huron, to the northward of the Isle Philippeaux, in Lake Superior ; and that from thence the said line shall proceed to the bottom of West Bay, in the said lake ; and from thence, in a due west course, to the river of the Red Lake ; or eastern branch of the Mississippi ; and down the said branch to the main river of the Mississippi ; and that, as well on the said branch, as on (—— or —— through Lake Superior ; and from thence to the water communication between the said lake, and the Lake of the Woods, to the point where the said water communication shall be intersected by a line running due north from the mouth of the River St. Croix, which falls into the Mississippi below the falls of St. Anthony, and that the boundary line shall proceed from such point of intersection, in a due southerly course, along the said line to the Mississippi, and that, as well on the said

water communication, as on) every part of the Mississippi
where the same *bounds the territory* of the *United States*, the
navigation shall be free to both parties, and His *Majesty's
subjects* shall *always* be admitted to enter freely into the
bays, ports, and creeks, on the *American* side, and to land
and dwell there for the purposes of their commerce ; and,
for greater certainty, the undersigned ministers have annexed to each of the copies of this treaty a copy of the
map made use of by them, with the boundaries marked
thereon, agreeably to this article ; and the boundaries of
the United States, as fixed by the said treaty of peace, and
by this treaty, together with all the other articles of the said
treaty, are hereby recognized, ratified and forever confirmed.

Art. 3. Whereas it is alleged, by divers British merchants and others, His Majesty's subjects, that debts, to a
considerable amount, which were *bona fide* contracted before
the peace, still remain owing to them by citizens or inhabitants of the United States, and that, by the operation of
various lawful impediments since the peace, not only the
full recovery of the said debts has been delayed, but also
the security and value thereof has been impaired and lessened, and that, in many instances, the British creditors cannot now obtain, by the ordinary course of judicial proceedings, full and just relief for the loss and damage so sustained
by them, it is agreed, that, in all cases where such relief cannot, for whatever reason, be now had by British creditors,
in the ordinary course of justice, the United States of America will make full and complete satisfaction to the said creditors ; and that, for this purpose, commissioners shall be
appointed and authorized to act in America, in manner following, that is to say: two commissioners shall be named
by His Majesty, and two by the United States, and a fifth by
the unanimous choice of the other four; but, if they shall not
agree in such choice, then one name shall be proposed by
the British commissioners, and one by the commissioners of

the United States, and one of the two names so proposed shall be drawn by lot, in the presence of the said original commissioners; and in case of death, sickness or necessary absence, the places of the said commissioners shall be respectively supplied in the same manner as such commissioners respectively were first appointed. The said five commissioners shall be sworn to hear all such complaints as shall, within the space of eighteen months from their first sitting, or within such further time as they shall see cause to allow for that purpose, be preferred to them, by British creditors, or their representatives, in virtue of this article, and impartially to determine the same, according to the true intent of this article, and of the treaty of peace.

And the said commissioners, in awarding such sums, as shall appear to them to be due to the said creditors by virtue of this article, are empowered to take into their consideration, and to determine, all claims, on account either of principal or interest, in respect of the said debts, and to decide respecting the same, according to the merits of the several cases, due regard being had to all the circumstances thereof, and as equity and justice shall appear to them to require; and the said commissioners shall be empowered to examine all persons, on oath, touching the premises, and also to receive in evidence, at their discretion, and according as they shall think most consistent with equity and justice, all written depositions, or books, or papers, or copies, or extracts thereof, every such deposition, book, paper, copy or extract, being duly authenticated, according to the legal forms now respectively existing in the two countries, or in such other manner as the said commissioners shall see cause to prescribe and require.

Three of the said commissioners shall constitute a board, and be empowered to do any act appertaining to the said commission; provided that in every such case, one of the commissioners named on each side, and the fifth com-

missioner, chosen as above, shall be present; and all decisions shall be made by the majority of voices of the commissioners then present.

The award of the said commissioners, or any three of
them, as aforesaid, shall, in all cases, be final and conclusive,
both as to the justice of the claim, and to the amount of the
sum to be paid to the claimant; and the United States
undertake to cause the same to be paid to such claimants,
without deduction, in sterling money and in such place or
places, and at such time or times, as shall be awarded by the
said commissioners; and on condition of such releases to be
given by the claimant of his demands against individuals, as
to them shall appear just and reasonable.

Art. 4th. Whereas complaints have been made by divers
merchants and others, citizens of the United States, that,
during the course of the war in which His Majesty is now
engaged, they have sustained considerable loss and damage,
by reason of irregular or illegal captures, and condemnation
of their vessels, under color of authority or commission from
His Majesty; and that, from various circumstances belonging to the said cases, adequate compensation for the said
losses cannot now be obtained by the ordinary course of
judicial proceedings, it is agreed that, in all such cases,
where adequate compensation cannot, for whatever reason,
be now *had* by the said merchants and others, full and complete satisfaction will be made by the British Government,
to the said complainants; and that, for this purpose, commissioners shall be appointed and authorized to act, in
London, in the same manner, and with the same powers and
authorities, and subject to the same restrictions as the commissioners named in the third article of this treaty; and
that the award of the said commissioners shall, in like manner, be final and conclusive in all respects. And His Britannic Majesty engages to cause to be paid to such complainants, respectively, the amount of all sums so awarded, with-

out deduction, in *sterling* money, and at such time or times, and in such place or places, as shall be awarded by the said commissioners, and on condition of such releases, on the part of the complainants, of their demands against individuals, as to the said commissioners shall appear just and reasonable.

And it is further agreed that, if it shall appear that, in the course of the war, loss and damage has been sustained by His Majesty's subjects, by reason of the capture of their vessels and merchandise, such capture having been made, either within the limits of the jurisdiction of the said States, or by vessels armed in the ports of the said States, or by vessels commanded or owned by the citizens of the said States, the *United States* will make full satisfaction for such loss or damage, the same being to be ascertained by commissioners, in the manner already mentioned in this article.

Art. 5th. It is agreed that, with respect to the neutral commerce which one party may carry on with the *European* enemies of the other, when engaged in war, the principles to be observed by Great Britain towards the United States, and reciprocally by the United States towards Great Britain, shall always, and in all points, be the same as those which shall at that time be observed by the said parties, respectively, towards the most favored neutral nations of Europe, with the exception of such particular privileges as may, before the commencement of the war to which the same shall apply, have been granted, by special treaty, to particular European nations, and with such extensions or modifications as may occasionally be established by special treaty, between Great Britain and the United States, for their mutual convenience.

Art. 6th. It is agreed that, in all cases where vessels shall be captured or detained, on just suspicion of having on board enemies' property, or of carrying to the enemy any of the articles which are *contraband* of war, the said vessels shall be brought to the nearest or most convenient port ; and that all proper measures shall be taken to prevent delay in deciding the case of ships so brought in for adjudication, and in the payment or recovery of any indemnification adjudged or agreed to be paid to the masters or owners of such ships.

Art. 7th.   When one of the contracting parties is engaged in war, and the other remains neutral, the said neutral Power shall not suffer the ships, vessels, goods, or merchandise of the other, which may be taken at sea or elsewhere, by the enemy, to be brought into any of its ports or dominions, and much less to be there sold or exchanged ; but shall publicly forbid anything of that kind to be done.   And if any ships, vessels, goods, or merchandise, of either of the contracting parties, or their people, or subjects, so taken, at sea, or elsewhere, shall be carried into the ports or countries of the other, by the enemy, neither the same, nor any part thereof, shall be allowed to be sold or exchanged in that port, or in any other place in the dominion of the said neutral party.   The master of the ship or vessel so taken, as also the mariners and passengers of every description, shall, as soon as they arrive, be immediately set at liberty ; and the said ship or vessel so brought, shall not be permitted to stay in that harbor, but shall be obliged immediately to leave the port, with her goods, merchandise, and lading, and without being allowed to return to the same, or to any other port in the dominions of the said neutral party ; Provided, nevertheless, that nothing in this article shall be construed to derogate from the public treaties which have already been entered into by either of the contracting parties with other nations ; but in so far as such treaties do not interfere, and *in all cases to which they do not apply*, the above article shall remain in full force, and shall be executed accordingly. And the contracting parties will not, in future, conclude any treaty in derogation of this article.

Art. 8th. It is agreed that the subjects and inhabitants of the kingdoms, provinces, and dominions, of the contracting parties, shall exercise no acts of hostility or violence against each other, either by sea or by land, or in rivers, streams, ports, or havens, under any color or pretence whatsoever, and particularly, that the subjects or people of either party shall not receive any patent, commission, or instruction, for arming, and acting at sea as privateers, or any letters of reprisal, as they are called, from any Prince or States, enemies to the other party ; neither shall they arm ships in such manner as is above said, nor go out to sea therewith, for the purpose of exercising any act of violence against the subjects or people of the other contracting party ; nor shall they, in any manner, molest or disturb the said subjects or people ; to which end sufficient laws and regulations shall, if necessary, be provided ; and, as often as it is required by either party, strict and express prohibitions shall be renewed and published, in all the territories, countries, and dominions, of each party, wheresoever, that no one shall, in any wise, use such commissions, or letters of reprisal, or engage in any such acts of hostility as aforesaid, under the pain of severe punishment, to be inflicted on the transgressors, besides their being liable to make full restitution and satisfaction to those to whom they have done any damage. Neither shall any letters of reprisal be hereafter granted by either of the said contracting parties, to the prejudice or detriment of the subjects of the other ; except, only, in such case wherein justice is denied or delayed ; which denial or delay of justice shall not be regarded as verified, unless the petition of the person who desires the said letters of reprisal shall be communicated to the minister residing there on the part of the Government against whose subjects or people they are granted, that, within the space of four months, or sooner, if it be possible, they may manifest the contrary, or procure the satisfaction which may be justly due.

Art. 9th. Neither of the said contracting parties shall permit the ships or goods, belonging to the subjects of the other, to be taken within the limits of their respective jurisdictions, on their coasts, nor in the ports or rivers of their dominions, by ships of war, or others, having commission from any prince, republic, or city, whatsoever ; but, *in case* it should so happen, both parties shall employ their *united force* to obtain reparation of the damage thereby occasioned.

Art. 10th. If it should unfortunately happen that a war should break out between Great Britain and the United States, all merchants and others residing in the two countries, respectively, shall be allowed nine months to retire with their effects, and shall be protected from capture on their way home : Provided, always, that this favor is not to extend to those who shall act contrary to the established laws. And it is further agreed, that neither *debts due* from *individuals* of the one nation to individuals of the other, nor shares or moneys which they may have in the *public funds*, or in the *public* or *private banks*, shall ever, in any event of war or national differences, be sequestered or confiscated ; it being both unjust and impolitic that debts and engagements contracted and made by individuals, having confidence in each other, and in their respective governments, should ever be destroyed or impaired, by national authority, on account of national differences and discontents.

Art. 11th. It is agreed that British subjects, who now hold lands in the territories of the United States, and American citizens, who now hold lands in His Majesty's dominions, shall continue to hold them, according to the nature and tenure of their estates and titles therein ; and may grant and sell, and devise the same, as, and to whom, they please, in like manner as if they were natives ; and that neither they, nor their heirs or assigns, shall, so far as may respect the said lands, and the legal remedies incident thereto, be regarded as aliens.

Commercial Projet.

The Preamble.

Art. 1st. It is agreed that there shall be, between the dominions of His Britannic Majesty in Europe, and the territories of the United States, a reciprocal and perfect liberty of commerce and navigation, and a free admission of all ships belonging to either party, whether the same be ships of war or merchant vessels; and that the subjects and inhabitants of the two countries, respectively, shall have liberty, freely and securely, and without hindrance or molestation of any kind, to come, with their said ships and their cargoes, to the lands, countries, cities, ports, places, and rivers, within the dominions and territories aforesaid; to enter into the same, to resort thereto, and to remain and reside therein without any limitation of time; also, to hire, purchase, and possess, houses and warehouses, for the purpose of their commerce; and, generally, that the merchants and traders, on each side, shall enjoy the most complete protection and security for their commerce; but subject always, as to what respects this article, to the general laws and statutes of the two countries, respectively.

Art. 2nd. It shall be free for the two contracting parties, respectively, to appoint consuls for the protection of trade, to reside in the dominions and territories aforesaid, the same being of the nation on whose behalf they shall be so appointed, and not otherwise; and such consul shall enjoy the liberties and rights which belong to them by reason of their functions; but either party may except, from the general liberty of residence of such consuls, such particular places as such party shall judge proper to be so excepted.

Art. 3rd. The vessels of the two contracting parties, respectively, coming to the dominions or territories aforesaid, shall enjoy the same liberty in respect of the entry and discharge of their lawful cargoes, and all other regulations which respect the general convenience and advantage of commerce, as now are, or shall, at any time, be enjoyed by any other foreign nation, which shall be the most favored in that respect; and no distinction shall exist, of tonnage or other duties, (such light house duties excepted as are levied for the profit of individuals or of corporations) by which the vessels of the one party shall pay, in the ports of the other, any higher or other duties than shall be paid, in similar circumstances, by the vessels of the foreign nation the most favored in that respect, or by the vessels of the party into whose ports they shall come.

Art. 4th. No article, being of the growth, produce, or manufacture, of any of the dominions or territories of the one party, shall pay, on being imported directly from the said territories or dominions, into the ports of the other, any higher or other duties than shall be there paid for the like articles, on importation from any other foreign country.

Art. 5th. No new prohibition shall be laid in any of the territories or dominions aforesaid, by one of the contracting parties, on the importation of any article, being of the growth, produce, or manufacture, of the territories or dominions of the other; nor shall articles, being of the growth, produce, or manufacture, of any other country, be prohibited to be imported into the dominions of one of the contracting parties, by the vessels of the other, except such articles only as are now so prohibited.

Art. 6th. With respect to the territories and dominions of His Britannic Majesty in the West Indies, the following arrangements have been agreed to by the contracting parties.

His Majesty consents that it shall and may be lawful, during the time hereinafter limited, for the citizens of the United States of America to carry to any of His Majesty's islands and ports in the West Indies, from the United States, in their own vessels, not being above the burthen of seventy tons, any goods or merchandise being of the growth or produce of the said States, which it is or may be lawful to carry to the said islands and ports from the said States in British vessels and that the said American vessels and their cargoes shall pay there no other or higher duties than shall be payable by British vessels, in similar circumstances: And that it shall be lawful to the said American citizens to purchase, load, and carry away, in their said vessels, to the United States, from the said islands and ports, all such articles, being of the growth and produce of the said islands, as may, by law, be carried from them to the said States in British vessels; and subject only to the same duties and charges on exportation to which British vessels are or shall be subject in similar circumstances. Provided, always, that they carry and land the same in the United States only; it being expressly agreed and declared that, during the continuance of this article, the United States will prohibit the carrying any West India productions or manufactures in American vessels, either from His Majesty's Islands, or from the United States, to any part of the world except the United States—reasonable sea stores excepted, and excepting also rum made in the United States from West India molasses.

It is agreed that this article, and every matter and thing therein contained, shall continue to be in force during the continuance of the war in which His Majesty is now engaged, and also for two years from and after the day of the signature of the preliminary articles of peace by which the same may be terminated.

And it is further agreed, that, at the expiration of the said term, the two contracting parties will treat further concerning the arrangement of their commerce in this respect, according to the situation in which His Majesty may then find himself as with respect to the West Indies, and with a view to the mutual advantage and extension of commerce.

Art. 7th. This treaty, and all the matters therein contained, except the sixth article, shall continue to be in force for twelve years from the day of the exchange of the ratifications thereof ; and if, during the continuance of this treaty, there shall arise, on either side, any complaint of the infraction of any article thereof, it is agreed that neither the whole treaty, nor any article thereof, shall, on that account, be suspended, until representation shall have been made to the Government by the Minister of the party complaining ; and even if redress shall not then be obtained, four months' notice shall be given previous to such suspension.

To the before mentioned letter I returned the following answer, viz. :

PALL-MALL, ROYAL HOTEL,
September 1, 1794.

MY LORD :

I was yesterday honoured with your Lordship's letter of the 30th August, with the projets and map which accompanied it. I consider the articles in these projets as being (like those in our conversations) merely for mutual consideration.

In these projets several parting points present themselves ; some of them, I presume, may be easily accommodated, but there are others which create in my mind serious apprehensions. One of these articles (being without the limits of my authority) I think I ought now to particularize ; it is the one which proposes a cession of territory in the northwestern corner of the United States. It is proper, also, that I should say with frankness that, in my opinion, many circumstances and considerations which shall be submitted to your Lordship will restrain the United States from such a cession.

This article would entirely frustrate my hopes, if I had not reason to persuade myself that the enlarged and enlightened policy of excluding *secondary* from a competition with *primary* objects will always harmonize with your Lordship's mind. The present occasion is great, and, though critical, yet auspicious to the establishment of confidence and friendship between the two countries. With the magnitude and importance of these objects, the projets in question really do not strike me as being commensurate. I am aware that, in forming them, your Lordship had many difficulties growing out of the subject, and probably some others to encounter, and that your attention was constantly divided between a multitude of great and pressing affairs.

The negotiation now becomes delicate, and I should experience more than a proportionate embarrassment were it not for my confidence in your Lordship's candour and liberality, and for those sentiments of esteem, as well as respect, with which I have the honour to be, etc.

The Rt. Hon. Lord GRENVILLE, etc.

The proposed alterations in our northwestern boundary, and the consequential cession and dereliction of territory, appeared to me to be a point which I ought, without delay, to state to his Lordship in the light in which it appeared to me. I therefore prepared and sent him enclosed in a note, the following remarks, viz. :

Royal Hotel, Pall-Mall,
4th September, 1794.

Mr. Jay presents his compliments to Lord Grenville, and requests the favor of his Lordship to name a time for receiving Mr. Jay on the subject of the proposed treaties. In the meantime Mr. Jay has the honour of submitting the remarks herewith enclosed to his Lordship's consideration.

Remarks on that part of the second article of the projet of a treaty for terminating all differences between Great Britain and the United States of America, which purports a cession or dereliction by the latter of the country lying to the westward and northward of either of the two lines therein proposed and described.

For this cession or dereliction two reasons are assigned, viz. :

1st. That it is now understood that the river Mississippi would, in no part thereof, be intersected by a west line from the Lake of the Woods.

2d. That it was stipulated by the treaty of peace that the navigation of the river Mississippi should be free to both parties.

Admitting the fact in the *first* of these reasons to be well founded, it shows *only* that the northern and western lines of the United States do not meet and close, and, therefore, that it is necessary to fix on a line for closing them. But no argument thence results that either Great Britain or the United States ought to cede or to acquire any territory further than what such closing line may possibly render unavoidable.

That the Mississippi would, in no point thereof, be intersected by a west line from the Lake of the Woods is a fact involved in too much uncertainty to be assumed as a foundation for national stipulation ; for however it may be conjectured or supposed, yet it still remains to be ascertained.

The map sent to Mr. Jay by Lord Grenville, viz., Faden's, published in 1793, informs us that the river Mississippi has been ascended only as far up as about the forty-fifth degree of north latitude—that is, about a degree above the Falls of St. Anthony, so that its further extent and course towards the north *are yet to be discovered.*

On the same map, Faden lays down a stream connected with the marshy lake, near the forty-fifth degree of latitude, and thus denominates it : " *Mississippi by conjecture.*"

He also lays down on the same map a stream connected with the White Bear Lake, near the latitude forty-six, and thus denominates it : " *Mississippi by conjecture.*"

He also lays down on the same map a stream connected with the Red Lake in latitude forty-seven, and thus denominates it : " Red Lake River, *or Lahonton's* Mississippi."

Inasmuch, therefore, as three different streams, found in the immense wilderness above latitude forty-five, are *conjectured* to be the Mississippi, it is plain that, so far from being certain how far that river runs to the north, we really are yet to learn where it does run, and which of the rivers in that wilderness it is. How then can it be assumed, as a fact resting on good evidence, that the Mississippi would at no point thereof be intersected by a west line from the Lake of the Woods?

Individuals differing about boundaries depending on the course and extent of brooks and streams, settle questions of that kind by actual surveys. States usually, and with good reason, do the same. Why be content with delusive conjectures and probabilities when absolute certainty can easily be had? Let a survey be accurately made by joint commissioners, and at joint expense. The United States are ready to adopt that measure and to enter into the necessary stipulations and arrangements.

If it should appear on such a survey that the west line would intersect the Mississippi, no room for further question or dispute will remain; but if the contrary should prove to be the case, then, as the northern and western lines of the United States would not close, the manner of closing them will naturally and necessarily come under consideration. Several modes of closing them may be devised, neither of which may be altogether agreeable to both parties. Unless they shall be able to agree, let joint commissioners, at joint expense, and upon oath, fix a closing line in the manner which they shall judge most consonant with the true meaning and intent of the treaty of peace. The United States are ready to enter into such eventual stipulations as may be necessary for that purpose.

The *second* reason assigned for this cession is, " that

it was stipulated by the treaty of peace that the navigation of the Mississippi should be free to both parties."

From this stipulation it is argued, as a natural and necessary inference, that it was in the expectation and intention of the parties that they should and would both border, not only on the river, but also on the *navigable* part of it.

This inference seems to be violent. A right freely to navigate a bay, a strait, a sound, or a river is perfect without, and does not *necessarily* presuppose the dominion and property of lands *adjacent* to it.

But, although, from a right to navigate the river Mississippi, a right to adjacent lands cannot be inferred, yet, when that right is connected with the circumstance that both parties were to be bounded by a line terminating at the river, it is thought to be thence presumable that the parties expected and intended the said line would and should terminate at a navigable part of it. They might or might not have intended it. Whether they did or not can only be discovered from their concomitant *words* and *actions*. On looking into the treaty for *words* indicating such intention, our search proves fruitless ; there are no such *words* in it, nor the least shadow of a stipulation or declaration on the point. If we review the plain and manifest design of the treaty relative to boundaries, we find the idea of such intention uniformly contradicted. The treaty, in delineating the boundaries of the United States, passes from the northwest angle of Nova Scotia to the head of the Connecticut River; then down that river to the fifty-fifth degree of latitude; then on that line of latitude to the River Iroquois; then (quitting that line of latitude) to Lake Ontario; then, from lake to lake through their connecting waters, until it arrives at the Lake of the Woods, and passing through it to the northwesternmost point thereof, proceeds on a due west course to the Mississippi, etc.

Now it was always well known, and the maps show it, that the *Lake of the Woods* is situated at a great distance in the north, above the latitude of the Falls of St. Anthony, which interrupt the navigation of the Mississippi, and consequently that a *due* west line from the Lake of the Woods must of necessity strike the river above those falls, and as far above them as the latitude of the lake is above the latitude of the falls.

Again, it was not then known, nor is it yet known, how far the Mississippi runs navigable beyond those falls, nor whether any, or how many, other falls intervene between them and its source. The parties therefore being entirely ignorant of the extent and of the course and of the character of the river high above the falls, could not possibly have judged, or divined, or guessed whether the place or part of the river at which the west line would strike it was navigable or not. How, then, could they expect or intend anything about it? Nothing could be more obvious than that a *due* west line might terminate on the river at a place *not navigable*, and had navigation been in view it seems strange that the treaty should not contain a provision that if the said west line, on being actually run, should strike the river at a place where it was not navigable, then the said line should be declined so many degrees southerly as might be necessary to bring it to the first navigable water of the river. Yet nothing like this is to be found in the treaty.

It is not difficult to discern from the treaty, and so was the fact, that other ideas and views governed the direction of the boundary lines.

The question then was, where would it be most convenient to both parties, and, all things considered, where would be most wise and prudent, that the boundaries between them should be fixed? Two lines were proposed and considered, one from the point before mentioned, on Connecticut River, and running straight on the line of the forty-fifth degree of latitude, west to the Mississippi; the other was the one adopted and established by the treaty. The official papers of the British ministers which respect that negotiation will probably show that Great Britain had the choice of these two lines, and that she preferred the latter.

This choice and preference gives no support to the idea that she then contemplated navigable water in that part of the Mississippi which was supposed to penetrate into Canada. The first line, if adopted, would have favoured it, and fair presumption might have classed that among the reasons of preference; but notwithstanding this, Great Britain did not prefer it; on the contrary, as the waters would form a line which never could be mistaken, and afforded great conveniences to both parties, the line of the waters was preferred by both. This water line was, by mutual consent, terminated at the northwesternmost point of the Lake of the Woods ; it was agreed that the Mississippi should bound the United States on the west, nothing then remained but to agree on the course which the closing line, from the lake to the river, should run ; and a due west course was agreed upon, without any expectation or design that it would or should there meet the navigable water. The truth is, that the stipulation respecting the navigation of the river, being free to both parties, was an afterthought, and gave occasion to a new and subsequent article, viz., the eighth. Even in the drawing of that article, when the navigation of the river became an object of contemplation, no connection was introduced between the right mentioned in that article and the boundaries designated in the second article ; no facilities were asked, or proposed, or stipulated, for a water or any other communication between Canada and the navigable water of the Mississippi, which doubtless would have been the case had such a communication been then in view, especially considering the absolute uncertainty and extreme improbability of that river being navigable above the high latitude of the Lake of the Woods.

From the before mentioned circumstances and considerations it seems fairly to result that the *two* reasons assigned for the cession in question, as a matter of equity and right, do not afford it a solid foundation.

If this conclusion be just, it precludes the necessity of showing at large that none of the inferences ascribed to the said *two* reasons involve a claim to tracts of country so extensive as either of the two proposed and marked on the map, each of which includes more than thirty thousand square *miles ;* and that without taking into computation the extensive country lying between (what in the subjoined diagrams are for the purpose of computation regarded as) the west sides of these tracts and the Mississippi, and to the southward of the west line form the Lake of the Woods, and which country would on either of these plans become also annexed to Canada.

In order that you may have an accurate idea of the lines proposed by Lord Grenville, I here insert copies of the diagrams mentioned in the foregoing remarks. (Nos. 1 and 2.)

On the 5th of September Lord Grenville wrote me the following note, viz. :

DOWNING STREET, September 5, 1794.

Lord Grenville presents his compliments to Mr. Jay. He has received Mr. Jay's note, with the enclosed remarks, and will be glad to see him at his office tomorrow, at twelve o'clock. Lord Grenville has, in the mean time, the honor to enclose to Mr. Jay some observations which have occurred to him on the perusal of the paper which he received from Mr. Jay.

The observations enclosed with this note were as follows, viz. :

*Observations Respecting the Northwestern Boundary of the
United States of America.*

It cannot for a moment be admitted, that the proposed
arrangement on the subject of the Northwestern boundary,
is properly to be considered in the manner in which it is
spoken of by Mr. Jay, namely, as a cession, or dereliction
of territory on the part of the United States.

Their boundary to the northwest, as fixed by the treaty,
is a line " to be drawn from the Lake of the Woods, in a
due west course to the Mississippi." There are in this
agreement two distinct parts :

1st. That the boundary line should be drawn in a due
westerly course from the Lake of the Woods ; and,

2d. That it should likewise be drawn in a due westerly
course to the Mississippi.

If such a line cannot in fact be drawn, between those
points, there can be no ground for considering one part of
this stipulation as more permanently fixed than the other,
or as affording a more equitable ground for any future
arrangement ; and it would be quite as reasonable for
this country to consider as a cession of territory, on our
part, the adoption of any other boundary than that of a
due westerly line striking the Mississippi, as for the United
States to urge that such a cession exists on their part, if
such a line is not drawn from the Lake of the Woods.

To this consideration must be added, that which so
plainly results from the article respecting the free navigation of the Mississippi ; on which head it seems sufficient
for the present to remark that such a right evidently and
necessarily implies the possibility of access to that river,
without passing through a foreign territory.

Little objection occurs to making an actual survey,
except that of delay. If, on that survey, the stipulations
in the treaty should be found to be compatible with the

real geography of the country, it is certain that no further dispute could exist on that point.

But, if we have from the best information on the subject sufficient reason to believe that no such line can be drawn as mentioned in the treaty, it cannot be desirable, when all the interests of the two countries with relation to each other are under discussion, with a view to lasting friendship, to leave unsettled so material a ground of difference as that of an unascertained boundary. The mode of settling that point is necessarily connected with the general result of the present negotiation. If no more can be accomplished on any other point, than the doing strict justice between the parties, according to existing treaties and the laws of nations, the appointment of commissaries, as proposed by Mr. Jay, does not appear ill adapted to obtain the same object as to this point : provided that those commissaries are distinctly enabled to take into their consideration the 8th article, and to give to that stipulation such effect as they shall think it ought in justice to have, in the formation of a new boundary line.

But, if the negotiation should lead to new stipulations of mutual advantage, no subject appears more proper for the application of that principle, than one in which there exist two doubtful and contradictory claims, founded on an agreement which cannot by any possibility be executed ; especially if it be true, as it is considered here, that this is a point where any advantage, whatever it should be, which Great Britain might acquire, would, under all circumstances, be found at least equally beneficial to the United States.

Downing Street, 5*th September*, 1794.

Expecting that when we met, the first of the above projets would, as first in the order of things, be first considered, my attention was more immediately confined to it ; but the time consumed in preparing the remarks before mentioned left me very little leisure to employ in forming satisfactory opinions on the different parts of this projet; several, however, occurred to me, of which I made short notes; they are as follows. You will find the numbers marked in the margin of the projet.

Note 1. In what capacity are they so to remain? As British subjects or American citizens? If the first, a time to make their election should be assigned.

2. If his Majesty's subjects are to pass into the American territories for the purposes of Indian trade, ought not American citizens to be permitted to pass into His Majesty's territories for like purposes.

3. If the American Indians are to have the privilege of trading with Canada, ought not Canada Indians to be privileged to trade with the United States?

4. If goods for Indian trade be introduced *duty free* by British traders, how is the introduction of other goods with them to be prevented? And for this privilege, operating a loss to American revenue, what reciprocal benefit is to be allowed?

5. Why should the commissioners for ascertaining the river St. Croix, meet and decide in London? Is it not probable that actual views and surveys, and the testimony and examination of witnesses on the spot, will be necessary?

6. Why confine the mutual navigation of the Mississippi to where the same *bounds the territory of the United States?*

7. Why should *perpetual* commercial privileges be granted to Great Britain on the *Mississippi, etc.,*

when she declines granting *perpetual* commercial privileges to the United States *anywhere ?*

8. This preamble, connected with the silence of the treaty as to the negroes carried away, implies that the United States have been aggressors; it also unnecessarily impeaches their judicial proceedings.

9. On no principle ought more to be asked, than that the United States indemnify creditors for losses and damages caused by the impediments mentioned.

10. The word *had* is not sufficiently definite; the object being not only sentence, decree, or judgment, but payment and satisfaction.

11. Sterling money fluctuates according to exchange; this should be *fixed.*

12. Why not place these captures on the footing with the others, and charge the United States only in cases where justice and complete compensation cannot be had from judicial proceedings?

13. Why provide only for neutral commerce with *European* enemies? The whole of this article is so indefinite as to be useless.

14. What are or shall be deemed *contraband* in the sense of this article?

15. As the United States have permitted the French to sell prizes in the United States, should not the restriction not to do it in future commence at the expiration of the present war?

16. There should be an article against the impressment of each other's people.

17. This united force should be confined to the *moment* of aggression.

18. The confiscation of debts, etc. This article should be in the *treaty of commerce.*

On the 6th of September, agreeable to Lord Grenville's appointment, I waited upon him; we spent several hours in discussing the several topics which arose from these notes, and some others, which in the course of the conversation occurred. He promised to take what I had offered into consideration, and manifested throughout the conversation every disposition to accommodate that could be wished : we may not finally be able to agree. If we should not, it would, in my opinion, occasion *mutual* regret, for I do believe that the greater part of the Cabinet, and particularly Lord Grenville, are really disposed and desirous not only to settle all differences amicably, but also to establish permanent peace, good humor, and friendship between the two countries.

On the 8th of September I received from Lord Grenville the following letter, enclosing the papers mentioned in it, viz. :

ST. JAMES'S SQUARE, Sept. 7, 1794.

SIR : In order to narrow as much as possible the objects of our discussions, I have stated in the enclosed paper what occurs to me on the different points to which your notes apply, except the second, third, and fourth articles of those notes, which I have reserved for further examination and inquiry. I expect that, by Tuesday or Wednesday at furthest,I shall be able to converse further with you on those points, as well as with respect to what you suggested on the subject of the East Indies. The points in discussion will then be reduced within a small compass, but they certainly do not relate to the least important parts of our negotiation.

With respect to them, I can only say, that you shall continue to find in me the same openness of discussion, and the same desire to state to you, without reserve, what I think may be conceded to the object of speedy conciliation, and what the interest and honor of my country, and the duty which I owe to the king, oblige me to insist upon, as necessary for that object. It is with sentiments of very real esteem and respect, that I have the honor to be, &c., &c.

GRENVILLE.

P.S.—I also send a note of two alterations to be made in the commercial projet in consequence of our conversation of yesterday. G.

To the Hon. Mr. JAY, &c.

Observations Enclosed with the Above Letter.

No. 1. In consequence of the observation contained in the first remark, Lord Grenville proposes to add, in the first article of the projet, after the words, " property thereof," at the end of the first paragraph, these words : "and such of them as shall continue to reside there for the purposes of their commerce, shall not be compelled to become subjects of the United States, or to take any oath of allegiance to the Government thereof, but shall be at full liberty so to do (if they think proper) within one year after the evacuation of the posts, which period is hereby assigned to them for making their choice in this respect." Considering the length of the first article, now increased by this addition, it may be better to divide it into two—the second beginning with the words, " It shall at all times be free " &c. &c.

Articles, 2, 3, and 4 reserved for further examination.

5. The meeting of the commissioners respecting the river St. Croix is proposed to be in London, because it is supposed that the great mass of evidence on the subject is here. A power may be given to them, either to direct a local survey,

or to adjourn to America, but it seems very unlikely that this would become necessary.

6. No idea was entertained of confining the mutual navigation of the Mississippi to that part of the river where it bounds the territory of the United States. That qualification was intended only to have reference to the free admission of British merchants and ships, into the bays, ports, and creeks of the United States, on the Mississippi; nor would it have been proposed at all, to repeat in this article, what is so distinctly stipulated in the treaty of peace, respecting the free navigation of the Mississippi, except for the purpose of expressly extending that stipulation to every part of the waters now proposed to form a part of the boundary.

7. The right of admission into ports, &c. for the purposes of trade, and the general liberty of commerce, spoken of in this article, are not considered as commercial privileges, such as are usually made the subject of temporary regulation by special treaties of commerce. Great Britain by no means declines to give the same rights permanently to America, as with respect to those parts of her dominions which are open to foreign commerce. These rights are, indeed, now generally acknowledged to be incident to a state of amity and good correspondence; and if it is proposed to particularize them, as with respect to the Mississippi, this is done only with the view of removing the possibility of such doubts as were formerly raised here upon the subject.

8. On the fullest reconsideration of this preamble, Lord Grenville sees no ground to think it liable to the objection made by Mr. Jay, particularly when compared with the preamble proposed for the fourth article. The proceedings in both articles are grounded on the allegations of individuals. The truth of those allegations is referred to the decision of the commissioners. Lord Grenville's opinion respecting the prior aggression of the United States, as well as his

reasons for that opinion, are well known to Mr. Jay; but he has no wish to introduce into the proposed treaties any discussion of that point. He is therefore very ready to consider any form of words which Mr. Jay may suggest for those articles, as better suited to the two objects to which they are directed—those of justice to individuals, and conciliation between the Governments; and this applies equally to the remarks Nos. 9 and 10.

11. The substitution of the word *specie*, as suggested by Mr. Jay, seems fully to meet the object here mentioned.

12. What Mr. Jay here desires, was intended to be done, and was indeed conceived to be implied in the general words at the end of the article. But Lord Grenville sees no objection to the insertion of express words for the purpose.

13. Lord Grenville explained to Mr. Jay, this morning, the reason of the insertion of the word European, in the place here referred to. The subject is connected with the larger consideration to which their conversation led, and from the further discussion of which Lord Grenville is inclined to hope that mutual advantage may arise. Mr. Jay will observe, that the subject to which his remark, No. 15, applies, is one instance among many, which might be brought to show that this article would not be inefficient.

14. To meet the object which was this morning suggested in conversation on this article, Lord Grenville would propose the adoption of the following additional article, to come in immediately after the eighth. Lord Grenville has, in conformity to what was mentioned by Mr. Jay, used the words of *Vattel :*

" In order to regulate what is in future to be esteemed contraband, it is agreed that, under the said denomination shall be comprised all arms and implements serving for the purposes of war, by land or sea, such as cannon, muskets, mortars, petards, bombs, grenades, carcasses, saucisses, carriages for cannon, musket rests, bandeliers, gunpowder, match, saltpetre, ball, pikes, swords, headpieces, cuirasses, halberds, lances, javelins, horses, horse furniture, holsters, belts, and generally all other implements of war; as also timber for shipbuilding, tar, or rosin, sheet copper, sails, hemp, and cordage, and generally whatever may serve directly to the equipment of vessels; unwrought iron and fir planks only excepted. And all the above articles are hereby declared to be just objects of confiscation, whenever they are attempted to be carried to an enemy.

"And whereas corn, grain, or provisions, can be considered as contraband in certain cases only, namely, when there is an expectation of reducing the enemy by the want thereof, it is agreed that, in all such cases, the said articles shall not be confiscated; but that the captors, or, in their default, the government under whose authority they act, in this respect, shall pay to the masters or owners of such vessels the full value of all such articles, together with a reasonable mercantile profit thereon, and also the freight and demurrage incident to their detention."

15. It seems by no means unreasonable, that the effect of this stipulation should be extended to the existing war, as a natural consequence of the good understanding to be established by this negotiation, and by the removal of all existing differences. And it would tend to prevent so many occasions of acrimony and dispute, on both sides, that Lord Grenville thinks it highly desirable to maintain this article in its present form.

16. Lord Grenville sees no reason whatever to object to this article.

17. This remark seems also perfectly just, and will be best met by omitting the concluding part of this article.

18. Lord Grenville rather thinks this article ought to be permanent, for the mutual interest of both countries; but he is content to leave this point to the decision of Mr. Jay, who is much too enlightened not to see the effect which a

contrary conduct to that here prescribed must produce as with respect to America.

Commercial Projet—Observations.

Art. 2. Omit these words: "the same being of the nation on whose behalf they shall be appointed, and not otherwise"; and insert, in lieu thereof, "the same being first approved by the government of the country in which they shall be so appointed to reside, and not otherwise."

Art. 3. The last sentence to run thus: "by which the vessels of the one party shall pay, in the ports of the other, any higher or other duties than shall be paid in similar circumstances by the vessels of the foreign nation the most favored in that respect, or any higher or other duties than shall be paid in similar cases by the vessels of the party itself into whose ports they shall come."

Thus, sir, I have given you a very particular and correct account of the negotiation. Many observations and explanatory remarks might be added. I might also inform you, that I had strenuously urged the justice of compensation for the detention of the posts; and that I consider the privilege of trading to the West Indies as providing for claims of that kind. On this privilege, and the probability of its being revived after the expiration of the term assigned for its duration, I could enlarge, but it does not strike me as necessary to go into further details, nor indeed could I at present find time for the purpose.

It will not escape you that the articles, now under consideration, will doubtless undergo many alterations, before they assume that final form in which they will either be accepted or rejected; and, *there-*

fore, that it would not be proper to publish them at present. I think that, in the course of a few weeks, the questions, now under discussion, will be decided. No time shall be lost in communicating to you the result.

Another subject remains to be mentioned. It appeared to me advisable that our people should have precise and plain instructions relative to the prosecution of appeals and claims, in cases of capture. For that purpose, I applied to Sir William Scott, and requested him, in concert with Dr. Nicholl, to prepare them. We conversed on the subject, and I explained to him my views and objects.

On the 10th of September I received them, enclosed with the following letter from Sir William, which I insert on account of the friendly disposition towards our country which it manifests, and which appears to me to be less uncommon here than we generally suppose, viz. :

To his Excellency, John Jay, Esq., etc.

SIR :

I have the honor of sending the paper drawn up by Dr. Nicholl and myself ; it is longer and more particular than, perhaps, you meant, but it appeared to be an error on the better side rather to be minute, than to be too reserved, in the information we had to give ; and it will be in your excellency's power either to apply the whole or such parts as may appear more immediately pertinent to the objects of your inquiry.

I take the liberty of adding that I shall, at all times, think myself much honored by any communications from you, either during your stay here, or after your return, on any subject in which you may suppose that my situation can give me the power of being at all useful to the joint interests of both countries: if they should ever turn upon points in which the duties of my official station appear to me to impose upon me an obligation of reserve, I shall have no hesitation in saying that I feel them to be such. On any other points on which you may wish to have an opinion of mine, you may depend on receiving one that is formed with as much care as I can use, and delivered with all possible frankness and sincerity.

I have the honor to be, with great respect, &c.

WILLIAM SCOTT.

COMMONS, September 10, 1794.

Paper Enclosed in the Foregoing Letter.

SIR:

We have the honor of transmitting, agreeably to your excellency's request, a statement of the general principles of proceeding in prize causes, in British courts of admiralty, and of the measures proper to be taken when a ship and cargo are brought in as prize within their jurisdictions.

The general principles of proceeding cannot, in our judgment, be stated more correctly or succinctly, than we find them laid down in the following extract from a report made to His late Majesty, in the year 1753, by Sir George Lee, then Judge of the Prerogative Court, Dr. Paul, His Majesty's Advocate General, Sir Dudley Ryder, His Majesty's Attorney General, and Mr. Murray (afterwards Lord Mansfield), His Majesty's Solicitor General:

"When two powers are at war, they have a right to make prizes of the ships, goods, and effects, of each other, upon the high seas. Whatever is the property of the enemy may be acquired by capture at sea; but the property of a friend cannot be taken, provided he observes his neutrality.

" Hence, the law of nations has established, that the goods of an enemy, on board the ship of a friend, may be taken.

" That the lawful goods of a friend, on board the ship of an enemy, ought to be restored.

" That contraband goods going to the enemy, though the property of a friend, may be taken as prize ; because supplying the enemy with what enables him better to carry on the war is a departure from neutrality.

" By the maritime law of nations, universally and immemorially received, there is an established method of determination, whether the capture be, or be not, lawful prize.

" Before the ship or goods can be disposed of by the captor, there must be a regular judicial proceeding, wherein both parties may be heard, and condemnation thereupon as a prize, in a court of admiralty, judging by the law of nations and treaties.

" The proper and regular court for these condemnations is the court of that State to whom the captor belongs.

" The evidence to acquit or condemn, with, or without, costs and damages, must, in the first instance, come merely from the ship taken, viz. : the papers on board, and the examination, *on oath*, of the master, and other principal officers ; for which purpose, there are officers of admiralty in all the considerable seaports of every maritime power at war, to examine the captains, and other principal officers, of every ship, brought in as a prize, upon general and impartial interrogatories ; if there do not appear from thence ground to condemn, as enemy's property or contraband, goods going to the enemy, there must be an acquittal, unless, from the aforesaid evidence, the property shall appear so doubtful, that it is reasonable to into further proof thereof.

" A claim of ship r goods must be supported by the oath of somebody, at ' as to belief.

" The law of ons requires good faith ; therefore, every ship must be ovided with complete and genuine papers, and the master, at least, should be privy to the truth of the transaction.

" To enforce these rules, if there be false or colorable papers; if any papers be thrown overboard; if the master and officers, examined *in preparatorio*, grossly prevaricate; if proper ship's papers are not on board; or if the master and crew cannot say whether the ship or cargo be the property of a friend or enemy, the law of nations allows, according to the different degrees of misbehavior or suspicion, arising from the fault of the ship taken, and other circumstances of the case, costs to be paid, or not to be received, by the claimants, in case of acquittal and restitution: on the other hand, if a seizure is made without probable cause, the captor is adjudged to pay costs and damages: for which purpose, all privateers are obliged to give security for their good behavior; and this is referred to and expressly stipulated, by many treaties.

" Though, from the ship's papers, and the preparatory examinations, the property does not sufficiently appear to be neutral; the claimant is often indulged with time to send over affidavits to supply that defect: if he will not show the property, by sufficient affidavits, to be neutral, it is presumed to belong to the enemy. Where the property appears from evidence not on board the ship, the captor is justified in bringing her in, and excused paying costs, because he is not in fault; or, according to the circumstances of the case, may be justly entitled to receive his costs.

" If the sentence of the court of admiralty is thought to be erroneous, there is, in every maritime country, a superior court of review, consisting of the most considerable persons, to which the parties, who think themselves aggrieved, may appeal; and this superior court judges by the same rule which governs the court of admiralty, viz.: the law of nations, and the treaties subsisting with that neutral Power, whose subject is a party before them.

" If no appeal is offered, it is an acknowledgment of the justice of the sentence by the parties themselves, and conclusive.

" This manner of trial and adjudication is supported, alluded to, and enforced, by many treaties.

" In this method, all captures at sea were tried, during the last war, by Great Britain, France, and Spain, and submitted to by the neutral Powers; in this method, by courts of admiralty acting according to the law of nations, and particular treaties, all captures at sea have immemorially been judged of in every country of Europe. Any other method of trial would be manifestly unjust, absurd, and impracticable."

Such are the principles which govern the proceedings of the prize courts. The following are the measures which ought to be taken by the captor, and by the neutral claimant, upon a ship and cargo being brought in as prize :

The captor, immediately upon bringing his prize into port, sends up, or delivers upon oath, to the registry of the court of admiralty, all papers found on board the captured ship. In the course of a few days, the examinations in preparatory, of the captain and some of the crew of the captured ship are taken upon a set of standing interrogatories, before the commissioners of the port to which the prize is brought, and which are also forwarded to the registry of the admiralty, as soon as taken ; a monition is extracted by the captor from the registry, and served upon the Royal Exchange, notifying the capture, and calling upon all persons interested to appear, and show cause why the ship and goods should not be condemned ; and at the expiration of twenty days, the monition is returned into the registry with a certificate of its service, and, if any claim has been given, the cause is then ready for hearing, upon the evidence arising out of the ship's papers, and preparatory examinations.

The measures taken on the part of the neutral master, or proprietor of the cargo, are as follows:

Upon being brought into port, the master usually makes a protest, which he forwards to London, as instructions (or with such further directions as he thinks proper) either to the correspondent of his owners, or to the consul of his nation, in order to claim the ship, and such parts of the cargo as belong to his owners, or with which he was particularly entrusted; or the master himself, as soon as he has undergone his examination, goes to London to take the necessary steps.

The master, correspondent, or consul, applies to a proctor, who prepares a claim, supported by an affidavit of the claimant, stating briefly to whom, as he believes, the ship and goods claimed, belong, and that no enemy has any right or interest in them. Security must be given, to the amount of sixty pounds, to answer costs, if the case should appear so grossly fraudulent on the part of the claimant as to subject him to be condemned therein.

If the captor has neglected, in the meantime, to take the usual steps (but which seldom happens, as he is strictly enjoined, both by his instruction and by the prize act, to proceed immediately to adjudication) a process issues against him on the application of the claimant's proctor, to bring in the ship's papers and preparatory examinations, and to proceed in the usual way.

As soon as the claim is given, copies of the ship's papers and examinations are procured from the registry, and upon the return of the monition, the cause may be heard. It, however, seldom happens, (owing to the great pressure of business, especially at the commencement of a war,) that causes can possibly be prepared for hearing immediately upon the expiration of the time for the return of the monition. In that case, each cause must necessarily take its regular turn; correspondent measures must be taken by the neutral master, if carried within the jurisdiction of a vice-admiralty court, by giving a claim, supported by his affidavit, and offering security for costs, if the claim should be pronounced grossly fraudulent.

If the claimant be dissatisfied with the sentence, his proctor enters an appeal in the registry of the court where the sentence was given, or before a notary public, (which regularly should be entered within fourteen days after the sentence,) and he afterwards applies at the registry of the lords of appeal in prize causes (which is held at the same place as the registry of the high court of admiralty) for an instrument called an inhibition, and which should be taken out within three months, if the sentence be in the high court of admiralty, and within nine months, if in a vice admiralty court, but may be taken out at later periods if a reasonable cause can be assigned for the delay that has intervened. This instrument directs the judge, whose sentence is appealed from, to proceed no further in the cause. It directs the registry to transmit a copy of all the proceedings of the inferior court; and it directs the party who has obtained the sentence to appear before the superior tribunal to answer to the appeal. On applying for this inhibition, security is given on the part of the appellant, to the amount of two hundred pounds, to answer costs, in case it should appear to the court of appeals that the appeal is merely vexatious. The inhibition is to be served upon the judge, the registrar, and the adverse party and his proctor, by showing the instrument under seal, and delivering a note or copy of the contents. If the party cannot be found, and the proctor will not accept the service, the instrument is to be served *viis and modis ;* that is, by affixing it to the door of the last place of residence, or, by hanging it upon the pillars of the Royal Exchange. That part of the process above described, which is to be executed abroad, may be performed by any person to whom it is committed, and the formal part at home is executed by the officer of the court; a certificate of the service is endorsed upon the back of the instrument, sworn before a surrogate of the superior court, or before a notary public, if the service is abroad.

If the cause be adjudged in a vice admiralty court, it is usual, upon entering an appeal there, to procure a copy of the proceedings, which the appellant sends over to his correspondent, in England, who carries it to a proctor, and the same steps are taken to procure and serve the inhibition, as where the cause has been adjudged in the high court of admiralty. But if a copy of the proceedings cannot be procured in due time, an inhibition may be obtained, by sending over a copy of the instrument of appeal, or by writing to the correspondent an account only of the time and substance of the sentence.

Upon an appeal, fresh evidence may be introduced, if, upon hearing the cause, the lords of appeal shall be of opinion that the case is of such doubt as that further proof ought to have been ordered by the court below.

Further proof usually consists of affidavits made by the asserted proprietors of the goods, in which they are sometimes joined by their clerks, and others acquainted with the transaction, and with the real property of the goods claimed. In corroboration of these affidavits may be annexed original correspondence, duplicates of bills of lading, invoices, extracts from books, &c. These papers must be proved by the affidavits of persons who can speak to their authenticity; and if copies or extracts, they should be collated and certified by public notaries. The affidavits are sworn before the magistrates or others, competent to administer oaths in the country where they are made, and authenticated by a certificate from the British consul.

The degree of proof to be required depends upon the degree of suspicion and doubt that belongs to the case. In cases of heavy suspicion and great importance, the court may order what is called " plea and proof "; that is, instead of admitting affidavits and documents introduced by the claimants only, each party is at liberty to allege, in regular pleadings, such circumstances as may tend to acquit or condemn the capture, and to examine witnesses in support of the allegations, to whom the adverse party may administer interrogatories. The depositions of the witnesses are taken in writing. If the witnesses are to be examined abroad, a commission issues for that purpose ; but in no case is it necessary for them to come to England. These solemn proceedings are not often resorted to.

Standing commissions may be sent to America, for the *general* purpose of receiving examinations of witnesses in all cases where the court may find it necessary, for the purposes of justice, to decree an inquiry to be conducted in that manner.

With respect to captures and condemnations at Martinico, which are the subjects of another inquiry contained in your note, we can only answer, in general, that we are not informed of the particulars of such captures and condemnations: but as we know of no legal court of admiralty established at Martinico, we are clearly of opinion that the legality of any prizes taken there, must be tried in the high court of admiralty of England, upon claims given, in the manner above described, by such persons as may think themselves aggrieved by the said captures.

We have the honor to be, &c.,

WM. SCOTT.

JOHN NICHOLL.

COMMONS, September 10, 1794.

I take the liberty of advising that these instructions with a proper title prefixed, be printed in a pamphlet, and published for general information.

You will find herewith enclosed a copy of the instructions of the king and council, revoking the order to capture neutral vessels laden with corn, etc., bound to France. A gazette of 6th September, containing an order restraining impressments, etc., and a gazette of 9th September, containing a copy of the order of 6th August, relative to appeals and claims, of which copies have already been sent to you.

I have the honour to be, etc.,

JOHN JAY.

JAY TO ALEXANDER HAMILTON.

LONDON, 17th September, 1794.

DEAR SIR:

I had last week the pleasure of receiving from you a few lines by Mr. Blaney. You will receive this letter by the hands of Mr. Morris. He will also be the bearer of my despatches to Mr. Randolph. They will be voluminous, particular, and in many respects, interesting. It should not be forgotten that there is irritation here as well as in America, and that our party processions, toasts, rejoicings, etc., etc., have not been well calculated to produce good-will and good-humour. The government, nevertheless, distinguish between national acts and party effusions, and have entertained hitherto an opinion and belief that the president and our government and nation in general, were really desirous of an amicable settlement of differences, and of laying a foundation for friendship as well as peace between the two countries.

The secretary's letters by Mr. Monroe, and his speech on his introduction to the Convention, have appeared in the English papers. Their impression in this country may easily be conjectured. I wish they had both been more guarded. The language of the

United States at Paris and London should correspond with their neutrality. These things are not favourable to my mission. A speedy conclusion to the negotiation is problematical, though not highly improbable. If I should be able to conclude the business on admissible terms, I shall do it and risk consequences, rather than by the delay of waiting for and governing myself by opinions and instructions, hazard a change in the disposition of this court; for it seems our country, or rather some part of it, will not forbear asperities. I hear that Virginia is taking British property by escheat; and other things which in the present moment are *unseasonable*, are here reported.

As the proposed articles are under consideration—as they have already undergone some alterations, and as I am not without hopes of other and further amendments, I really think they ought not to be published in their present crude state, especially as in the course of a few weeks I expect to be able to communicate their ultimate form. If they should not appear to me to be such as I ought to sign, I will transmit them, and wait for further instructions.

Adieu, my dear sir.

Yours, sincerely,
JOHN JAY.

JAY TO ALEXANDER HAMILTON.

LONDON, 17th September, 1794.

DEAR SIR:

There is something very pleasant in the reflection, that while war, discord, and oppression triumph in so many parts of Europe, their domination does not extend to our country. I sometimes flatter myself that Providence, in compassion to the afflicted in these countries, will continue to leave America in a proper state to be an asylum to them.

Among those who have suffered severely from these evils, is Monsieur De Rochefoucauld Liancourt, formerly president of the National Assembly of France. His rank and character are known to you. He will be the bearer of this letter, and I am persuaded that his expectations from it will be realized.

Yours, sincerely,

JOHN JAY.

JAY TO LORD MORNINGTON.[1]

ROYAL HOTEL, PALL-MALL,
September 22, 1794.

Mr. Jay presents his compliments to Lord Mornington, and has the honour of informing him that an American gentleman, in whom Mr. Jay has confidence, purposes to go, in the course of this week, to Paris. Should his Lordship wish to honour this gentleman with any commands, Mr. Jay (being persuaded they would be cheerfully received and properly executed) will, with great pleasure, take the necessary measures.

LORD MORNINGTON TO JAY.

SIR :
BRIGHTHELMSTON, September 25th, 1794.

I return you many thanks for the honour of your note, which I received last night upon my arrival at this place,

---

[1] Brother of the Duke of Wellington. A third brother, Sir Henry Wellesley, and his sister, Lady Fitzroy, referred to in the following letters, had been taken prisoners by a French man-of-war while on their passage from Lisbon to England, and carried to France.

and I request you to be assured that I shall always retain a grateful sense of your humane attention to the application, which I took the liberty of making to you in favour of my brother and sister.

In a matter of such extreme delicacy, and which is so much involved in difficulties on all sides, I had determined, after our conversation at Dropmore, to wait the event of your application for the release of the young person detained at Boulogne, and to be guided by that event with respect to the form of any memorial to the French government with which I might hereafter trouble you, according to your kind permission. But the circumstance which you mention in your note seems to offer so evident an advantage, and of a nature so little likely to recur within any short time, that I have determined not to lose it by giving way to any further doubt or hesitation. I am convinced that any gentleman in whom you have confidence must possess all those qualities of discretion and discernment which are necessary for the conduct of such an affair. I have therefore written a narrative of the misfortunes of my sister and of my brother, with no other observations than such as appeared to me to be necessary to explain the peculiar hardship of their case. I have translated this narrative into French ; and you will very much add to the kindness which I have already received from you, if you will have the goodness to read over these papers, and if you find any thing imprudent or superfluous, to strike it out. I would then request you to deliver these papers to the gentleman who is going to Paris, and to induce him to exercise his judgment as well on their contents as on the use to be made of them. If he thinks it useful to present the French paper to the government at Paris, or if he should be of opinion that my object would be better attained by communicating the facts relating to my brother and sister in any other mode, I should wish him to act entirely according to his view of circumstances upon the spot. If it should unfortunately happen to be his opinion, that any application in favour of the prisoners would only tend to draw them into more particular notice, and to expose them to more rigorous treatment, my wish then would be that he should not even mention their names; and painful as this termination of my endeavours to obtain their liberty must be to my mind, the opinion of a gentleman of such a character as you describe will satisfy me that the best decision has been taken which circumstances would admit.

With respect to the conditions which might be annexed to their liberty, I imagine they can be only of but two kinds,—either an exchange of French prisoners in the place of my brother and sister and their servants, or a pecuniary consideration in the way of ransom. The first would not be a matter of much difficulty, although it cannot be done under the authority of government; but I think it might easily be accomplished through the agents for prisoners at Jersey or Guernsey, and at St. Malo. With regard to a ransom, I am ready to pay it if it should not be scandalously exorbitant; although I cannot but say that I think such a transaction would be highly disgraceful to the French government.

If there should appear a disposition to release my brother and sister, I should hope they might be allowed to freight a neutral ship at Brest for some English port: this would be the safest as well as the most expeditious mode of returning home. But if this should be refused, they might still be permitted to return through Switzerland.

I trust you will have the goodness to pardon the length of this detail; I thought it necessary for the information of the gentleman who has the kindness to charge himself with this commission; and I am persuaded the same sentiment of humanity which induced you to give your favourable attention to my first application, will plead my excuse for the tediousness of this letter.

I shall naturally be very anxious to learn the result of this affair, in which I am so deeply interested ; and I hope you will allow me to have the honour of paying my respects to you in London from time to time for that purpose.

Believe me, sir, with the most sincere respect and esteem,

Your much obliged and obedient servant,

MORNINGTON.

P.S. I have taken the liberty of enclosing with the narrative a letter to my brother, which I request your friend to put in the post either at Paris or anywhere in France. It contains nothing but common family intelligence, and some expressions of surprise at the long detention of the two prisoners. If your friend could only find means of obtaining conveyance for a letter from my brother to me, it would be a great object, as I have not heard from him since the 10th of July. I have carefully abstained from giving the least hint in my letter of the kindness of your friend.

LADY MORNINGTON TO JAY.

No 3, CAVENDISH-SQUARE
Thursday, Oct. 2d, 1794.

Lady Mornington presents her respectful compliments to Mr. Jay, and takes the liberty of enclosing a few lines for her daughter, to inform her that her children and friends are well. Lady Mornington begs leave to assure Mr. Jay, that she is most gratefully sensible of his humane attention to Lord Mornington's application respecting his brother and sister, and she cannot resist giving way to a hope, that Mr. Jay's doing her unfortunate children the honour to interest himself about them may be successful.

JAY TO LADY MORNINGTON.

Mr. Jay presents his respectful compliments to Lady Mornington. Immediately on receiving the note with which her Ladyship honoured him to-day, he sent the letter that was enclosed in it to the gentleman who is expected to carry it to France.

The measure of arresting and confining all the English without discrimination who were found in France indicates a policy and a disposition unfavourable to Lady Fitzroy's liberation. Whether the existing administration will, if so inclined, find it safe and prudent to relax in these respects is doubtful; especially considering the influence which popular opinions, jealousies, and resentments frequently have on popular chiefs and leaders.

Mr. Jay forbears, therefore, to flatter either Lady Mornington or himself with expectations which, however pleasing, are too precarious to be greatly indulged in.

ROYAL HOTEL, PALL-MALL, October 2, 1794.

JOHN SLOSS HOBART TO JAY.

THROGGS NECK, 16th October, 1794.

MY DEAR SIR,

I should have written to you sooner but have been out of town when opportunities offered to England; besides I could not help hoping, even against hope, that your mission would prove so short that you might return before the cold season set in. . . .

I am much obliged for the returned cyder; you shall

know when you come home how much it has improved by
the voyage. Good as it is (and Chief Justice Morris has
given it his fiat) it would have been better if it had not been
bottled so soon. Your visit to Sir John Sinclair was truly
a feast. The lock of wool you was good enough to inclose
me has been examined and admired. Is it practicable to
obtain a few such sheep from Spain ? if not, could not some
of the breed be procured to be brought from Saxony to
Hamburg to which place we have some constant traders ?
I am much pleased with the plan of the Board of agriculture and mean to avail myself of the advantages to be
derived from their reports.

On this side the water the spirit of enterprise progresses.
The cotton manufactories at Paterson and Horn's hook
have produced some specimens which appear to be well
executed. The waters of the Bronks are in great demand
for manufacturing purposes. A company of Frenchmen
are errecting a manufactory of hardware on an extensive
scale on that river in the neighbourhood of Mr. Cox. Oliver
Delancy has sold the house in which he lives together with
100 acres of land extending on both sides the river for
£1,500 for which I am told he would have taken £800 not
long since. Mr. Izard mentioned to me a few days ago that
£6,000 had been offered for the mills independent of the
orchard. Last spring you abandoned your building in
Stone Street on account of the enhanced expenses; *that*
has since greatly increased, and yet the rage for building
has increased at a greater rate. Houses start up as it were
by enchantment and still the demand for them every month
is greater than the last. Our friend Troup sold his dwelling
house in August for about £1,500; the purchaser within a
month was asked to take £1,800 for it. It is impossible to
conjecture when this will stop, unless a stop should be put
to the flood of Emigrants and specie with which we are at
present inundated. This being our present situation, while

the success of your negotiation is uncertain I could build a monstrous fabrick contemplating them concluded to our wishes—*sed hac*. Please to present my respects to our friends Trumbull and Jay and believe me with sincere esteem,

Dear Sir,

Your faithfull friend

JNO. SLOSS HOBART.

JAY TO PRESIDENT WASHINGTON.

LONDON, 29th October, 1794.

DEAR SIR :

I have been honoured with yours of the 5 September ; want of leisure constrains me to be concise.

I am authorized by Lord Grenville to assure you in the most explicit terms that no instructions to stimulate or promote hostilities by the Indians against the United States have been sent to the King's officers in Canada. I am preparing an official representation to him on this subject and he will give me an official answer to it, but as this cannot be done in season to forward by this vessel (for letters after this day will be too late to go by her) his Lordship was permitted to make this informal communication to you for your satisfaction. I am to lay before him a statement of the evidence relative to the interference complained of, to the end that it may be sent to Canada and strict enquiry made into the truth of the allegations and facts in question. They would have been done sooner, but for reasons which shall be explained to you. The Treaty is drawing to a conclusion, and unless some difficulties yet to be removed prove insuperable, will speedily be completed. My letter to Mr. Randolph will contain all the information which I can find here at present to communicate. Be assured, my dear sir, of the perfect respect, esteem, and attachment with which I am,

Your obliged and obedient servant,

JOHN JAY.

JAY TO EDMUND RANDOLPH.

LONDON, October 29, 1794.

SIR :

I have been favoured with yours of the 15th, 18th, and 30th August, and of the 5th, 12th, 17th, and 20th of September last.

Although I have materials for another letter as long and particular as the one which I had the honour of writing to you on the 13th of September, yet sufficient time for details cannot possibly be spared from the business of the negotiation. I must confine myself to generals, and postpone a minute statement of the transactions which have taken place since the date of that letter to a future opportunity.

You have been informed that we had agreed to incorporate the two projets, viz. : of a settlement and of a commercial treaty. I undertook this business, and prepared a draught, including most of the articles in those two, and adding several others, but all of them for mutual consideration. From these Lord Grenville, extracting several, omitting some, and adding others, formed a new draught. Difficulties have appeared, and been discussed; some have been removed, some lessened by proposed modifications, and a few still remain. It was proposed that goods for the Indian trade should pass from Canada to the Indians within the United States, *duty free :* to this I could not consent. It has been proposed that alien tonnage and impost should cease : to this there also appeared to me to be very strong objections.

I think the former may be yielded, in some degree, to us ; as to the latter, I cannot yet form a judgment.

We spent several hours, on Friday and yesterday, in these discussions, and they will be resumed tomorrow morning. I perceive nothing that indicates a desire to protract, and I think it cannot be long before the negotiation terminates either in a treaty, or in a certainty that an amicable settlement is impracticable.

All propositions relative to a new line in our northwestern corner are suspended. We have agreed that the river shall be surveyed and its source ascertained. I think Canada and its Indian trade will be opened to us, but not the navigation of the St. Lawrence from the sea.

Although a more early day than June 1, 1796, cannot be had for the evacuation of the posts (for reasons which shall hereafter be mentioned), yet we agreed yesterday to add, " the United States, in the meantime, extending their settlements to any parts within their boundaries, except within the precincts of any of the posts."

I wish to take particular notice of your letters, but, really, sir, I cannot do it now.

I feel very sensibly the confidence reposed in me by the permission to take such notice of my reception here as I might judge proper. The following is a copy of the letter which I have written to Lord Grenville on that subject.

ROYAL HOTEL, PALL MALL, October 27, 1794.

MY LORD :

The President having been informed of the gracious reception with which their Majesties were pleased to honour me, has made it my duty to assure them of the sense he entertains of that pleasing mark of attention to the United States. He flatters himself that a negotiation, commenced under such favorable auspices, and conducted with a correspondent disposition to conciliation, will terminate in a settlement mutually satisfactory and beneficial.

He requests his Majesty to be persuaded that he will continue to promote every measure that may conduce to this desirable event ; and that the United States will, with pleasure and alacrity, cherish the concord and good-will which will naturally result from it. I am convinced, my Lord, that this communication will derive advantages from the manner in which you will convey it to their Majesties ; and I am the more gratified in addressing it to your Lordship, as an additional opportunity is thereby afforded me of assuring you of the respect and esteem with which I have the honour to be your Lordship's, etc.

The Right Honourable Lord GRENVILLE, etc.

I am preparing an official representation, touching unfriendly interferences with the Indians, and I have reason to believe that a satisfactory answer will be given to it.

LORD GRENVILLE TO JAY.

DOWNING STREET, Oct. [30 ?], 1794.

SIR,

I have taken the earliest opportunity to lay before the King your letter of the 27th instant, and I have it in command to express to you the satisfaction which His Majesty has derived from the sentiments which you have been charged to convey to me on the part of the President of the United States, and to assure you that there exists on His Majesty's part the same disposition towards the object of conciliation and friendship. I trust you are convinced of the satisfaction which those who are honored with His Majesty's confidence will always feel in executing to the best of their power His Majesty's intentions in this respect.

It has on that account been matter of the greatest satisfaction to me that, in the course of a negotiation directed to the attainment of this desirable object, I have to treat with a Minister whose dispositions and conduct are so well calculated to promote it. I trust with no small degree of confidence that the final issue of our joint endeavours will be such as I am persuaded we both wish ; but, in every case, I shall always retain those sentiments of the most sincere respect and esteem with which I have the honor to be,

Sir,

Your most obedient, humble servant,

GRENVILLE.

JOHN DRAYTON [1] TO JAY.

Octr. 30th, 1794, CHARLESTON, S. C.

MY DEAR AND RESPECTED SIR,

With the regard almost of a son, and the sincere esteem of a friend, permit me again to borrow a little from the moments which are precious to you, while I indulge the sweet pleasure, of an imaginary conversation. . . .

. . . Permit me to offer for your perusal at a leisure moment, a publication of mine, respecting matters which struck my attention during my northern jaunt. You will find by it, that so far from giving up writing, the itch of scribbling still continues to affect me : and that from a newspaper writer, I have now stept forth, the author of a small book. I assure you I tremble at the step I have taken ; but the thing is done ; and all that remains for me is to hope for the best. Before the publication of this book, I wrote several numbers, which were published in our paper under the signature of " A native of Charleston, and one of its representatives in the Legislature " upon the Subject of representation, which took very well, insomuch, that at the last election for the legislature, I had 410 votes, where before I had only 165 ; and in this last election all the violent French party were opposed to me. This subject of representation takes up much of the public attention. The people in the back country wish to alter our present representation, and make it only upon a ratio of white population. Those of the low country in whose favor I am, are for property having a proportionate representation in the Legislature. It will be warmly advocated in the Legislature of this State, in the next Month.

Judge Wilson and his Lady are at present here ; I flatter

[1] Subsequently Governor of South Carolina. As a young man he attempted authorship, and, among other productions, published some letters descriptive of a visit to New York, Newport, Boston, and other places in 1793.

myself they will have no reason to complain of the inattention of the citizens.

He has much business to transact, both in the federal, civil, and criminal court.

Wishing you, my Dear Sir, an honorable negotiation and happy return to your family and friends I have the honor to subscribe myself,

   Your sincere friend and most
     Obedient and very humble Servt.,
        J. DRAYTON.

PRESIDENT WASHINGTON TO JAY.

[PRIVATE.]

       PHILADELPHIA, Novr. 1st, 1794.

MY DEAR SIR,

On Tuesday last I returned from my tour to the westward. On Monday Congress, by adjournment, are to meet; and on the day following, Mr. Bayard, according to his present expectation is to leave this city for London.

Thus circumstanced (having so little time between my return, and the opening of the session, to examine papers, and to prepare my communications for the legislature) you will readily perceive that my present address to you must be hurried;—at the same time, my friendship and regard for you, would not let an opportunity, so good as the one afforded by Mr. Bayard, pass without some testimony of my remembrance of you; and an acknowledgement of the receipt of your private letters to me, dated the 23d of June, 21st of July and 5th and 11th of August.—These comprehend *all* the letters I have received from you since your arrival in England, to the present date.

That of the 5th of August, dawns more favorably upon the success of your mission, than any that had preceded it;

and for the honor, dignity and interest of this country, for your own reputation and glory, and for the peculiar pleasure and satisfaction I should derive from it, as well on private, as on public considerations, no man more ardently wishes you *complete* success than I do.   But as you have observed in some of your letters, that it is hardly possible in the early stages of a negotiation to foresee all the results —so much depending upon fortuitous circumstances and incidents which are not within our controul—so, to deserve success by employing the means with which we are possessed to the best advantage, and trusting the rest to the All wise Disposer, is all that an enlightened public, and the virtuous and well disposed part of the community can reasonably expect ; nor in this, will they, I am sure, be disappointed.   Against the malignancy of the discontented, the turbulent, and the vicious, no abilities, no exertions, nor the most unshaken integrity, are any safeguard.

As far as depends upon the Executive, measures preparatory for the worst, while it hopes for the best, will be pursued ; and I shall endeavor to keep things in *statu quo* until your negotiation assumes a more decisive form, which I hope will soon be the case, as there are many hot-heads and impetuous spirits among us, who with difficulty can be kept within bounds.   This, however, ought not to precipitate your conduct, for as it has been observed, there is a " tide in human affairs " which ought to be watched ; and because I believe all who are acquainted with you will readily concede that considerations, both public and private, combine to urge you to bring your mission to a close with as much celerity as the nature of it will admit.

As you have been, and will continue to be, fully informed by the Secretary of State of all transactions of a public nature, which relate to, or may have an influence on, the points of your mission, it would be unnecessary for me to touch upon any of them in this letter, was it not for the presumption, that the insurrection in the western counties of this State has excited much speculation, and a variety of opinions abroad, and will be represented differently according to the wishes of some, and the prejudices of others, who may exhibit it as an evidence of what has been predicted "that we are unable to govern ourselves." Under this view of the subject I am happy in giving it to you as the general opinion, that this event having happened at the time it did, was fortunate, although it will be attended with considerable expence.

That the self created societies which have spread themselves over this country, have been labouring incessantly to sow the seeds of distrust, jealousy, and, of course discontent, thereby hoping to effect some revolution in the government, is not unknown to you.—That they have been the fomenters of the western disturbances admits of no doubt in the mind of any one who will examine their conduct; but fortunately they precipitated a crisis for which they were not prepared, and thereby have unfolded views which will, I trust, effectuate their annihilation sooner than it might otherwise have happened. At the same time it has afforded an occasion for the people of this country to shew their abhorrence of the result and their attachment to the constitution and the laws ;—for I believe that five times the number of Militia that was required, would have come forward if it had been necessary, in support of them.

The spirit which blazed out on this occasion, as soon as the object was fully understood, and the lenient measures of the government were made known to the people, deserve to be communicated ; for there are instances of General officers going at the head of a single troop, and light companies ;—of field officers, when they came to the places of rendezvous and found no companies for them in that grade turning into the ranks, and proceeding as private soldiers, under their own captains ; and of numbers, possessing the first fortunes in the country, standing in the ranks as private men, and marching day by day with their knapsacks and haversacks at their backs, sleeping on straw, with a single blanket in a soldier's tent, during the frosty nights we have had, by way of example to others ; nay more, of many young Quakers (not discouraged by the Elders) of the first families, characters and properties, having turned into the ranks, and marching with the troops.

These things have terrified the insurgents, who had no conception that such a spirit prevailed, but while the thunder only rumbled at a distance, were boasting of their strength, and wishing for, and threatening the militia, by turns ; intimating, that the arms they should take from them would soon become a magazine in their hands.—Their language is much changed indeed, but their principles want correction.

I shall be more prolix in my Speech to Congress on the commencement, and progress of this insurrection than is usual in such an instrument, or than I should have been on any other occasion ; but as numbers (at home and abroad) will hear of the insurrection and will read the Speech, that may know nothing of the documents to which it might refer, I conceived it would be better to encounter the charge of prolixity by giving a cursory detail of facts (that would shew the prominent features of the thing) than to let it go naked into the world, to be dressed up according to the fancy or inclinations of the readers, or the policy of our enemies.

I write nothing in answer to the letter of Mr. Wangenheim (enclosed by you to me). Were I to enter into correspondencies of that sort (admitting there was no impropriety in the measure) I should be unable to attend to my ordinary duties. I have established it as a maxim, neither to invite, nor to discourage, emigrants. My opinion is that they will come hither as fast as the true interest and policy of the United States will be benefited by foreign population. I believe many of these, as Mr. Wangenheim relates, have been, and I fear will continue to be, imposed upon by speculators in land, and other things.

But I know of no prevention but caution nor any remedy except the laws. Nor is military, or other employment so easy to obtain as foreigners conceive in a country where offices, and the seekers of them, bear no proportion to each other.

With sincere esteem and great regard,

I am, Dear Sir,

Your Affectionate Servant

G. WASHINGTON.

P. S. 4th Novr.

Your correspondance with New York is, I am persuaded, too regular and constant to leave you in any doubt as to the health of Mrs. Jay. Yet, as I was told yesterday by Mrs. King that she and all your family were well, I chose to mention it.

For want of a Senate, Congress have not yet proceeded to business.

G. W.

JAY TO OLIVER ELLSWORTH.

LONDON, 19th November, 1794.

DEAR SIR:

The negotiation is terminated by a treaty. It will, with this letter, go by the packet, which, in expectation of this event, has been detained above a week.

In my opinion we have reason to be satisfied. It is expedient that the ratification should not be unnecessarily delayed. The best disposition towards us prevails in the cabinet, and I hope they will have reason to be content with the delicacy and propriety of our conduct towards them and the nation. Further concessions on the part of Great Britain cannot, in my opinion, be attained. The minister flatters himself that this treaty will be very acceptable to our country, and that some of the articles in it will be received as unequivocal proofs of good-will. We have industriously united our efforts to remove difficulties, and few men would have persevered in such a dry, perplexing business, with so much patience and temper as he has done.

I could write you a long letter on these topics, but I have not time. Believe me to be, with great esteem and regard, dear sir,

Your most obedient and humble servant,

JOHN JAY.

JAY TO PRESIDENT WASHINGTON.

LONDON, 19th November, 1794.

DEAR SIR :

A letter which I wrote to you on the 29th October last, contained the following paragraph, viz. :

" I am authorized by Lord Grenville to assure you, in the most explicit terms, that no instructions to stimulate or promote hostilities by the Indians against the United States, have been sent to the king's officers in Canada. I am preparing an official representation to him on this subject, and he will give me an official answer to it ; but as this cannot be done in season to forward by this vessel (for letters after this day will be too late to go by her), his Lordship has permitted me to make this informal communication to you for your satisfaction. I am to lay before him a statement of the evidences relative to the interferences complained of, to the end that it may be sent to Canada, and strict inquiry made into the truth of the allegations and facts in question."

My time and thoughts have ever since continued to be so entirely engrossed by the treaty which is now concluded, and was this day signed, as that it really has not been in my power to finish and present this representation.

As to the treaty, it must speak for itself. A hasty letter which I have written to Mr. Randolph, contains some remarks on a few of the articles in it. That letter is far from being so particular as I could wish, but I cannot help it. My whole time has been employed. To do more was not possible. I wish that I could accompany the treaty, but I feel that I ought not to expose myself to the severities of a winter's voyage.

I am exceedingly anxious to return ; for although I have every other reason to be satisfied with my situation, yet I am not at home. I ought not to conceal from you, that the confidence reposed in your personal character was visible and useful throughout the negotiation.

If there is not a good disposition in the far greater part of the cabinet and nation towards us, I am exceedingly deceived. I do not mean an ostensible and temporizing, but a real good disposition. I wish it may have a fair trial. With perfect respect, esteem, and attachment,

I am, dear sir,

Your obliged and obedient servant,

JOHN JAY.

JAY TO ALEXANDER HAMILTON.

LONDON, 19th November, 1794.

MY DEAR SIR :

My task is done ; whether *finis coronat opus*, the president, senate, and public will decide.

This letter goes by the packet, and the treaty with it ; some parts of it require elucidation to common readers. I have not time for comments ; Lord Grenville is anxious to dismiss the packet ; I therefore write in haste. If this treaty fails, I despair of another. If satisfactory, care should be taken that the public opinion be not misled respecting it, for this reason the sooner it is ratified and published the better. I really think the good disposition of this country should be cherished. I came here in the moment of exultation and triumph on account of Lord Howe's victory. From that day to this I have experienced no change in sentiments or conduct relative to the negotiation. I must, though not without reluctance, conclude ; not being fit for a winter voyage, I shall stay here till spring. Indeed, I shall want repairs before I am quite fit for any voyage. God bless you.

Yours,

JOHN JAY.

JAY TO RUFUS KING.

LONDON, 19th November, 1794.

DEAR SIR :

I send by the packet the fruit of my negotiation —a treaty. I wish that I could go with it, as well that I might again be in my own country, as that I might answer questions on the subject. The draft has undergone several editions, with successive alterations, additions, etc. This shows that time and trouble have not been spared. I have just finished a hasty letter to Mr. Randolph. It will be thought slovenly, but I cannot help it. The packet must go. If I entirely escape censure, I shall be agreeably disappointed. Should the treaty prove, as I believe it will, beneficial to our country, justice will *finally* be done. If not, be it so—my mind is at ease : I wish I could say as much for my body, but the rheumatism will not permit me. Health and happiness to you, my good friend.

Yours, sincerely,

JOHN JAY.

JAY TO THOMAS PINCKNEY.

PALL MALL, 19th November, 1794.

DEAR SIR :

The Treaty is signed. I am just returned from Lord Grenville, and going to dine out of town. Being persuaded that this event will give you pleasure I write these few lines in haste to inform you of it, and to present to you my thanks and acknowledgments for the friendly aid I have received from you in the course of the negotiation.

Be assured of the very sincere esteem and regard with which I am, dear sir,

Your friend and humble servant,
JOHN JAY.

JAY TO EDMUND RANDOLPH.

LONDON, 19th November, 1794.

SIR :

The long-expected treaty accompanies this letter; a probability of soon concluding it has caused the packet to be detained for more than a week. The difficulties which retarded its accomplishment, frequently had the appearance of being insurmountable; they have at last yielded to modifications of the articles in which they existed, and to that mutual disposition to agreement which reconciled Lord Grenville and myself to an unusual degree of trouble and application. They who have levelled uneven grounds, know how little of the work afterwards appears.

Since the building is finished, it cannot be very important to describe the scaffolding, or go into all the details which respected the business. Explanatory remarks on certain articles might be useful, by casting light on governing principles, which, in some instances, are not so obvious as to be distinctly seen on first view. Feeling the want of leisure and relaxation, I cannot undertake it in this moment of haste. I must confine myself to a few cursory observations, and hope allowances will be made for inaccuracies and omissions.

My opinion of the treaty is apparent from my having signed it. I have no reason to believe or conjecture that one more favourable to us is attainable.

Perhaps it is not very much to be regretted that all our differences are merged in this treaty, without having been decided ; disagreeable imputations are thereby avoided, and the door of conciliation is fairly and widely opened by the *essential* justice done, and the conveniences granted to each other by the parties.

The term limited for the evacuation of the posts could not be restricted to a more early day ; that point has been pressed. The reasons which caused an inflexible adherence to that term, I am persuaded, were these, viz. : That the traders have spread through the Indian nations goods to a great amount ; that the return for those goods cannot be drawn into Canada at an earlier period ; that the impression which the surrender of all the posts to American garrisons will make on the minds of the Indians cannot be foreseen. On a former occasion it was intimated to them (not very delicately) that they had been forsaken, and given up to the United States ; that the protection promised them on our part, however sincere, and however, in other respects, competent, cannot entirely prevent those embarrassments which, without our fault, may be occasioned by war ; that, for these reasons, the traders ought to have time to conclude their adventures, which were calculated on

the existing state of things ; they will afterward calculate on the new state of things ; but that in the
meantime, the care of government should not be
withdrawn from them.

The third article will, I presume, appear to you in
a favourable light ; a number of reasons which, in my
judgment, are solid, support it. I think they will, on
consideration, become obvious. It was proposed and
urged that the commercial intercourse opened by this
article ought to be exempted from all duties on either
side. The inconveniences we should experience from
such a measure were stated and examined. It was
finally agreed to subject it to native duties. In this
compromise, which I consider as being exactly right,
that difficulty terminated ; but for this compromise
the whole article would have failed, and every expectation of an amicable settlement been frustrated.
A continuance of trade with the Indians was a
decided ultimatum ; much time and paper, and many
conferences were employed in producing this article ;
that part of it which respects the ports and places on
the eastern side of the Mississippi, if considered in
connection with the —— article in the treaty of peace,
and with the article in this treaty which directs a
survey of that river to be made, will, I think, appear
unexceptionable.

In discussing the question about the river St. Croix,
before the commissioners, I apprehend the old French
claims will be revived. We must adhere to Mitchell's
map. The Vice-President perfectly understands this
business.

The 6th article was *sine qua non*, and is intended as well as calculated to afford that justice and equity which judicial proceedings may, on trial, be found incapable of affording. That the commissioners may do exactly what is right, they are to determine according to the merits of the several cases, having a due regard to all the circumstances, and as justice and equity shall appear to them to require.

It is very much to be regretted that a more summary method than the one indicated in the seventh article could not have been devised and agreed upon for settling the capture cases; every other plan was perplexed with difficulties, which frustrated it. Permit me to hint the expediency of aiding the claimants, by employing a gentleman, at the public expense, to oversee and manage the causes of such of them as cannot conveniently have agents of their own here; and whether in some cases pecuniary assistance might be proper. I do not consider myself at liberty to make such an appointment, nor to enter into any such pecuniary engagements. It would probably be more easy to find a proper person on your side of the water than on this. Here there are few fit for the business, and willing to undertake it, who (having affairs of their own to attend to) would not be tempted to consider the business of the claimants in a secondary light. Several objections to giving him a fixed salary are obvious. In my opinion a moderate commission on the sums to be recovered and received, would be a more eligible method of compensating him for his services. Our consul here talks, and, I believe, in earnest, of returning to America, or I should expect much advantage from his zeal and endeavours to serve such of the claimants as might commit their business to his management.

You will find in the 8th article a stipulation, which, in effect, refers the manner of paying the commissioners very much to our election. I prefer paying them jointly. The objection to it is, that the English pay high. I have always doubted the policy of being *penny-wise.*

The Lord Chancellor has prepared an article respecting the mutual admission of evidence, etc., which we have not had time fully to consider and decide upon ; it contains a clause to abolish *alienism* between the two countries. His Lordship's conduct and conversation indicate the most friendly disposition towards us. A copy of his article shall be sent, and I wish to receive precise instructions on that head.

The credit of some of the States having, to my knowledge, suffered by appearances of their being favourable to the idea of sequestrating British debts on certain occasions, the 10th article will be useful. People wishing to invest their property in our funds and banks, have frequently applied to me to be informed whether they might do it without risk of confiscation or sequestration. My answer has been uniform, viz., that, in my opinion, such measures would be improper ; and, therefore, that, in my opinion, they would not be adopted. Some pressed me for assurances, but I have declined to give any.

The 12th article, admitting our vessels of seventy

tons and under, into the British islands in the West Indies, affords occasion for several explanatory remarks. It became connected with a proposed stipulation for the abolition of all alien duties of every kind between the two countries. This proposition was pressed, but strong objections opposed my agreeing to it. A satisfactory statement on this point would be prolix. At present I cannot form a very concise one, for that would not require less time. The selection and arrangement necessary in making abridgments cannot be hastily performed. The duration of this article is short, but if we meet the disposition of this country to good humour and cordiality, I am much inclined to believe it will be renewed. The duration of the treaty is connected with the renewal of that article, and an opportunity will then offer for discussing and settling many important matters.

The article which opens the British ports in the East Indies to our vessels and cargoes, needs no comment. It is a manifestation and proof of good-will towards us.

The questions about the cases in which alone provisions become contraband, and the question whether, and how far, neutral ships protect enemy's property, have been the subjects of much trouble, and many fruitless discussions. That Britain, at this period, and involved in war, should not admit a principle which would impeach the propriety of her conduct in seizing provisions bound to France, and enemy's property on board neutral vessels, does not appear to me extraordinary. The articles, as they now stand, secure compensation for seizures, and leave us at liberty to decide whether they were made in such cases as to be warranted by the *existing* law of nations ; as to the principles we contend for, you will find them saved in the conclusion of the 12th article, from which it will appear that we still adhere to them.

The articles about privateers were taken from the treaty of commerce between Great Britain and France, and the one for treating natives, commanding privateers, as pirates, in certain cases, was partly taken from ours with Holland.

The prohibition to sell prizes in our ports had its use ; and we have no reason to regret that your instructions to me admitted of it.

Various subjects which have no place in this treaty, have, from time to time, been under consideration, but did not meet with mutual approbation and consent.

I must draw this letter to a conclusion ; Lord Grenville is anxious to dismiss the packet as soon as possible.

There is reason to hope that occasions for complaint on either side will be carefully avoided. Let us be just and friendly to all nations.

I ought not to omit mentioning the acknowledgments due from me to Mr. Pinckney, with whom I have every reason to be satisfied, and from whose advice and opinions I have derived light and advantage in the course of the negotiation. His approbation of the treaty gives me pleasure, not merely because his opinion corresponds with my own, but also from the sentiments I entertain of his judgment and candor.

It is desirable that I should have the earliest advice of the ratification ; and be enabled to finish whatever may be expected of me, in season to return in one of the first spring vessels. My health is not competent to a winter's voyage, or I should be the bearer of the treaty. This climate does not agree with me, and the less so on account of the application and confinement to which it was necessary for me to submit.

I had almost forgotten to mention that, on finishing and agreeing to the draft of the treaty, I suggested to Lord Grenville, as a measure that would be very acceptable to our country, the interposition of his Majesty with Algiers, and other states of Barbary, that may be hostile to us. This idea was favourably received, and it is my opinion that this court would, in good earnest, undertake that business, in case nothing should occur to impeach the sincerity of that mutual reconciliation which it is to be hoped will now take place.

It will give you great pleasure to hear that great reserve and delicacy have been observed respecting our concerns with France. The stipulation in favor of existing treaties was agreed to without hesitation ; not an expectation, nor even a wish, has been expressed that our conduct towards France should be otherwise than fair and friendly. In a word, I do not know how the negotiation could have been conducted, on their part, with more delicacy, friendliness, and propriety, than it has been from first to last.

I have the honour to be, etc.,

JOHN JAY.

JAY TO LORD GRENVILLE.

ROYAL HOTEL, PALL MALL,
22d November, 1794.

MY LORD :

I have had the pleasure of receiving the letter which your Lordship did me the honour to write yesterday, enclosing a copy of one that you had written to Mr. Hammond.[1] Marks of confidence from those who merit it are grateful to the human mind ; they give occasion to inferences which by soothing self-love produce agreeable emotions.

Being aware that our mutual efforts to restore good humour and good-will between our two countries should be continued beyond the date of the treaty, I am happy that our sentiments in this respect coincide.

The letters I have written to America with the two copies of the treaty, which are already despatched, leave me little to add on the subject of your Lordship's letter ; they are indeed concise, for I had not time to amplify ; they will be followed by others less general and more pointed. There are men among us to whom these ideas will be familiar, and who will not omit to disseminate them. Their opinions and example will have influence, but it will be progressive, not sudden and general. The storm, I hope and believe, will soon cease ; but the agitation of the waters will naturally take some time to subside ; no man can with effect say to them, ' Peace, be still.' By casting *oil* upon them, they will doubtless be the sooner calmed. Let us do so.

[1] The British Minister to the United States.

I have a good opinion of Mr. Hammond ; nay, more, I really wish him well ; the asperities, however, which have taken place, lead me to apprehend that official darts have frequently pierced through the official characters and wounded the men. Hence I cannot forbear wishing that Mr. Hammond had a better place, and that a person well adapted to the existing state of things was sent to succeed him.

My Lord, I make this remark on the most mature reflection, and found it on those active principles in human nature which, however they may be repressed, cannot easily be rendered dormant, except in cases of greater magnanimity than prudence will usually allow us to calculate upon.

It is not without reluctance that I give this remark a place in this letter. I class Mr. Hammond among those who I think are friendly to me. I have experienced his attentions and hospitality : not an unkind idea respecting him passes in my mind. Public and common good is my object and my motive.

That official letters and documents have been prematurely and improperly published in America is evident. I have not been sparing of animadversions on this head, and flatter myself that more circumspection will in future be used.

The consuls and other public officers and agents in the two countries will have it much in their power (especially in America, from the nature of the government and state of society) to promote or check the progress of conciliation and cordiality.

I have but imperfect knowledge of those now in the United States, except Sir John Temple, whose conduct and conversation appeared to be conciliatory. I have been informed very explicitly that Mr. ———, the consul in Virginia, is not esteemed, and that his private character is far from being estimable. I mention this as meriting inquiry.

There being no French merchant-ships in the American seas, the privateers must either prey on neutral vessels or return without spoil. Hence they become exposed to temptations not easy for them to resist.

The privateers of two hostile nations have no desire to seek and to fight each other. Between mere birds of prey there are few conflicts. If they were recalled, their crews might be usefully employed in ships of war or of commerce. Pardon the liberty of these hints, they occurred to me, and I let my pen run on —perhaps too far.

Permit me to assure you, my Lord, that my endeavours to cultivate amity and good-will between our countries and people shall continue unremitted ; and that they will not cease to be animated by your Lordship's co-operation. To use an Indian figure, may the hatchet henceforth be buried for ever, and with it all the animosities which sharpened, and which threatened to redden it. With the best wishes for your happiness, and with real esteem and regard, I am, my Lord,

Your Lordship's most obedient servant,

JOHN JAY.

COLONEL JOHN TRUMBULL TO JAY.

[LONDON], December 10, 1794.

SIR,

In consequence of your directions, I spoke to Mr. Burges of the propriety of making some acknowledgement on your part to the two clerks who wrote the copies of the treaty, and in consequence of our conversation I have this morning enclosed ten pounds to him, with a request that he will divide it to the two, according to their merits.

This conversation introduced the general subject of presents, when Mr. Burges informed me that it was the established custom here to present to the Foreign Minister who conducted a treaty the portrait of the king elegantly set ; " and on this occasion," added he, " I have by Lord Grenville's direction already given Orders to the King's Jeweller to have the picture and box which is to enclose it, finished immediately. It is also customary to make a proportional present to the Secretary of such Minister ; and these are given on the Exchange of the Ratifications." I answered that I believed it to be otherwise with us, and that the Officers of the United States were even prohibited to receive presents of any kind, from any foreign Prince or State.

I submit to your Judgement how far my answer was right ; and how far it was intended by the Constitution to prohibit the Ministers of the United States receiving presents of this Nature.

I am, with every sentiment of respect,

Your most obliged servant,

JNO. TRUMBULL.

JAY TO JOHN QUINCY ADAMS.

LONDON, 13th December, 1794.

DEAR SIR :

I am much obliged by your letter of the 2d of this month; your letter to Mr. Randolph goes by the *Aurora* to New York; we have had several late arrivals from thence and from Philadelphia. In the *Adriana* from the latter place Mr. Samuel Bayard came passenger; he is appointed by the government to superintend the prosecution of claims and appeal in the capture causes. The insurrection in Pennsylvania was dissipating fast, and government will derive strength from its suppression. The general irritation had considerably abated; specie and emigrants were daily arriving; trade brisk and the prices of all our productions unusually high. It was believed that there would be a large majority of federal representatives returned to Congress. Mr. Smith of South Carolina was re-elected. Notwithstanding the efforts of our Jacobins, affairs in general had assumed a more favourable aspect.

Appearances here indicate another campaign; the issue of it cannot fail of being important in its consequences. If the United States preserve peace and tranquillity, they will have reason to be thankful. I become daily more and more convinced that the best disposition towards us prevails here. Remember me to your brother, and be assured of the esteem and regard with which I am, dear sir,

Your most obedient and humble servant,

JOHN JAY.

PRESIDENT WASHINGTON TO JAY.

[PRIVATE.]

PHILADELPHIA, Decr. 18th, 1794.
MY DEAR SIR,

Since writing to you by Mr. Bayard, about the first of November, I have been favored with your letter of the 13th of September and 2d of October.

As the sentiments contained in the first of these respecting the communications of Mr. Monroe to the National Convention of France were also transmitted in a *private* letter from you to the Secretary of State, and replied to by him (both of which I have seen) I shall dwell no longer on that subject than just to observe 1st, that considering the place in which they were delivered, and the neutral policy this country had to pursue, it was a measure that does not appear to have been well devised by our Minister ; 2d, aware of this himself, and that his conduct would be criticised, he has assigned reasons for its adoption, a summary of which are, that the Navy officers and privateers-men of France who had resorted to our ports, and had been laid under such restrictions as neutral policy required altho' disagreeable to them, had represented this country (and not without effect) as unfriendly to the French revolution. To do away which he found himself necessitated to counteract them by strong assurances of the good dispositions of the people of these United States towards that nation. And 3dly, although I think with you that in order to accomplish this he has stepped beyond the true line, yet, under the then existing circumstances, the expression of such reciprocal good will, was susceptible of two views—one of which even in the pending state of the negotiation (by alarming as well as offending the British Ministry) might have no unfavorable operation in bringing matters to a happy and speedy result, than which nothing is more desirable, or can be more ardently wished for by the friends of peace and good order in this country.

As the Secretary of State has written to you several times since the receipt of your statement of the negotiation on the 13th of September, I shall add nothing to the observations which were contained in his letters on this subject thereof. The business of the Session hitherto has been tranquil, and I perceive nothing *at this time*, to make it otherwise, unless the result of the negotiation (which is anxiously expected by all) should produce divisions. As yet no details have been handed to Congress on this subject; indeed, no communication of that business has been made to anybody except those immediately about me in the executive department. A paragraph, of which the enclosed is a copy, is running through all our Gazettes, accompanied with a report that the United States are contemplated as mediator between France and England. To ascertain by what authority the first was inserted, Bache, in whose paper it first appeared, has been called upon by the Secretary of State, but no satisfactory answer has been obtained from him as yet. With respect to the other it seems to have originated on the other side of the water, and is of a delicate nature, the very idea of which, under the present successes of the French arms (admitting it should be agreeable to the other power) would, it is conceived, convey unpleasant sensations, and be viewed in an evil light by that nation, unless intimations to the contrary should first come from them.

The Virginia escheats of British property do not, as I am informed, stand upon the ground as related to you; but as I am not accurately enough read in the law respecting these escheats to be precise in my recital of it, I will request the Secretary of State to give you the principles thereof.

As I expected, and as you have been informed the result would probably be, so it has happened that, the western insurrection has terminated highly honorable for this country, which by the energy of its laws, and the good disposition of its citizens, have brought the rioters to a *perfect* sense of their duty without shedding a drop of blood. In the eyes of foreigners, among us, this affair stands in a high point of respectability. With great truth I remain,

Dear sir,

Your affectionate,

G. WASHINGTON.

JAY TO TENCH COXE.

LONDON, 18th December, 1794.

DEAR SIR :

Accept my thanks for your obliging letter of the 8th of last month, and for the book which accompanied it. As yet, I have not had time to give it that regular and attentive perusal which it appears to merit. It certainly contains much interesting information, and from your accuracy, I presume that the facts and statements in it are correct. It will naturally lead both our own people and foreigners to form a favourable and just estimate of the United States, and show in a strong light the policy of maintaining that respect for our government and laws, without which our local and other advantages can neither be enjoyed nor improved.

The manner in which the insurrection has been dissipated gives me pleasure ; and there is reason to hope that the arts and counsels which produced it, will not be able to operate such another.

Our affairs relative to this country have a promising

aspect. The best disposition towards us prevails here, and the indications and proofs of it daily increase. I do really believe, that this government means to give conciliatory measures with the United States a full and fair trial. I wish it may be reciprocated on our part. It never can be wise to cast ourselves into the arms and influence of any nation ; but certainly it is wise and proper to cherish the good-will of those who wish to be on terms of friendship and cordiality with us. It may seem strange, and yet I am convinced, that next to the king, our president is more popular in this country than any man in it.

With the best wishes, and with sentiments of esteem and regard, I am, dear sir,

Your most obedient servant,

John Jay.

JAY TO JOHN HARTLEY.

London, 8th January, 1795.

Dear Sir :

Accept my thanks for the pamphlet you were so obliging as to send me. It does not appear probable to me that Europe is very speedily to be blessed with a general and lasting peace, or that the period has already arrived when reason and virtue will govern the conduct of the mass of mankind. There is much reason to believe that the majority of men are neither reasonable nor virtuous ; and hence it has happened, that so many systems which were calculated on the supposed prevalence of reason and virtue, have proved delusive.

The time, doubtless, will come, and is approaching, when a new order of things will be introduced, and when, as the human passions and vices cease to predominate, the checks necessary to control them will become proportionably less necessary. To see things as being what they are, to estimate them accurately, and to act accordingly, are requisites no less essential to sound politics than to sound philosophy or religion.

These are general remarks, and not made with reference to the political questions agitating in this kingdom, and with which (being a citizen of another country) it would not become me to interfere. With the best wishes for your health and happiness, I am, dear sir,

Your friend and obedient servant,

JOHN JAY.

JOHN QUINCY ADAMS TO JAY.

HAGUE, January 9, 1795.

DEAR SIR,

Mr. M'Evers has just delivered me your favours of the 13th and 14th of last month, and I take the earliest opportunity to acknowledge the obligation, which delay might prevent me from transmitting.

Mr. Schermerhorn some time since handed me also a letter of introduction from you. Please to accept my thanks, Sir, for the accquaintance of these gentlemen. I shall esteem myself fortunate in any opportunity to render them a service to which your recommendation so fully entitles them.

Nothing could be more grateful to my feelings than the intelligence from America, which you are pleased to communicate. The suppression of the insurrection, the return of conciliatory dispositions, the growing prosperity of commerce, and the prevalence of national principles, demonstrated by the re-election of good men for the ensuing Legislature, are all promising indications that our country will get to be flourishing, united, and happy.

The friendly dispositions, of which the result of your late negociation, and your observations since that period have tended to confirm your opinion, give us an additional ground of satisfaction. It may be expected that the treaty has by this time arrived in America. It is my cordial wish and hope that it will be received with a temper similar to that which formed and acceded to its arrangements, with that combination of firmness and of generosity which is so well calculated to terminate with honour our foreign differences, and which has so happily succeeded in suppressing internal dissension.

The value of peace and neutrality is nowhere more forcibly felt than at this moment in the country where I am. Its situation becomes more and more critical from day to day. In the terrible agitation between the dismal alternative of conquest or civil war, it feels at the same moment all the terrors of a torrent rushing from without, and a volcano bursting from within.

The alarm at this place is great. The emigrants who have the means are hurrying away. The British Ambassador is gone to meet the future Princess of Wales ; the Spanish, Portuguese, and Prussian Ministers are gone. But the Stadtholder and his family still remain, determined, it is said, to stay at all events, and partake of the common destiny. There is yet no intelligence from the Commissioners gone to Paris. Some hopes are still entertained of their success, which are strengthened by the moderate and rainy weather, which will impede for the moment the further progress of the French armies.

Requesting you to present my cordial remembrances to Col. Trumbull and to your son, I remain with every sentiment of respect and attachment,

Dear Sir, your very humble and obedient servant,

JOHN Q. ADAMS.

JAMES MONROE TO JAY.

PARIS, January 17th, 1795.

SIR,

Early in December last, English papers were received here, containing such accounts of your adjustment with the British administration as excited much uneasiness in the councils of this government; and I had it in contemplation to despatch a confidential person to you, for such information of what had been done as would enable me to remove it. At that moment, however, I was favoured with yours of the 25th November, intimating that the contents of the treaty could not be made known until it was ratified, but that I might say it contained nothing derogatory to our existing treaties with other powers. Thus advised, I thought it improper to make the application, because I concluded the arrangement was mutual, and not to be departed from. I proceeded, therefore, to make the best use in my power of the information already given.

To-day, however, I was favoured with yours of the 28th of the same month, by which I find you consider yourself at liberty to communicate to me the contents of the treaty; and as it is of great importance to our affairs here to remove all doubt upon this point, I have thought fit to resume my original plan of sending a person to you for the necessary information, and have, in consequence, despatched the bearer, Mr. John Purveyance, for that purpose. I have been the more induced to this, from the further consideration that in case I should be favoured with the communication promised in cipher, it would be impossible for me to comprehend it, as Mr. Morris took his off with him.

Mr. Purveyance is from Maryland, a gentleman of integrity and merit, and to whom you may commit whatever you may think proper to confide, with perfect safety. 'T is necessary however to observe, *that as nothing will satisfy this government but a copy of the instrument itself*, and which as our ally it thinks itself entitled to, so it will be useless for me to make to it any new communications *short of that*. I mention this that you may know precisely the state of *my engagements here*, and how I deem it my duty to act under them, in relation to *this object*. I beg leave to refer you to Mr. Purveyance for whatever other information you may wish to have, either on this subject, or the affairs more generally of this republic.

> I have the honour to be
> > With great respect, &c. &c. &c.
> > > JAMES MONROE.

JAY TO JAMES MONROE.

LONDON, February 5, 1795.

SIR :

I have received the letter you did me the honour to write on the 17th of last month by Mr. Purveyance.

It is much to be regretted that any unauthorized accounts in English newspapers, of my " adjustment " with the British administration, should " have excited much uneasiness in the councils of the French government "; and the more so as it does not imply that confidence in the honour and good faith of the United States which they certainly merit.

You must be sensible that the United States, as a free and independent nation, have an unquestionable right to make any pacific arrangements with other powers which mutual convenience may dictate, provided those engagements do not contradict or oppugn their prior engagements with other states.

Whether this adjustment was consistent with our treaty with France, struck me as being the only question which could demand or receive the consideration of that republic; and I thought it due to the friendship subsisting between the two countries, that the French government should have, without delay, the most perfect satisfaction on that head. I therefore, by three letters, viz., of 24th, 25th, and 28th November, 1794, gave you what I hoped would be very acceptable and satisfactory information on that point. I am happy in this opportunity of giving you an exact and literal extract from the treaty. It is in these words, viz. :

" Nothing in this treaty contained, shall, however, be construed or operate contrary to former and existing public treaties with other sovereigns or states."

Considering that events favourable to our Country could not fail to give you pleasure I did intend to communicate to you concisely some of the most interesting particulars of this treaty, but in the most *perfect confidence*, as that instrument has not yet been ratified nor received the ultimate forms necessary to give it validity; as further questions respecting parts of it may yet arise and give occasion to further discussion and negotiations, so that if finally concluded at all it may then be different from what it now is, the impropriety of making it public at present is palpable and obvious. Such a proceeding would be inconvenient and unprecedented. It does not belong to ministers who negotiate treaties to publish them even when perfected, much less treaties not yet completed and remaining open to alteration or rejection. Such acts belong exclusively to the governments who form them.

I cannot but flatter myself that the French government is too enlightened and reasonable to expect that any consideration ought to induce me to overleap the bounds of my authority or to be negligent of the respect which is due to the United States. That respect, and my obligations to observe it, will not permit me to give without permission of their government a copy of the instrument in question to any person or *for any purposes ;* and by no means for the purpose of being submitted to the consideration and judgment of the councils of a *foreign nation* however friendly.

I will, sir, take the earliest opportunity of transmitting a copy of your letter to me, and of this in answer to it to the Secretary of State, and will immediately and punctually execute such orders and instruction as I may receive on the subject.

I have the honour to be, with great respect, sir, your most obedient and humble servant,

JOHN JAY.

JAY TO PRESIDENT WASHINGTON.

LONDON, 25th February, 1795.

DEAR SIR :

Your very friendly letter of the 1st November last gratified me not a little. The insurrection had caused disagreeable sensations in this country. The objects and efforts of the Jacobin societies in America were well known here ; and the fate of our government was considered as being involved in that of the insurrection. The manner in which it has terminated has given sincere satisfaction to this government, to whom all disorganizing innovations give alarm, and their confidence in your wisdom and decision and energy has been confirmed by the event.

The institution and influence of such societies among us had given me much concern ; and I was happy in perceiving that the suppression of the insurrection, together with the character and fall of similar ones in France, would probably operate in the extinction of these mischievous associations in America.

Your remarks relative to my negotiations are just and kind. I assure you nothing on my part has been wanting to render the conclusion of them as consonant as was possible to your expectations and wishes.

Perfectly apprised both of my duty and responsibility I determined not to permit my judgment to be influenced by any considerations but those of public good under the direction of my instructions. *I knew and know that no attainable settlement or treaty would give universal satisfaction ;* and I am far from expecting that the one I have signed will not administer occasion for calumny and detraction.

These are evils which they who serve the people will always meet with. Demagogues will constantly flatter the passions and prejudices of the multitude, and will never cease to employ improper arts against those who will not be their instruments. I have known many demagogues, but I have never known one honest man among them. These are among the other evils which are incident to human life, and none of them shall induce me to decline or abandon any pursuits in which I may conceive it to be my duty to embark or persevere. All creatures will act according to their nature, and it would be absurd to expect that a man who is not upright, will act like one who is. The time will come when all books and histories and errors will be consumed, and when from their ashes truth only will rise and prevail and be immortal.

I observe from Mr. Randolph's letter that certain articles in the treaty will be considered as more objectionable than they appear to me. Before answers to his letters arrive its fate will be decided, and if it should not be ratified I presume explicit instructions will immediately be sent to me on the points in question, and I will do my best endeavours to adjust them accordingly.

Among my despatches to Mr. Randolph by this ship is a copy of a letter I have received from Mr. Monroe at Paris, and of two which I have written to him. The expediency of correcting the mistakes which the French Convention seem to have imbibed will doubtless strike you. From the last of my two letters to Mr. Monroe you will remark that Col. Trumbull is going to Stutgard with my consent; his presence there is necessary about some plates which our engraver there has nearly finished for him. Be pleased to present my best compliments to Mrs. Washington, and be assured of the perfect respect, esteem, and attachment with which I am,

Dear sir,

Your obliged and affectionate servant,

JOHN JAY.

JAY TO PRESIDENT WASHINGTON.

[PRIVATE.]

LONDON, 6th March, 1795.

DEAR SIR :

After considering all that I have heard and seen on the subject, it is my opinion that the common and popular (not official) language of America, relative to Great Britain, manifested such a disposition as to create serious apprehensions in this country that we should join with the French in the war; that these apprehensions gave occasion to secret designs, calculated on such an event; that in proportion as your views and counsels became developed, these apprehensions gradually subsided; that my mission was regarded as a strong proof of your desire to preserve peace, and that the perfect and universal confidence reposed in your personal character excluded every doubt of your being sincere; and that this government is not yet entirely convinced that a pacific and conciliatory system will be supported by the inclination and correspondent conduct of the great body of the people. Various circumstances, however, induce me to believe, that the Cabinet ultimately determined to give conciliation a fair experiment, by doing us substantial justice and by consenting to such arrangements favourable to us, as the national interests and habitual prejudices would admit. To relax the navigation act was to alarm these prejudices, and therefore was a measure which required caution and circumspection, especially in the first instance. To break the ice was the difficulty. To enlarge the aperture afterward would be more easy ; and it will probably be done, if we should be reasonably temperate and prudent. To admit us into their East and West India dominions, and into all their continental American territories, under any modifications, were decided deviations from their former policy, and tended to shock ancient prejudices. Yet these things have been done. None but a strong administration would have ventured it. These are offerings to conciliation, and include, though not confessedly, satisfaction to our claims of justice.

What passed at Paris on Mr. Monroe's arrival, I am persuaded made a strong and disagreeable impression ; and had not your private character prevented those transactions from being imputable in any degree to your orders, I do believe that the system of conciliation would have been instantly abandoned.

What would have succeeded it cannot be easily conjectured ; certainly no treaty so favourable to us as the present would then have been attainable. Whatever the American opinion of it may prove to be, the administration here think it very friendly to us; and that it could not in the present moment have been made more so, without exciting great discontent and uneasiness in this country.

The present situation of Great Britain may to us and others appear to be perilous, but the ministry seem to have no such fears. They have been uniformly bent on prosecuting the war with vigour, and since my arrival I have observed no change in that resolution. Even a distinguished leader in the opposition lately told me that the French could not possibly injure the vitals of this country. Let it be infatuation or what it will, the government and the great majority of this nation meant and mean to continue the war. I will mention a striking anecdote.

You have doubtless heard that the merchants concerned in the American trade gave me a dinner. The principal Cabinet Ministers were present, and about two hundred merchants. Many toasts were given. When "The President of the United States" was given, it was proposed to be with three cheers, but they were prolonged (as if by preconcert, but evidently not so) to six. Several other toasts passed with great acclamation, particularly "The wooden walls of Old England." Almost every toast referable to America, and manifesting a desire of conciliation and cordiality, met with general and strong marks of approbation. Towards the conclusion of the feast, I was asked for a toast. I gave a neutral one, viz., "A safe and honourable peace to all the belligerent powers." You cannot conceive how coldly it was received, and though civility induced them to give it three cheers, yet they were so faint and single as most decidedly to show that peace was not the thing they wished,—these were *merchants*. Mr. Pinckney was struck as forcibly by it as I was ; and we both drew the same conclusions from it.

Except an inconsiderable number, the men of rank and property, and all whom they can influence throughout the kingdom, think the war is indispensable to their safety. The dread of Jacobin politics and Jacobin scenes, and the expectation that the pecuniary resources of this country will ultimately render them superior in the contest, appear to be their prevailing motives.

It was expected by some that the loss of Holland would have damped this spirit. It has had only a partial effect. We find the Ministry and Parliament have been stimulated by it to greater efforts.

All the members who voted for what are called the pacific resolutions were not moved, as many of them certainly were, by a mere desire of peace, but by the policy of professing a readiness to make peace, in order that, if spurned by the French, the nation might continue in the war with more constancy and unanimity. They did not suppose that an acceptable peace could, in the present moment, be obtained.

This people appear to think their constitution and property and national character and importance as being all at stake, and on that stake to be inflexibly determined to risk everything.

Of the great number who advocated a reform in Parliament, there is a portion (but how great cannot easily be ascertained) who are so sore and mortified and vexed, that in my opinion the French successes give them as much pleasure as pain. There are men among them whose designs as well as whose fortunes are desperate, as well as men who have honest designs and good fortunes. These people are at present kept from action by the energy of the government, and the unanimity of the great majority of the nation as to the necessity of the war.

The French Jacobins have greatly injured the cause of rational liberty. The detestable massacres, impieties, and abominations imputable to them, excited in the people here the most decided hatred and abhorrence ; and the government by that circumstance rendered the war popular. But the system of moderation and justice lately adopted in France, the suppression of the Jacobins, and the strict discipline observed in their armies will doubtless have an influence on the sentiments of this nation. I think I see traces of this influence already on minds not suspected of it.

The present war system, however, strikes me as being less firm, consolidated, and formidable than it appears to be. The administration has been composed more with a view to the conciliation of parties than the efficiency of measures. I think the system is liable to fluctuation and derangement, from a variety of events and circumstances. Opposition to reform, as leading to innovations, is doubtless carried too far, and may produce serious consequences. Ideas of the rights of man, and the inferences deducible from them, are spreading among the people. Veneration for royalty, abstractedly considered, has abated ; and although the king is popular, yet it is said that the Prince of Wales and the Duke of York are not. The prosperity of Britain results from and depends on many causes ; complicated machines are most liable to derangement. Should there be a scarcity of corn, want of employment to the manufacturers, or signal convulsions or disasters in the East or West Indies, or in Ireland, or on the sea, the government would find their task very arduous. Alarm and distress will abate pride and obstinacy ; and when the multitude begin to feel severely, their passions frequently take a new and dangerous direction.

The Minister would, I think, have stood on stronger ground, if he had taken the first good opportunity of saying explicitly in the House of Commons, that it was France who declared war against Great Britain, and not Great Britain against France; and that the government was disposed and ready to make peace whenever France would do it on terms compatible with honour and the essential interests of Great Britain. To put an enemy in the wrong is to obtain great advantages. The placing and so long continuing Lord Chatham at the head of the admiralty—the putting the Duke of York at the head of the army— the improper liberties taken with neutral nations, for which the Danes and Swedes on their part are not yet satisfied—the strange measures relative to Ireland, and many other things which strike me as blunders, indicate a defect either in the Cabinet or in the Minister. Although united as to the war, yet as to the mode of conducting it, the wisest counsels may not always prevail. Upon the whole, I shall be surprised if, in the course of this war, Britain does not reap more thorns than laurels.

I have great reason to believe that the king, the Cabinet, and nation were never more unanimous in any system than in that of conciliation with us ; even Lord Hawkesbury does not oppose it. If it should not succeed, they will naturally pass, like a pendulum, to the other extreme.

This system rests principally on their confidence in the uprightness, independence, and wisdom of your conduct. No other man enjoys so completely the esteem and confidence of this nation as you do ; nor, except the king, is any one so popular. The idea which everywhere prevails is, that the quarrel between Britain and America was a family quarrel, and that it is time it should be made up. For my part, I am for making it up, and for cherishing this disposition on their part by justice, benevolence, and good manners on ours. To cast ourselves into the arms of this or any other nation would be degrading, injurious, and puerile ; nor, in my opinion, ought we to have any political connection with any foreign power.

Before I came here, I had no idea that the king was so popular as he is ; his reign having been marked by national calamities produced by reprehensible measures. But his popularity is owing to his private rather than his official character. As a man, there is much in him to commend ; and I have not heard any vice imputed to him. As a domestic man, affectionate and attentive to his queen and children, and affable to all about him, he is universally esteemed. Few men are so punctual in all things. He patronizes the arts and sciences. He pays uncommon attention to agriculture, and delights in his farms. He lays out about ten thousand pounds a year in improving and embellishing the royal estates. He is industrious, sober, and temperate, and has acquired much various knowledge and information. He converses with ease, and often with adroitness, and has an uncommon memory ; they who ought to know him concur in these accounts. That he is a great and a wise king, I have not heard asserted. That he does (to use a vulgar expression) as well as he knows how, seems not to be doubted ; but yet some say that he occasionally is cunning instead of being wise. I have heard him described as being a great man in little things, and as being generally well-intentioned, pertinacious, and persevering.

I congratulate you and our country on the bloodless issue of the insurrection ; it is very reputable to the government and to the people, and exalts both in the estimation of this and other nations.

The tranquillity of the present session of Congress is a pleasing circumstance ; but I suspect it has proceeded more from their having nothing to differ about, than from a spirit of forbearance or a desire of unanimity. The result of my negotiations will doubtless produce fresh disputes, and give occasion to much declamation ; for *I have no idea that the treaty will meet with Antifederal approbation.* Besides, men are more apt to think of what they wish to have, than of what is in their power to obtain. How far the rejection of such a treaty would put the United States in the wrong ; whether it is consistent with our honour, engagements, and important interests ; whether it is preferable upon the whole to a war,—are questions which require much cool and deliberate consideration, as well as more information than many who will decide upon them possess. I regret not having had time to make my letter, which accompanied the treaty, more full, so as to have particularized and explained the reasons which relate to the several articles in it. Then I had not leisure ; to have done it since would have been too late, as the fate of the treaty would probably be decided before subsequent letters could arrive. I still have thoughts of reducing them to writing ; and yet there are some among them which should not be published, lest the future measures, which they also respect, should be thereby marred. I allude, for instance, to the free navigation of the St. Lawrence.

Mr. Randolph does not see the West India article in the same light that I do ; it breaks the ice—that is, it breaks in upon the navigation act. The least stream from a mass of water passing through a bank will enlarge its passage. The very article stipulates that the arrangements to succeed it shall have in view the *further extension* of commerce. This should not be too nicely discussed in American or English newspapers; for though liberal and enlightened people will admit such extensions of commerce to be beneficial to both countries, yet all ancient prejudices must be delicately managed. There are many men who have less wisdom than power, and more integrity than political information. The restriction not to carry certain articles to Europe, etc., is confined to the United States and the British islands. From *other* places, we may freely carry them. Deposits of French and Spanish sugars, etc., may be made in the Dutch, Danish, or other islands, and thence carried where we please. English sugars, cotton, cocoa, and coffee will probably not be more than our consumption requires; and all *cotton* brought into our country should be there manufactured.

Thus, my dear sir, I have passed part of this day very agreeably in writing to you this long letter; and the pleasure is increased by the opportunity it affords me, of assuring you how cordially and sincerely I am

Your obliged and affectionate friend and servant,

J<small>OHN</small> J<small>AY</small>.[1]

---

[1] Mr. Jay's son, Peter, writing to his mother on the 7th says:

"We begin now to be a little anxious to hear the fate of the treaty, which must by this time have been decided. It has doubtless been productive of much declamation, clamor and abuse; and I presume a certain party in New York, with a worthy Senator at their head, have been the most forward to reprobate and oppose it. Let them, however, remember that should it, thro' their machinations, be rejected, upon *their* heads will be all the bloodshed and calamities which must ensue. We are the more anxious for the arrival of the treaty,

THOMAS PINCKNEY TO JAY.

LONDON, 10th April, 1795.

MY DEAR SIR:

In answer to the question you have proposed to me, concerning the propriety of the diplomatic agents of the United States receiving from the court to which they have been sent the present which it is customary to offer them at the conclusion of their mission; I have to inform you that before I left America I had a conversation with Mr. Jefferson, then secretary of state, on this subject, and that it was his opinion that the present might with propriety be received. The reasons in support of this opinion are principally these,—that the acceptance of the present can have no influence on the conduct of the minister (which it is to be presumed the article of the constitution means to guard against), because it is given indiscriminately to all foreign ministers; that it is of equal value to all of the same rank, whether their conduct has been pleasing or otherwise to the court to which they have been delegated; that it is only given at the conclusion of their mission; that it may be placed on the same footing with the privileges, received by all foreign ministers, of exemption from the payment of duties on the importation of certain articles for their use; that it may be considered in the nature of a retribution for the Christmas-boxes, and other customary perquisites which it is usual for foreign ministers to give to the inferior attend-

---

since that is now the only obstacle to our return; we shall sail in the very first vessel after receiving it."

On the 13th he adds:

"By papers which came in this ship we learn that the account of the treaty's having been concluded had arrived in America, but not the treaty itself; and also the more mortifying intelligence of the success of the Antifederal party in the elections of Congress men. Col. Trumbull a few days ago left us to go to Germany, in order to superintend the plate of his *Bunker's Hill* which is there engraving. By this circumstance I have now to do what he formerly did."

ants of the sovereign at whose court they reside ; that the refusal might be considered as an offensive peculiarity in the ministers of the United States ; that it has hitherto been received by our ministers at foreign courts, notwithstanding the article in the old confederation, similar to that in our present constitution ; and lastly, that it is an established custom with our government to make similar presents to the ministers of foreign powers delegated to them.

Here are more reasons, my dear sir, than an object of so little importance seems to merit : you will, however, shortly have an opportunity of knowing the present sentiments of our government on the subject, which you will oblige me by communicating for the direction of my conduct.

Believe me to be, with the sincerest esteem and true respect,

My dear sir,

Your faithful and obedient servant,

THOS. PINCKNEY.

LORD GRENVILLE TO JAY.

DOVER STREET, May 11, 1795.

MY DEAR SIR,

I cannot resist the desire I feel of availing myself of the opportunity of the first packet since your departure, to express to you how happy you would make me by allowing me occasionally to recall to your recollection in this manner one who will always entertain for you the most sincere esteem and friendship. I am particularly anxious to hear of your safe arrival, and that you have found your family and friends well. These are points paramount to all other considerations, but I know your return to your country will not be fully satisfactory to you unless you have also found the state of public affairs such as to promise the continuance of good order and tranquility. That it may be so no one more sincerely wishes than myself, and it would be a great satisfaction to me to hear it from you.

Since you left us the news of the arrival of the treaty in America has reached us. We were singularly unfortunate in the loss of the Tankenville packet. By a strange negligence the November and December mails from hence were both put on board that ship without our having any notice of it from the Post office, so that while I thought we were sending duplicates by two different conveyances, we were in fact sending them by the same Vessel. My letters to Governor Simcoe which I have frequently mentioned to you, and my despatches to Mr. Hammond on the subject of the treaty, were on board the same ship; so that this accident has thrown us far back in the arrangement of many material points. I hope, however, that with attention, and a continuance on the part of the two Governments of the same disposition which actuated all our communications and negotiations here, the great work which we have begun will be carried to its full extent.

I have not been inattentive to the points which remain to be settled here. One of the most material is, I flatter myself, at length in a train of being well arranged, I mean that which relates to the Admiralty Courts in the West Indies, which it is in contemplation immediately to diminish in point of number so as to have them only at Jamaica, Barbados, Grenada, Antigua, and Martinique. Knowing as I do how much evil has been produced by the multiplication of these Courts I look to this reduction with very sanguine hopes. But I hope the regulation will not stop there, but that the effect of it may lead to render the practice of those which still remain, more correct and cautious than I fear it has hitherto been.

The impossibility of our receiving the ratification of the treaty till quite the end of July, leaves us no chance of being able to propose to Parliament during the present session those matters connected with the treaty in which the interference of the legislature is necessary. I know that this delay will be misconstrued on your side of the water, but it is unavoidable. I requested Mr. Pinckney before he went to Spain to write to America on this point in order that the explanation of it might not rest merely on the communications of our Minister there. You will be able to speak with still more knowledge and effect to the same point. Whatever does not depend on the repeal or alteration of existing laws will be immediately executed on the receipt of the ratification.

The public papers and the communications will inform you fully of the state of affairs in Europe. The dispositions of the people in France are evidently turning very fast towards the establishment of some settled state of order which may relieve them from the miseries of their present anarchy. In a similar situation in this Country we experienced the advantage of a known and moderate form of government under which the Nation had before been happy, and to which therefore it returned with enthusiasm and almost with unanimity. The want of such a standard to resort to is now, as far as I can judge, the great obstacle to the restoration of order in France, and consequently of peace in Europe. Mild as their old government was in its practice it was attended with many circumstances the renewal of which creates great apprehension and uneasiness; and there is no authority of sufficient weight to prescribe the form and limits of any change. Some of the belligerent powers are, as you will have seen, too impatient to wait the results of this doubtful issue. To others all idea of peace which shall not give better security than the signature of the Committee of Safety, or the ratification of the Convention, seems delusive and dangerous ; and to this sentiment I profess myself strongly inclined. You are happy in America if you can avoid, as I trust you will, the dangers of the war and of the peace.

With the sincerest wishes for your prosperity, believe me, Sir,

Your most attached and faithful humble servant,

GRENVILLE.

JUDGE WILLIAM CUSHING TO JAY.

June 18th, 1795.

DEAR SIR,

I heartily congratulate you on your return to your own country, after the fatigue of the seas, and your exertions abroad for its prosperity, I hope, without injury to your health.[1] What the treaty is, is not come to us with authenticity; but whatever it be, in its beginning, middle or end, you must expect to be mauled by the sons of bluntness—one of the kinds of reward which good men have for their patriotism. Peace and American interests are not the objects with some.

I cannot so heartily relish the gubernatorial office, which is presented to you, and with so much advantage in the choice. It will doubtless be for the good of New York, as well of the public in general; and what is of some consequence, more for your ease and comfort, than rambling in the Carolina woods in June.

If you accept, as the newspapers seem to announce, I must, though reluctantly, acquiesce.

I was in hopes to get clear of going to Philadelphia this hot season, but suppose it well not to do, to risque the

---

[1] Mr. Jay returned to New York May 28th, 1795, and received a warm welcome from his fellow-citizens—a welcome the more heartily tendered in view of his election two days before to the governorship of the State. His acceptance of this new office necessitated his resignation of the chief-justiceship of the United States, as mentioned in the succeeding letter.

want of a quorum, unless you give me permission to stay at home. A Virginia cause was continued to August term for your presence; whether that will be consistent with your situation, I know not. The middle circuit will of course fall to me next; in the summer or fall I expect the pleasure of calling to pay my respects to you.

Mrs. Cushing joins in sincere regards and respects to you, Mrs. Jay, and Mrs. Ridley and family.

Yours &c. affectionately,

WM. CUSHING.

JAY TO PRESIDENT WASHINGTON.

[PRIVATE.]

NEW YORK, 29 June, 1795.

MY DEAR SIR:

The enclosed contains my resignation of the office of Chief Justice. I cannot quit it, without again expressing to you my acknowledgments for the honour you conferred upon me by that appointment, and for the repeated marks of confidence and attention for which I am indebted to you. It gives me pleasure to recollect and reflect on these circumstances, and to indulge the most sincere wishes for your health and happiness, and to assure you of the perfect respect, esteem and attachment with which I am,

Dear Sir,

Your obliged and affectionate friend and servant,

JOHN JAY.

JAY TO GENERAL HENRY LEE.

NEW YORK, 11th July, 1795.

DEAR SIR:

Accept my cordial thanks for the friendly congratulations expressed in your obliging letter of the 30th of last month, which I received yesterday.

It was obvious to me, when I embarked on my late mission, that so many circumstances combined to render *pacific* arrangements with Great Britain unwelcome to certain politicians and their partisans, both here and elsewhere, that their approbation of any treaty whatever with that nation was not to be expected.

Apprised of what had happened in Greece and other countries, I was warned by the experience of ages not to calculate on the constancy of any popular tide, whether favourable or adverse, which erroneous or transitory impressions may occasion.

The treaty is as it is; and the time will certainly come when it will very universally receive exactly that degree of commendation or censure which, to candid and enlightened minds, it shall appear to deserve. In the meantime I must do as many others have done before me—that is, regretting the depravity of some, and the ignorance of a much greater number, bear with composure and fortitude the effects of each. It is as vain to lament that our country is not entirely free from these evils, as it would be to lament that our fields produce weeds as well as corn.

Differences in opinion, and other causes equally pure and natural, will unavoidably cause parties; but

departure from the instructions you had given me, he ultimately determined not to receive from me the proposed information. That I should be there, be seen frequently with him, and he remain ignorant on such a subject, would have increased the jealousies which already existed; and for this there was no remedy but in observing the utmost distance and coldness:—Of course the whole weight of suspicion and ill will was accumulated upon me, and my situation became very awkward and unpleasant.—I thought it, however, prudent to remain as long as my business required, contenting myself with repeating on all occasions that the treaty contained nothing contrary to the engagements of the existing treaties; and that whenever the contracting Government should see fit to make it public, I had no doubt but it would meet the approbation of all reasonable men.

We are now in hourly expectation, of hearing the result of the deliberations of the Senate, as we have accounts down to the 15th June and know that the *Asia* was to sail from Phila about the 20th with Mr. Allan's and Mr. Hammond's families:—I hope the late Orders, for bringing in neutral Ships bound with Provisions to France and the continued Captures on the Coast of America, will not prove the source of new misunderstandings.—I yesterday breakfasted with Sir William Scott, and had some conversation on this Subject;—I ventured to say to him, that, having just arrived from France I could assure him that as a measure of military policy the bringing in of Neutral Ships was utterly useless, as great quantities of foreign Corn had been received and the harvest was begun in the South; that if the want of bread here operated as a reason for the measure, I was sorry it had not been announced in another way, as we should have been equally ready to sell to this Country as to any other; that I dreaded the Effect this Measure might have upon the public mind in America, for although

I trusted it would not prevent the ratification of the Treaty, yet the loss falling upon the same important Class of men who had already suffered so severely, I did apprehend, that unless great dispatch in the settlement of this business and great liberality in payment were experienced, it would have the Effect to counteract in a very great degree that return of Amity and neutral kindness which I had supposed to be the great object of the treaty; and to render all that had been done a mere palliative and momentary business.

Sir William assured me that the necessities of the Country were to a certain degree the Cause of the existing Orders; that, at the same time Government considered themselves as in the Exercise of one of the rights of war common to all Nations, and which they should not think of contesting, were we or any other Nation to exercise the same hereafter in similar circumstances, with respect to the Ships of this Nation ; that Government had instructed him (and he should most faithfully and with pleasure execute those instructions) to give all possible dispatch to the business, as well as the utmost latitude to payments consistent with reason. In the mean time our people are very much dissatisfied both here and on the Continent.

A body of Emigrant Troops have lately been landed in Quiberon Bay, from whose cooperation with the disaffected people of La Vendee and Brittany, much has been expected ;—but I believe little will be done ; we already hear of several revolts, and additional troops are known to be on their March from the North and East of France, where hostile operations are at present suspended.

The Public opinion of France, no longer controul'd by the Guillotine and patriotic Baptisms, is now as loudly pronounced against the Atrocious consequences of Jacobinism, as that of England or America ever were ; and if they now Err in their criminal prosecutions it is by employing a formality and caution which one can scarce refrain from blaming, when exercised towards such a wretch as Joseph Le Bon, or Fouquier Tinville.

The Constitution of which I sent you a Copy, is still under discussion ; several amendments (as we think them) have been, and it is probable that others will be, adopted ; and I am not without a hope, and even an Expectation that within a few Months we shall see a form of Government in operation in France which altho' not altogether meeting our views of Wisdom, will yet be a prodigious approach towards it ; and such a declaration of intentions towards other Nations as will show more Moderation than might have been expected from a people covered with so many Victories.

My plate at Stutgard I found not so nearly finished, as I had hoped, and of course the publication cannot take place this Winter.   I shall send in a few days to Mr. Pinfield an impression of it in the State it was last January, as well as a finished one of Montgomery, from which my friends, I hope, will be induced to have a little longer patience ; they cannot be so much hurt at the delay as I am.—I beg my respects to Mrs. Jay and Peter, as well as to Mr. Benson, King, Hobart, &c.   I am with all respect,

Dear Sir, your Humble Servant,

JN. TRUMBULL.

TIMOTHY PICKERING [1] TO JAY.

[PRIVATE.]

SIR,   PHILADELPHIA, Aug. 14th, 1795.

No man can be more anxious for the fate of the treaty with Great Britain than you ; and the wanton abuse heaped upon you by the enemies of their country, gives you a

---

[1] Secretary of War.

right to the earliest possible relief. The treaty will be ratified. This day the president finally sanctions a memorial announcing it to the British minister Mr. Hammond. The ratification will conform to the advice and consent of the Senate, unembarrassed with any other condition.

Permit me to suggest to your consideration the expediency—perhaps I should say the necessity, at this time of general ferment, when the grossest falsehoods, the most infamous calumnies, are industriously disseminated to render suspected and odious the real friends to their country— of a solemn public declaration by the president of the principles of his administration, and of his appealing to the train of actions which have marked his whole life, for the purity and patriotism of his conduct on the present occasion. Something of the kind seems due to himself, and to the early, determined, and uncorrupted patriots who have supported him.

The post is on the point of departure, which obliges me to conclude abruptly.

With great and sincere respect,

I am yours,

TIMOTHY PICKERING.

JAY TO TIMOTHY PICKERING.

[PRIVATE.]

NEW YORK, 17th August, 1795.

SIR :

Accept my thanks for your obliging letter of the 14th inst. The friendly motives which induced you to communicate to me the information contained in it shall be remembered. The President's firmness on this occasion adds new honours to his character and confers new obligations on his country.

Of the expediency of an address I am not perfectly satisfied ; although I think it would in many respects be useful. It appears to me to be a good *general* rule, that the President should very rarely come forward except officially. A degree of reserve seems necessary to the preservation of his dignity and authority ; any address would be exposed to indecent strictures. Many of our presses are licentious in the extreme, and there is little reason to presume that regard to propriety will restrain *such* parties, and *so* hostile to the constitution and government, from acting improperly.

My opinion of the existence, and of the views and practiecs of the leaders of these parties, or rather factions, is not of recent date. Nothing in their present conduct strikes me as singular, except their more than ordinary indiscretion. Industrious they are and will be, and no activity or *means* will be spared to gain *a majority in Congress at the ensuing session.* To render this attempt abortive the proposed address will doubtless conduce. The President's speech may indeed comprise his sentiments and remarks on the subject, but then by that time the mischief may be advanced and ripened. A more early address, by correcting public opinion, would render it a check on the conduct of some representatives who might otherwise favour the opposition. There are men who will go with the stream, whatever its course may be ; and there are others who will act right when they see no advantage to themselves in acting wrong. Snares and temptations will be spread; in a word, this address has its pros and cons; but it is a point on which I should confide in the President's judgment, which I think very seldom errs.

Ancient as well as very modern history teaches us lessons very applicable to the present times; and points out the necessity of temper, activity, and decision. I think that the President, with the blessing of Providence, will be able to carry his country safe through the storm, and to see it anchored in peace and safety: if so, his life and character will have no parallel. If, on the contrary, the clubs and their associates should acquire a decided ascendency, there will be reason to apprehend that our country may become the theatre of scenes resembling those which have been exhibited by their brethren in France; and that, to justify themselves, their utmost malice and art will be employed to misrepresent and vilify the government, and every character connected with it.

God governs the world, and we have only to do our duty wisely, and leave the issue to him.

I have the honour to be, etc.,

JOHN JAY.

P. S.—I do not learn that there is much uneasiness or defection in the counties of this State, except in places where Jacobin societies have been set up, or in neighbourhoods where some leading malcontents have influence. Late accounts from Albany on these topics are agreeable.

JAY TO EDMUND RANDOLPH.

[PRIVATE.]

NEW YORK, 20th August, 1795.

SIR :

I have been honoured with yours of the 16th instant, and thank you for the interesting information detailed in it.

Knowing that my opinions and sentiments relative to the treaty cannot easily be supposed to be free from the influence of personal considerations, I have been so reserved as that since my arrival I have neither written a line to the President, nor been the author of a single anonymous paper on the subject of its merits.

However much I regret the ferment which it has been made the occasion of inciting in certain places, and among certain people, yet I confess few circumstances have occurred which I did not expect. I carried with me to Europe, and I brought with me from thence, a fixed opinion, that no *treaty whatever* with Great Britain would escape a partial but violent opposition. I did clearly discern that any such treaty would be used as a pretext for attacks on the government, and for attempts to diminish the confidence which the great body of the people reposed in it.

In the history of this country, posterity will have much to admire and commend ; and I shall be mistaken if they have not also much to censure and deplore. Be that as it may, I shall continue to possess my mind in peace, and be prepared to meet with composure and fortitude whatever evils may result to me from the faithful discharge of my duty to my country. The history of Greece, and other less ancient governments, is not unknown to either of us ; nor are we ignorant of what patriots have suffered from domestic factions and foreign intrigues in almost every age.

It is pleasing, however, to reflect that our country possesses a greater portion of information and morals than almost any other people ; and that although they may for a time be misled and deceived, yet there is reason to expect that truth and justice cannot be long hid from their eyes.

I am, dear sir,

Yours truly,

JOHN JAY.

PRESIDENT WASHINGTON TO JAY.

[PRIVATE.]

PHILADELPHIA, 31st August, 1795.

MY DEAR SIR,

You will have learned from the public gazettes, and through other more authentic channels, that all that rested with me to do, to give ratification to the treaty with this country and Great Britain, is already accomplished.

Mr. Pinckney's absence from the court of London, the information and aids it was expected he would derive from Mr. Short's presence at that of Madrid, the pecuniary situation of our affairs in Holland requiring the attention of Mr. Adams in that country, and the little knowledge we had of the character and qualifications of Mr. Deas, have occasioned no little embarrassment in this business. However, a mode is adopted which, I hope, will be effectual.

It has not been among the smallest of these embarrassments that the domineering spirit of Great Britain should revive just at this crisis, and the outrageous and insulting conduct of some of her officers should combine therewith, to play into the hands of the discontented, and sour the minds of those who are friends to peace, order, and friendship with all the world. But this by-the-bye.

The object of this letter is to pray you to aid me with hints relative to those points which you conceive to be fit subjects for the further friendly negotiations on the West India trade with Great Britain, agreeably to the recommendation of the Senate ; and which appear to have been in contemplation by the concluding part of the treaty signed by yourself and Lord Grenville.

I intended to have asked this favour of you at an earlier day ; but a coincidence of unexpected circumstances has involved me in so much business and perplexity, that it has been delayed from time to time (since my arrival in this city) until the present moment. But as nothing is now asked that you have not, I am sure, revolved over and over again during your negotiation, and since the decision of the Senate thereon, I persuade myself it will require but little time for the digest I ask ; and which I beg to receive as soon as you can make it convenient to give me, circumstances rendering it necessary for me to leave this place, if possible, on Monday next for Virginia, in order to bring back my family ; but instructions for the new negotiator *must* be prepared before I go.

With great esteem and regard,

I remain, my dear sir,

Your affectionate and obedient servant,

GEORGE WASHINGTON.

JAY TO PRESIDENT WASHINGTON.

NEW YORK, 3d September, 1795.

DEAR SIR :

I have been honoured with yours of the 31st of last month. The article in the treaty, to which you allude, viz. the *last*, was proposed by me to Lord Grenville, because it seemed probable that, when the treaty should for some time have been in operation, defects might become manifest, and further arrangements become desirable, which had not occurred to either of us ; because no plan of an article relative to impressments, which we could devise, was so free from objections as to meet with mutual approbation ; and because the Lord Chancellor's proposed article, relative to alienism and other interesting objects, was of such magnitude that I did not think any stipulations respecting them should be ventured until after that article had received the most mature consideration of our government.

I think that in endeavouring to obtain a new modification of the 12th Article, an extension of tonnage from 70 to 100 tons should be attempted ; for although this was strenuously pressed before, yet I can see no inconvenience in repeating it, by way of experiment—not insisting on it as an ultimatum. In my opinion, it would also be expedient that the new article should *specify* the particular commodities which our vessels shall be permitted to carry from the United States to the British islands, and import from the latter into the former.

As to the *impressment* of seamen, the forming of

any very satisfactory arrangement on that head will, I fear, continue to prove an arduous task. In my opinion, Great Britain should at present agree not to take any seamen from our vessels on the ocean, or in her colonial ports, on account of the injuries thence resulting to our navigation. It would be difficult to support the position, that she ought to agree not to seek for and take her own seamen on board of any merchant vessel in the ports of Great Britain or Ireland.

In the India, or 13th Article, "It is expressly agreed, that the vessels of the United States shall not carry any of the articles, exported by them from the said British territories, to any port or place, except to some port or place in *America*, where the same shall be unladen." I would propose that after the word America be added, "or to some foreign port or place in Asia." There is, indeed, nothing in the article as it now stands which restrains the India Company's government from continuing to permit our vessels to carry cargoes from India to China ; but it would be better, if possible, to establish this as a right by express agreement.

For my own part, I regard the present moment as unfavourable for negotiations with Great Britain. Although she has reason not only to approve but to admire the conduct of our government, yet while it appears doubtful to her whether the sentiments and dispositions of the great body of our people are pacific and friendly or otherwise, it seems natural to suppose that it will be her policy to be reserved. To multiply engagements with and facilities to us under such circumstances might be ascribed to her apprehensions ; and as her government will doubtless perceive this risk, I suspect they will be strongly inclined to avoid it. Besides, I should doubt the policy of introducing into the negotiation at present either so many or such propositions as may defer the ultimate ratification so late as to prevent orders to evacuate the ports by the 1st of June next from being sent in due season.

The commercial part of the treaty may be terminated at the expiration of two years after the war ; and in the meantime a state of things more auspicious to negotiation will probably arrive, especially if the next session of Congress should not interpose new obstacles.

I am, dear sir,

Your faithful friend and obedient servant,

JOHN JAY.

JAY TO JAMES DUANE.

NEW YORK, 16th September, 1795.

DEAR SIR :

I read your kind and affectionate letter of the 31st of July last with great satisfaction and sensibility, and I thank you for it. It is pleasing to see friendship, like an evergreen, bid defiance to the vicissitudes of seasons.

The opposition to which you allude, except as to its degree of malignity, was not unexpected. When the mission to England was pressed upon me, it was perceived that there were parties who would endeavour to wound the government through the sides of the envoy, and either depreciate his success or censure his want of it.

It had long been obvious that negotiations relative to the posts would unavoidably extend to the complaints of Great Britain relative to the debts, and that every idea of paying them would be offensive to the Southern States.

The attempts of the French to plunge us into the war were well known, and it was equally plain that they would not cease to be hostile to an amicable settlement of our differences with Great Britain.

The Constitution still continued to be a rock of offence to the Antifederalists ; and the funding system, by affording support to the government, had become exceedingly obnoxious to that party. It was evident, then—

That a treaty with Great Britain, by preventing war, would disappoint the Southern debtors of the receipts in full, with which they flattered themselves from a war.

That it would displease the French, by lessening our supposed dependence on them for protection against Great Britain, by diminishing their influence in our councils, and by making us friends with their enemies.

That it would discontent the Antifederalists, by disarming them of their affected complaints against the government on account of the posts, and commerce, etc., and by giving additional strength to the administration, etc., etc.

Hence there was reason to apprehend that a treaty with Great Britain would become a signal to the Antifederalists, the debtors, and the French, to unite their efforts to prevent its taking effect, and to embarrass its execution if ratified, and to conduct their opposition in a manner most injurious to the Constitution and to the administration and to all the men who are attached or give support to either. That with these parties would naturally be associated the Jacobin philosophers, the disorganizing politicians, and the malcontents of various descriptions ; together with the many who have little to lose and much to covet, and those who regard war as speculation, and prefer spoil and plunder to patient industry and honest gains. To these also may be added the numerous herd of those who blindly follow their leaders, who judge without understanding, who believe without evidence, and who are to their demagogues what some other animals are to their riders.

On the other hand, the highest confidence was reposed in the wisdom and firmness of the government, and in the virtue and good sense of the great mass of our people, who (especially in the Eastern and Middle States) possess a degree of information and steadiness not to be found in other countries. This confidence I then entertained and still retain. I persuade myself it will be justified by the event, and that the delusion which certain spirits are spreading to deceive the people, will not invest the sound part of the nation. If, however, this persuasion should prove to be ill founded, we may expect to see our country afloat on a sea of troubles. But having been conversant with difficulties, we are apprised that it is more proper as well as more useful to turn our faces than our backs to them.

As to the treaty, it must and will speak for itself; it has been maliciously slandered, and very ably defended. But no calumny on the one hand, nor eloquence on the other, can make it worse or better than it is. At a future day it will be generally seen in its true colours and in its proper point of view.

Strenuous efforts will be made to *gain* and *mislead* a majority of the House of Representatives at the ensuing session of Congress; and if they succeed, many perplexities and embarrassments may be expected. But perplexities and embarrassments are incident to human affairs; and while *moral* evil remains in the world it will constantly generate political ones.

Whenever I visit Albany, I shall certainly make an excursion to Duanesburgh. Your family are taking deep root there; and they have my best wishes that they may there be and remain "*like a tree planted by the water-side, whose leaf shall not wither.*"

I am, dear sir, your friend and servant,

JOHN JAY.

JUDGE HOBART TO JAY.

THROGGS NECK, 18th November, 1795.

DEAR SIR,

I have read with pleasure your excellency's proclamation for a day of thanksgiving and prayer; the causes are well assigned, and the petitions well adapted.[1] Everybody will agree that we have received great and undeserved mercies, as a society, from our Creator; and that it is fit and proper we should, as a society, acknowledge and implore the continuance of them. But by whose authority shall the times and seasons for the purpose be pointed out?

I wot that in good olden time it was the peculiar province of holy church, and so continued till Henry the 8th, of *pious* memory, made a kind of hotch-pot business of it, by uniting the ecclesiastical and civil power in his own hands. His example has been followed by his successors to the present day: they issue their proclamations appointing days for public fasting, humiliation, and prayer in times of public calamity, and for public thanksgiving and praise upon signal instances of public mercies. It may be said their proclamations are authoritative, ours only recommendatory. But I ask, if the recommendation does not partake of the nature of a *conge d'elire?*—and who will be hardy enough to neglect an acknowledged duty when recommended from such high authority? Am I mistaken, or do my glasses magnify too much when I fancy I see the cloven foot of *monarchy* in this business? Alas! where are the direful effects of this extraordinary envoyship to end?—the benefits of our commerce transferred to Britain—the usurpations of its monarchy transferred to us. Nor is this all: the poor clergy

---

[1] Judge Hobart refers here to Governor Jay's proclamation recommending the observance of Thursday, Nov. 26, 1795, as a day of public thanksgiving throughout the State. The opposition papers assailed his action. See Jay's "Life of Jay," vol. i., pp. 385–86.

are by the constitution confined to the cure of souls. They may not intermeddle with the political concerns of the community; the door is for ever barred against them. Let who may be rulers, they *must* be subject. And shall the poor pittance of power, arising from the authority of calling their congregations together, to observe particular days for religious purposes, be thus wrested from them? It is in vain to say that no interference with their authority is intended; for whether intended or not, it may happen that our civil governor may recommend a thanksgiving to be celebrated on the same day which our spiritual governors had set apart for fasting. The case I observe has actually happened in the present instance; and I applied yesterday to the casuistry of the parson of the parish to decide for me between them, and tell which ought to be obeyed. He, good man, entered an *advisari*, and may eventually take it *ad referendum*. It seems this power ought to be exercised by the spiritual or the civil rulers solely: it is an *hereditament* of which they cannot be seized as *tenants in common*, unless there should be formed such an intimate *alliance* between church and state as to prevent all possibility of interference.

If Camillus can dispose of these objections to the proclamation in as handsome a manner as he has those to the treaty, I shall tremble for the fate of my country when you are sent on an extra mission to the court of Rome, lest the same spirt of imitation might produce a bull, constituting another *defender*, though I trow not of the faith.

Yours, most sincerely,
JOHN SLOSS HOBART.

His excellency Gov. JAY.

19th.—I find by the Daily Advertiser that the proclamation, no more than the treaty, is to escape the shafts of envy and malevolence.

JAY TO PRESIDENT WASHINGTON.

New York, 14th December, 1795.

DEAR SIR:

.   .   .   .

I have lately received much intelligence from several quarters. Some allowances are to be made for zeal; but all my accounts agree in representing the public mind as becoming more and more composed, and that certain virulent publications have caused great and general indignation, even among many who had been misled into intemperate proceedings, and had given too much countenance to factious leaders. The latter, however, persevere with great activity, though with less noise and clamour. These are political evils, which, in all ages, have grown out of such a state of things, as naturally as certain physical combinations produce whirlwinds and meteors.

With perfect respect, esteem, and attachment,

I am, my dear sir,

Your obliged and affectionate servant,

JOHN JAY.

PRESIDENT WASHINGTON TO JAY.

[PRIVATE.]

PHILADELPHIA, 21st Dec., 1795.

MY DEAR SIR,

Your two letters of the 14th instant came duly to hand. With respect to Mr. ———, I beg you to be persuaded, that if all things in his favour are equal, your mentioning of him will have its weight. But in appointments of the sort he solicits, many matters must be attended to ; and as I am sure we have the same wishes respecting them, namely, to fix on characters who, under all circumstances, are most likely to answer the objects of their appointment, and to meet general approbation, I must endeavour to be circumspect in the selection ; and that I may have the greater variety to choose from, I would thank you and my other friends for giving me the names of such gentlemen as may occur, and are most prominent and fit to discharge the duties of commissioners.

My information with respect to the general disposition of the people, accords with yours ; and I have little doubt of a perfect amelioration of sentiment, after the present fermentation (which is not only subsiding, but changing) has evaporated a little more. The dregs, however, will always remain, and the slightest motion will stir them up. With sincere esteem, and affectionate attachment,

I am always yours,
GEORGE WASHINGTON.

JAY TO ROBERT GOODLOE HARPER.[1]

NEW YORK, 19th January, 1796.

SIR :

A friend of mine lately sent me your address to your constituents relative to the treaty. I have read it with pleasure. Had all the publications on that subject been written with equal knowledge and attention, or with equal candour and decorum, more truth would have been disseminated, and less irritation excited.

---

[1] Member of Congress. This letter was published by Mr. Harper, at Mr. Jay's request.

I observe in it the following paragraph, viz.:

"Objections both personal and constitutional have been made to Mr. Jay. He has been said to be prepossessed in favour of Britain, and an avowed enemy to France. If this had been true, it would have been a sufficient reason for rejecting him—but it is not true. I can contradict it, and do, on my own knowledge. I heard Mr. Jay express, in public and private, and those who have been much more and much longer acquainted with him, assure me that he always has expressed the utmost pleasure in the French Revolution, and the warmest wishes for its success, the greatest dislike for the former government, and sentiments of the highest esteem and respect for the nation."

I am much obliged to you, sir, for this vindication ; but it being summary and in general terms, and comprehending only one of the points, I think it best, in order to obviate all further questions, to state particularly my sentiments relative to them both.

It has, for obvious reasons, been judged convenient to represent me as being strongly attached to the interests of Britain, and as being equally hostile to those of France. Before I take notice of either, I will premise that, as it is my duty, so it is my inclination and resolution, never to be a partisan of any foreign court or nation, but to be and remain with those independent and genuine Americans, who think it unwise and improper to meddle in foreign politics, and who regard all foreign interference in our counsels as derogatory to the honour and dangerous to the best interests of the United States.

Not being of British descent, I cannot be influenced by that delicacy towards their national character, nor that partiality for it, which might otherwise be supposed not to be unnatural. I nevertheless continue to concur in, and to express those sentiments of esteem for that nation, which are expressed, and I believe with great sincerity, in the early Journals of Congress.

It is not from the characters of this or that administration, or prevailing party in the government, that the character of a nation is to be inferred. A true judgment of it can no otherwise be formed than by observing the general tenor of their dispositions and conduct, viewed under all their circumstances and in all their relations during a long course of time. It certainly is chiefly owing to institutions, laws, and principles of policy and government, originally derived to us as British colonists, that, with the favour of Heaven, the people of this country are what they are.

Notwithstanding the tendency which all arbitrary governments, and particularly the long reign of such a monarch as Louis the Fifteenth, have to debase and corrupt their subjects, the people of France continued to be highly distinguished by their talents, and by their progress in the arts both of peace and of war.

It is true that I returned from that country to this, with opinions unfavourable to their court; but not only without a wish unfriendly to them, but, on the contrary, with sentiments of good-will and regard. That I have from early life expressed a strong dislike to the former arbitrary government of France, is well known. The more I became acquainted with it, the more it appeared to me to be a government always dreadful in theory, and always more or less so in practice, according to the characters of those by whom its powers were exercised.

In the revolution which put a period to it, I did cordially rejoice : I mean the one which limited the power of the king, and restored liberty to the people. The patriotic Assembly which concerted and accomplished that revolution, and the people and army who concurred in and supported it, did themselves immortal honour ; and impressed me (although my judgment did not accord with all their acts) with great respect and esteem for them, and with the warmest wishes for the ultimate success and perfection of the constitution and government which they established.

The successors of that memorable Assembly produced another revolution. They abolished the constitution and government which had been just established, and brought the king to the scaffold.

This revolution did not give me pleasure. I derived no satisfaction from the disastrous fate of a prince who (from whatever motives) had done us essential services, and to whom we had frequently presented the strongest assurances of our attachment and affection. This revolution had, in my eye, more the appearance of a woe than a blessing. It has caused torrents of blood and of tears, and been marked in its progress by atrocities very injurious to the cause of liberty and offensive to morality and humanity.

But this revolution having abolished the monarchy declared France a republic, and received the general concurrence of the nation, a new constitution became indispensable : and as, in case this revolution should be overthrown by the combined powers, they would doubtless dictate what that new constitution should be (an interference not to be submitted to), I wished success to the revolution, so far as it had for its object not the disorganizing and managing of other states, which ought neither to be attempted nor permitted, but the exclusive ordering of all internal affairs, and the establishment of any constitution which the nation should prefer. It gives me pleasure to find that one has lately been so established ; and I sincerely wish it may be the means of giving permanent peace, liberty, and good government to France.

As to the issue of the war, I am far from desiring that either France, Britain, or Germany, or any other power, should acquire a decided preponderance in Europe. In my opinion, it would conduce more to the welfare and peace of those nations, and also of the United States, that they should remain in capacity to limit and repress the ambition of each other.

I will conclude this letter with an extract from one which I wrote to the late Secretary of State, dated at London on 21st November, 1794, viz.:

" I daily become more and more convinced of the general friendly disposition of this country towards ours ; let us cherish it. . . . Let us cultivate friendship with all nations. By treating them all with justice and kindness, and by preserving that self-respect which forbids our yielding to the influence or policy of any of them, we shall, with the Divine blessing, secure peace, union, and respectability."

With sentiments of esteem and regard, I have the honour to be, sir,

Your most obedient and humble servant,

JOHN JAY.

JAY TO REV. UZAL OGDEN.

NEW YORK, 14th February, 1796.

DEAR SIR:

I am much obliged to you for the books you have been so kind as to send me, and which, with your friendly letter of the 11th instant, were delivered to me yesterday. Except while at church I have employed this day in reading the first and part of the second volume, and expect to finish the perusal of the remainder next Sunday. I have long been of opinion that the evidence of the truth of Christianity requires only to be carefully examined to produce conviction in candid minds, and I think they who undertake that task will derive advantages from your enumeration of many interesting facts, your remarks on various heads and topics, and from your references to numerous authors proper to be consulted, and some of whom are but little known.

As to " The Age of Reason," it never appeared to me to have been written from a disinterested love of truth or of mankind, nor am I persuaded that either of those motives induced certain characters to take such singular pains to distribute and give it reputation and currency in this country. Religion, morality, and a virtuous and enlightened clergy will always be impediments to the progress and success of certain systems and designs, and therefore will not cease to experience both direct and indirect hostilities from those who meditate or embark in them.

With the best wishes for your health and happiness, I am, dear sir,

Your most obedient and humble servant,

JOHN JAY.

JAY TO JUDGE LOWELL.

DEAR SIR:

NEW YORK, 29th February, 1796.

I have been favoured with yours of the 15th inst. by Mr. Parkman; am much pleased with him and his fellow-traveller, Mr. Cooledge. Their representation of the state of things in Massachusetts corresponds with the hints on that head suggested in your letter. There is too much intelligence in the Northern States to admit of their being greatly and long deceived and misled; and I hope the same remark will in time become equally applicable to all the others. Considering the nature of our governments, a succession of demagogues must be expected; and the strenuous efforts of the wise and virtuous will not cease to be necessary to frustrate their artifices and designs. They will always be hostile to merit, because merit will always stand in their way; and being actuated by envy, ambition, or avarice, and not unfrequently by them all, will be diligently at work, while better men will take their rest.

It seems strange, but so it is in all republics, that many excellent men who are happy in their families and fortunes and in the esteem of society and of their friends, who enjoy their villas and their gardens and neglect not to guard their trees and vines from caterpillars and their favourite plants and flowers from nipping frosts, yet omit attending to the political grubs, who are constantly and insidiously labouring to wound and prey upon the roots of all their temporal enjoyments. Several gentlemen of this description with us becoming alarmed have been very useful; and I presume this has been, more or less, the case in other States.

Be assured of the esteem and regard with which I am,

Yours, etc.,

JOHN JAY.

LORD GRENVILLE TO JAY.

CLEAVELAND-ROW, March 17th, 1796.

DEAR SIR,

I cannot let Mr. Liston go, without taking the occasion of his departure to recommend him to you, and to express my hope that his character and conduct will be found well calculated to continue and promote that harmony, which it was the object of our labours to establish. I have, since you left us, taken one occasion to renew to you my assurances of the sincere esteem and friendship with which your whole conduct has impressed me, and of the high sense which I entertain of your virtues and talents. It is a great satisfaction to one, when, in the course of so many unpleasant discussions as a public man must necessarily be engaged in, he is able to look back upon any of them with as much pleasure, as I derived from that which procured me the advantage of friendship and intercourse with a man valuable on every account. You, I trust, saw enough of me to know that these expressions are not, on my part, compliments of course, but that they proceed from sentiments of real esteem and regard.

I need not tell you with how much pleasure, on every account, I have learned that the public in the United States are recovering from the delusion into which they had been led, and that justice is now done by the country at large, as it was before by well informed and well principled men, to the uprightness and ability of your conduct. I, on my part, should have thought, that I very ill consulted the interests of my own country, if I had been desirous of terminating the points in discussion between us, on any other footing than that of mutual justice and reciprocal advantage; nor do I conceive that any just objection can be stated to the great work which we jointly accomplished, except on the part of those who believe the interest of Great Britain and the United States to be in contradiction with each other, or who wish to make them so.

It would be a great gratification to me to learn occasionally that you are well, and that you retain a friendly recollection of one who is, with the greatest sincerity,

> Most truly and faithfully,
> Your obedient humble servant,
> GRENVILLE.

PRESIDENT WASHINGTON TO JAY.

PHILADELPHIA, 31st March, 1796.

Accept, my dear sir, my thanks for your note of the 25th inst., enclosing a copy of Mr. Bayard's letter to you. The purport of it is pleasing; but the conduct of the British armed vessels in the West Indies is intolerable beyond all forbearance.

My answer, given yesterday to the House of Representatives' request for papers, will, I expect, set a host of scribblers to work: but I shall proceed steadily on in all the measures which depend on the executive, to carry the British treaty into effect.

This reminds me of the name of ————., who some time ago you mentioned as a commissioner; but upon inquiring of his countrymen, it was found he was unfit.

Be assured of the affectionate regard of

GEORGE WASHINGTON.

JAY TO LADY AMHERST.

Mr. Jay presents his respectful compliments to Lady Amherst, and returns many thanks to her Ladyship for the prints which she did him the honour to send. It was not until last week that they came to his hands. The respect entertained in this country for his Lordship's character and services render them very interesting. Among the agreeable moments which Mr. Jay passed in London his recollection often dwells on those for which he is indebted to the obliging attentions of Lord and Lady Amherst. His son retains similar sentiments and impressions, and they both unite in the best wishes for the health and happiness of Lord and Lady Amherst, and of the young ladies.

NEW YORK, 12th April, 1796.

WALTER ROBERTSON TO JAY.

Mr. Walter Robertson presents his respects to the Governor and begs leave to inform him that he is very desirous of having his portrait, for the purpose of being engraved as a companion to two prints of the President and Col. Hamilton. Mr. Robertson has already sketched the Governor's features from an unfinished portrait of Mr. Stewart's, and now takes the liberty of requesting to know at what time his Excellency can make it convenient to honor him with a sitting either at the Government House or at his house, No. 3 Stone Street.

Friday, 15 Apl., 1796.

JAY TO PRESIDENT WASHINGTON.

NEW YORK, April 18, 1796.

DEAR SIR :

You can have very little time for private letters, and therefore I am the more obliged by the one you honoured me with on the 31st of last month. Your answer to the call for papers meets with very general approbation here. The prevailing party in the House of Representatives appear to me to be digging their political grave. I have full faith that all will end well, and that France will find the United States less easy to manage than Holland or Geneva.

The session of our Legislature is concluded, and nothing unpleasant has occurred during the course of it. I think your measures will meet with general and firm support from the great majority of this State. There is no defection among the Federalists ; as to the others, they will act according to circumstances.

These contentions must give you a great deal of trouble ; but it is apparent to me, that the conclusion of them, like the conclusion of the late war, will afford a train of reflections which will console and compensate you for it.

Attachment to you, as well as to our country, urges me to hope and to pray that you will not leave the

be checked by fresh obstacles, permit me, my Lord, to submit to your consideration the prudence, as well as justice of strong measures, to prevent, as far as possible, those very exceptionable impressments, and other severities, which too often occur. They may give occasion, and I am persuaded will continue to give occasion to more clamour than facts will justify ; but it is certainly true that much just cause for complaint does exist, and that there are persons here who would rejoice if there was much more. There is reason to believe, that certain individuals in the British service have been irritated, by the improper things said and published in this country, to indiscreet acts of resentment ; not considering, and probably not suspecting, that they were said and published for the purpose of provocation. It is to be wished that they had recollected that these things were not said and published by our government, nor by those who desire to promote, and who do promote, peace and harmony with Great Britain, nor by those who are actuated by zeal for the honour and interests of their *own* country.

We have aimed at and laboured for the restoration of mutual justice and mutual good-will between our countries. The greatest difficulties are surmounted, and perseverance, with prudence and temper on both sides, will ensure success. Would not orders to discharge all impressed Americans, and enjoining a just and friendly conduct towards the people of this country, cherish their confidence, and manifest that disposition to conciliation, which repeated instances of violence and severity enable designing men (and with great appearance of reason) to draw into question ? Would not friendly assurances on these points to our government tend greatly to impress the public with still more favourable opinions of the propriety and policy of their measures ; and consequently diminuish the credit and influence of those who seize every occasion of impeaching their wisdom and your sincerity ? These men have, indeed, for the present missed their object, but they have not abandoned their designs. I mean the leaders, not the rank and file of the party. Among the latter are many misled, honest men, who, as they become undeceived, will act with propriety.

Pardon, my Lord, the liberty I take in these observations. I write freely because I confide fully in your candour, and because I flatter myself that you confide in mine. I have not leisure, at this moment, to be more particular. This letter will soon be followed by others.

With great and sincere esteem and regard, I have the honour to be, my Lord,

Your Lordship's most obedient

And humble servant,

JOHN JAY.

PRESIDENT WASHINGTON TO JAY.

PHILADELPHIA, 8th May, 1796.

MY DEAR SIR,

You judged very right when in your letter of the 18th ulto. you observed I " can have very little time for private letters." But if my friends will put up with the hasty and undigested ones I can write, under such circumstances, there are a few of them (among whom allow me the gratification to place you) with whom I should feel very happy to correspond: and while I hold my present office to learn their sentiments upon any of the important measures which come before the Executive of the United States.

I am *sure* the mass of Citizens in the United States *mean well*,—and I firmly believe they will always *act well* whenever they can obtain a right understanding of matters; but in some parts of the Union, where the sentiments of their delegates and leaders are adverse to the government, and great pains are taken to inculcate a belief that their rights are assailed, and their liberties endangered, it is not easy to accomplish this;—especially (as is the case invariably) when the inventors, and abettors of pernicious measures, use infinitely more industry in disseminating the poison, than the well disposed part of the community do to furnish the antidote.—To this source all our discontents may be traced, and from it our embarrassments proceed.—Hence serious misfortunes, originating in misrepresentations, frequently flow, and spread, before they can be dissipated by truth.—

These things do, as you have supposed, fill my mind with serious anxiety.—Indeed the trouble and perplexities which they occasion, added to the weight of years which have passed upon me, have worn away my mind more than my body;—and render ease and retirement indispensably necessary to both, during the short time I have to remain here.—

It would be uncandid therefore, and would discover a want of friendly confidence (as you have expressed a solicitude for my (at least) riding out the storm) not to add, that nothing short of events—or such imperious circumstances (which I hope and trust will not happen) as might render a retreat dishonorable, will prevent the public annunciation of it in time, to obviate waste or misapplied votes at the Election of President and Vice President of the United States in December next, upon myself. I congratulate you on the tranquil session, just closed in your State, and upon the good dispositions, generally, which I am informed prevail among the citizens thereof.

With most friendly sentiments I remain, dear Sir,

Your obedient and affectionate Servant,

GEO. WASHINGTON.

JAY TO TAMMANY SOCIETY.

The Governor has taken into consideration the request signified to him by a committee of the Tammany Society in this city : That he would order the flags on Governor's Island, and also on the Battery, to be hoisted on the day of their anniversary, vizt. the 12th May instant. It appears to him that if such a compliment be paid to the Tammany, it ought not to be refused to any other of the numerous societies in this city and State. Arbitrary preferences would be partial and unjust, and to discriminate on any principle of comparative utility or respectability would be a task too invidious to be undertaken for an object like the present. He doubts the policy and prudence of making such marks of public respect more general than they now are ; and thinking it his duty to observe the limits which usage and acknowledged propriety prescribe, he presumes that his declining to give the orders in question will, on being maturely considered, meet with approbation.

NEW YORK, 11th May, 1796.

The President and Members of the Tammany Society
in the City of New York.

JAY TO REV. DR. THATCHER.

New York, 26th May, 1796.

Dear Sir :

Mr. Thomas Hancock delivered to me yesterday your obliging letter of the 23d of last month.   I shall always be happy in opportunities of manifesting to the family of the late Governor Hancock my respect for his memory.   We were fellow-labourers in the American Revolution, and I reflect with pleasure on the good understanding which subsisted between us, and the friendly attentions with which he uniformly honoured me.   Permit me to add that my esteem and regard for you would not only ensure a welcome reception to this amiable young gentleman, but to any others you may recommend.

The approbation of one judicious and virtuous man, relative to the conduct of the negotiations in which I was lately engaged, affords me more satisfaction than all the clamours raised on that subject by intrigue and passion have given me concern.   It was foreseen that a strenuous opposition would be excited, and I was disappointed only in this, that the management of it has been less circumspect and politic than I had supposed.   There was little reason to expect that any treaty of amity with Great Britain, which our constituted government could form, would be acceptable to those Anti-federalists, whose prejudices, instead of being removed, but gathered strength and malignity from the failure of their predictions ; to debtors, anxious by any means to elude payment ;

or to partisans of a *foreign power*, which had systematically and industriously laboured to keep us in the condition of a satellite, and prevent our ever diverging from the sphere of her attraction and governing influence.

Believing the people of this country too intelligent to be long deceived, and not sufficiently vicious to require great national calamities, I hope and trust that Providence will continue to bless us with as much prosperity as will be good for us ; I say as will be good for us, for in my opinion Agur's prayer is not less suitable for nations than for individuals. With the best wishes for your health and happiness, I am, dear sir,

Your most obedient and humble servant,

JOHN JAY.

JAY TO WILLIAM VAUGHAN.

NEW YORK, 26th May, 1796.

DEAR SIR :

The letters of the 24th and 28th November last, with which you favoured me, have remained long unanswered, though not forgotten ; my time having, since my arrival, been so occupied by public concerns, that I have had no leisure to attend to my private affairs or correspondence.

As to political reformations in Europe or elsewhere, I confess that, considering men as being what they are, I do not amuse myself with dreams about an age of reason, prior to the millennium, which I believe will come, though I cannot tell the precise time when. Until that period arrives I expect there will be wars, and commotions, and tyrants, and factions, and demagogues, and that they will do mischief as they may have opportunity. Human knowledge and experience will doubtless continue to do good, in proportion to their extent and influence, but that they will ever be able to reduce the passions and prejudices of mankind to such a state of subordination to right reason as modern philosophers would persuade us, I do not believe one word of.

I should not think that man wise who should employ his time in endeavouring to contrive a shoe that would fit every foot; and they do not appear to me much more wise who expect to devise a government that would suit every nation. I have no objections to men's mending or changing their own shoes, but I object to their insisting on my mending or changing mine. I am content that little men should be as free as big ones and have and enjoy the same rights; but nothing strikes me as more absurd than projects to stretch little men into big ones, or shrink big men into little ones. Liberty and reformation may run mad, and madness of any kind is no blessing. I nevertheless think that there may be a time for reformation and a time for change, as well as for other things; all that I contend for is that they be done soberly, by sober and discreet men, and in due manner, measure, and proportion. It may be said that this cannot always be the case. It is true, and we can only regret it. We must take men and things as they are, and act accordingly—that is, circumspectly.

With the best wishes for your health and happiness,

I am, dear sir, your most obedient servant,

JOHN JAY.

JAY TO THE MAYOR OF NEW YORK.

NEW YORK, 7th June, 1796.

SIR :

Considering the works erected on Governor's Island, and the obvious objections to having a lazaretto near a garrison, I am solicitous to procure some other place for that purpose.

You are apprised of the difficulty or rather impossibility of purchasing from individuals any ground in a convenient situation for a lazaretto on account of the popular prejudices against having such an establishment in their neighbourhood.

As Bedloe's Island, which belongs to the Corporation, has heretofore been used and considered as a proper place for the purpose I think it would be agreeable both to the State and to the citizens of New York that it should be purchased by the State, and the intended lazaretto built there in preference to Governor's Island, in case the French intend soon to remove from it as I have understood they purpose to do ; for I have no desire to interfere with any arrangements between the Corporation and them relative to it. Be pleased therefore to lay this letter before the Corporation, and to inform me whether they will sell it to the State and at what price. Considering that this city

is more immediately interested in the precautions
necessary to be taken against the introduction of con-
tagious disorders by vessels arriving in this port than
the more distant parts of the State, I flatter myself
that the terms will be moderate, and such as the
Legislature would approve of my acceding to.[1]

I have the honour to be with great respect,

Sir, your most obliging and humble servant,

JOHN JAY.

The Honourable the Mayor of the
City of New York.

JAY TO GEORGE HAMMOND.[2]

NEW YORK, 15th June, 1796.

DEAR SIR :

Accept my thanks for your friendly letter of the
14th March last. I am happy in resuming my correspondence with my friends in England, and regret
that it has been so long suspended. As Mr. King
will be the bearer of this letter, I refer you to him for
information respecting the state of affairs here. You
have heard of the appointment of this gentleman to
succeed Mr. Pinckney. You are well acquainted with
his qualifications for that place, and with his character
public and private.

I thank you for making to Lord Grenville the inti-
mation I requested relative to the intended present. I

---

[1] The City Corporation granted the island to the State about three weeks.
ater.

[2] Late British Minister in the United States.

shall deem myself sufficiently honoured and gratified, if my endeavours should prove conducive to permanent peace and conciliation between our countries. This can, and I hope will, be accomplished. Nature has made few difficulties within the sphere of honest and rational policy, that are insuperable to prudence and perseverance. Mutual justice, mutual kindness, and a little mutual forbearance will ensure success. But it is to be remembered that political, like other fields, require constant attention ; when neglected, they soon become unproductive, and fresh weeds, briers, and thorns will gradually spring up.

The tide in human affairs, of which the poet speaks, now runs favourably, and will present a proper occasion for arranging our West India commerce. The war has, in a great degree, suspended the importance of it to us. When that suspension ceases, a strong sense of it will return, and will excite uneasiness which should be obviated or allayed by regulations as satisfactory as can well be made. Although a system more liberal than that in the twelfth article, if it had been immediately made, might have been ascribed to the pressure of circumstances, rather than to motives more pleasing and friendly ; yet that objection has nearly lost its force, and passed its time ; for the treaty is now in operation, with the approbation of a decided and great majority of the people, and success attends your arms.

While America has no just cause of complaint against Britain, nor Britain against America, their commercial and friendly relations will operate freely and effectually, and the designs of those who aim at discord between them will prove abortive.

I am, dear sir,

Yours very sincerely,

JOHN JAY.

LORD GRENVILLE TO JAY.

DROPMORE, July 9th, 1796.

MY DEAR SIR,

It is a great satisfaction to me to have to acknowledge two of your letters, and to be allowed the hope of hearing from you more frequently. I should have been very sorry to think that I was wholly out of your recollection, as I frequently reflect with pleasure on the opportunity I had of becoming acquainted with a character which I saw so much reason to esteem.

Mr. Gore delivered to me, a few days ago, your letter of introduction. He seems to be a sensible and moderate man, and I shall have great pleasure both in facilitating, as far as may depend on me, the public objects of his mission, and in showing him any private attention and civility that may be in my power. I think he and his colleague will be well satisfied with the choice which has been made here for that commission. Both Dr. Nicoll and Mr. Ansty are known (in some degree) in America, the former by character, the latter personally ; and I trust the appointment has proved the spirit in which it was made. If I do not deceive myself, the choice of the commissioners who are going to America will not be less satisfactory. Their names are not yet announced, but I look upon the appointment as very nearly, if not quite, fixed.

Your letter of the 1st of May was delivered to me two days ago, and I take the opportunity of this mail to answer it. I have the greatest pleasure in hearing from you, that you consider the questions which have agitated America since your arrival as determined. I think we always felt that even after the great points were adjusted, and a foundation of solid friendship laid, something must be still left for the operation of time and temper. Where so much heat has prevailed, irritation will remain among individuals, and will occasionally produce inconvenience and embarrassment to both governments. Mutual good disposition and confidence, a uniform and steady conduct in great points, and moderation respecting those of less importance, must ultimately surmount these difficulties, as they have already surmounted others which were much greater.

With respect to the impressments, I am confident that such orders as you speak of have been more than once repeated. I speak from general impression, not having had opportunity to ascertain the fact since I received your letter. But I think I can answer for it that they shall be renewed. In this country, much of the detail of that business has fallen within my own knowledge; and I can say positively, that I do not think one instance can be brought where a seaman has not been discharged, who could produce, I do not say proof, but any probable, or even plausible ground for supposing him a native citizen of the United States, or a resident there at the time of the separation from this country. In some instances, the conduct observed has been so favourable, that within the last week, before I received your letter, two men were discharged, one on producing a certificate of an American consul here, which did not recite on what grounds or from what proof it was given, but merely asserted the fact that the bearer was an American citizen; and the other, on producing a paper neither certified nor attested, but purporting to be a discharge from an American regiment of militia,—a paper, which, even if genuine, may, as you will easily see, have passed into twenty hands before it was produced here.

I saw in the proceedings of the last session of the Congress, some steps taken towards a regular establishment for the granting certificates. If such an establishment were formed, with proper and sufficient checks to prevent its being abused, the effect would be to do away the greatest part of our difficulties on the subject. But I much fear that the ideas prevalent in America on the subject of emigration, will prevent this ever being well or satisfactorily done.

I have been led into this discussion by what you say of the advantage which might arise from giving orders, which I am confident have been repeatedly given. The assurances of Mr. Liston on the subject will also, I trust, be such as you seem to desire.

I beg you to believe that you cannot do a thing more agreeable to me, or, perhaps, more useful to the interest of both our countries, than in expressing to me at all times, freely and without reserve, your opinion as to the means of maintaining that spirit which we jointly laboured to establish. This may be a means of rendering our correspondence greatly and permanently beneficial. Agreeable to me it can never fail to be, while it conveys to me information of your welfare, and gives me the opportunity of assuring you of the very sincere esteem and regard with which I have the honour to be, my dear sir,

Your most faithful and obedient humble servant,

GRENVILLE.

DIRCK TEN BROECK TO JAY.

ALBANY, 14th December, 1796.

I have the honor to acquaint your Excellency that I have procured two rooms in the house of Mr. Rooseboom, for your accommodation in this place this winter, and am in hopes the exertions of the family will contribute much to your ease, and comfort, both Mr. and Mrs. Rooseboom assuring us that nothing shall be wanting on their part to make every thing agreeable to you. I shall be highly gratified, in finding the result, correspond with my wishes on this subject. On Monday last, I dispatched a sledge for the cask of porter you had consigned to my care, which arrived here last evening; I have had it put into Mr. Rooseboom's cellar.

Your Excellency's letter of the 10th instant, was handed to me last Eve by the two Mohawk Indians, (accompanied by another of the Chiefs of that Nation, being the father of John, who handed me the letter). Agreeable to your directions I've procured decent lodgings for them, and shall have an eye towards them, for fear they should make too free with the *strong waters* of their host.

It is with singular satisfaction I can now inform you, that the Citizens of Albany are making every exertion to accommodate the Gentlemen of the Legislature, and I feel satisfied that their exertions will not be in vain. The rooms in our Court-house have been put in ample order for the reception of both branches of the Legislature, and I conclude we shall find ourselves comfortably and conveniently situated.

Any commands your Excellency shall please to honor me with, will be punctually attended to, and executed to the best of my ability.

I am, Sir, with respect and esteem,

Your most obedient servant &c.,

DIRCK TEN BROECK.

JAY TO REV. JEDEDIAH MORSE.

ALBANY, 28th February, 1797.

DEAR SIR :

I have been favoured with yours of the 14th ultimo, and also with the one which accompanied the set of your Geography, for which be pleased to accept my thanks.

It gives me pleasure to learn that you will endeavour at least to prepare for a history of the American Revolution. To obtain competent and exact information on the subject is not the least arduous part of the task ; it will require much time, patient perseverance, and research. As the Revolution was accomplished by the councils and efforts of the *Union*, and by the auxiliary councils and efforts of each individual *State or colony*, it appears to me that your inquiries will necessarily be divided into those *two departments*. The first of them will of course include foreign affairs, and both of them will naturally divide into two others— viz., the *civil* and the *military*. Each of these, you know, comprehends several distinct heads, which are obvious.

So much of our colonial history as casts light on the Revolution, viewed under its different aspects, and considered in all its anterior relations, will be essential. I think our colonial history is strongly marked by discriminating circumstances relative to our political situation and feelings, at three different periods : 1st, down to the revolution under King William ; 2d, from thence to the year 1763 ; and 3d, from that year to the union of the colonies in 1774. Want of leisure will not permit me to go into details.

As to documents—*public* and *private* journals of Congress ; the papers mentioned or alluded to in them, such as certain reports of committees ; letters to and from civil and military officers, ministers, agents, State governors, etc. ; the proceedings of the standing committees for marine, commercial, fiscal, political, and foreign affairs,—all merit attention.

The journals and papers of State conventions, and councils of safety, and of some of the standing and other committees, during the revolutionary government, contain much interesting information.

There are also diaries and memoirs and private letters, which would give some aid and light to a sagacious and cautious inquirer ; for experience has convinced me that they are entitled to no other respect or attention than what they derive from the well established characters of the writers for judgment, accuracy, and candour. As to characters, I have, throughout the Revolution, known some who passed for more than they were worth, and others who passed for less. On this head great circumspection is particularly requisite. It is to be regretted, but so I believe the fact to be, that except the Bible there is not a true history in the world. Whatever may be the virtue, discernment, and industry of the writers, I am persuaded that truth and error (though in different degrees) will imperceptibly become and remain mixed and blended until they shall be separated forever by the great and last refining fire.

I remain, my dear sir,

Your very obedient servant,

JOHN JAY.

JAY TO DR. BENJAMIN RUSH.

ALBANY, 22d March, 1797.

DEAR SIR :

I have received and read with pleasure your elegant eulogium on the late Mr. Rittenhouse. Such attentions to worthy characters cherish and encourage modest merit. As a man and a philosopher, his title to esteem and praise is, I believe, universally acknowledged.

The " Illustrations of the Prophecies," which you mention, I have not seen. On my return to New York I will inquire for it. The author's applying certain of the prophecies to certain recent events renders his work the more interesting. I have frequently known this to be done with more imagination than judgment, but from your account of the book I presume it is not liable to that remark. The subject naturally excites attention, and the present extraordinary state of things permits an idea to slide into the mind that even additional events, admitting of a like application, may precede a general peace.

We live, my dear sir, in times that furnish abundant matter for serious and profound reflections. It is a consolatory one that every scourge of every kind by which nations are punished or corrected is under the control of a wise and benevolent Sovereign.

With sincere esteem and regard, I am, dear sir,
Your faithful and obedient servant,
JOHN JAY.

JAY TO LORD GRENVILLE.

MY LORD: NEW YORK, 4th June, 1797.

A long interval has passed between the date of my last letter, and that of this. They would have been more frequent, had they been exposed to less risk of interception.

My respect and esteem for your Lordship remain unabated, and I yet flatter myself with the pleasure of becoming a better correspondent. It will give you satisfaction to know that the letters I have received from Mr. King and Mr. Gore, make honourable mention of the candour and good faith of your government. They both appear to be well pleased, and I am glad of it. The proceedings of the Congress now in session will doubtless be sent to you. There appears to be a general disposition to pacific measures throughout our country. If it procures peace, so much the better; if not, we shall be the more united. To put our adversaries in the wrong is always a valuable point gained, especially as the forbearance necessary for the purpose will not in the present instance be prompted by fear, nor produce dejection.

In every event, some malcontents are to be expected; and it is remarkable that *patriots* born in British dominions, are very distinguishable among those who the most invariably oppose our government and its measures. They appear to be as little disposed to promote good-will between our two countries, as the French; indeed, they seem to like our government as little as they did their own.

I have the honour to be, with very great respect, esteem, and regard, my lord,

Your lordship's most obedient servant,

JOHN JAY.

RUFUS KING TO JAY.

LONDON, June 10, 1797.

DEAR SIR:

I have the honor to introduce to you General Kosciusko. He will pass some time at New York, and possessing every claim to esteem and respect, he will, I am certain, experience every act of kindness and attention that can be shewn to him.

The General is accompanied by two of his countrymen and friends, one of whom, Mr. Julien Niemceuriz, is likewise his kinsman. I take the liberty to recommend him and them to your esteem and friendship, and remain with perfect respect, Dear Sir,

Your obedient, faithful servant,

RUFUS KING.

JAY TO JAMES SULLIVAN.

NEW YORK, 28th July, 1797.

SIR :

I have been favoured with yours of the 30th of last month, informing me of the necessity of my being at Boston on the 14th of August next, to give testimony to the Commissioners appointed to determine what river was intended by the river St. Croix in the treaty of peace.

If on further consideration my personal attendance should be judged indispensable, I shall certainly think it my duty to attend. But really, sir, when I reflect on the nature of my evidence, it appears to me that my affidavit or answers to written interrogatories would be sufficient and satisfactory.

My testimony would amount to this, vizt., that in the negotiations for peace, the river St. Croix, as forming part of our eastern boundary came into question ; that several rivers in those parts were said to have that name ; that much was urged and argued on that topic ; that Mitchell's map was before us, and frequently consulted for geographical imformation ; that both parties finally agreed that the river St. Croix laid down on that map, was the river St. Croix which ought to form a part of that boundary.

It may be asked, Did you at that time understand that the river St. Croix, laid down on Mitchell's map, was then so decidedly and permanently adopted and agreed upon by the parties, as conclusively to bind the two Nations to that limit, even in case it should afterwards appear that Mitchell had been mistaken, and that the *true* river St. Croix was a different one from that which he had delineated on his map by that name ?

To this question I answer, that I do not recollect nor believe that such a case was then put or talked of. [1]

With the best wishes for your health and happiness, I have the honour to be, Sir, your most obedient and humble servant, JOHN JAY.

---

[1] Respecting the long disputed "northeastern boundary" of the United States, see Mr. Gallatin's paper read before the New York Historical Society, in 1843, and published in its proceedings for that year. The discovery or production of Mr. Jay's copy of Mitchell's map, was the occasion of the address. Mr. Sparks published an article on the subject in the *North American Review* for 1843, vol. lvi.

JAY TO BENJAMIN VAUGHAN.

New York, 31st Aug., 1797.

Dear Sir:

I had this afternoon the pleasure of receiving your favour of the 18th inst. Mrs. Jay joins me in sincerely congratulating you and your amiable family on your arrival in this country; may your expectations of happiness in it be fully realized.

The reasons which have determined you to settle on the Kennebeck, I can easily conceive are cogent; but I flatter myself you will sometimes find leisure for excursions this way.

I presume that our political sentiments do not differ essentially. To me it appears important that the American government be preserved as it is, until mature experience shall very plainly point out very useful amendments to our constitution; that we steadily repel all foreign influence and interference, and with good faith and liberality treat all nations as friends in peace, and as enemies in war; neither meddling with their affairs nor permitting them to meddle with ours. These are the primary objects of my policy. The secondary ones are more numerous, such as, to to be always prepared for war, to cultivate peace, to promote religion, industry, tranquillity, and useful knowledge, and to secure to all the quiet enjoyment of their rights, by wise and equal laws irresistibly executed. I do not expect that mankind will, before the millennium, be what they ought to be; and therefore, in my opinion, every political theory which.

does not regard them as being what *they are*, will prove delusive.

It will give me pleasure to receive the publication you mention ; being from your pen, it will, I am persuaded, be interesting. Be pleased to present our best compliments to Mrs. Vaughan and your sister.

I am, dear sir,

Your affectionate and humble servant,

JOHN JAY.

JAY TO COL. JOHN TRUMBULL.

ALBANY, 27th October, 1797.

DEAR SIR :

I received, three days ago, by the post, your letter of the 7th of August, in which was a copy of the one you had written on the 20th of July, and the original of which I had received and read with pleasure.

The difficulty and delicacy of your task, my good friend, are obvious ; but I flatter myself the reputation to be derived from it will soften the trouble and anxiety it gives you. It was not to be expected that the judgments of the commissioners would not frequently differ, for the best judges sometimes vary in opinion from each other ; but it is to be expected, as well as wished, that their decisions may bear the test of the severe examination which they will certainly at one time or other undergo.

The delays of the court of admiralty do not surprise me. I have no faith in any British court of admiralty, though I have the greatest respect for, and the highest confidence in their courts of *justice*, in the number of which, those courts do not deserve to be ranked. I do not extend this stricture to the lords of appeal.

The question you hint at is interesting. Perhaps a mode might be devised for making and receiving claims *de bene esse;* but if any thing of that kind should be done, it should be on more mature consideration than that on which I suggest it; it is a thought which just occurred to me, and which I have not examined.

I am settled here with my family, at least for the winter. The Legislature have determined that this city shall be the seat of government, and that the principal public offices shall be here.

As to politics, we are in a better state than we were: but we are not yet in a sound state. I think that nation is not in a sound state whose parties are excited by objects interesting only to a foreign power. I wish to see our people more Americanized, if I may use that expression; until we feel and act as an independent nation, we shall always suffer from foreign intrigue.

Whether peace in Europe would ensure peace to America, is a question on which doubts are entertained. In my opinion, it will depend on circumstances, and not on any right or wrong about the matter.

Remember me to our friends, Mr. King, and Mr. Gore. I owe letters to them, and to others, but the

fate of letters has been so precarious, that I have
written much fewer than I should otherwise have done.

I am, dear sir, yours sincerely,

JOHN JAY.

JAY TO TIMOTHY PICKERING.

ALBANY, 13th November, 1797.

DEAR SIR :

I consider myself much obliged by your friendly
and interesting letter of the 28th ult. From Talleyrand's expressions and conduct it seems, and I infer,
that he will act as favourably towards us as may consist with his personal views, for I have very little
confidence in his being *governed* by any moral principles, further than they may be *conveniently* adopted.
As to Otto and La Forest, I entertain of them in that
respect very similar sentiments ; they will probably
be inclined towards us as far as may suit them.

The recent explosion at Paris has cast most of our
calculations and conjectures, relative to the issue of our
negotiations with the Directory, very much into the air.
A complete state of defence at home appears to me
to be the only solid foundation on which to rest our
hopes of security, and I regret that more has not been
done towards it. But until our people become more
united, and feel more sensibly the pride and the duties
of independence, our Jacobins will not cease to perplex the measures of our government, however wise
and salutary. It is pleasing to observe, that notwithstanding their efforts to mislead, the public mind is

gradually recovering from its errors, and to this end your public reports and letters have essentially contributed. Your answer to the Spanish minister's factious and indecent letter, has made stronger impressions than he and his counsellors probably suspect.

Yours, very sincerely,

JOHN JAY.

RUFUS KING TO JAY.

LONDON, Jan. 14, 1798.

DEAR SIR,

The faint remaining hope of an amiable settlement with France is extinguished. On the 4th instant the Directory sent a message to the council of 500 which contains the following paragraph: "The Directory is of opinion that it is indispensably necessary to enact a law declaring that the question whether a ship is neutral or otherwise, shall be decided by her Cargo; that the Cargo shall no longer be freed by the flag, and consequently that every ship found at sea, having on board a Cargo consisting wholly or in part of English commodities and merchandize shall be declared a lawful prize, whoever may be the owner of these commodities or merchandizes, which shall be reputed contraband, on this single fact, that they are the Product of England or of her Possessions." There is no doubt that the Councils will without delay pass a law conformable to the Message.

I know not what will be the conduct of Denmark and Sweden on this occasion. The law will reach all neutral nations, but will be most mischievous to us. I understand that the Swedes and Danes have made great supplies to France for which they have not been paid; and like our

Merchants, have in a great measure relinquished the trade. We have heard nothing from our Envoys since the 30th ult., when they were not received nor likely to be so. Every article of intelligence from the continent proves the ascendency of France. In a late address by the Directory to the people, we have a new theory for the future quiet and happiness of Europe, which is to be compleatly so, when France has nothing to ask, and the rest of Europe nothing to give.

Adieu, my Dear Sir,

I am your faithful Servant,

RUFUS KING.

COLONEL TRUMBULL TO JAY.

72 WELBECK ST., LONDON,
March 6th, 1798.

DEAR SIR,

The last letter which I have had the honor to receive from you is dated in Albany, the 27th Octr., and the last which I wrote to you was of the 10th December. Our Commissioners have not been received to an Audience in Paris, nor has any Negotiation with them been fairly opened. Decrees more offensive than all the acts of which they had to complain have been passed under their Eyes, and to me it appears, that we are in fact at war.

I have at length the satisfaction of informing you, that my two American plates are finished and in a style perfectly satisfactory to me. I had hopes of sending out their impressions to my subscribers by this Convoy, but it has been impossible to print a sufficient number to deliver to all, and as I can make no distinctions, I must suffer the whole to wait another Convoy when they will all be sent. In the mean time I have shipped on board the *Mary*, Capt. Allyn, a Case directed for you of which the Bill of Lading is inclosed to D. Penfield, Esq., with directions to convey it to you, and which contains a pair of proofs of these Prints, which I beg you will do me the honor to accept.—I have to regret that the talents which I had to employ in this work were not more equal to the dignity of the subject ;—and that the times in which I live are so little favorable to its successful continuation.

With the highest respect I am, Dear Sir,
                    Your obliged Servant and Friend,
                                        JNO. TRUMBULL.

TIMOTHY PICKERING TO JAY.

PHILADELPHIA, April 9th, 1798.

DR. SIR,

The dispatches from our envoys in Paris being published this morning, I do myself the pleasure to inclose you a copy. Unless the corruption of the French Government and their unjust, tyrannical, rapacious and insulting conduct towards the United States shall rouse the indignant spirit of the *people*, our independence is at an end. The leaders of the opposition in Congress, while thunderstruck with the exhibition of these dispatches, acknowledge the justice and moderation and sincerity of the Executive in his endeavours to accommodate our differences with France : but to all appearance, they will still oppose efficient measures even of defence, certainly by sea, and perhaps by land. Galatin professes to believe that our envoys have entered on a negociation, and that a treaty has ere this time been conducted. Mr. Jefferson says there is no evidence that the Directory had any knowledge of Talleyrand's unofficial negociations!

I am with great respect,
                    Your obedient servant,
                                        T. PICKERING.

RUFUS KING TO JAY.

LONDON, April 9, 1798.

DEAR SIR,

After every possible intrigue to divide our Envoys, and thereby to divide our Country, I have reason to believe that it has been determined to send two of our Envoys away, and to allow the third (Mr. Gerry) to remain with assurances that negociations shall commence as soon as the Directory shall have sufficient leisure. After all that has past, and with the lesson of Switzerland under our eyes, is it possible that this treacherous plan can succeed?—

We must banish internal divisions for our only safety is in Union.

Very truly your obedient servant,

RUFUS KING.

JOHN SLOSS HOBART TO JAY.

PHILADELPHIA, April 11, 1798.

MY DEAR SIR:

Soon after my arrival here I was informed of Mr. Troup's intention to resign,[1] by letter from our excellent friend Schuyler, who urged me to secure the appointment for myself ; this, I declined for a variety of reasons which I detailed to him, and which he had the goodness to approve of in very flattering terms. In the course of two or three weeks Mr. Laurence applied to me at the request of Mr. Bogert, who was sollicitous for the appointment if he could obtain it upon certain conditions, but in no event would he be considered as a candidate if it would be agreeable to me to accept the office. I told Mr. Laurence I wished to defer a

---

[1] The United States District Judgeship.

determination on that subject, if possible, till the result of the effort then making at Albany should be known. As soon as I heard of the decision of the Assembly I told him I would accept if the office was offered to me. He this morning waited upon the President, and in a conversation respecting Mr. Troup's resignation, gave it as his opinion that it would be generally agreeable to the people of the State should I be his successor. Whereupon the President sent a message to the Senate announcing Mr. Troup's resignation and nominating me to succeed him.

From this narration you will infer the probability that my next may bring you my resignation,[1] and that you will have to appoint a Senator. There is much sollicitude here to know on whom that appointment will fall. All enquirers express a confidence that he will be a good man, yet they can't help asking who will be sent.

Please to present my best respects to Mrs. Jay and the young ladies.

With sentiments of the most grateful friendship,

I am, yours

JNO. SLOSS HOBART.

PETER AUGUSTUS JAY TO JAY.

NEW YORK, 26 April, 1798.

DEAR PAPA:

. . . .

I have just returned from the Society for free debate, and tho' it is very late, I cannot forbear to mention the occurences that have just happened there. This Society was lately instituted, in all probability with the intention that

---

[1] As one of the United States Senators from New York.

it should be converted into a Jacobin Club. A Committee
of Managers was appointed consisting, with only one or
two Exceptions, of Violent Democrats; these preside in rota-
tion. Every Person who will pay a Shilling becomes for
that evening a Member. The Chairman for this Meeting
happened to be John Swarthout. one of the Antifederal
candidates as Assemblyman. Upon going into the room
almost by accident, I found it entirely filled by a great
crowd of people who were listening to a discussion of this
question : " Is it most expedient under existing Circumstances to lay an Embargo, or to arm our Vessels in defence of
our carrying trade ? " A Mr. Davis, One Butler, an Irish Shoe-
maker, and Dr. Smith, brother to the late Chief Justice of
Canada, supported the propriety of an Embargo in long and
inflammatory speeches, and were answered by Mr. Brown,
a sensible Quaker, McDougal, a Painter, and a young, but
really eloquent man of the name of Howe, a student at
Princeton College.

It was easy to perceive from the applauses and hisses be-
stowed upon the Speakers that tho' the Question had been
chosen with a View to influence the Election and a great
number of Democrats were present, that a vast Majority
were Federalists and would decide in favor of arming. The
Chairman was in many instances evidently partial, and in all
of them overruled (tho' not without much Noise and riot)
by the Society. Finding how Matters were going, he proposed that on account of the lateness of the hour, the final
decision should be deferred until the next Meeting ; this
being negatived he took the question on a Motion for Adjournment which being also lost, he by Virtue of a power
which he said was vested in him by the Constitution adjourned us.

The Society nevertheless remained and directed the Constitution to be read which was found to confer no such
Authority. The Chairman was then obliged to resume the

Chair and put the final question which was carried in favor of arming by at least five to one. Having pronounced the decision with an Appearance of extreme mortification and anger, he refused to hear any other Motion and again left the Chair. Mr. Howe then moved that a Committee should be appointed to form an Address from the Meeting to the President and Congress of the U. S. approving of the Measures which have been pursued with respect to France and expressing a determination to support them. Col. Morton being placed in the Chair, the Motion was carried, and Mr. Cozine, Col. Morton, Mr. Evertson, Col. Stevens and Mr. Hoffman appointed the Committee; And then after a fruitless attempt by Peter R. Livingston to call another Meeting to consider the Address which might be reported and after three Cheers the Society seperated.[1]

This Circumstance induces me to give more Credit to the Assertions of our friends who are confident that the whole of the Federal ticket will be carried in this City.

I am your Affectionate Son

PETER AUGUSTUS JAY.

---

[1] On May 6th, young Jay describes another meeting he attended: " I mentioned in a former letter the proceedings had at a Meeting of the Society for free debate. On last Thursday the Democrats mustered their whole strength to carry a Vote of Censure on those proceedings. The Federal party apprised of the design appeared also in great force to frustrate the attempt. The Democrats tho' the smaller Number, with surprising impudence, placed Commodore Nicholson in the Chair and by this procedure occasioned a Scene of the greatest Noise and Confusion I have ever witnessed. The adverse parties were frequently on the point of a general engagement. Many of our most respectable people were present; but no one was heard. If a Speaker began by addressing himself to the Chairman he was stopped by one party and by the other if he did not. After this State of Confusion had continued from before Nine till long past Eleven, the Federalists divided from their Opponents and having an evident (tho' not large) Majority, the Commodore adjourned the Meeting which immediately dissolved. . . . Betts to a great Amount have been laid on your Election at the odds of ten to one in your favor."

Governor Jay who had been renominated for the office in April of this year was re-elected by a large Federal majority over Chancellor Livingston.

JAY TO TIMOTHY PICKERING.

13th May, 1798.

DEAR SIR :

It is said that the Naturalization Act is to be revised and amended. Permit me to suggest an idea which I have for many years deemed important. We doubtless may grant to a foreigner just such a portion of our rights and privileges as we may think proper. In my opinion it would be wise to declare explicitly, that the right and privilegeof being elected or appointed to, or of holding and exercising any office or place of trust or power under the United States, or under any of them, shall not hereafter be granted to any foreigner ; but that the President of the United States, with the consent of the Senate, be nevertheless at liberty to appoint a foreigner to a military office.

I am, dear sir,

Your most obedient servant,

JOHN JAY.

WILLIAM NORTH [1] TO JAY.

[PHILADELPHIA,] June 6, 1798.

DEAR SIR,

The bill for prohibiting all intercourse with France is now before us, and will probably pass. The Alien Bill has passed the Senate ; Webster will have it in his paper. The act for raising, when it may be thought necessary, 10,000 men with permission to the President to receive such Volunteers as

---

[1] United States Senator from New York.

may offer, is, I believe, published; and there is now a bill for completing the marine Corps to 500 men. In addition to these and others providing for defence, certain resolutions have been laid before the other house to declare the Treaty void, and to grant letters of marque and reprisal; this step, however, has been thought by a majority of our friends at a private meeting to be rather premature. They will not be withdrawn, but remain with the committee of defence for future occasion. The warm spirits in this and the other house perhaps wish to run faster than is necessary; those who oppose the government would never stir a step. It is true the head of the government has given and daily gives us to understand that we are already at war; witness his answer to the address from Duanesbrugh and others. Whether there is a necessity for this open language you are a better judge than I can pretend to be; but it strikes me that it is never worth while to speak plain while you are in a measure prepared to ward off the blow which your antagonist is ready to strike.

The military department has at its head a man who is said to be not the most competent to its great and various duties; what ability the new minister of Marine may possess I know not. It is regretted much that Mr. Cabbot would not accept the appointment—The situation of our Militia is bad, both with respect to discipline and arms. I find that there is no likelihood of Congress being brought to do any thing in the business; the eastern men say (perhaps for fear of taxing themselves for the Southern States who will receive the greater benefits) their Militia is well armed, they want no assistance, they are disciplined, they want no further laws on the subject, and that if they did, the States individually have, if not full, a concurrent power with Congress to do what is necessary. I believe it would be a wise step, if our legislature meets, to erect, or by encouragement, by loan or otherwise, induce individuals to erect manufactories of small arms, powder and salt-petre. I will endeavour to get a bounty allowed on the manufacture of those articles. The spirit of the people of New York seems to be exerting itself for the safety of the City. I have sent to Col. Hamilton Baron Steuben's ideas on the subject and also have given them to Mr. McHenry, who is to go to New York next week, and fortunately is in possession of certain plans and maps, made by a Mr. Smith, and approved by Montressor and a board of engineers, intended to point out the proper place and the best method of fortifying the harbour of New York.

. . . .

I am with respect, Dear Sir,
Your obedient Servant,
W. NORTH.

WILLIAM NORTH TO JAY.

[PHILADELPHIA,] June 22, 1798.

DEAR SIR,

I have only time to enclose your Excellency the last communication of the President and to say that a bill is now before the Senate to declare the treaty with France void. This step I believe proper and shall support it; but we shall go farther, and before we adjourn probably declare War. This, it appears to me, there is no occasion for and that no good will result from it.

Your opinions I have the greatest respect for and should be happy to know your sentiments on this and every other occasion.

I am with respects, Dear Sir,
Your obedient Servant,
W. NORTH.

JAY TO WILLIAM NORTH.

New York, 25 June, 1798.

Dear Sir :

On my arrival here the day before yesterday I had the pleasure of receiving your letter of the 22d inst. enclosing the President's last communication, for which accept my thanks. The others which I received just before I left Albany, being in my trunk which I expect this morning, I cannot now answer particularly.

In my opinion it would be both just and proper to declare the treaty with France to be void, but I think it would be more advisable to direct reprisals than to declare war at *present*, for the public mind does not appear to me to be quite prepared for it. Of this however you are better informed, and therefore can judge better than I can. Should it be the case, the Jacobin leaders will continue to persuade their deluded followers that the Government is chargeable not only with participation, but with a desire to prevent an accommodation, which they affect to believe practicable notwithstanding the treatment of our Envoys, etc., etc.

When the mass of our people are convinced that war would be just, necessary and unavoidable, they will be content that it should be declared, and will support it vigorously ; but I doubt whether that connection, however well founded, is as yet so prevailing and general as it ought to be, and as it would be, but for the arts practised to retard and prevent it. To me there seems to be reason to apprehend that there

are characters to whom revolution and confiscation
would not be disagreeable.   Nothing should be omitted to frustrate their endeavours to deceive ; every
thing should be done to inform the people, and cause
them to see things as they are.   Mr. Gerry's remaining in France is an unfortunate circumstance—it
tends to prolong vain hopes, to cherish old divisions,
and to create new ones ; he was doubtless actuated by
the best intentions but I think he committed a mistake.   If both Houses should concur in opinion that a
declaration of war would be *seasonable,* I hope the
minority against it will not be so considerable as to
give countenance to a contrary opinion.

There are attempts to make mischievous use of
Talleyrand's letter.

I am, dear sir, etc.,

JOHN JAY.

·P : Ought War to be declared by such thin Houses ?

JAY TO THE JUSTICES AND SELECTMEN OF THE TOWN
OF NORWALK, CONN.

NEW YORK, 2d July, 1798.

GENTLEMEN :

I have received the petition by which you and other
inhabitants of the town of Norwalk request that a
pardon may be granted to Stephen Belknap, who was
lately convicted of attempting, in concert with other
prisoners, to effect their escape from the jail of this
city by force of arms.   The jail of the city was broken,

the citizens alarmed, one of them was shot and severely wounded, and the lives of others of them greatly endangered. For this offence he was sentenced to imprisonment and hard labour in the state-prison for eighteen months, and to a fine of no great amount.

This correct and well-written petition appears to have been dictated by pure and commendable motives. From the characters of the subscribers I am convinced that entire credit is due to the facts stated in it, and that the reputation, circumstances, and connections of Stephen Belknap are truly represented.

I feel the force of the considerations you urge, and sincerely sympathize with the young man's father in the affliction which he must necessarily experience from so distressing an event.

It is true that I have authority to grant him a pardon ; but that authority, you well know, gentlemen, is to be considered as a *trust* to be executed, not according to my will and inclination, but with sound discretion, and on principles which reconcile mercy to offenders, with the interests of the public.

In free states the laws alone bear rule ; and, to that end, respect for and obedience to them is indispensable to the order, comfort, and security of society. Belknap's offence includes disrespect to the laws, opposition and defiance to their authority, and a most unjustifiable combination to break from their control by force of arms, and without regard to the blood and lives of faithful officers and innocent citizens.

The punishment to which he has been adjudged is mild, and they who visit the state-prison will find that he has nothing but his confinement to complain of. After having very maturely considered this case, it appears to me that the nature of his offence is such as that a pardon would not be a prudent or a seasonable measure. The civil magistrates and ministers of justice must be protected, and that so decidedly as to let it be seen and felt, that violences and outrages against them cannot be committed with impunity. To pardon and discharge such an offender almost directly after his commitment to the state-prison would, instead of producing the proper impressions on him and others, naturally excite disgust and indignation in the peace-officers, and be censured, if not generally, at least by those who think our present penal code too mild. Besides, should a pardon be granted to Belknap and refused to his fellow-offenders, it would be difficult so to discriminate him from all the others as to avoid that partiality and respect to persons which both justice and policy forbid. Although too much severity is inhumanity, yet unless mercy is extended with great discretion, it will encourage offences and ultimately multiply punishments.

It also merits consideration, that many judicious and well-disposed citizens among us think that more sanguine expectations are entertained from our present mild or (as some call it) relaxed system of punishments, than will ever be realized. Prudence directs that it should have a fair trial, and therefore that the supposed objections to it should not be permitted to derive strength and support from the frequency of pardons, in cases where the propriety of them is justly liable to doubt and question.

I submit these reflections to your candid consideration ; and I assure you that I sincerely regret their constraining me to forego the satisfaction I should derive from a compliance with your request.

It is pleasant to gratify those who wish us well, and whom we esteem and respect ; but there are occasions when we must, however reluctantly, deny ourselves that pleasure.

I have the honour to be, gentlemen,

Your humble servant,

JOHN JAY.

JAY TO PRESIDENT ADAMS.

SIR : ALBANY, 21st August, 1798.

I have the honor of transmitting to you herewith enclosed an address from the Senate and Assembly of this State which passed and was agreed to *unanimously.*

It gives me pleasure to reflect that, from the numerous other expressions of the public sentiment relative to the reprehensible conduct of France towards our country, you may rely on the decided co-operation of the nation in the measures necessary to protect the rights and maintain their honour and independence.

I have too long known and too often been a witness to your patriotic and successful exertions not to be convinced that you will deserve both confidence and gratitude, and it is but doing them justice to say that no republics have given to their patriots and benefactors less cause of complaint than the United States of America.

I have the honour to be with great respect and esteem, sir, your most obedient and most humble servant, JOHN JAY.

JAY TO ALEXANDER HAMILTON.[1]

ALBANY, 30th August, 1798.

DEAR SIR :

I was this morning favoured with yours of the 27th inst. I regret the circumstances which prevented our seeing each other when you were here. There are several topics on which I wish to converse with you, and particularly respecting military arrangements at New York. The rifle corps and a few of the new light-infantry companies are established. There were reasons, which I shall mention when we meet, which induced me to suspend a decision relative to the others for the *present*. The objections stated in the petition are not, in my judgment, conclusive. So soon as the commissions advised by the council are despatched, I propose to set out for New York. The defence of the port, etc., in my opinion, should be under your direction. The measures will be concerted between us. The council will meet again

---

[1] Hamilton had lately been appointed Inspector-General of the United States Army with the rank of Major-General.

before the session, and all such new corps as ought to be established will then without difficulty be organized ultimately. I think with you on the subject of resignations.

It is with me a question whether any person convicted of *forgery* ought to be pardoned at *present*, when offences of that kind abound. As yet I have not pardoned any convicts of that description, except in cases where the convictions turned on a balance of evidence, and where guilt was probable, but not certain. Mr. Murray has just been with me on this subject. I shall take it into further consideration, but fear the objections will prove insuperable. The young man's father and family are to be pitied, but the power to pardon is a *trust* to be exercised on principles of sound discretion, combining policy, justice, and humanity ;—we will talk this matter over. I have an idea of putting the light corps into a regiment, and making our friend Troup colonel of it.

I am, dear sir,

Yours sincerely,

JOHN JAY.

JAY TO PRESIDENT ADAMS.

ALBANY, 26th September, 1798.

DEAR SIR :

During the late special session of the Legislature of this State an act was passed for the further defence of this State, of which a copy is herewith enclosed. The first section of this act appropriates a sum not exceeding 150,000 dollars towards the defence of the city and port of New York, and provides that the said sum shall be expended under the direction of the President of the United States.

In pursuance of another section of this act I have lately obtained on loan 100,000 dollars of the above-mentioned sum, and should have immediately gone to New York on this and other business, had not a circumstance occurred which made it necessary for me to summon the members of the Council of Appointment to meet here on the eighth day of next month.

It appears to be the intention of the Legislature that this money shall be laid out only in the manner which the national government will recognize as useful and advisable ; I therefore take the liberty of submitting to your consideration whether, as Major General Hamilton is a national officer in whom great confidence may be reposed, it would not be expedient to authorize him to concert with me the plan of laying out this money to the best advantage and to appoint him to superintend the execution of it. I think it would be best that I should leave the money in the Bank of New York, and appoint a proper person to audit and keep the accounts of the expenditures directed from time to time by General Hamilton relative to the works, and pay them as they become due by checks on the bank.

I have the honor to be with great respect and esteem, dear sir, your most obedient and humble servant, JOHN JAY.

JAY TO REV. DR. MORSE.

ALBANY, 30th January, 1799.

DEAR SIR:

You will herewith receive copies of the acts of our two last sessions. A variety of official and other affairs, which, although in numerous instances of little importance, yet required to be dispatched with punctuality, induced me, from time to time, to postpone replying to your obliging letter of the 19th November, and to thank you for the interesting pamphlets you were so kind as to send with it.

We see many things, my dear sir, which might be altered for the better, and that, I believe, has been the case at all times. But at this period, there certainly are an uncommon number and series of events and circumstances which assume an aspect unusually portentous. The seeds of trouble are sowing and germinating in our country as well as in many others ; they are cultivated with a zeal so singularly blind as not, in many instances, to be easily accounted for. Infidelity has become a political engine, alarming both by the force and the extent of its operations. It is doubtless permitted to be used for wise ends, though we do not clearly discern them ; when those ends shall be accomplished, it will be laid aside.

Much ill-use has been and will yet be made of secret societies. I think with you that they should not be encouraged, and that the most virtuous and innocent of them would do well to concur in suspending them for the present.

What precisely is to be understood of the death and resurrection of the witnesses, will probably be explained only by the *event.* I have an idea, that either the Old and New Testaments, or the moral and revealed law, are the two witnesses : witnesses to the existence, attributes, promises, and denunciations of the Supreme Being. Atheism is now killing these witnesses. That all true and pious apostles or believers are everywhere or generally to be slain, seems hardly credible. Whatever or whoever the witnesses may be, it is certain that the slaughter is not yet perfected. I much doubt whether, in any view of the subject, the clergy of the Church of Rome are of the number.

The Pope has lost his triple crown, and his spiritual dominion is rapidly declining. The Turk is now a party to the war ; whether any or what consequences will result from it to Mahomet, is yet to be seen. Wide is the field open for *conjectures.*

That our country is to drink very deep of the cup of tribulation, I am not apprehensive ; but that we shall entirely escape, does not appear to me very probable. I suspect that the Jacobins are still more numerous, more desperate, and more active in this country than is generally supposed. It is true, they are less indecorous and less clamorous than they have been. How few of their *leaders* have abandoned their errors, their associations, their opposition to their own government, and their devotion to a foreign one ! Why, and by whom, were the Kentucky and Virginia resolutions contrived, and for what purposes?

I often think of Pandora's box ; although it contained every kind of evil, yet is it said that *hope* was placed at the bottom. This is a singular fable, and it admits of many, and some of them very extensive, applications.

With very sincere esteem and regard, I am, dear sir, your most obedient servant,

JOHN JAY.

ALEXANDER HAMILTON TO JAY.

NEW YORK, February 12, 1799.

DEAR SIR:

The survey of this port to the Narrows inclusively has been executed and the expense defrayed out of the funds of the Corporation.   But it is interesting to the question of the defence of our port to have a survey of the bay below the Narrows to Sandy Hook.   There are sand banks critically situated which merit consideration as proper sites for fortification.   Such a survey was made under the direction of the British commanders and a Mr. *Hill* possesses a draft of that part of the bay.   He will not take less for it than 800 dollars ; am told the survey of the upper part cost 600 dollars.   In proportion, that of the part below will be moderate at 800. I enquired of General Clarkson as to the provision of funds for this object.   He answered that he had no more than 500 dollars at command.   If you agree in opinion with me that it will be well to obtain the draft in question for the price demanded, you will be so obliging as to give orders for the payment.

With great respect and esteem, dear Sir,

Your obedient

A. HAMILTON.

RUFUS KING TO JAY.

LONDON, March 18th, 1799.

DEAR SIR:

The opposition of Virginia, and of her offspring, Kentucky, appears bolder and more considerable than I had apprehended. The reform that seems to have taken place in the Carolinas is, however, a consoling and important circumstance. I have been inclined to believe that the Congressional election was the principal object of these inflammatory proceedings, which discredit and injure us so much abroad, and when passed, that these States would display less turbulence. According to present appearances, the war must recommence between France and Austria, if it has not already begun ; but that an honest and solid confederacy against France is likely to take place between the great powers, is more than I dare even to expect. Russia is uncommonly zealous. Passawan Ouglou has accepted pardon and promotion ; and it is just now said, how accurately is another point, that Prussia and Austria are to lay aside their mutual jealousy and to consult and act together for their common safety.

The commercial condition of England is extremely prosperous, and notwithstanding the hazardous and really dreadful situation of Ireland, this country is united in an uncommon degree, and appears resolved to persevere in the war. The minister, at the opening of his budget, estimates the total income of all the people of Great Britain at a hundred million per annum ; and it is confidently expected, that the taxes of this year will considerably exceed one-third of this sum. The Directory lately hold a language respecting America more moderate, but not less artful and dangerous. Whether any change in their privateering laws will be made, I think uncertain ; if my conjectures respecting the views of the Directory are correct, these laws will be now modified, or at least for a time suspended. After the experience we have had, it will be humiliating if we are deceived by the artifices that will be practised among our people.

I am always and sincerely, dear sir,

Your obedient and faithful servant,

RUFUS KING.

JAY TO BENJAMIN GOODHUE.

ALBANY, 29th March, 1799.

DEAR SIR :

The letters which you were so obliging as to write to me from Philadelphia have been received, and disposed of in the manner you requested. The information communicated in those letters has given me much concern. The expediency of the President's declaration, that he would not send another minister to France, until he should receive assurances, etc., was not, in my judgment, unquestionable. There are political considerations against it, and there are others in its favour. Such a declaration, however, was made, and the propriety of it seems to have been acquiesced in. It is to be wished that Mr. Murray had been more reserved in his conversations with the French secretary, on the subject of our national differences. These matters were foreign to his department, and I presume they were not within his instructions. Those conversations have facilitated overtures, which are calculated, and I believe designed, to perplex and divide our councils, and to mislead public opinion.

The manner in which Mr. Murray transmitted these overtures to the President is such a deviation from the official and customary course as (unless adopted for extraordinary and substantial reasons) is certainly exceptionable. Nor does any reason occur to me why the President thought it proper to omit communicating the overtures to the Secretary of State. Such is my confidence in the patriotism of the President, and also of the secretary, that every indication of want of confidence between them appears to me singular, and to be regretted.

Whether these overtures (considered in connection with the before-mentioned declaration of the President and other existing circumstances) should have been accepted, or encouraged, or rejected, or neglected, are questions not free from doubts. I am inclined to think that *immediate* attention to them was neither necessary nor advisable, and that they had not as yet acquired such a degree of maturity as to call for any formal, national act. But viewing this subject in all its various relations, I suspect it is one of those on which statesmen might naturally be led to opposite opinions, by the difficulty of estimating the precise weight and balance of the many and diverse considerations comprehended in it.

Much might be said, but not to much purpose; for whatever remarks may be applicable to the origin, progress, and present state of this perplexing affair, *it is as it is.* Nothing therefore remains but to make the best of the situation into which we are carried, and to avail ourselves of all the advantages to be derived from the united talents and efforts of the best friends to our country and government. The apprehensions entertained from the projected negotiation may not be extensively realized, and events may yet arise to press the Directory into proper measures relative to this country—measures not to be expected from their sincerity or sense of decorum or justice.

I am for aiding and adhering to the President, and for promoting the best understanding between him and the heads of the departments. Notwithstanding what has happened I hope his real friends will not keep at a distance from him, nor withhold from him that information which none but his friends will give him. Union, sedate firmness, and vigorous preparations for war generally afford the best means of counteracting the tendencies of insidious professions, and of too great public confidence in them.

With great esteem and regard,
I am, dear sir,
Your most obedient servant,
JOHN JAY.

JAY TO WILLIAM WILBERFORCE.

ALBANY, September 3, 1799.

DEAR SIR :

It was not until the last week that I had the pleasure of receiving from Mr. Naylor your obliging and very friendly letter of the 24th February, 1799. Accept my thanks for it.

Permit me to congratulate you on the promising aspect of affairs in Europe. England stands high, and while just, no one ought to repine at her prosperity. In my opinion she does not pass for more than she is worth. Your tax on income does honor to the minister who devised it, to the parliament who adopted it, and to the people who bear it. If hereafter accommodated to a state of peace, it would be a powerful auxiliary to your sinking fund.

Our conversation here turns so much on Great Britain and (as some phrase it) her *doings*, that I find myself insensibly led to this interesting topic. Not only Great Britain, but every other civilized country will have reason to rejoice when the present atrocious war, and the pestiferous principles which generated and have protracted it, shall cease to distress and corrupt mankind. May that happy period not be distant. With great esteem and regard, and the best wishes for your health and happiness,

I am, dear sir,

Your most obedient and faithful servant,

JOHN JAY.

ROBERT TROUP TO JAY.

NEW YORK, 23d Dec., 1799.

DEAR SIR:

On Tuesday last I wrote you a few lines informing you of the probability of General Washington's death. The truth of this melancholy event is confirmed beyond all possibility of doubt. We are taking measures here to pay suitable honors to the memory of this greatest and best of men. Our whole city appears to be penetrated with the profoundest grief. Our churches are in mourning; our bells are muffled and toll every day at 12 o'clock. Our citizens wear mourning. Mr. Gouverneur Morris, at the request of the Corporation, is to pronounce an oration. Committees are forming to concert a general plan for the expression of our grief, and I have no doubt we shall transmit to our posterity the most honorable proof of the consideration in which we hold the illustrious founder of our liberties. I hope our friends at Albany will not be inferior to us in zeal and patriotism upon this truly mournful occasion.

In great haste, I am, dear sir,

Very truly yours,

ROBERT TROUP.

JAY TO ROBERT TROUP.

ALBANY, December 28, 1799.

DEAR SIR :

I have been favoured with yours of the 23d inst., and with the one mentioned in it. The subject of them both is indeed an affecting and unexpected one. I perfectly concur in the sentiment that we should transmit to our posterity the most honourable proofs of the veneration in which we hold the memory of that singularly virtuous and great man whose death we lament. The idea of the Corporation respecting an oration meets with my approbation ; and from the talents and taste of the gentleman who is to compose and pronounce it, I expect it will be such an one as it ought to be. I hope it will not be *hurried;* it had better be a little delayed than not be finished.

I am, dear sir,

With great esteem and regard, yours,

JOHN JAY.

JAY TO REV. SAMUEL MILLER.

ALBANY, 28th February, 1800.

SIR :

Accept my thanks for the sermon on the death of General Washington, which you were so obliging as to send me. In my opinion it abounds in excellent sentiments, well arranged and expressed. Writing thus freely, I think it candid to observe that in some instances ideas are conveyed which do not appear to me to be correct ; such, for instance, as " our glorious *emancipation* from Britain." The Congress of 1774 and 1775, etc., regarded the people of this country as being free ; and such was their opinion of the liberty we enjoyed so late as the year 1763, that they declared the colonies would be satisfied on being replaced in the political situation in which they then were. It was not until after the year 1763 that Britain attempted to subject us to arbitrary domination. We resisted the stamp with energy and success, and when afterwards she claimed to bind us in all cases whatever, the same spirit of resistance animated our councils and our conduct ; when she recurred to arms to put a yoke upon us, we recurred to arms to keep it off. A struggle ensued which produced the Revolution, and ended in an entire dissolution of all the political ties which had before subsisted between the two countries. Thus we became a distinct nation, and I think truth will justify our indulging the pride of saying that we and our ancestors have kept our necks free from yokes, and that the term *emancipation* is not applicable to us.

Speaking of the measures of General Washington's civil administration, you observe, and it is the fact, "that there is less unanimity among her countrymen with respect to these, than with respect to his military services." But do facts warrant our ascribing this diminution of unanimity entirely to doubts respecting the wisdom of those measures? The Revolution found and left only two primary parties, viz., the Whigs who succeeded, and the Tories who were suppressed. The former were unanimous in approving the leading measures, both civil and military, which gave them victory. When the adoption of the new Constitution afterwards came into question, the Whigs divided into two parties, one for and the other against it. The party for the Constitution prevailed; and they have with as great unanimity approved of General Washington's civil, as of his military measures and services. The party opposed to the Constitution disapproved of the government established by it, and there are very few of the important measures of that government which have escaped their censure.

I take the liberty of making these remarks from the respect I have for your talents, and an opinion that, with due circumspection, they will promote the great interests of truth, virtue, and national liberty. Receive them, therefore, as marks of the esteem with which I am, sir,

Your most obedient servant,

John Jay.

REV. SAMUEL MILLER TO JAY.

New York, March 17, 1800.

Dear Sir:

. . . .

With regard to your observation, on the manner in which General Washington's political character and services are taken notice of in the sermon, though I receive it, and consider the motive by which it was dictated, with profound respect, yet you will pardon me if I hesitate to adopt your opinion in the same unqualified manner, in this, as in the preceding instance.

On the occasion on which the sermon was delivered I was unwilling to touch upon any thing connected with party animosity. Had I, therefore, perfectly agreed with you in sentiments, with regard to the parties which have for several years divided the citizens of the United States, it would not have been thought proper by me, to introduce such sentiments, or indeed any other, involving the political polemics of the day, into a pulpit exercise. But, sir, I had a more powerful reason for speaking as I did. To avoid giving offence to an audience will always, I hope, be a secondary object with me to the duty of a candid expression of my sentiments, when such expression is demanded. I am one of those who do not entirely approve the measures of the late venerable President, and although I am persuaded that multitudes have opposed them from a fixed principle of hostility to the constitution and in a very unreasonable and criminal manner, yet, after as impartial an examination of my own mind as I am able to institute, I cannot believe that my disapprobation arises from any other source than "doubts of the wisdom of those measures." My doubts, indeed, may be wholly groundless; and give me leave to say, that few things have more frequently tempted me to suspect that this might be the case, than a recollection of the splendid talents and (in my view) the unquestionable uprightness, which have been engaged in carrying on the measures referred to. Still, however, these doubts exist, though, I hope, they are entertained, and generally expressed, without obstinacy and without malevolence.

With respect to the last idea suggested in your letter, that the party who originally approved the Constitution have unanimously continued to approve the Government established by it, considered as a general remark, it is probably just. But many exceptions are certainly to be found. Being only a lad of seventeen years of age when the Constitution was adopted, it would be improper to speak of my own sentiments at that time. I was then residing in Delaware, my native State. In that State, you recollect, the Constitution was adopted promptly and unanimously. Among the number of its warmest admirers and most zealous supporters were my family and particular friends ; and in the same class I have, ever since, considered myself. It is, moreover, beyond all question true, that many of the first characters, for talents, virtue, and property, in that State, who then took side in favour of the constitution with great decision, and who have uniformly professed themselves to be its friends to the present day, are now to be ranked with what is called the *opposition.* I have taken my examples from Delaware, as being better able to compare the different parts of the conduct of her principal citizens, for the last twelve years, than to do the same with regard to my adopted State. I am well aware that those who came under the description which has been mentioned, are charged with being *inconsistent* men, and with having *changed their ground.* That some have given reason for bringing this charge against them, and for suspecting their motives, I do not deny. But that disapproving parts of the conduct of Administration always implies enmity to the constitution, I am not convinced, and, therefore, am not ready, at present, to concede.—

You will, perhaps, be somewhat surprized at my taking the liberty to trouble you with these expositions and details of my sentiments, in answer to your remarks. I am sensible it is of little importance what my political opinions are. They have been generally held in a moderate and inoffensive manner, and both my profession and inclination forbid me to take an active part in the civil concerns of my country. It is, indeed, my wish to abstract myself more and more from party politics. But several reasons induced me to acknowledge the receipt of your remarks, and in doing this my first resolution was to be unreserved. You had given an example of candour too flattering and instructive not to be imitated. I have only to add, that, if I do not deceive myself, my highest ambition is to promote "the great interests of Religion, Virtue, and rational Liberty;"—that if any of my principles have a different tendency, I shall be among the first to abhor them on making the discovery; and that he who corrects any errors into which I may fall, will always be considered by me as my truest friend and benefactor.

I have the honor to be, with sentiments of very high respect,

Your Excellency's much obliged and humble Servant,

SAML. MILLER.

JAY TO REV. DR. MORSE.

ALBANY, 24th April, 1800.

DEAR SIR :

Several affairs, more interesting to others than to me, have for some months past so pressed upon me as, together with official busines, to leave me little leisure to attend even to my own concerns. Hence I have been constrained into delays respecting my correspondents, which could not have been less agreeable to their feelings than to my own.

Accept my thanks for the several communications with which you have favoured me. The fact which you have given to the public relative to the conduct of France in our Revolution, as well as your strictures on the designs and intrigues of the Illuminés, have, to a certain extent, been useful. They have made proper impressions on many sedate and candid men, but I suspect they have detached very few of the disciplined adherents of the party. As yet, there appears but little reason to believe that philosophism is losing ground in this country. There is indeed less said about it, but indications of immorality are neither less frequent nor more odious and disgraceful in common estimation than heretofore. A moral epidemic seems to prevail in the world. What may be its duration, or the limits of its ravages, time only can ascertain.

The approaching general election in this State will be unusually animated. No arts or pains will be spared to obtain an anti-federal representation, in order to obtain an anti-federal President, etc., and through him divers other objects.

The late revolution in France does not appear to have dissipated the clouds which veiled from our view the fate of that and other countries. As yet, I see little reason to expect the restoration of the Bourbon family; nor is it certain that great good would result from it. Of the issue of the present interesting campaign, no satisfactory conjectures can yet be formed; and nothing at present appears which presents a fair prospect of a speedy termination of the miseries of Europe. Our envoys in France will probably succeed; but whether that success would ultimately promote our tranquillity and happiness, is a point on which many judicious men differ in opinion.

We have lost much in General Washington, whose death you and others have made the subject of eloquent discourses. From the state of our parties and affairs, some are persuaded that he has been taken from *evil to come.* It may be so; but I fear that such apprehensions are sometimes indulged too far, and that they often disqualify men from meeting either good or evil in a becoming manner.

With great esteem and regard, I am, dear sir, your most obedient servant,

JOHN JAY.

THEOPHILUS PARSONS TO JAY.

NEWBURYPORT, May 5th, 1800.

SIR:

The Rev. Mr. Andrews of this town, intending to visit Albany, during a journey he is now contemplating, I have taken the liberty to trouble you with a line by him containing a short statement of the political sentiments of Massachusetts at the present moment, as our public papers will not give a correct view of them. Opinions, formed from the general appearance of our papers, in favour of the great prevalence of artificial sentiments, would be as unjust as, in fact, they are ill founded. The votes for Governor are generally returned, and it is now certain that Mr. Gerry is not elected; and it is extremely probable that Mr. Strong is. As our constitution requires a majority of votes, it is perhaps possible that there may be a few scattered votes, in addition to the number already known, which may defeat an election by the people. But my principal motive in troubling your Excellency, was to explain the motives, which induced so large a number of the electors to support Mr. Gerry, consistently with the great predomination of Federal principles in Massachusetts.

Mr. Gerry was believed to be a Federalist by one half of the electors who supported him. This opinion resulted from several causes. He was considered as an ardent revolutionary Whig. He had publickly professed the strongest attachment to Mr. Adams' administration. The President had appointed him an Envoy to France; and it was reported and by some believed, that he approved of his conduct in that mission, and still continued strongly attached to him. The mercantile towns were also told that Mr. Gerry was educated a merchant, and consequently would promote the commerce of the country; that Mr. Strong, living in a remote part of the State, all executive business would be impeded by his distance from the centre of the Government. In addition to these causes another was also invented, that the legislature had recommended him, and had thus invaded the rights of the electors; and that to spurn at the commendation would effectually prevent any future invasion. Arguments of a very different nature were industriously and privately circulated among the anti-Federalists. They were informed, that Mr. Gerry was an anti-Federalist, opposed originally to the Federal constitution, and never after reconciled to it, that he went to France merely to preserve peace with our republican allies, that he would have succeeded had he gone alone, that he was opposed to war, to a standing army, to a funding system, was no stock-holder, was unconnected with commerce, and attached to the agricultural interest. An attention to the votes for senators, will clearly evince the fact that a great part of the electors for Mr. Gerry were Federalists. In every senatorial district, the anti-Federalists ran a rival ticket with great zeal and confidence. But in every district, except three, the Federal ticket had a majority, and, in most of them, great majorities. In Norfolk the anti-Federal ticket prevailed thro' the influence of our general, the famous Heath; in the other two, from a division of sentiments, there was no choice. In Middelsex, where Mr. Gerry had the strongest support, and in which he resides, the Federal senators were chosen, when at the last election, from the prevalence of Jacobinism, the anti-Federal ticket had the greater number of votes.

I fear I shall be tho't impertinent in descending to these minute observations; but our passions have been exceedingly engaged in the progress of the election and we are very apprehensive that an opinion, prevailing in the neighbouring states, that anti-Federalism was taking strong ground in Massachusetts, would give activity and resolution to a restless, desperate faction, to be found in every part of the Union. It seems, to have set up its gods in Virginia; whose reason and law, wisdom and patriotism, honor and integrity, are immolated upon their Altars.

The next election of President will be an important event. If I had not already imposed on your Excellency's patience beyond all reasonable limit, I would state the views and intentions of the Federalists in the State, upon that subject. I will now only say, that a number of them have felt exceedingly hurt at the persevering plan of the new French mission, and have also been chagrined at the political importance the President's nomination gave to Mr. Gerry, a man, who in their opinion, was undeserving of any public notice. The impressions appear now to be much worn out; and I believe that at this time the universal sentiment of the Federalists is, to support Mr. Adams, with all the activity and perseverance such a measure deserves. The Jacobins appear to be completely organized throughout the United States. The principals have their agents dispersed in every direction; and the whole body act with a union to be expected only from men, in whom no moral principles exist to create a difference of conduct resulting from a difference of sentiment. Their exertions are bent to introduce into every department of the State governments unprincipled tools of a daring faction, to render more certain the election to the Presidency, of the great arch priest of Jacobinism and infidelity. God grant that they may be caught in their own craft, and that shame and confusion may overwhelm these base plotters against the peace, safety and felicity of the United States.

As Mr. Andrews, who obliges me by taking charge of this letter, is very solicitous to pay his personal respects to your Excellency, I presume he will deliver it himself. I hope your Excellency's indulgence for the trouble I have given you, and that you will please to attribute it to my anxiety for the prosperity of our common country, an anxiety which sometimes oppresses me, when I dare to look at what may be the fate of the United States. But your Excellency will not do me justice, unless by the persuasion that I am, with the utmost respect and sincerity,

Your Excellency's most obedient, and humble servant,

THEOP. PARSONS.

ALEXANDER HAMILTON TO JAY.

DEAR SIR: NEW YORK, May 7, 1800.

You have been informed of the loss of our election in this City. It is also known that we have been unfortunate throughout Long Island and in Westchester. According to the returns hitherto, it is too probable that we lose our Senator for this District.

The moral certainty, therefore is that there will be an Anti-Federal Majority in the ensuing legislature, and the very high probability is that this will bring *Jefferson* into the Chief Magistracy, unless it be prevented by the measure which I shall now submit to your consideration, namely the immediate calling together of the existing legislature.

I am aware that there are weighty objections to the measure; but the reasons for it .appear to me to outweigh the objections; and in times like this in which we live, it will not do to be overscrupulous. It is easy to sacrifice the substantial interests of society by a strict adherence to ordinary rules.

In observing this, I shall not be supposed to mean that anything ought to be done which integrity will forbid, but merely that the scruples of delicacy and propriety, as relative to a common course of things, ought to yield to the extraordinary nature of the crisis. They ought not to hinder the taking of a *legal* and *constitutional* step, to prevent an *atheist* in Religion and a *fanatic* in politics from getting possession of the helm of the State. You, Sir, know in a great degree the Anti-Federal party, but I fear that you do not know them as well as I do. 'T is a composition indeed of very incongruous materials but all tending to mischief—some of them to the overthrow of the Government by depriving it of its due energies, others of them to a Revolution after the manner of Buonaparte. I speak from indubitable facts, not from any conjectures and inferences. In proportion as the true character of the party is understood is the force of the considerations which urge to every effort to disappoint it; and it seems to me that there is a very solemn obligation to employ the means in our power. The calling of the Legislature will have for object the choosing of Electors by the people in districts. This (as Pennsylvania will do nothing) will insure a majority of votes in the United States for a Federal candidate. This measure will not fail to be approved by all the Federal Party ; while it will no doubt be condemned by the opposite. As to its intrinsic nature it is justified by unequivocal reasons of public safety. The reasonable part of the world will, I believe, approve it. They will see it as a proceeding out of the common course but warranted by the particular nature of the crisis and the great cause of social order. If done the motive ought to be frankly avowed. In your communication to the Legislature they ought to be told that temporary circumstances had rendered it probable that without their interposition the executive authority of the General Government would be transferred to hands hostile to the system heretofore pursued with so much success and dangerous to the peace, happiness and order of the country; that under this impression from facts convincing to your own mind you had thought it your duty to give the existing legislature an opportunity of deliberating whether it would not be proper to interpose and endeavour to prevent so great an evil by referring the choice of electors to the people distributed into districts.

In weighing this suggestion you will doubtless bear in mind that popular governments must certainly be overturned, and while they endure prove engines of mischief, if one party will call to its aid all the resources which vice can give, and if the other, however pressing the emergency, confines itself within all the ordinary forms of delicacy and decorum. The legislature can be brought together in three weeks, so that there will be full time for the object; but none ought to be lost.

Think well, my Dear Sir, of this proposition. Appreciate the extreme danger of the crisis, and I am unusually mistaken in my view of the matter if you do not see it right and proper to adopt the measure.

Respectfully and affectionately yours,

A. HAMILTON.[1]

---

[1] Jay endorsed this letter : " Proposing a measure for party purposes, which I think it would not become me to adopt."

GENERAL SCHUYLER TO JAY.

DEAR SIR :   NEW YORK, May 7th, 1800.

Our Federal friends in Congress, extremly allarmed at the Success of the Anti-Fedarilsts in the recent elections in this state, and dreading the results which they are persuaded will follow the Election of Mr. Jefferson to the Presidency of the United States, has induced several of them to intrust me to write to your Excellency and to sollicit you to convene the Legislature in the hopes that an Act may be passed directing the appointment of Electors by district elections, in which case they are perfectly confident that Mr. Jefferson's Election will be defeated and equally so that Mr. Adams and Mr. Pinkney will be elected. I am well aware, my dear Sir, that convening the Legislature for this express purpose involves embarrassment, but your enemies who are also the enemies of order and good government will be loud in their censures on the Measure, whilst, on the contrary, your friends will justify it as the only way to save a nation from more disasters, which it may and probably will experience from the mis-rule of a Man who has given such strong evidence that he was opposed to the salutary Measures of those who have been heretofore at the helm, and who is in fact pervaded with the mad French philosophy. Indeed, my Dear Sir, it is impossible to appreciate all the painful results which may ensue from Mr. Jefferson's conduct, should he be president ; the Country may be by this means involved in a war with Britain. It seems to me that these considerations will justify the Measure of calling the Legislature.

I am, my Dear Sir, with perfect Esteem.

         Your Excellency's Obedient Servant,

                 PH. SCHUYLER,

P. S.—Mr. Marshall is one of those who has recommended the measure above mentioned.

JAY TO THEOPHILUS PARSONS.

SIR :   ALBANY, 1 July, 1800.

On my return from New York on Friday last, your obliging letter of the 5th of May, which arrived here during my absence, was delivered to me. I am much gratified by the information it contains, and thank you for it.

Serious apprehensions were entertained that anti-Federalism had gained considerable ground in Massachusetts ; but I am happy to find from the facts you state, that appearances do not warrant the conclusions which have been drawn from them. The present aspect of our affairs is far from being agreeable. Although peculiarly blessed, and having abundant reason for content and gratitude, our nation is permitting their happiness to be put in jeopardy by the worst passions, inflamed and directed by the most reprehensible means. Whether the good sense of the people will avert the dangers which threaten them is yet to be seen.

If the sound and leading friends of their country could concur in opinion as to men and measures, their efforts would probably be successful ; but unfortunately there is too little unanimity in many points, and the want of it exposes us to the hazard of many evils.

It really appears to me that the mission of our Envoys to France has been treated with too much asperity. The President declared to the Congress, that he would never send another Legation to Paris until he received assurances that it would be properly respected. As that declaration seemed to imply that when he should receive such assurances he would again send Envoys, it was not unnatural that he should conceive himself in honour bound to do so. His attachment to the dictates of honour and good faith, even supposing it to have been too scrupulous, is amiable and praiseworthy. Whether that declaration was advisable, and whether the nomination of the Envoys was made exactly in season, are questions which, like others of the same kind, may receive different answers from different men ; but having nominated the Envoys and received the requisite assurances, I for my part consider the sending them as a matter of course, and I do not concur in opinion with those gentlemen who think they should nevertheless have been detained.

I regret that my absence deprived me of the pleasure of seeing the Rev. Mr. Andrews, and the more so as he would have answered my inquiries respecting many of my friends at Boston, and informed me of your health.

With the best wishes that you may now and long enjoy that valuable blessing,

I am, sir, your most obedient servant,

JOHN JAY.

JAY TO HENRY VAN SCHAACK.

DEAR SIR : ALBANY, 23d September, 1800.

Mr. Beers, in compliance with your request, has delivered to me an extract from the Albany *Register*, of the 15th of last month, which contains the following erroneous statement of the expenses incurred by the United States for negotiating the treaty with Great Britain, viz. :

Mr. Jay, for his outfit to make the treaty -	-	-	$18,000 00
For his passage to Europe	-	-	3,708 52
To pay incidental expenses	-	-	10,000 00
To do. in negotiating the treaty -	-	-	5,000 00
To get paper of captures -	-	-	16,012 83

$52,721 35

This statement is not a new one; it appeared in Greenleaf's paper in March, 1797. It is calculated, and doubtless was designed, to impress an opinion that the administration of President Washington was too prodigal of the public money in the negotiation with Great Britain, and that I derived extravagant emoluments from it.

Calumny, my dear sir, has been an engine of party in all countries, and particularly in elective governments. It is an evil which, originating in the corruption of human nature, is without remedy, and consequently is to be borne patiently. The esteem of the wise and good is valuable, and to acquire and preserve it is all that ambition ought to aim at.

As to the statement in question, you are desirous to know exactly how far it deviates from the truth; and to gratify this desire I will give you a concise and accurate state of the facts.

Being at Philadelphia on official business, in May, 1794, President Washington desired me to go as Envoy to Great Britain. I earnestly endeavoured to fix his attention elsewhere ; but he persevered, and I found it impossible to reconcile it with my duty to persist in declining the appointment. Circumstanced as I was, and aware of the nature of the business, of the temper of the times, and of the union of certain interests against any amicable settlement with Great Britain, personal considerations opposed my undertaking the task. When I finally yielded to the President's request, I told him that I declined any compensation for my services—that my necessary and actual expenses only should be paid ; but that my stated salary as chief justice must be continued. A vessel in ballast was chartered to carry me to England, for you will recollect that an embargo was then in operation ; but in contracting for paying for this vessel, I had no agency.

The Secretary of State gave me a bill for eighteen thousand dollars, towards the expenses of the mission, and for which I was to account. All my expenses of every kind as Envoy to Great Britain, including the salary of my secretary, the expense of my passage home, and £63 sterling paid in counsel fees respecting capture cases, amounted to the sum of twelve thousand dollars and thirty-six cents; which being deducted from the before mentioned eighteen thousand dollars, left in my hands a considerable balance due to the United States.

This balance I accounted for, and settled with the Treasury in the following manner, viz. :

By cash advanced to an American gentleman in the service of the United States, and whose account with the public was charged with it by the Treasury   - $233 33

By amount of my order on the banker in favour of Mr. Pinckney, who was then the American Minister at London, towards a fund for expenses respecting capture cases, to be accounted for by him with the Treasury   -   -   -   -   -   -   5,270 22

By cash paid by me to the Treasurer   -   -   496 09

5,999 64

12,000 00

$18,000 00

These facts are verified by the Treasury report of the account between the United States and me, marked No. 7373; by the auditor's report marked No. 8330, on which is endorsed the Comptroller's certificate; and by the Register's certificate of the final settlement of the account.

With sentiments of esteem and regard

I am, dear sir,

Your most obedient servant,

JOHN JAY.

JAY TO RICHARD HATFIELD.[1]

ALBANY, 8th November, 1800.

SIR :

Being engaged with company this evening when the committee appointed by the respectable meeting of citizens from various parts of the State, of which

---

[1] This letter is in reply to the expressed wishes of Mr. Jay's Federalist friends that he would accept a renomination for the State governorship.

you were chairman, presented to me their address, I could only return them a verbal answer. But it appears to me proper to answer it in writing, as well to evince my respect, as that my sentiments on the subject may be the better ascertained.

In the sincerity of the assurances with which they honor me, I have perfect confidence ; they have heretofore been verified by uniform manifestations of esteem and attachment, which I shall always remember with grateful sensibility. The period is now nearly arrived at which I have for many years intended to retire from the cares of public life, and for which I have been for more than two years preparing. Not perceiving, after mature consideration that any duties require me to postpone it, I shall retire accordingly ; but I shall retain and cherish the warmest affection for my country, as well as the esteem which I entertain for many, and the good-will which I bear to all my fellow-citizens.

On this occasion various reflections crowd into my mind, but I doubt the utility under existing circumstances of expressing them. Time and experience will correct many errors which ought not to have been introduced into public opinions. What the price of that experience may be, cannot be foreseen. They who are convinced that our constitutions ought to be maintained inviolate, and that the rights of persons and of property cannot be preserved without government constituted with power and administered with determination to secure them, will steadfastly oppose whatever may have a contrary tendency. It is not to be expected that parties will never be intemperate, but overbearing intemperance or violence in individual leaders ought neither to appal nor inflame good citizens. On the contrary, such violations of propriety should be met with temper and moderation, as well as with increased union and firmness.

I declare to you explicitly that in my opinion we ought to resist innovations, to adhere to our constitutions and governments, to give them a fair trial, and to amend them from time to time according to the dictates of experiences, and not according to the views of demagogues or the visions of theorists. On this head much might be said ; but in seasons like the present, truth and admonitions seldom make strong or general impressions.

I have the honour to be with great respect, sir,
Your most obedient servant,
JOHN JAY.

JAY TO SIR JOHN SINCLAIR, LONDON.

ALBANY, 16th December, 1800.
SIR :

I had yesterday the pleasure of receiving from the Secretary of State the letter which you did me the honour to write on the 22d of May last.

They who feel an interest in the honour of this country cannot fail of being gratified by every mark of respect to the memory of our late President. The tribute of commendation paid to his merits by so many respectable persons in Great Britain is no less honourable to them than to him ; and I very sin-

cerely concur with you in wishing that the best
understanding may always subsist beween our two
nations.

The *fac-simile* copies of the letters appear to me to
be well executed, but I am not certain that the taste
of this country is such as to produce a considerable
demand for them. I shall immediately put the cards
and subscription papers into the hands of such persons here, and at New York, as I think most likely
to promote the object of them. For my own part, I
am preparing and expect to retire in the spring to my
estate at Bedford, in the County of Westchester,
about fifty miles from the city of New York. I shall
request the persons to whom the subscription papers
will be delivered, to transmit them to Mr. Hugh
Gaine, a bookseller of reputation at New York ;
and shall request him to communicate the result to
Messrs. Nicoll, etc., in London.

Having, since my return to England, been constantly engaged in official affairs, I have had little
leisure for other pursuits ; so much so that I have not,
from that time to this, visited my estate more than
twice in any one year.

A member of your board (of whose address I took
a memorandum, which I have since often looked for
without success) was so obliging as to send me a cask
of *English* gypsum. I promised to try it, and inform
him whether it succeeded. It was ground, and sent
to my farm, where a part of it was used in like manner
with French and Newfoundland gypsum, but not
with the like success ; it produced no visible effect.

On being acquainted with this, I directed the remain- der to be saved, in order that on my removal there it might be tried under my own direction ; if I live, this shall be done.

I last evening read with attention your proposal for an experimental farm. The objects in view are certainly very interesting, and to a considerable degree attainable under the direction of such a manager as I suspect it would be more easy to describe than to find. It would probably be advisable to make him a handsome allowance per cent. on the profits, besides a liberal stated salary.

This country will derive advantages from all your improvements relative to the breed and management of live stock. But I apprehend that, from the difference between your climate and ours, it will in some respects be less easy for us to apply and put into practice your improvements respecting the growth and cultivation of plants.

In the year 1784 I had an interesting conversation with one of your intelligent farmers in Essex. He was surprised that we in this country seldom sowed more than one bushel of wheat on an acre. On being told that in our good land one seed would produce many shoots or straws, he observed that we had better sow an additional bushel, for that these shoots were generally less productive than single straws from single grains. On my return that year to this country, I mentioned the remark to some of our best farmers. One of them in particular gave it a fair trial for several years. He increased his seed in various experiments, from one bushel to above two bushels per acre ; but he finally found and was convinced that not more than one bushel and a half per acre could be sowed on his farm with advantage ; any quantity above that filled the field with too much straw. Hence I conclude that (all other things being equal) the same number of grains of seed wheat will throw out more shoots in this climate than in yours. But to return to the experimental farm : it appears to me that such an establishment comes naturally within the department of the agricultural society ; and if instituted by *them,* would enjoy greater advantages than such an establishment if entirely independent and distinct from them would possess.

The more food Great Britain produces the better ; and it is plain that by cultivating all your waste lands, and by still greater improvements in husbandry, the quantity annually produced may and will be exceedingly augmented ; yet, sir, it is not quite clear to me that Great Britain can always continue to produce more food than she will consume. You now manufacture for about five millions of people in this country, and for many millions in other countries. Consider the rapidity of population in this country, and in some parts of your extensive empire. Your manufacturers must increase and they must have food. On this topic much might be said which will readily occur to you.

With great respect and esteem, I am, sir,
Your most obedient servant,
JOHN JAY.

PRESIDENT ADAMS TO JAY.

DEAR SIR: WASHINGTON, Dec. 19th, 1800.

Mr. Ellsworth afflicted with the gravel and the gout, and intending to pass the winter in the south of France, after a few weeks in England, has resigned his office of chief justice, and I have nominated you to your old station. This is as independent of the inconstancy of the people as it is of the will of a president. In the future administration of our country, the firmest security we can have against the effects of visionary schemes or fluctuating theories, will be in a solid judiciary ; and nothing will cheer the hopes of the best men so much as your acceptance of this appointment. You have now a great opportunity to render a most signal service to your country. I therefore pray you most earnestly to con-sider of it seriously, and accept it. You may very properly resign the short remainder of your gubernatorial period, and Mr. Rensselaer may discharge the duties. I had no permis-sion from you to take this step, but it appeared to me that Providence had thrown in my way an opportunity, not only of marking to the public the spot where, in my opinion, the greatest mass of worth remained collected in one individual, but of furnishing my country with the best security its inhabi-tants afforded against the increasing dissolution of morals.

With unabated friendship, and the highest esteem and respect,   I am, dear sir, yours,

JOHN ADAMS.

P. S. Your commission will soon follow this letter.

JAY TO PRESIDENT ADAMS.

DEAR SIR :   ALBANY, 2d January, 1801.

I have been honoured with your letter of the 19th ult. informing me that I had been nominated to fill the office of Chief Justice of the United States, and yesterday I received the commission. This nomination so strongly manifests your esteem, that it affords me particular satisfaction.

Such was the temper of the times, that the Act to establish the Judicial Courts of the United States was in some respects more accommodated to certain prejudices and sensibilities, than to the great and obvious principles of sound policy. Expectations were nevertheless entertained that it would be amended as the public mind became more composed and better informed ; but those expectations have not been realized, nor have we hitherto seen convincing indications of a disposition in Congress to realize them. On the contrary, the efforts repeatedly made to place the judicial department on a proper footing have proved fruitless.

I left the bench perfectly convinced that under a system so defective it would not obtain the energy, weight, and dignity which are essential to its affording due support to the national government, nor acquire the public confidence and respect which, as the last resort of the justice of the nation, it should possess. Hence I am induced to doubt both the propriety and the expediency of my returning to the bench under the present system ; especially as it would give some countenance to the neglect and indifference with which the opinions and remonstrances of the judges on this important subject have been treated.

Altho' I wish and am prepared to be and remain in retirement, yet I have carefully considered what is my duty, and ought to be my conduct, on this unexpected and interesting occasion. I find that, independent of other considerations, the state of my health removes every doubt, it being clearly and decidedly incompetent to the fatigues incident to the office. Accept my warmest acknowledgments for the honour you have done me, and permit me to assure you of the respect, esteem, and regard with which I am,

Dear sir, etc.,

JOHN JAY.

COMMITTEE OF FEDERAL FREEHOLDERS OF THE CITY OF NEW YORK TO GOVERNOR JAY.

NEW YORK, 13th January, 1801.

SIR:

Our feelings too well accord with those that dictated the resolutions of which we have the honor to transmit a copy, not to render the execution of the task committed to us particularly agreeable.

We have been long accustomed to contemplate, with sentiments of exalted satisfaction, the virtues, public and private, which adorn your character, and the distinguished talents and services which place you in the first rank of citizens eminently useful to their Country. To attempt to retrace the variety of arduous and honorable exertions which have marked your public career, would be an office to which we do not feel ourselves equal. Neither does it require our testimony to record, what will ever find an indelible memorial in the minds and hearts of the enlightened and just, that in the great events which accomplished the American Revolution, you were among the most conspicuous, and that your abilities, patriotism and energy, then and since, have been repeatedly displayed with lustre, as well in the councils of this State and of the United States, as in the different diplomatic trusts confided to your charge. The part you acted in forming the constitution of the State, and in promoting the adoption of the National Government, the important treaty which terminated the controversy for independence, and the Convention which lately preserved your Country from being involved in a pernicious war (defeating the predictions of evil, and confirming the anticipations of good), are a few of the many Acts that bear witness to the truths we have mentioned.

Having now declared your intention to resign the cares of public life, envy and ill will can scarcely deny that the most recent scene of it has exhibited all the valuable characteristics proper to the situation—prudence, moderation and rectitude. It will at least be no small consolation to yourself and to your friends, to reflect, that the *purity* of your administration imposes silence on the tongue of detraction.

To time, the best arbiter of human pretentions, it may safely be left to liquidate the true merit of your actions, and to erect a monument to your fame beyond the reach of jealous or malevolent cavil.

With the most respectful consideration we have the honor to be, Sir,

> Your Excellency's obedient Servants,
> COM. RAY,
> ROB. TROUP,
> ARCH. GRACIE,
> RICH. HARISON,
> WILLIAM W. WOOLSEY,
> JAMES M. HUGHES,
> JAMES WATSON.

JAY TO THE COMMITTEE OF FEDERAL FREEHOLDERS OF
THE CITY OF NEW YORK.

ALBANY, 27 January, 1801.

GENTLEMEN :

I have received the letter which you did me the
honour to write on the 15th, inclosing a copy of a
resolution of the Federal freeholders of the city of
New York, of the 13th instant.

Permit me, through you, to assure them of the high
sense I entertain of the honour they have done me by
the sentiments respecting my public services which
are expressed in that resolution ; and be pleased,
gentlemen, to accept my warmest acknowledgments
for the friendship and attachment which your letter
evinces. Considering the relations in which I have
stood to those of my fellow-citizens who are denomi-
nated Federalists, I take the liberty of submitting to
their consideration a few remarks.

It is an agreeable circumstance that the prosperity
of our country since the institution of the present
government justifies the support and confidence we
have given to those by whom it has hitherto been administered. But general prosperity does not invariably produce general content, nor will public opinion,
perplexed by the different lights and shades in which
men and measures are often placed and seen, always
remain steady and uniform. These observations are
confirmed by events of no inconsiderable importance,
which have recently occurred. They place us in a
new situation, and render it proper for us to consider
what our conduct under it should be. I take the lib-

erty, therefore, of suggesting, whether the patriotic principles on which we profess to act do not call upon us to give (as far as may depend upon us) fair and full effect to the known sense and intention of a majority of the people, in every constitutional exercise of their will, and to support every administration of the government of our country which may prove to be intelligent and upright, of whatever party the persons composing it may be.

With the best wishes for the happiness of your constituents, and with great personal respect and regard for yourselves,

I have the honor to be, Gentlemen,

Your obliged and obedient servant,

JOHN JAY.

JAY'S MESSAGE TO THE LEGISLATURE OF NEW YORK IN THE MATTER OF APPOINTMENTS TO OFFICE, FEBRUARY 26, 1801.[1]

GENTLEMEN :

It has generally and justly been considered as highly important to the security and duration of free states, that the different departments and officers of government should exercise those powers only which are constitutionally vested in them ; and that all controversies between them respecting the limits of their

---

[1] In regard to this controversy see Jay's *Jay*, vol. i., pp. 423–427. It remained unsettled during the remainder of Governor Jay's term, and for several months no appointments of town and county officers were made. Jay transmitted a second message to the Legislature, containing his correspondence in the case with the judges of the Supreme Court. This was first published in a supplement to the *Albany Centinel*, March 31, 1801.

respective jurisdictions and authorities be circumspectly and speedily settled. There are few constitutions or other instruments, however carefully framed, which are entirely free from ambiguity, and do not contain paragraphs liable to different constructions. Defects and obscurities have been observed in the constitution of this State, and on certain occasions they have produced inconveniences.

The 23d Article of it ordains : " That all officers, other than those who by this Constitution are directed to be otherwise appointed, shall be appointed in the manner following, to wit. The Assembly shall, once in every year, openly nominate and appoint one of the Senators from each District, which Senators shall form a Council for the appointment of said officers, of which the Governor for the time being, or the Lieutenant Governor, or the President of the Senate, when they shall respectively administer the Government, shall be President, and have a casting Voice, but no other Vote, and with the *advice and consent* of the said Council, shall *appoint* all the said officers."

Doubts have long existed whether by this article the right of nomination was exclusively vested in the Governor, or whether it was vested concurrently in him and the council. Questions arose on this article during the administration of my predecessor, and in the month of March, 1794, gave occasion to animated discussions between him and the then Council.

When I came to the government my official duty made it proper for me to form as correct a judgment on the subject as I possibly could. After having deliberately considered this article, I became fixed in the opinion that it vested the right of nomination exclusively in the Governor, and for this, among other reasons, that the right to *appoint* necessarily included the right to *select* and *nominate ;* and it gave me pleasure to find, on conferring with my predecessor, that this opinion was strengthened by his informing me that he had always claimed this right, and never yielded or conceded it to be in the Council.

Nevertheless, as respectable members of the former Council, acting under their oaths to support the constitution, had adopted a different construction of this article, and had actually assumed and exercised this right, it was evident that this was a question on which upright and judicious men might differ in opinion. Being therefore apprehensive that it might, and probably would, again produce disagreeable disputes, I thought it advisable to insert the following paragraph in the first speech which I had the honour to make to both houses of the Legislature, viz. :

" There is an article in the constitution, which by admitting of two different constructions has given rise to opposite opinions, and may give occasion to disagreeable contests and embarrassments. The article I allude to is the one which ordains that the person administering the government for the time being, shall be president of the council of appointment, and have a casting voice, but no other vote, and with the advice and consent of the said council, shall appoint all the officers which the constitution directs to be appointed. Whether this does, by just construction, assign to him the exclusive right of nomination, is a question which, though not of recent date, still remains to be definitely settled. Circumstanced as I am in relation to this question, I think it proper to state it, and to submit to your consideration the expediency of determining it by a declaratory act."

Unfortunately this important question was permitted to continue undecided ; and, consequently, I could adopt no other rule for my official conduct than that construction of the article which appeared to me to be best founded, and which had been adopted as the true construction by my predecessor. I have, therefore uniformly held and exercised the exclusive right of nomination ; nor have any of the Council endeavoured to assume it, until the 24th day of this month, when the following occurrences took place, viz. :

The present sheriffs of New York and Queens, who had been nominated on the 11th instant, were negatived. Benjamin Jackson, who on the 17th instant was nominated for sheriff of Orange, was negatived. Certain other nominations were agreed to. Three persons were then successively nominated for the office of Schoharie—to wit, Wardell Green, John Ingold, and Benjamin Miles, and they were negatived. Col. William Falconer was then nominated for sheriff of Orange, and being negatived, I nominated Col. John Nicholson for that office. On this nomination the Council (except Mr. Sanders) explicitly refused to vote; and one of the members of the Council proceeded to nominate John Blake, Jun., for sheriff of that county. Judging it prudent to consider maturely what ought to be my conduct under such circumstances, the Council was adjourned.

After having well considered the subject, it appears to me proper to state these facts to you. While I think and believe, as I most sincerely do, that the right to nominate is vested exclusively in the Governor by the constitution, it ought not, and I am persuaded it will not be expected that I should, by conceding this right or power to any member of the Council, violate my oath to administer the government to the best of my knowledge, in conformity with the powers delegated to me by the constitution.

From what had formerly happened, it was not a matter of surprise to me that the Council should claim concurrent right on nomination with me; but the refusal to vote on one of my nominations, and, while it remained undecided, to nominate another person for the same office, were measures which, going to the exclusion of even a concurrent right in the Governor, appeared to me not a little extraordinary.

Many appointments exceedingly interesting to the public ought soon to be made; but while those gentlemen persist in the course of proceeding which they have adopted, that business must necessarily remain subjected to impediments not in my power to obviate or remove. I therefore submit to your consideration, whether it has not become indispensable that the merits of these opposite and interfering claims to the right of nomination should be ascertained and decided without delay.

In whatever constitutional way, whether by a declaratory statute or by judgment of law, a decision may be made; and whether it should or should not correspond with the opinion I have expressed, I shall certainly acquiesce in and regulate my conduct by it.

JOHN JAY.

THE MAYOR AND ALDERMEN OF THE CITY OF ALBANY TO JAY, MAY 11, 1801.

To his Excellency, John Jay, Esquire, Governor of the State of New York.

SIR—

We, the Mayor, Aldermen and Commonalty of the City of Albany in Common Council convened, cannot forbear at the moment of your departure from this city to retire voluntarily from an elevated official situation into the shades of private life, to express our unfeigned regret for the loss of so estimable a citizen, and such an eminently valuable public servant, and to offer you our sincere thanks and respectful consideration for the various and important services you have performed for your Country.

In rendering this grateful tribute to your virtues, talents and patriotism the members of the Common Council indulge at once a lively sensibility as Freemen, and a peculiar pride as Citizens of your native State. We leave it with the pen of the faithful historian to delineate the distinguished course of your political life, conscious that it will not be forgotten, so long as the glorious epoch of the American revolution is remembered and admired.

The period of your administration of the government of this State, and the integrity of your example, are too strongly marked to escape the attention of future patriots and statesmen, and exhibit useful patterns for their imitation, while at the same time they have engaged our warmest affections. Under these impressions, and as a farther testimony of the high sense the Common Council entertain of your Excellency's exalted character, we beg leave to present you with the Freedom of the City.

We fervently pray that the benevolent Author of all our blessings, may sweeten your retirement with the rich reward due your merits, and when your course shall be finished here, receive your immortal spirit among the Saints in everlasting Glory.

By order of Common Council.

JAY TO ROBERT LENOX.

BEDFORD, 3d April, 1802.

SIR :

I have been favoured with yours of the 5th ult. Immediately on receiving the letter of Mr. Colles [1] which informed me that Mr. Vanderlyn was ready to take

---

[1] John B. Colles, as chairman of a committee of the Common Council of New York, had written to Jay, February 6th, as follows :

"Some time in the last year the Common Council of this city entered into a resolution to procure your portrait at full length, for the purpose of placing it in one of the publick rooms.

"Richard Varick, Esq., then Mayor, communicated to you this resolution, and you were pleased to inform him that you would sit for this purpose when necessary. Mr. Stewart, residing at Philadelphia, has been applied to to paint this portrait, but has delayed coming here as he had promised to do, and a Mr. Vanderline, born at Esopus, who has been in France for a number of years, having returned to this State, with a high reputation as a painter, and having seen some of his performances in this line, I have engaged him. He is now ready to commence this painting. I have, therefore, now to request the favour of you to come here for the above purpose as early as you can make it convenient."

my portrait, I wrote to him that as soon as roads would admit of it I would go to New York. I accordingly set out in February by the way of Rye; while there the late long storm came on, and before it ended I was taken with an intermittent fever, which rendered it prudent for me to return home. On finding this to be the case, I mentioned it to Mr. Colles by letter before I left Rye. Although since my return I have been less unwell than I was there, yet my health neither is, nor probably will be, in such a state as to permit me to visit New York at a period so early as Mr. Vanderlyn's convenience may require. This delay is unavoidable as well as embarrassing, and I regret it the more, as it may countenance conjectures not consistent with the sense I entertain of the honour intended me by the corporation of my native city—a corporation which, for many years, has been entitled, not only to my respect, but to my sincere and grateful attachment.

Yours, etc.,

JOHN JAY.

JAY TO PROFESSOR HENRY DAVIS.[1]

SIR : BEDFORD, 10th February, 1803.

This letter will be delivered to you by my son William, whom, agreeable to President Dwight's recommendation and advice, I commit to your care.

---

[1] Professor of Divinity, Yale College. Mr. Jay had previously written to President Dwight, inquiring whether he would receive his son into his family. Dr. Dwight replied that he would be unable to do so, and referred Mr. Jay to Prof. Davis as follows, January 3 :

" Mr. Henry Davis, senior tutor of this College and Professor of Divinity

He has hitherto been so good a boy as to render any degree of severity unnecessary ; even private and gentle admonitions have very rarely been requisite, and have, in no instance, proved ineffectual. I regret that since the death of the Rev. Mr. Ellison, circumstances occurred which prevented his being regularly employed. Habits of punctuality and industry are so important through life that they cannot be too early and carefully formed. Although it never appeared to me useful to confine boys to their books for more hours than can possibly be attentively employed, yet I think it indispensable that they do study in study times, and that exact punctuality to all appointments be rigidly insisted upon. I herewith inclose fifty dollars ; out of this money be pleased from time to time to provide for him such clothing and other articles as may be requisite and proper ; also make him a weekly allowance of one quarter of a dollar, to spend without account for postage of letters and otherwise as he may choose. In my opinion, boys ought not to be kept entirely without money on the one hand, nor profusely supplied with it on the other. Let me request of you to favour me now and

elect, has a family of a few boys, whom he is preparing for a collegiate education ; among them are a son of Mr. Senator Hillhouse. No person, within my knowledge, is more competent to perform this business, both kindly and skillfully. Mrs. Davis is a daughter of Judge Treadwell, of this State, and is a very respectable and amiable woman. The terms on which Mr. Davis will board and instruct your son, should you wish to place him under his care, are two and a half dollars, exclusive of washing, firewood, and candles, and threefourths of a dollar for his instruction, a week. His washing, firewood, and candles, will amount to a moderate sum only. Should you determine to send your son to Mr. Davis, he will receive him at the beginning of February. Should you determine otherwise, and should you think of any way in which I can be of service to you, please to command me."

then with a candid account of my son's progress and behaviour—that if delinquencies or errors should take place, I may co-operate with you in correcting them. Hitherto I have not perceived in him the least propensity to any vice ; and I pray God to render your endeavours to preserve him from it effectual. I am exceedingly solicitous that his college education be perfected by the time he shall be eighteen years old. He will be fourteen next June. He has been, unfortunately, though unavoidably, retarded by Mr. Ellison's death and other circumstances. That loss of time may, I think, be retrieved, but as it can only be done by more than ordinary attention on your part, I ought not only to request that favour of you, but also to express my readiness amply to remunerate it.

> I am, sir,
> Your most obedient servant,
> JOHN JAY.

JAY TO GENERAL SCHUYLER.

BEDFORD, 25th July, 1804.

MY DEAR SIR :

The friendship and attachment which I have so long and so uniformly experienced from you will not permit me to delay expressing how deeply and sincerely I participate with you in the afflicting event [1] which the public are now lamenting, and which you have so many domestic and particular reasons to bewail.

---

[1] Death of Hamilton.

The philosophic topics of consolation are familiar to you, and we all know from experience how little relief is to be derived from them. May the Author and only Giver of consolation be and remain with you.

With great esteem and affectionate regard, I am, dear sir,

Your obliged and obedient servant,

JOHN JAY.

JAY TO MRS. BANYER.

BEDFORD, 2d November, 1804.

MY DEAR DAUGHTER :

I passed a part of yesterday morning very agreeably in writing a letter to you. Happy to learn from your brother and sister that your health was fast improving, and well knowing the innocent gratifications you were deriving, probably "in long perspective" from your dear little boy, my letter insensibly grew long, nor could I easily quit these pleasing topics.

Last night I received Mr. Banyer's letter of the 27th. You can judge of my feelings on the occasion. It has cast a gloom on both families. I have to lament the departure of my only grandson, as well as the affliction of my dear and affectionate daughter. It is natural that such events should excite grief in a high degree ; I know this by experience, and I know by experience also, that no consolation is to be derived from any other source than acquiescence in and resignation to the will of God, without whose appointment or permission nothing comes to pass.

Our Heavenly Father has called this child *home*, and the very best wish that you or I could have formed for him was that, after a long an virtuousd abode here, he might be where he now is. We have indeed reason to grieve for the comforts we lose by his absence, but not that he is where he is. His happiness is now certain, complete, eternal. Happy shall we all be to arrive finally at the same blest abodes ; and there to be received by him, and many others of our best and dearest friends and kindred.

Let us all endeavour to become the wiser and better for these chastisements ; and remember the expressions of Job when all his children were taken away from him. I wish, my dear Maria, to comfort both you and myself. Let us both consider these things, and hold fast our confidence in Him who alone can console and bless us.

> I am, my dear Maria,
> Your very affectionate father,
> JOHN JAY.

JAY TO LINDLEY MURRAY.

DEAR SIR :   BEDFORD, 12th June, 1805.

I ought sooner to have written to you and thanked you for the books you sent me, and for the kind letter which accompanied them.

For a considerable time I had not leisure to pay sufficient attention to your work respecting our language. It has been much commended, and I think with much reason. Within thirty years past eloquence has made great progress in this country. Governments like ours are favourable to it. Every work which really facilitates the attainment of that influential science will meet with notice and respect. Some of our compositions, however, are not free from marks of incorrect taste, such as high-wrought verbiage and too little simplicity; new words have been admitted into our language incautiously, and in some instances old words are used in senses which did not formerly belong to them. It is to be wished that no alteration in the English language may take place in Britain or in America but such as the best writers in both countries will adopt.

Being retired from the fatigues and constraints of public life, I enjoy with real satisfaction the freedom and leisure which has at length fallen to my lot. For a long course of years I had been looking forward with desire to the tranquil retirement in which I now live, and my expectations from it have not been disappointed. I flatter myself that this is the inn at which I am to stop in my journey through life. How long I shall be detained is uncertain, but I rejoice in the prospect of the probability of being permitted to pass my remaining time in a situation so agreeable to me. Do not conclude from this that I am without cares and anxieties exclusive of those which are more or less common to all men. I have an excellent son, who has been obliged, by hectic complaints, to relinquish business and to pass two winters abroad. I hope he will recover his health, but until all doubts are removed some solicitude will remain. The truth is, that although in numerous respects I have abundant reason to be thankful, yet in others I experience the necessity and the value of patience and resignation.

That you may long continue in a capacity to do good, and to enjoy good, is the sincere wish of

Dear sir,

Your friend,

JOHN JAY.

JAY TO JOHN MURRAY, JUN.

SIR: BEDFORD, 18th October, 1805.

I have been favoured with your letter of the 2d ult. respecting the "African free school" in the city of New York. It is in my opinion a charitable and useful institution, and well entitled to encouragement and support. From your account of its present embarrassments I am induced to think that, in order to its being and remaining on a respectable and permanent footing, some vigorous and well devised measures should be taken to obtain adequate and durable funds. The uncertain donations occasionally solicited and expected from charitable but scattered and unconnected individuals will probably be always incompetent, and must obviously be too precarious to afford ground for reasonably calculating the prudence and extent of expenditures.

The existing debts should doubtless be paid; indeed, they cannot be paid too soon, and it is desirable that new ones be not contracted. For my part I am persuaded that it can very, very seldom be discreet for institutions depending on charity to contract debts, and then apply to charity to pay them.

What should be done ? is the question. Two things occur to me, which I will take the liberty to suggest.

First : The Society of Friends in general, and particularly those in New York, have given more patronage to the objects connected with the school than any other society or denomination in the State, and from circumstances peculiar to their association and discipline they are enabled to pursue and accomplish their objects with more than ordinary union and effect. Hence I am led to believe that if those of your society in New York would recommend this school to the notice and liberality of their brethren in the country, and desire them also to request the aid of all well disposed persons of other denominations, in their respective neighbourhoods, a considerable sum might be collected ; especially considering the prudence as well as zeal with which your affairs are usually managed. On this or any other plan which would in some degree be general throughout the country, I would readily be one of the contributors.

Secondly : I submit to your consideration the expediency of regularly putting at interest one tenth of the annual income of the school, whatever it may be and whencesoever it may arise ; and invariably to bring the yearly expenses of the school to a level with the remaining nine tenths.

On this plan both the principal of the stable funds and the income of the school (so far as it comprehended the interest of the funds) would increase from year to year. In time the interest alone would form an income so considerable as to be productive of more good than if the institution had continued to depend and subsist on scanty and precarious supplies. It may also be well to consider whether the benevolent objects of this institution might not be promoted by an act of incorporation, with such provisions in it as would conduce to its stability and extend its usefulness.

Be pleased to inform me whether any particular attention is paid by the superintendents to the children after they have left it, and whether it is part of the plan to endeavour to have them bound out to trades or to service in decent families. To me it appears important that they be not left entirely either to their parents or to themselves, it being difficult to give them good morals, manners, or habits in any other way than by placing them under the care and direction of persons better qualified for those purposes than their parents generally are.

With esteem and regard I am, sir,

Your obedient servant,

JOHN JAY.

WILLIAM WILBERFORCE TO JAY.

ELMDON-HOUSE, NEAR BIRMINGHAM,
November 7th, 1805.

MY DEAR SIR:

I am willing to flatter myself you have not quite forgotten the person who is now beginning to address you. He certainly has not forgotten you; on the contrary, he retains

a lively recollection of the pleasure he derived from your
society during your residence in this country, and still more
of the benefit he received, especially on one important
occasion, from your judicious and friendly counsel. He has
never since ceased to embrace every opportunity of inquiring
after you, and to take an interest in your well-being.

After this preamble, I proceed to state, that my object in
now taking up the pen is, to recommend earnestly to your
serious perusal and impartial consideration, a pamphlet
which I will take the liberty of transmitting to you, lately
published, entitled " War in Disguise, or the Frauds of the
Neutral Flags." It is spoken of in high terms by the most
intelligent and respectable men I know, and is written, as I
think you will agree with me, with considerable knowledge
of its subject, as well as with great spirit and eloquence.
Its general tenor is so clearly indicated by its title, at least
to you who are experimentally acquainted with the topics
of which it treats, that I need say nothing on that head ; I
will only beg leave to assure you, that I took it up with
very strong prejudices against the conclusions which I understood the author endeavoured to establish, on account of
the strong disposition I invariably feel to cultivate and promote a friendly connexion between our two countries. I
cannot but be anxious to hear what reception it meets with
on your side of the Atlantic. That those whose interest is
at stake will endeavour to raise a cry, is no more than what
we must expect. Happy shall I be, if this is countervailed
by the opposite opinion of men of sense, knowledge, and
impartiality. Nothing could have brought me over to the
doctrines the pamphlet lays down, but a deliberate and firm
persuasion, that on our practical adoption of them (I would
not hastily affirm to what extent) depends, according to all
human appearances, not merely the maritime superiority,
but the very existence of this empire. The author appears
to me to have left very short that part of his work in which
he speaks of the effects, on our marine and our maritime

interests, of the continuance of the present abuses. The work, I happen to know, was written in haste, and in a bad state of health ; and though the production of a man who was actuated by a sense of duty, and had taken great pains to inform himself, it is in some parts faulty, in the composition and language especially ; but knowing to whom I am writing, it would be mere impertinence to do more than introduce it to your notice. I leave it, not without solicitude, but yet with good hope, to your intelligence, experience, equity, and temper.

I heartily wish this may find you in the enjoyment of good health and personal comfort. You will not, I trust, think it improper egotism if, relying on your friendly remembrance, I add, that I thank God I am favoured with great domestic felicity,—having a wife and five children, the youngest born only about two months ago. I should scarcely know where to leave off, if I allowed myself to touch on any of those numerous and interesting topics which press themselves on my attention while writing to you. I will, however, abstain from them all, and take my leave ; assuring you that I am ever, with cordial esteem and regard, my dear sir,

Yours very sincerely,

W. WILBERFORCE.

P. S.—If you do me the favour to answer this letter, my address is always London.

JAY TO WILLIAM WILBERFORCE.

BEDFORD, WESTCHESTER COUNTY, STATE OF NEW YORK,
14th April, 1806.

DEAR SIR :

It was not until within a week that I received your friendly letter of the 7th November last. It expresses sentiments of esteem and regard which, being mutual, excite agreeable recollections and emotions.

"War in Disguise," of which you were so good as to enclose a copy, has given occasion to uneasiness relative to the matter and design of it. It contains marks of ability, but the author has not been entirely circumspect. I enclose an answer to it, written, as is supposed, and I believe, by a gentleman of excellent talents and good dispositions.[1]

It appears to me, that every *independent* state has, as such, a perfect right at all times, whether at war or at peace, to make grants to and treaties with any other independent state; but then those acts, in order to be valid, must consist with justice, and be in no respect fraudulent. To the validity of such grants and treaties, no third power, whether belligerent or neutral, can, in my opinion, have reasonable cause to object.

When such acts are fraudulent, and injurious to others, those others are justifiable in regarding them as being what they are (that is, fraudulent), and in acting accordingly. When such acts are just and fair, but abused to the injury of others, those others have a right to complain of and to attack the *abuse*, but not the thing abused.

Whether this or that particular act (of the description alluded to) be fair or fraudulent, is a question to be decided by evidence internal and external, according to the rules and maxims of the laws of nations relative to such cases.

Believing these principles to be well founded, they do not permit me to adopt some of the opinions of this ingenious writer, nor to approve of all the latitude

---

[1] Gouverneur Morris.

contended for by some of his opponents. To view in their various lights and relations and to examine properly all the doctrines and positions in question, cannot be done within the compass of a letter.

Your disposition and desire to promote good-will between our two countries exactly accord with my own. It is to be wished that each of them may ever be mindful, that the preservation of friendship between nations, as between individuals, requires justice and prudence always, and even forbearance sometimes; for states, as well as persons, commit errors. It is our lot to live in perplexing and eventful times. The passions of men are not good counsellors, and never less so than when agitated and inflamed.

We have seen concluded, with the treaty of Amiens, the *first* act of the astonishing tragedy which the French Revolution has introduced on the theatre of the world. The present and succeeding acts will probably be highly interesting and impressive. In this prodigious drama, Great Britain still sustains a conspicuous and important part; perhaps she may be employed to restrain the "remainder of wrath." Whether this distant nation is to appear among the *dramatis personæ*, cannot now be known. We certainly do not desire it.

The inconveniences apprehended from the death of Mr. Pitt will doubtless be diminished, if not obviated, by the general confidence reposed in your new administration. I am glad to find that Lord Grenville holds a distinguished place in it. My respect and esteem for him continue undiminished.

Very sincerely do I congratulate you on your domestic felicity. May it continue and increase. I thank you for what you have briefly remarked on that topic ; for you have given me pleasure, by letting me see how much reason you have to be pleased.

With true esteem and regard, I am, dear sir,

Your faithful and obedient servant,

JOHN JAY.

P. S.—As your letter was so long on the way, this answer will arrive, if it arrives at all, much later than you expected. Being anxious to remove appearances of inattention, I shall send a duplicate by another vessel. There will then be a double chance of its coming to your hands.

JAY TO PETER VAN SCHAACK.

BEDFORD, May 4, 1807.

DEAR SIR:

Accept my thanks for your friendly letter of the 18th of last month.

As to the *election*, it is not clear to me what will be its precise effect in relation to the Federalists. If as a *party* they judged it to be expedient to favour Mr. Lewis, I think they should as a *party* have *openly* and decidedly declared and resolved that they would support him. The language of the Federal leaders to the party seems to amount to this, viz. : On this occasion you may leave your standard ; you may go home, and every man is at liberty to do what may be right in his own eyes, but we nevertheless intimate to you, as an opinion to which we *incline*, but do not explicitly adopt, that it may be better for us to have

Mr. Lewis than Mr. Tomkins for our Governor. I do not like measures of this kind. I fear that they tend to disorganize and sever us, and that they do not manifest that degree of resolution, self-respect, and dignity which our motives, objects, and situation demand. Had the party resolved to support Mr. Lewis, I certainly should have voted for him. As a mere individual, judging what was proper for me to do, I declined voting for either of the candidates.

I did hope that your letter would have encouraged me to expect Mrs. V. Schaack here this season with you, and such of the children as you could conveniently bring. Such a visit would be exceedingly grateful to me and my family.

For some weeks during the winter I was much indisposed ; at present my health is much as it usually is, and probably as good as it ever will be. My children join with me in assuring you and Mrs. V. Schaack and your family of our regards and best wishes.

Peter's health has for some time past been gradually improving. I mention this because I am sure it will give you pleasure.

I am, dear sir,

Your affectionate friend,

JOHN JAY.

JAY TO GOUVERNEUR MORRIS.

DEAR SIR : BEDFORD, 15th September, 1807.

I have received your letter of the 2d inst., and expected to have answered it this week in person. My health had so much mended that, on Friday last, I rode to Bedford for the first time since my return. That night, rheumatic pains in my head, neck, and shoulders came on. They have somewhat abated, but still confine me to the house. In our journey through life, as in other journeys, our wishes cannot always be gratified. Travellers must expect to live and fare like travellers.

You have the gout, and you extract consolation from it; this is good moral chemistry. My rheumatism and your gout may perhaps carry us home the farthest way round, but not in an easy chair. When we "ruminate past enjoyments," we taste that tincture of melancholy which their departure and other associated circumstances infuse; it nevertheless affords a kind of pleasure which, like some medical wine, is not only better than no wine, but perhaps in some respects more salutary than pure wine.

The half a century you speak of has given us some knowledge and experience, both of men and things. That experience leads me to concur cordially in your idea of cultivating sentiments of friendship, and particularly to cherish those with which I am

Yours, very sincerely,

John Jay.

JAY TO JUDGE RICHARD PETERS.

BEDFORD, 30th 'August, 1808.

Dear Sir:

Accept my thanks for your obliging letter of the 9th ult., which was lately sent to me, and for the memoirs of your Agricultural Society, which accompanied it. Marks of friendly attention from those we esteem are particularly grateful, and I have delayed making my acknowledgments to you because I wished to first read the memoirs; this I have done with pleasure.

As to what you have heard of my living very retired, it is to a certain degree true.[1] The fact is, that I live very much as I have long wished to do. I have a pleasant situation, and very good neighbours. I enjoy peace and a competency proportionate to my comforts and moderate desires, with such a residue of health as, while it constantly whispers "*memento mori,*" still permits me to see my friends with cheerfulness and pleasure. The burthen of time I have not experienced; attention to little improvements, occasional visits, the history which my recollections furnish, and frequent conversations with the "mighty dead," who in a certain sense live in their works, together with the succession of ordinary occurrences,

---

[1] In his letter of July 9th Judge Peters wrote to Jay from his home at Belmont, Penn.:

"It is said that you have turned hermit, and I am not much behind you. Both of us are old enough to wish for repose; but the disturbed state of the world will not permit us to enjoy it. Old Gates used to tell me in 1776 that if the bantling Independence lived one year, it would last to the age of Methuselah. Yet we have lived to see it in its dotage, with all the maladies and imbecilities of extreme old age. Quacks and empirics are not likely to prolong its existence. Those who laboured in bringing this bantling into the world, and nursed and fostered it in its infancy, have not the less merit, because, in its manhood, it has lived too fast and got into bad company. Theories and wild speculations are the order of the day, and we must submit with as good a grace as we can. When present circumstances are disgusting, I endeavour to re-enjoy what is past. Among these retrospective pleasures is the sincere satisfaction produced by the recollection of the constant regard with which I have been, and still remain, very affectionately yours."

preserve me from *ennui.* They who endeavour to grow wiser and better as their years wear away, feel little temptation to permit the fable of the country-man and his ass to be applicable to them. So much respect only is due to the dictums of the day as they may be worth; everything beyond it is mⴲre *vox et prœterea nihil.* Party feuds give me concern, but they seldom obtrude upon me. The mass of the people of this town were steady Whigs during the Revolution, and have been steady Federalists since the date of our new Constitution. They live so peaceably that their law business would scarcely afford wages to an attorney's clerk.

.   .   .   .   .   .

With the best wishes for the health and happiness of yourself and family, and with great esteem and regard, I am, dear sir,

Affectionately yours,
JOHN JAY.

JAY TO MORRIS S. MILLER.[1]

DEAR SIR: BEDFORD, 22d May, 1809.

I have received by the last mail, and have read with great pleasure your obliging letter of the 11th inst.

---

[1] Mr. Miller, of Utica, N. Y., wrote to Jay as follows, May 11th :

"Permit me to advise you of the result of the election in the Western District. For the first time in eight years the triumph of correct principles is complete. In the year 1808 the Democratic Senators succeeded by a major-ity of about two thousand nine hundred ; the Federalists are elected this year by a majority of at least six hundred.

"It is with peculiar pleasure I inform you that in every part of the District the election has been bottomed and conducted on decided Federal principles :

The information it conveys cannot fail of being grateful to all who prefer the wise and upright policy which distinguished the administration of Washington to that which of late has distressed and disgraced our country. How far the favorable changes which have taken place are imputable to patriotic and correct principles, time and experience only can decide. Sincerely do I wish that all our elections may manifest the prevalence of such principles ; but I am not sanguine in my expectations of it. Personal and pecuniary considerations appear to have acquired a more than ordinary degree of influence ; many sacrifices of public good have and will yet be made to them. On the exertions of the virtuous and intelligent much will always depend ; should they become relaxed by a sense either of security or of fatigue, we shall probably lose the ground we have gained. I brought with me into retirement the same affection for our country by which I have always been actuated, and you rightly judge that nothing which is of importance to the public can be a matter of indifference to me.

---

in no County has there been any arrangement or concert with either section of the Democratic party. The result of this election therefore may be fairly attributed to the increasing prevalence of those principles on which the patriotic framers and supporters of the Constitution have uniformly acted. I hope, sir, you will excuse the liberty I have taken in thus trespassing on your time and attention. Altho' you have in a great measure withdrawn from public life, and stand aloof from the bustle of political contests, yet after having made so many sacrifices for the public good, and contributed so much to the dignity and prosperity of this country, it is not to be believed you can be indifferent to the revival of those principles which you have so successfully inculcated and on which the future destinies of the United States so much depend."

Miss Jay joins with me in assuring you and Mrs. Miller of our best wishes for your prosperity.

I am, dear sir, with sincere esteem and regard,

Your obedient servant,

JOHN JAY.

JAY TO JUDGE PETERS.

BEDFORD, 24th July, 1809.

DEAR SIR:

Soon after receiving your letter of the 18th September last I was called to Albany by the death of the only remaining child of my daughter, whose grief for the loss of her son and of her husband was still fresh and severe.

I returned on the 3d of November with a pain in my side, which the doctor ascribed to an obstruction in the liver. The complaint increased, and kept me in close confinement during the winter and spring ; it reduced me to such a state of debility that I have as yet regained only sufficient strength to ride two or three miles at a time. I am better but not well, and it is uncertain whether I ever shall be ; such mementos are useful, though unpleasant, and therefore I ought to make the best of them.

Your remarks relative to plaster will induce me, if I live, to extend the application of it to the various objects you mention. I have directed it to be freely used in the garden this spring, and am pleased with the results. I have heard a strange story, and apparently from good authority. A person who suspected that plaster promoted vegetation by means of the air and not of the earth, placed at every hill in several rows of corn some plaster in clam shells—the rest of his corn field he plastered in the common way ; the crop was just as good in the one case as in the other. Can this be so ? perhaps the rain washed much of the plaster out of the shells.

The effect of plaster in vegetation is to me a mystery ; if it acts only by attracting water, why does the ground (as some say) grow *tired* of it, and require a supply of common manure to renew the efficacy of it ? Often repeated experiments and long-continued observation naturally lead to important discoveries, but the very limited duration of human life rarely allows sufficient time for the talents and perseverance of any individual to arrive at their *ne plus.* Here the antediluvians had the advantage of us, and many of them doubtless made the most of it. Hence it may be inferred that they carried many of the useful arts, as well as those which belong to the departments of vice, to a higher degree of perfection than they are at present. To me it does not appear improbable that the celebrated works of remote antiquity were not a little indebted to information which passed through the flood.

National interest unites with other considerations in drawing our attention to agriculture. I think it has greatly improved in our country since the Revolution, and there is reason to believe that the " resuscitation " which you are attempting would be generally useful. I wish it may be effected, but unless a number of gentlemen well qualified for the purpose will heartily and diligently unite with you, I fear your endeavours will not be so successful as they are commendable.

You are right in supposing that we are much of an age; in December next I shall have lived sixty-four years—a long course of years when to come—a dream when past. But whether life is or is not composed of " such stuff as dreams are made of," it is a valuable gift, and is capable of many enjoyments, to be found by all who rationally seek and use them. Among the enjoyments which men derive from each other, those which arise from *such* social intercourse as you allude to certainly are to be placed in the first class. This class, however, like the first class of almost every other species of good, has more items in theory than in actual experience.

I think with you that the Spaniards deserve credit for the spirit they have exhibited. There are fine points in their character. In a conversation respecting them, with the late Abbé Mably, he said : " *Monsieur, ils sont plus hommes que nous.*" This was a great deal for a Frenchman to say. I sincerely wish them success, but my expectations of it have not been sanguine. Their hatred of France and their attachment to their religion, etc., may continue to stimulate their indignation and their valour ; but it does not appear to me that their opposition has been, or probably will be, so managed as to prove effectual. As yet there has been no display of civil or military talents *equal to the occasion ;* we may guess, but we cannot prophecy.

Perilous times have descended upon all Europe, and Bonaparte seems to be the Nebuchadnezzar of the day. Divines say that in prophetic language nations are called seas. According to that language, Europe is a tempestuous and a raging ocean ; and who can tell which of the governments afloat upon it will escape destruction or disaster ? Some dark clouds from that tempest have reached and lately obscured our political sky ; nor has it again become quite serene and clear. This country, as well as others, will experience deep distress, but I do not believe that you or I will live to see it. From transitory and ordinary evils we cannot expect to be exempt. We may suffer from rash experiments, from the pressure of fraternal embraces or resentments, from the machinations of demagogues, and gradually from the corruption incident to the love of money, but for my own part I do not apprehend the speedy approach of anything like "overturn." You have had a democratic tornado at Philadelphia : it did but little harm ; perhaps it did some good. I found it gave you something to do, and I found also, as I expected, that you did it. Too many in your State, as in this, love pure democracy dearly—they seem not to consider that *pure* democracy, like *pure* rum, easily produces intoxication, and with it a thousand mad pranks and fooleries. Ebriety, whether moral or physical, is difficult to cure ; and the more so as such patients cannot easily be convinced of the value and the necessity of temperance and regimen.

I observe that I have written a long letter ; feeling

you. His piety gives unfading charms to his compositions. But I am in danger of expending all the time for which I must venture to detain you, without proceeding to the business which gives me occasion, an occasion which, I own, I am glad to seize, to address you after so long a silence. I am aware, indeed, that your retirement may prevent your taking any part in public, even in the case I am about to mention ; still your opinion, your good wishes, may be useful to us. Since the abolition of the slave-trade, an institution has been formed consisting of a considerable number of the most respectable members of both houses of parliament, as well as of other men of consideration and worth, with the Duke of Gloucester at our head, for the purpose of promoting civilization and improvement in Africa. Of course, all our hopes are grounded and bottomed in the cessation of the slave-trade. Now, from the operation of the war, and of other causes, this traffic is stopped, with a very trifling exception, which, though trifling, we are trying, and that successfully, to do away throughout all that immense part of the continent of Africa which is north of the line, and indeed much further ; unless as it may be carried on by your countrymen and our own, in direct violation of the laws of both countries. We trust we shall be able, by sending ships of war to scour the coast of Africa, to suppress the British slave-trade ; but this will be of little avail, if the traffic may still be carried on in fact, though prohibited by law, by the American slave-trader ; nor do I see any prospect of preventing this abuse, unless a convention could be made between the two countries, by which the ships of war of each should be authorized and even encouraged (by the hopes of gaining by the forfeitures) to seize and bring in for adjudication the vessels of the other, when prosecuting this unlawful commerce. I rather believe there is another particular in which it still remains for your country to render its law similar to ours, by subjecting to forfeiture any ship of any country, and under any flag, which is fitted out in and cleared out from an American port. Now, my dear sir, may I hope for your assistance towards the production of the effects I have specified? Knowing to whom I am writing, I will say no more on this head.

I cannot address you without tracing my way to the period when we were last together, through the long and interesting interval which lies between that and the present moment. What events have since happened! What events may take place in the same number of years yet to come! How many whom we loved have gone in the last thirteen years! How many will go in the next! How strongly, my dear sir, are we admonished to place our happiness on a firmer and more secure basis, than it can enjoy in this world, which never more than of late verified the character given of it by one of our greatest and best churchmen, Hooker, that it is full (made up, I think he says) of perturbations. How astonishing is it to see men of penetrating understandings, and of deep and large views, confining their regards to this limited scene, apparently insensible to the existence of any thing beyond it! But I beg pardon for thus running on, and I stop before my pen has got the mastery of me. I will detain you no longer than while I express my hopes that you are well and happy, and assure you that I shall never cease to take an interest in your welfare.

I remain, with respect and regard,

My dear sir,

Your obliged and faithful servant,

W. WILBERFORCE.

P. S. If you favour me with a reply, may I take the liberty of asking after your family? I married about two years after you left England, and am surrounded, I thank God, by an excellent wife and children. I trust I do not deceive myself in the persuasion that you will not be un-interested in this statement, for which therefore I will not use the affectation of apologizing. I will take the liberty of sending you a copy of the African Institution's reports. You will also see in it a list of the members.

JAY TO REV. DR. JEDEDIAH MORSE.

BEDFORD, 16th August, 1809.

DEAR SIR:

I this morning received your letter of the 9th inst. with the interesting sermon which it enclosed, and I thank you for them both.

A proper history of the United States[1] would have much to recommend it : in some respects it would be singular, or unlike all others ; it would develop the great plan of Providence, for causing this extensive part of our world to be discovered, and these " utter-most parts of the earth " to be gradually filled with civilized and *Christian* people and nations. The means or second causes by which this great plan has long been and still is accomplishing, are materials for

---

[1] Dr. Morse had written to Mr. Jay from New Haven, August 9th : " I have undertaken, should I have leisure to continue, *A General History of the United States* (particularly in reference to remarkable interpositions of Divine Providence in favor of this country, from its settlement to this day), begun by Revd. Dr. Trumbull, and which he has brought down to the year 1766, in MSS. ready for the press. With events in our country since that period, you, Sir, are more intimately acquainted than most other men. I have a great desire to avail myself of such information as to events and facts most prominent and interesting, as you possess, and shall be willing to communicate. In a personal interview I could more fully disclose my wishes and plan."

history, of which the writer ought well to know the use and bearings and proper places. In my opinion, the historian, in the course of the work, is never to lose sight of that great plan.

Remarkable interpositions of Divine Providence are fine subjects, but the exhibition cannot have a full effect, unless accompanied with a distinct view of the objects and state of things to which they relate ; it is by discerning how admirably they are accommodated and fitted to answer their intended purposes, that the reader is made to reflect and feel properly.

Few among us have *time* and *talent* for such a work. I am pleased with the prospect of your under-taking it ; and I do believe that, with a *due allowance of time*, that is, of several years, you would execute it well.

As to aid from me, I am far more willing than able to assist you. I became sick last autumn, and have not had a well day since. Although better, I am still feeble ; and can neither bear much exercise, nor much employment of any kind ; even in reading and in writing, I find it necessary to be abstemious.

I regret the circumstances which deprived me of the pleasure of receiving a visit from you ; for no conversations are more agreeable to me, than those with persons whom I esteem, and in which the *utile* and the *dulce* are blended. With the best wishes for your health and happiness,

I am, dear sir,

Your affectionate and obedient servant,

JOHN JAY.

JAY TO WILLIAM WILBERFORCE.

BEDFORD, N. Y., 8th November, 1809.

DEAR SIR :

On the 28th ult., I received your letter of the 1st of August last, and I thank you for it, and for the pamphlet enclosed with it.

I am well persuaded that your sentiments relative to me are such as you describe ; and I assure you that mine relative to you correspond with them.

The patrons of the Abolition Act and of the African Institution certainly do honour, and will probably do more than ordinary good, to Great Britain, against whom complaints have ascended both from Asia and Africa. It is pleasing to behold a nation assiduously cultivating the arts of peace and humanity in the midst of war, and while strenuously fighting for their all, kindly extending the blessings of Christianity and civilization to distant countries.

That your and our governments should co-operate in rendering their respective laws against the slave-trade effectual, is to me very desirable, and I believe that a convention for the purpose would be approved by all who think and feel as you and I do respecting that base and cruel traffic. Whether the times are propitious to such a convention, is another question. Negotiations are said to be pending between our government and Mr. Jackson. I can discern no objection to his being instructed to propose such a measure. They who offer to do what is fit and right to be done, cannot be losers by it. I can do but little—that little shall be done.

The information you give me respecting your family, and your friendly inquiries concerning mine, gratify me not a little. I rejoice that while perturbation reigns abroad, you enjoy in tranquillity at home the comforts mentioned in the 128th Psalm.

In my family there have been, since the date of my last letter, some painful and some pleasing events. Death has deprived my eldest daughter of an excellent husband, and of the only two children which she had. On the other hand, my son has gradually recovered his health, and has married an amiable young lady, who, about a year ago, brought him a son. My other children are well, and doing well.

As to myself, sickness confined me to the house last winter, and I am still more of an invalid than a convalescent. However difficult the task, such visitations should be received and borne with grateful as well as patient resignation.

The observation you cite from Hooker is very just, and so are your remarks on this turbulent and transitory scene. To see things as they are, to estimate them aright, and to act accordingly, is to be wise. But you know, my dear sir, that most men, in order to become wise, have much to unlearn as well as to learn, much to undo as well as to do. The Israelites had little comfort in Egypt, and yet they were not very anxious to go to the promised land. Figuratively speaking, we are all at this day in Egypt, and a prince worse than Pharaoh reigneth in it. Although the prophet "like unto Moses" offers to deliver from bondage, and invites us to prepare and be ready to go with him, under Divine guidance and protection, to the promised land, yet great is the number who prefer remaining in slavery and *dying* in Egypt.

If this letter should reach you, be so good as to let me know it, and name some person in London to whose care I may transmit future ones for you.

With the best wishes for your health and happiness, and with real esteem and regard, I am, dear sir,

Your faithful and obedient servant,

JOHN JAY.

PETER A. JAY TO JAY.

NEW YORK, 23d February, 1810.

DEAR PAPA:

The Washington Society requested me to deliver an oration on their Anniversary, and as you advised me not to be an insignificant Member, I was induced to consent, and accordingly spoke one Yesterday. I have of course been for some time busy in preparing it, and have on that account pressed the furnace business less than I should otherwise have done. The Celebration of yesterday has occasioned much exultation among the Federalists. The Society walked in procession and amounted to more than *two thousand*. Many Gentlemen kept aloof, but it was one of the most respectable assemblages of people that I have ever seen. It consisted of substantial Shop keepers and Mechanicks, of Men of the middling Class, and of a considerable Number of old Revolutionary officers and Soldiers. Almost all of them possess Influence and can bring to the poll other votes besides their own. In the Evening a grand

ball was given, not by the Society but by subscription. ...
My best love to William and Nancy.

> I am, my dear father,
>> Your affectionate son,
>>> PETER AUGUSTUS JAY.

JAY TO JUDGE PETERS.

BEDFORD, 26th February, 1810.

DEAR SIR:

After lingering through the summer I found my disorder gradually returning in the autumn. Since the middle of November I have been confined to the house; but have as yet suffered less this winter than I did the last; at times, however, I seemed to be approaching that state in which "a grasshopper is a burden." When I took up my pen it was not because it was pleasant, but because it was necessary. The late fine weather has done me good. I have walked on the piazza and breathed mild fresh air. I feel less relaxed, and think it probable that the spring will again relieve me. The *carpe diem* reminds me that I should take this opportunity of writing to you, and to a few others whom I have *apparently* neglected.

From your letter I can perceive what your feelings have been and are. When afflictions make us wiser and better, they answer their purpose; and they do so when they produce the acquiescence and resignation you mention. A traveller has great reason for regret when a faithful and affectionate friend and companion leaves him on the road; but that regret is softened by the expectation of meeting again at the end of the journey. To you it will readily occur, that we are all travellers, some in coaches, others on foot; some lodge in good inns, and others where the night finds them; some press forward with an eye to the " promised land," while many others loiter and revel on the way, with as little concern about where they are going as the horses by which they are drawn or carried, etc., etc. . . . He did not speak much at random who said that "the greatest miracle to man is man."

Our political sky still continues to grow more and more dark and threatening. Whether the clouds will quietly disperse and disappear, or whether they portend a storm, is uncertain. The present tempestuous state of the world does not encourage us to expect a long season of uninterrupted fair weather. If peace has been and is in our power, it would be mortifying to be involved in war unnecessarily. There came forth with the French Revolution a spirit of delusion, which, like an influenza, passed over and infected all Europe. Even our distant country has not entirely escaped. Great is the number among us, of whom it may be said that, "seeing they have not perceived, and hearing they have not understood." Delusions have their errands, and are sent for some purpose different from that of promoting unanimity and peace. But be these things as they may, it is a consoling reflection that He who rules all, rules wisely.

I will now turn to a more pleasing topic. On conversing with a gentleman who visited me last summer. about the damage said to be often done to pear-trees by lightning, he observed that the damage in question proceeded, in his opinion, more frequently from disease than from lightning. That on seeing the upper branches of one of his pear-trees to be withering, he examined them often, and found them to be dying from the extremities downwards. After some time he took off all those branches below the mortification, cutting through sound healthy wood. The tree soon began to flourish. It put forth new and strong shoots, and has since been as thrifty as the others.

Something a little like this happened last year in my garden. A frost took my watermelons when they were about as large as a marble. They turned black, and dropped off. The ends of the vines began to die, and continued to do so for some days. I then had the vines cut below the mortified part, and the whole well sprinkled with plaster. They recovered, and brought some, though not much, fruit to perfection.

I believe that you and I derive more real satisfaction from attending to our vines and fruit-trees, than most conquerors do from cultivating their favourite laurels.

At present I indulge the expectation of being able to bid a cheerful welcome to the spring, and to participate a little in the enjoyments of it, notwithstanding the wickedness or folly which may abound in high places. That you may share largely and for many years in these and other enjoyments, is sincerely the wish of,

Dear sir,

Your affectionate and obedient servant,

John Jay.

WILLIAM WILBERFORCE TO JAY.

KENSINGTON-GORE, near LONDON,
July 18th, 1810.

MY DEAR SIR:

Calling to mind the friendly spirit which animates your letters to me, I am not ashamed of being deemed impertinently selfish, when I commence my reply to your last very obliging communication of November, 1809, by telling you that about a year and three-quarters ago I changed my residence, and find myself in the habitation which my family now occupies, and which we find more salubrious than Clapham Common. We are just one mile from the turnpike gate at Hyde Park corner, which I think you will not have forgotten yet, having about three acres of pleasure-ground around my house, or rather behind it, and several old trees, walnut and mulberry, of thick foliage. I can sit and read under their shade, which I delight in doing, with as much admiration of the beauties of nature (remembering at the same time the words of my favourite poet: *nature is but an effect, whose cause is God)*, as if I were two hundred miles from the great city.

My parliamentary duties force me to be within easy reach of London all the winter, and even spring, and sometimes for a part of the summer. I have a very affectionate wife, who is always unwilling to be at a distance from me; and Providence has blest us with six children, the eldest of whom is not quite twelve, the youngest under two years of age. My family are breathing pure air, and taking exercise quietly and without restraint, while I am in the harness at St. Stephens or, to continue the metaphor, in a very good stable just opposite Westminster Hall, where I commonly, or rather chiefly, take both my food and rest during the whole session, often being unable to come over to Kensington-gore from Monday morning to Saturday night; always, however, within call, should domestic matters require my presence.

I was not aware that my egotism would be so tedious, yet again let me confess that I am not afraid of subjecting myself, with you, to any severity of censure. When I have a regard for any one, I like to know his habits of life, times, places, etc., and I recollect with pleasure, that you kindly gave me an account of your family matters, and of your present situation and pursuits. Let me beg you to be so obliging as to continue so to do, in any letter which you may do me the favour to write; next, let me not forget to inform you, that your friendly packet of the 8th November last, of which I received duplicates first, brought me two copies of your favour of 14th April, 1806, for which, however late, accept my best thanks. In conformity with the kind wish you express, that I should name to you some person in London to whom your letters may be addressed, let me name Robert Barclay, Esq. (the great brewer), or Samuel Hoare, Esq., the banker, both of whom I think you knew.

I wish I could recollect with certainty, how many of the reports of the African Institution I sent you. I will, however, transmit to you either to New York or Philadelphia, accordingly as on inquiry I shall judge best, all the reports but the first. Indeed on consideration I will send them all, as you may promote our common object, by giving away any copies you do not wish to retain.

I am grieved to tell you, that both your countrymen and my own are still carrying on the abominable traffic in human flesh, in spite of the abolition laws of their respective countries. I trust that a continuance of the vigorous methods we are using to carry our law into effect, will by degrees force our commercial men to employ their substance in some more innocent commerce. It has given me no little pleasure, to find all your several ministers (both Mr. King, Mr. Monroe, and Mr. Pinckney) warmly disposed to co-operate, so far as they properly could in their peculiar situation; and I am not without hopes of a practical, though not a formal adoption of the only effectual expedient for suppressing the slave trade, that of the armed vessels of both our countries taking the slave ships of the other as well as those of its own. There might be objections, though I own I can see none of sufficient importance to outweigh the countervailing benefits to a regular compact between our two countries for the above purpose; but it will answer the same end, provided we respectively abstain from claiming any of our vessels which may have been captured when engaged in the slave trade. I have received, within a few weeks, the opinion of your attorney-general in its practical tendency in favour of the system I am wishing to see established.

My dear sir, I know not how I have been able, with the pen in my hand, to abstain so long from expressing the sincere and great pleasure it has given me to find affairs taking a more favourable turn between our two countries. I can only account for my not breaking out on this topic, on my first sitting down to write to you, by the consideration that when once there is a favourable issue in any case, in which we have been receiving or communicating from time to time the tidings of the day, with extreme anxiety and earnestness (the French word *empressement* better expresses what I mean), as for instance in the case of the illness of a friend, we become so cool that we perhaps forget to inquire about, or to name at all, the very topic on which, during the state of suspense, we were continually asking for or giving intelligence with such feverish solicitude. Really, the idea of a war between our two countries is perfectly horrible; and I am really happy to say, that I think in this country this most just sentiment gains ground. Like all propositions which are founded in truth and reason, it gradually sinks into the minds of men, and, though perhaps slowly and insensibly, by degrees it leavens nearly the whole mass. It will tend to produce this friendly disposition on your side of the water, if more of your countrymen would come over and live awhile among us. We are not an idle people ; we are a busy people, and may not have leisure or disposition to pay all the personal attentions which politeness might prescribe ; but I am persuaded that any gentleman of character and moderation who should visit this country, would meet with such a friendly reception as would show him that the circumstance of our being the descendants of common progenitors is not forgotten, or rather, that it is reviving and diffusing itself with increasing force.

Before I conclude, let me express the satisfaction it gave me to find that you were safely laid up, if I may so express it, in a comfortable and tranquil harbour, after having figuratively as well as literally been so long, or at least so often, tossed on the stormy sea of public life. May I confess to you, at very near fifty-one only in years, but with only a weakly constitution and after having been in parliament very near thirty years, that I begin to look forward to the same secession from public life ; meaning, however, to form no positive determination for the future, but to follow the leadings of Providence, and do on the day the duties of the day.

In three or four years, my four boys, the eldest especially, will be attaining that period of life when a father's eye and tongue may be most useful and necessary to their future well-doing ; and really the business of parliament has increased so much of late years, as to render it next to impossible for any man who cannot live for six or seven months in every year with a very small proportion of food or sleep, especially the latter, to attend at all, as he would otherwise be glad to do, to domestic or social claims. Then let me add,—and if you will take it as intended in the way of a hint to yourself, excuse only my freedom in giving it, and you will not greatly mistake my meaning :

any man who has acted his part at all creditably on the stage of public life, may render very great service to mankind, especially to his own countrymen, with whose opinions, prejudices, and errors he is well acquainted, by his *pen;* for instance, by bearing testimony to the truth of the position which, however trite, it is still useful now and then to repeat and enforce, that honesty is the best policy, etc.

I happen to have just now many claims of an epistolary nature, which have been too long neglected, owing to my having left them, as in your case, to be attended to when the recess of parliament should afford me a little more leisure. Much writing also affects my breathing. I must therefore conclude. But before I lay down my pen, let me, recollecting your kindly opening your mind to me on one important occasion, in, I think, 1795 (or 1796), beg that when you next write to me, you would favour me by telling me how you would vote, etc., if you were in our House of Commons, on the question of parliamentary reform. I do not ask you to take the trouble of entering into a detailed statement of the premises which may lead you to form your judgment on that point, whatever it may be ; I wish only (unless you have a little leisure) for your conclusion. I will own to you, that one main motive with me for having supported, on a late occasion, the motion for parliamentary reform, was the persuasion that by taking away what must be confessed to be a blemish or blot, in an assembly which is professedly formed on the principle of representation, we are lessening the power of bad men to misrepresent and defame our constitution, and to mislead the well-intentioned but perhaps less acute and long-sighted, into a concurrence in their measures. 2dly, if the measure should be adopted at all, it is desirable that it should be so at a time when, as is really the case now, notwithstanding the confident assurances of such men as Cobbett and his adherents, the country feels coolly on the subject, and is therefore not likely to push its representatives to go dangerous lengths; for I think you will agree with me, that it is a species of reform, all things considered, concerning which, in this country and at this time, it is better of the two not to go quite far enough, than to go too far.

Farewell, my dear sir, and believe me, with cordial esteem and regard,

Your faithful servant,

W. WILBERFORCE.

P. S.—As I shall be sending you a parcel, and I do not recollect that I ever begged your acceptance of a religious publication, which I first sent into the world the year I married (and what I say of wedded life, I thank heaven I should not now alter), let me now transmit it as a testimony of my esteem and regard. It was, in truth, principally intended for the use of my friends, and therefore I may send it to you with great propriety. I will also accompany it with another on the slave trade. May these books preserve in your family the memorial of our friendly connexion, and if you will not call me impertinent, I will request from you some similar memorial.

JAY TO WILLIAM WILBERFORCE.

BEDFORD, 25th October, 1810.

DEAR SIR :

On the 13th instant I received and read with great pleasure your interesting and friendly letter of the 18th July last. There are several topics in it on which I should like to *converse* with you : they shall be noticed in some future letters. As I cannot write or read much at a time without fatigue, I shall confine myself at present to the one on which you express a wish to know my sentiments.

A satisfactory answer to the question of " REFORM," can only result from a judicious selection and combination of the reasons and circumstances which bear relation to it. Of many of these my information is so imperfect, that it would be rash to form a decided judgment. I have not sufficient *data* whereon to calculate, whether so much good may reasonably be expected from such a measure, as would justify the risk of inconveniences, to which every important innovation is more or less liable.

The principles of the English constitution appear to require that the whole number of representatives should be fairly apportioned among the whole number of electors. But I have observed nothing in it which even implies what is called " universal suffrage." It is not a new remark, that they who own the country are the most fit persons to participate in the government of it. This remark, with certain restrictions and exceptions, has force in it ; and applies both to the *elected* and the *electors*, though with most force to the *former*.

I do not know what the proposed plan of reform *precisely* is. If it be only to apportion the representatives among the counties, or other convenient election districts, whether now existing, or to be instituted, according to the number of their respective electors, I should consider it as being a just and constitutional measure, and should adopt it, unless some existing or impending circumstances should render it unseasonable. I am the more inclined to this opinion by the present state of your aristocracy, which is such, as not unnaturally to excite a jealousy that it will obtain, if it has not already obtained, an undue ascendancy. The French Revolution has so discredited democracy, and it has so few influential advocates in Europe, that I doubt its giving you much more trouble. On the contrary, there seems to be a danger of its depreciating too much. Without a portion of it there can be no free government. What that portion should be in England is a question to which your constitution affords, in my opinion, the best answer. To preserve balances in times like these, is difficult ; mere palliative, *pro-hac-vice* expedients seldom produce durable good. They so frequently violate sound established principles, as rarely to prevent more trouble than they cause. The fluctuation of human affairs occasionally imposes changes on nations as well as on individuals, to which they find it necessary and prudent to accommodate, by corresponding or by countervailing changes. These, if made considerately and in season, generally conduce to security and order. Whether, during the rage and range of democracy, your aristocracy received greater accessions of strength than the public safety and sound policy required, I do not know. There seems, however, to be reason to apprehend that, when things return to a calm and settled course, the Commons will feel the influence of the Lords out-of-doors, and consequently within doors, in a greater degree than the constitution allows.   If so, that consideration becomes an argument in favour of the proposed " reform."

I will add an observation which strikes me as having weight.   Some of the boroughs appear to have degenerated into a mere mean, by which opulent political leaders supply themselves with able and active partisans and advocates.   These, although received in parliament as members, are in fact and truth the representatives of their employers, and not of the nation.   It must be admitted that these employers have often taken into their service men of great talents, and in many instances of great worth. Wise and good borough-holders, like wise and good kings, doubtless wish and endeavour to make the best appointments ; but ought either borough-holders or kings to appoint representatives for the nation ?

With great esteem and regard, and the best wishes for the prosperity of yourself and family,

I am, dear sir,

Your most obedient and faithful servant,

JOHN JAY.

JUDGE PETERS TO JAY.

BELMONT, November 25, 1810.

DEAR SIR:

When I sent you, as a token of my constant remembrance, my *melange* about the Tunis sheep, I intended to have written a letter to accompany it.   But it seems that nothing must go with a pamphlet but the mere direction, under the pains and penalties of sousing the correspondent or *addressee* in all costs of enormous postage.   It is really true, that now, for nearly six years, I have abandoned wine and all stimulants, segars and rich food included. Every thing increasing and accelerating the blood is hostile to my health, and produces my constitutional malady, an accumulation of blood on the brain. This will, at the appointed time, produce my French-leave of all sublunary things. Finding that health and rich living were incompatible, I took the resolution to abandon old habits, and have sacredly kept it. I find myself, without abstemiousness in plain food, healthy generally, and, what I think contributes much to preserve health, innocently cheerful. I have now and then (in winter the worst) attacks of vertigo, which cupping or the lancet, timely applied, remove. This, you may say, is a history of my *secrets*. You and I are on a par in age and other circumstances, and may trust one another.

Speltz is an excellent and useful grain. You can see an account of it in our first volume, p. 260. I have often sowed it ; but, unless you are near a shelling-mill, you must give it to your horses. I abandoned the culture of it only because I had to send it a great distance for this operation. There is a great variety. Some produces whiter flour than wheat; some as black as rye. *Apropos :* General Armstrong sent from Paris to me about two quarts of the most extraordinary rye I ever beheld. Under my rage for diffusion, I gave away, in all quarters of our State, spoonfuls, till I left myself only half a pint, which is now vigorously growing. I wrote to him to procure a tierce or hogshead for me ; but I suppose my letter miscarried. I shall renew my request now he has got back to us. If he can spread this rye plentifully through our country, he will do more good than all our intercourse with the French Belial has done harm. The flour of this rye is like that of wheat, and it weighs sixty-four or sixty-five pounds per bushel. All our rye has depreciated here. You must make to me some *grains of allowance* for my antithesis about French intercourse; for this has done more harm than all their rye is worth. I find myself with a *wry* face whenever I think of our Gallic prostrations.

Our second volume is nearly finished. I have been obliged to write too much, to fill up the chasms. It is too Herculean a task to keep alive agricultural publications, and I shall give up a labour which rolls back on me like the stone of Sisyphus. I have just sent the preface to the press. You will see that for lack of a more tangible monument to our departed Confucius, I have erected one out of my ink-pot, with a goose's feather. You may say, when you see it, that any one could tell the feather belonged to a goose; but it will prove the scarcity of agricultural matter even for a preface. With all this, I think it will be a good publication, and much better than I expected. The great desideratum is, to get people to read such books. I have published with the memoirs—as the players say, by particular desire—my plaster book, newly vamped. Being tormented by excuses to dozens of requests to obtain new facts on plaster—the thorough-bass being dread of criticism—I have told a story for the petty critics in the preface (pushed for matter) which will probably bring the wasps on me, and not procure a single correspondent to satisfy my agricultural curiosity. When it is finished I will send it to you. I sincerely wish you may pass a better winter than you seem to express a hope of experiencing, and am,

Most affectionately, yours,

RICHARD PETERS.

P. S. Turn Pandora's box bottom upwards, and get hope out first. Dr. Logan called on me with a new-invented micrometer, to measure the filaments of wool, whereof he was the bearer for our society. The filament sent with the instrument was $\frac{16}{10000}$ parts of an inch in fineness, and no doubt selected. My Tunis wool is considerably finer. He

says they find in England that they have over-manufac-
tured, and the rage is turning to agriculture. There is no
bullion, and paper has depreciated. He saw store cattle
that would not sell here for more than $15, sell at fairs for
£15 sterling in paper. A milch cow and calf, worth here
$25, sold for £20 sterling. A universal wish to be in friend-
ship with us was expressed by all people of all grades in
society. Lord Wellesley told him that he had in his office
proofs of an offer from Bonaparte, to *divide* this country
with England. He gives me many entertaining pieces of
information which my paper obliges me to omit.

JAY TO JUDGE PETERS.

BEDFORD, January, 1811.

DEAR SIR :

I have received your letter of the 25th November.
Although the privations you voluntarily submit to,
exceed the *ne quid nimis* of the wise man, they evince
a sound mind, and will, I hope, tend to preserve it
long in a sound body.

My inquiries respecting speltz were in terms too
general. To sow wheat here is like taking a ticket in
a lottery ; more blanks than prizes. The fly destroys
more than we reap. A substitute therefore is desirable ; and if speltz, like rye, escapes the ravages of
that insect, it might be a good one. I did not recollect that it required a particular process for cleaning ;
as we have no mill here adapted to that purpose, it
would be useless to introduce it.

From your description of the rye sent to you from
France, it appears far to exceed the kind we have. I

wish that instead of dividing it, you had sowed the whole in your own ground, and distributed parcels of the increase. It is said that the quality of rye depends greatly on that of the soil. The prevailing opinion here is, that the rye of this country is all of one and the same species, and yet in some parts the rye bread is excellent, and in others black and strong. The weight and quality of the rye you mention lead me to suspect that it is of another species, or a distinct variety. I doubt there being danger of its depreciating, unless sown too near our own, or in particular cases of neglect. I know but of one kind of grain which, notwithstanding good management, depreciates here, and that is oats.

I am glad your second volume will soon be published. I expect to read it with pleasure, especially as there has been a hand in it which can make "a goose quill diffuse the *utile* and the *dulce*" through many a page. I suppose a number will be printed for sale ; if so, be so good as to desire the bookseller to send for me six sets (comprehending both volumes) directed to my son, Peter Augustus Jay, at New York, and to name to him some person there to receive the price of them. I mean to place a set in our town library, and to distribute others among certain persons in the neighbourhood who, in my opinion, would make a proper use of them.

Among the accounts you received from Doctor Logan, there are some which I did not expect, particularly those which respect the relative state of the manufactures and agriculture of England. In the present violent fluctuations of European affairs, it does not appear to me extraordinary that bullion should occasionally be scarce, and paper depreciate, even in England. I suspect it to be merely occasional and transient; for I have heard of no adequate cause which could produce and continue to produce such effects. That nation, I am persuaded, wish to be and remain on friendly terms with us. I have some reason to believe that the idea of "dividing" is not a new one. If the micrometer is practically accurate, the inventor has done more than I should have expected.

Civil discord, it seems, is assigning to Spanish America a part in the prodigious tragedy now exhibiting on the theatre of the world. We have seen and heard of strange things, and unless you should take your "French leave" before the curtain drops, you will doubtless see and hear of many more. I expect to take my leave more deliberately, but probably more early. Be that as it may, it is a comfortable reflection that when we do, hope will be the only article in Pandora's box that we shall take with us. Although a little more indisposed than I lately was, I am still less unwell than I was at this time last year, so that at present there is some prospect of my living to see further proofs of the perfectibility of human nature by modern philosophers, and of the increased illumination of this age of reason.

Adieu, my dear sir,

Yours sincerely,

JOHN JAY.

JUDGE PETERS TO JAY.

BELMONT, February 14, 1811.

DEAR SIR:

．　　　．　　　．　　　．　　　．　　　．　　　．

You will see that I wish, in my " Plaister " [1] book, though I had no premediated plan, to get among our farmers a *memento* of Washington's private character. I touch nothing of public character but what is connected with private virtues. It was an affair of the heart. His character is the only plank left for sinking patriotism to keep itself afloat *yet a little longer*. I am always hurt when I hear anything which tends to break what remains of the *charm* his name once possessed. I would not lie to support any position, but I would not tell mischievous truths. You see I have glanced at his " Farewell Address." It was meant to take off the edge of the unnecessary *buzz* that Hamilton wrote it. I do not believe he did more than *dress* it, and most likely weave in some good things. If I had it in his handwriting (Hamilton's) I would burn it. What good does the development of this fact do? Hamilton has fame enough. He can get no more from those who admire him, of whom I am one. He will not gain a feather from his, or the enemies of Washington's principles. But those principles would lose force by being ascribed to Hamilton and deducted from Washington. The circumstance of their being found in Hamilton's writing is not complete proof. I know that they are also found in the General's own hand writing. I aver that I have heard him in conversation express most of the sentiments ; and what I say about the bundle of letters (never intended to see the light) is strictly true. Mr. King, it is said, has a copy in Hamilton's writing. But I know there is also a complete

---

[1] See vol. ii. of the " Memoirs of the Philadelphia Society for the Promotion of Agriculture." Judge Peters prefaced it with some personal recollections of Washington and extracts from his letters.

copy in that of the General, as well as heads of most of the matter previous to composing it.

What I allude to in page v of the sketch, is the loss, by Genl. Greene's well intended pertinacity, of *Fort Washington*, of which I have a full account in Genl. W's letter. The instance of the foreign minister, who found fault with his want of graciousness, was that of *Hammond*.[1]

I knew Arnold to be a scoundrel; and detected him in pilfering the public stores. He hated me on this account. In Philadelphia I discovered his peculations, and gave orders (in conjunction, I believe, with Col. Pickering, who was then with me) to the staff departments, to supply him with only his rations. This was enough to raise his gall, you may be sure. When his villainy at West Point broke out, everybody was thunderstruck except Pickering and myself, to whom it was no surprise; tho' we could not have prophesied where, or when, he would betray his trust. I mention this (not having took notice of it publickly) because both Pickering and myself thought it a very indiscreet confidence placed in Arnold. But I have a letter of the General's [Washington], which completely exculpates him, in my mind. A most worthy and influential general officer and a Member of Congress, both of New York, recommended the measure very innocently; and they were presumed highly interested in the safety of the post. Neither they nor the General could have expected so horrid an abuse of the confidence. If Genl. W. ever explained this publickly, I never met with it. I believe he avoided any such exculpation of himself at other people's expence, tho' none were to blame. But I thought the affair of Fort Washington was enough.

I know that some of my friends do not believe the General was capable of composing, as I do. But this is an affair of critical taste, which I do not value myself upon. I had

[1] Minister from England during negotiations of the Jay treaty, 1794.

an early attachment to him. I remember Braddock's army, or the remnants of it (when I was 10 or 11 years old) crossing the Schuylkill and encamping below our city, where there are now squares of elegant houses. My uncle was Secretary of the Province, and hospitable. The officers frequented our house. They (the candid part of them) spoke in high approbation of Col. Washington. They attributed their salvation to his prowess and conduct. I wondered that any but a redcoat could be a soldier; some of them used to provoke my boyish playfulness, and I told them it was a shame to let Frenchmen beat them. They replied that Frenchmen could not have done it, but the *Indians* did it. I had a mortal dread of Indians, and excused the British on that account. I had a great longing to see this provincial soldier. When I was afterwards gratified, it fixed an habitual admiration on a youthful mind.

Yours very affectionately,
RICHARD PETERS.

JAY TO JUDGE PETERS.

BEDFORD, 29th March, 1811.

DEAR SIR :

I have received your letter of the 14th ult., and also the book on Plaster-of-Paris, which you were so obliging as to send me, and for which accept my thanks.

Your letter conveyed to me the first and only information I have received, that a copy of President Washington's valedictory address had been found among the papers of General Hamilton, and in *his* handwriting ; and that a certain gentleman had also a copy of it in the *same* handwriting.

This intelligence is unpleasant and unexpected. Had the address been one of those *official* papers which, in the course of affairs, the secretary of the proper department might have prepared, and the President have signed, these facts would have been unimportant ; but it was a *personal* act—of choice, not of official duty,—and it was so connected with other obvious considerations, as that he only could with propriety write it. In my opinion, President Washington must have been sensible of this propriety, and therefore strong evidence would be necessary to make me believe that he violated it. Whether he did or did not, is a question which naturally directs our attention to whatever affords presumptive evidence respecting it ; and leads the mind into a long chain of correspondent reflections. I will give you a summary of those which have occurred to me ; not because I think them necessary to settle the point in question, for the sequel will show that they are not, but because the occasion invites me to take the pleasure of reviewing and bearing testimony to the merits of our departed friend.

Is it to be presumed from these facts, that General Hamilton was the *real*, and the President only the *reputed*, author of that address ? Although they countenance such a presumption, yet I think its foundation will be found too slight and shallow to resist that strong and full stream of counter evidence, which flows from the conduct and character of that great man,—a character not blown up into transient splendour by the breath of adulation, but, being composed of his great and memorable deeds, stands, and will forever stand, a glorious monument of human excellence.

So prone, however, is "poor human nature" to dislike and depreciate the superiority of contemporaries, that when these facts come to be generally known (and generally known they will be) many, with affected regret and hesitation, will infer and hint that Washington had less greatness of talent, and less greatness of mind, than his friends and admirers ascribed to him. Nor will the number of those be few, who, from personal or party inducements, will artfully encourage and diligently endeavour to give currency to such imputations.

On the other hand, there are men of candour and judgment (and time will increase their number) who, aiming only at truth, will cheerfully trace and follow its footsteps, and on finding, gladly embrace it. Urged by this laudable motive, they will attentively examine the history of his life; and in it they will meet with such numerous proofs of his knowledge and experience of men and things in general, and of our national affairs in particular, as to silence all doubts of his ability to conceive and express every idea in that address. A careful perusal of that history will convince them, that the principles of policy which it recommends as rules for the conduct of others, are precisely those by which he regulated his own.

There have been in the world but two systems or schools of policy; the one founded on the great principles of wisdom and rectitude, the other on cunning parts, and who brought with them to the field all the license and all the habits which they had indulged at home? Could he, by the force of orders and proclamations, have constrained them to render him that obedience, confidence, and warm attachment which he soon acquired, and which, throughout all vicissitudes and distresses, continued constant and undiminished to the last? By what other means could he have been able to frustrate the designs of dark cabals, and the unceasing intrigues of envious competitors, and the arts of the opposing enemy? By what other means could he have been able, in so masterly a manner, to meet and manage all those perplexing embarrassments which the revolutionary substitution of a new government—which the want of that power in Congress which they had not, and of that promptitude which no deliberative body can have—which the frequent destitution, and constant uncertainty of essentials supplies—which the incompetency of individuals, on whom much depended, the perfidy of others, and the mismanagement of many, could not fail to engender? We know, and history will inform posterity, that, from the first of his military career, he had to meet and encounter, and surmount. a rapid succession of formidable dfficulties, even down to the time when his country was enabled, by the success of their arms, to obtain the honourable peace which terminated the war. His high and appointed course being then finished, he disdained the intimations of lawless ambition to prolong it. He disbanded the army under circumstances which

required no common degree of policy or virtue ; and,
with universal admiration and plaudits, descended
joyfully and serenely into the shades of retirement.
They who ascribe all this to the guidance and protection of Providence, do well ; but let them recollect,
that Providence seldom interposes in human affairs
but through the agency of human means.

When, at a subsequent and alarming period, the
nation found that their affairs had gone into confusion, and that clouds, portending danger and
distress, were rising over them from every quarter,
they instituted under his auspices a more efficient
government, and unanimously committed the administration of it to him. Would they have done this
without the highest confidence in his political talents
and wisdom ? Certainly not. No novice in navigation was ever unanimously called upon to take the
helm or command of a ship on the point of running
among the breakers. This universal confidence
would have proved a universal mistake, had it not
been justified by the event. The unanimous opinion
entertained and declared by a whole people in favour
of any fellow-citizen is rarely erroneous,—especially
in times of alarm and calamity.

To delineate the course and enumerate the
measures which he took to arrive at success, would
be to write a volume. The firmness and policy with
which he overcame the obstacles placed in his way by
the derangement of national affairs, by the devices
of domestic demagogues and of foreign agents, as
well as by the deleterious influences of the French

Revolution, need not be particularized. Our records and histories and memoirs render it unnecessary. It is sufficient to say, and it can be said with truth, that his administration raised the nation out of confusion into order, out of degradation and distress into reputation and prosperity. It found us withering—it left us flourishing.

Is it to be believed that, after having thus led the nation out of a bewildered state, and guided them for many years from one degree of prosperity to another, he was not qualified, on retiring, to advise them how to proceed and go on? And what but this is the object and the burden of his valedictory address? He was persuaded that, as the national welfare had been recovered and established, so it could only be preserved and prolonged by a continued and steady adherence to those principles of sound policy and impartial justice which had invariably directed his administration. Although the knowledge of them had been spread and scattered among the people, here a little and there a little, yet, being desirous to mark even the last day of his public life by some act of public utility, he addressed and presented them to his fellow-citizens, in points of light so clear and strong, as to make deep impression on the public mind. These last parental admonitions of this father of his country were gratefully received and universally admired. But the experience of ages informs us that it is less difficult to give good advice, than to prevail on men to follow it.

Such and so obvious is the force of the preceding

was to be presented to the whole nation, and on no common occasion; it was intended for the present and future generations; it was to be read in this country, and in foreign countries; and to be criticised, not only by affectionate friends and impartial judges, but also by envious and malignant enemies. It was an address which, according as it should or should not correspond with his exalted character and fame, would either justify or impeach the prevailing opinion of his talents and wisdom. Who, therefore, can wonder that he should bestow more thought, and time, and pains on that address than on a letter?

Although in the habit of depending ultimately on his own judgment, yet no man was more solicitous to obtain and collect light on every question and measure on which he had to decide. He knew that authors, like parents, are not among the first to discover imperfections in their offspring; and that consideration would naturally induce him to imitate the example of those ancient and modern writers (among whom were statesmen, generals, and even men of consular and royal dignity) who submitted their compositions to the judgment of their friends, before they put the last hand to them. Those friends would make notes of whatever defects they observed in the draught, and of the correspondent amendments which they deemed proper. If they found that the arrangement could be improved, they would advise certain transpositions; if the connection between any of the relative parts were obscure, they would make it more apparent; if a conclusion had better be left to implica-

tion than expressed, they would strike it out, and so
vice versa ; if an additional remark or allusion would
give force or light to a sentiment or proposition, they
would propose it ; where a sentence was too long,
they would divide it ; they would correct redundances ;
change words less apt, for words more apt, etc. To
correct a composition in this way, is to do a friendly
office ; but to prepare a new one, and offer it to the
author as a substitute for his own, would deserve a
different appellation.

Among those to whose judgment and candour
President Washington would commit such an interesting and delicate task, where is the man to be found,
who would have had the hardihood to say to him in
substance, though in terms ever so nice and courtly :
Sir, I have examined and considered your draught
of an address ; it will not do ; it is really good for
nothing. But, sir, I have taken the trouble to write
a proper one for you ; and I now make you a present
of it. I advise you to adopt it and to pass it on the
world as your own ; the cheat will never be discovered,
for you may depend on my secrecy. Sir, I have inserted in it a paragraph that will give the public a
good opinion of your modesty. I will read it to you ;
it is in these words :

" In the discharge of this trust, I will only say that
I have, with good intentions, contributed towards the
organization and administration of the government
the best exertions of which a *very fallible judgment*
was capable. Not unconscious, in the outset, of the

inferiority of my qualifications, experience in my own eyes, perhaps *still more* in the eyes of *others*, has strengthened the motives to diffidence of myself."

If it be possible to find a man among those whom he esteemed, capable of offering to him such a present, it is impossible to believe that President Washington was the man to whom such a present would have been acceptable. They who knew President Washington and his various endowments, qualifications, and virtues, know that, aggregately considered, they found a *tout ensemble* which has rarely been equalled, and perhaps never excelled.

Thus much for presumptive evidence. I will now turn your attention to some that is direct.

The history (if it may be so called) of the address is not unknown to me; but as I came to the knowledge of it under implied confidence, I doubted when I first received your letter whether I ought to disclose it. On more mature reflection, I became convinced that, if President Washington were now alive and informed of the facts in question, he would not only authorize but also desire me to reduce it to writing; that when necessary it might be used to invalidate the imputations to which those facts give colour. This consideration terminated my doubts. I do not consider that a disclosure is *necessary* at this moment, but I fear such a moment will arrive. Whether I shall then be alive, or in capacity to give testimony, is so uncertain that, in order to avoid the risk of either, I shall now reduce it to writing, and commit it to your care and discretion, *de bene esse*, as the lawyers say.

Some time before the address appeared, Colonel (afterward General) Hamilton informed me that he had received a letter from President Washington, and with it the draught of a farewell address which the President had prepared, and on which he requested our opinion. He then proposed that we should fix on a day for an interview at my house on the subject. A day was accordingly appointed. On that day Colonel Hamilton attended. He observed to me, in words to this effect—that, after having read and examined the draught, it appeared to him to be susceptible of improvement—that he thought the easiest and best way was to leave the draught untouched and in its fair state ; and to write the whole over with such amendments, alterations, and corrections as he thought were advisable ; and that he had done so. He then proposed to read it, and to make it the subject of our consideration. This being agreed to, he read it ; and we proceeded deliberately to discuss and consider it, paragraph by paragraph, until the whole met with our mutual approbation ; some amendments were made during the interview, but none of much importance. Although this business had not been hastily despatched, yet, aware of the consequence of such a paper, I suggested the giving it a further critical examination ; but he declined it, saying that he was pressed for time, and was anxious to return the draught to the President without delay. It afterward occurred to me that a certain proposition was expressed in terms too general and unqualified, and I hinted it in a letter to the President.

As the business took the course above mentioned, a recurrence to the draught was unnecessary, and it was not read. There was this advantage in the course pursued—the President's draught remained (as delicacy required) fair, and not obscured by interlineations, etc. By comparing it with the paper sent with it, he would immediately observe the particular emendations and corrections that were proposed; and would find them standing in their intended places. Hence he was enabled to review and to decide on the whole matter, with much greater clearness and facility than if he had received them in separate and detached notes, and with detailed references to the pages and lines where they were advised to be introduced.

> With great esteem and regard,
> I am, dear sir,
> Your obedient servant,
> JOHN JAY.

JAY TO JOHN BRISTED.

BEDFORD, 23d April, 1811.

SIR :

Accept my thanks for the book on the " Resources of Britain," which you were so obliging as to send me. It abounds in interesting matter, and if the facts and calculations stated in it are correct, there appears to be reason to conclude that Britain has less danger to apprehend from a long-continued war than from a premature peace.

In the twelfth page there is an anecdote which seems to refer to me ; if it does, it is proper for me to observe that your information on that head is not entirely accurate. While in France I was neither present at the death nor at the funeral of any French philosopher. During my residence there, I do not recollect to have had more than two conversations with atheists about their tenets. The first was this : I was at a large party, of which were several of that description. They spoke freely and contemptuously of religion. I took no part in the conversation. In the course of it, one of them asked me if I believed in Christ ? I answered that I did, and that I thanked God that I did. Nothing further passed between me and them or any of them on that subject. Some time afterward, one of my family being dangerously ill, I was advised to send for an English physician, who had resided many years at Paris. He was said to be very skilful, but, it was added, he is an atheist. I sent for him, and had reason to think very highly of his skill. For several weeks the patient required numerous visits, so that I saw the doctor often. He was a sedate, decent man. I frequently observed him drawing the conversation towards religion, and I constantly gave it another direction. He, nevertheless, during one of his visits, very abruptly remarked that there was no God, and he hoped the time would come when there would be no religion in the world. I very concisely remarked that if there was no God there could be no moral obligations, and I did not see how society could subsist without them. He did not hesitate to admit that, if there was no God, there could be no moral obligations, but insisted that they were not necessary, for that society would find a substitute for them in enlightened self-interest. I soon turned the conversation to another topic, and he, probably perceiving that his sentiments met with a cold reception, did not afterwards resume the subject.

I am, sir,

Your obliged and obedient servant,

JoHN Jay.

JAY TO PETER VAN SCHAACK.

BEDFORD, 28th July, 1812.

DEAR SIR :

I received on Saturday last your friendly letter of the 20th inst.

No event that is highly interesting to our country can be viewed with indifference by good citizens ; and there are certain occasions when it is not only their right, but also their duty, to express their sentiments relative to public measures.

As the war has been *constitutionally* declared, the people are evidently bound to support it in the manner which *constitutional* laws do or shall prescribe.

In my opinion, the declaration of war was neither necessary, nor expedient, nor seasonable ; and I think that they who entertain this opinion do well in expressing it, both individually and collectively, on this very singular and important occasion.

As to town meetings on the subject, the expediency of them depends much on the question whether and how far the inhabitants of the town concur or disagree in sentiment. When convened, their proceedings and resolutions should be decided and firm, and they should also be temperate and decent. There are few ideas which cannot be decently dressed. Harsh and violent expressions neither convince nor persuade. A Spanish proverb says : " We cannot catch flies with vinegar."

The irascible passions, when highly excited, are difficult to control, and sometimes produce or lead to events which are to be deprecated. Commotions tending to a dissolution of the Union, or to civil war, would be serious evils. A change of measures would result from a change of rulers, and public opinion is the proper means of effecting it.

I do not hesitate to express these sentiments on proper occasions ; but it would not be pleasant to be quoted in newspapers, or hand-bills, or public speeches.

Thus, my dear sir, I have complied with your request very clearly and explicitly. It would have given me pleasure to have done this in conversation, and to have talked over with you many other matters, both old and new.

I am, my good friend,
Yours, sincerely and affectionately,
JOHN JAY.

JAY TO GOUVERNEUR MORRIS.

BEDFORD, 21st September, 1812.

DEAR MORRIS :

I received on the 19th your letter of the 11th instant.[1] The diminution of my health since I left you leaves me very little reason to expect a return of such a degree of it as would enable me to attend to any business like that in question. To undertake a task without a prospect and probability of performing it properly, is to deviate from the path of prudence.

Your revolutionary services, the general confidence in your abilities and views, your standing in society and experience in affairs, your having much to preserve or to lose, are considerations which inspire trust and create influence.

In my opinion, the president of every county, State, or national convention should be a person fitted to receive and employ *authority* consistent with the laws and constitution. This idea, if placed in certain lights, may excite perplexing apprehensions, and therefore should be discreetly used. Let us have

---

[1] Morris had written Jay as follows on a proposition to hold a public meeting in New York, disapproving of the war, and recommending a general convention of the States :

"You will have learned that on my nomination you was chosen one of the delegates of Westchester county. If you should attend the first day, you would, I doubt not, be chosen president ; but I think this would not suit you ; neither would it coincide with my project, which is that you should be one of the delegates to the general convention. Tell me frankly your view of the subject, and who is in your opinion most suitable for the president. You know that a man raised to that point will not willingly afterward fall into the ranks.

P. S.   King is to go from Queens county."

efficient leaders, and place them where they will appear to be so.

Although the place of president of the proposed convention might not be agreeable to you or to Mr. King, yet it is desirable that you or he consent to accept it. Important matters may be matured in a committee of the whole house.

The convention should extend their views to what may be, as well as what is. Prudence looks all around—*before* as well as behind. Measures to favour system and organization should be adopted. Moderation, but no timidity—wisdom, but no cunning, should mark their proceedings. When the business of the session is finished, they should *adjourn*, not dissolve, and let the president be authorized to convene them if in his judgment an occasion to render it expedient should occur. Provision should be made for a new convention after the expiration of the year, in case affairs should then require a convention.

It is possible that a convention of delegates from the friends of peace in all the States, or a certain portion of them, may become advisable. A regular correspondence between the presidents of the State conventions should be maintained, and the state of public opinion and feeling be seasonably ascertained and attended to.

The French will not relax their efforts to render our nation subservient to their designs; and their political and pecuniary means will be industriously employed to effect it.

Besides, there may perhaps be an occurrence of peculiar circumstances inviting the use of means more palpable. This may or may not be. Anything like civil war or oppression is to be deprecated ; but it would be better to meet it as not unexpected, than be taken by surprise, or submit to be slaves or victims.

They who sail in hurricane seasons and latitudes should be prepared and vigilant.

Present my compliments and best wishes to Mrs. Morris.

Yours sincerely,
JOHN JAY.

JAY TO REV. CALVIN CHAPIN.

BEDFORD, 2d December, 1812.

REV. SIR:

I received by the last mail your letter of the 19th September, containing a copy of " An Act to Incorporate the American Board of Commissioners of Foreign Missions," and an abstract from their minutes, purporting, that at a meeting of the Board in September last, I had been elected a member of it.

Such institutions become the religion we profess, and the blessings we enjoy. Be pleased to assure the Board that I am very sensible of the honour they have done me ; and that I wish it was as much in my power, as it is in my inclination, to attend their meetings and take an active part in the business committed to them. For several years my health has been declining, and my age, as well as the nature of my complaints, do not permit me to expect the restoration of it.

Reflecting that they who consent to accept a place or office do impliedly engage to perform the duties of it, I think it right to delare my inability to perform those in question. If, therefore, any active services should be expected from me, I hope and request that the Board will consider themselves at liberty to give to this declaration the effect of a resignation, and proceed to elect another in my stead.

I am, reverend sir,

Your most obedient servant,

JOHN JAY.

JAY TO REV. DR. MORSE.

BEDFORD, 1st January, 1813.

DEAR SIR :

Accept my thanks for your friendly letter of the 17th ult., and for the sermon and report which accompanied it.

Whether our religion permits *Christians* to vote for *infidel* rulers, is a question which merits more consideration than it seems yet to have generally received, either from the clergy or the laity. It appears to me, that what the prophet said to Jehoshaphat about his attachment to Ahab,[1] affords a salutary lesson on another interesting topic.

Although the mere *expediency* of public measures may not be a proper subject for the pulpit, yet, in my opinion, it is the right and the duty of our pastors to press the observance of all moral and religious duties,

[1] "Shouldest thou help the ungodly, and love them that hate the Lord?" —2 *Chron.* xix., 2.

and to animadvert on every course of conduct which may be repugnant to them.

The Rev. Mr. Chapin informed me, that the American Board of Commissioners for Foreign Missions had done me the honour to elect me one of the members of it, and has also been so obliging as to send me copies of their last report. Institutions like this are not only to be approved and commended, but also to be sustained and assisted. As the declining state of my health will not permit me to render any active service, I feared that by retaining a place at the Board, I should exclude some other person who would be more useful. My answer, therefore, to Mr. Chapin referred it to the Board to do therein as they may judge proper.

The amount of the subscriptions exceeds what I had supposed, and manifests a spirit which I hope will become more universal.

Permit me to request the favour of you to procure for me two complete sets of the *Panoplist*, and to put my name on the list of subscribers for *two* of each of the future numbers. I propose to place one set of them in our town library : some good may result from it.

Such is your knowledge and information relative to the United States and their affairs, that I regret your finding it inconvenient to undertake the history you allude to. That it will be written at some future day is probable ; but when, or how well performed, is uncertain. Time will not wait, but will proceed in its usual way to impair memory, to diminish and obscure evidence, to introduce doubt, and enable error to impose on credulity, and acquire credit from currency. I presume, therefore, that a history (except as to great outlines) is the less to be depended upon, as its date is remote from the period of the transactions which it undertakes to narrate. How few have the talents, the patient diligence, and the love of truth which history requires.

The aspect of the times certainly continues portentous. To hope for the best and prepare for the worst, is a trite but a good maxim ; especially when associated with the reflection that He who governs the world can restrain the wrath of man as well as the rage of the ocean. It is a favourable circumstance, that the delusion which, like an epidemic, has prevailed throughout our country, is abating in many of the States. Calamities sometimes afford good remedies for national distempers.

My retirement has not disappointed me. As to my health, a complaint in the liver has for several years been impairing it. Medical prescriptions failing to remove it, relief could only be sought from palliatives ; and among these I find temperance, patience, and resignation to be the best.

I am glad, for her sake and for yours, that Mrs. Morse enjoys good health. I hope you do also. That you may both live to see many happy returns of this day, is very sincerely the wish of

Dear sir,

Your faithful friend,

JOHN JAY.

JAY TO JEREMIAH EVARTS.

BEDFORD, 12th January, 1813.

SIR :

I have received your obliging letter of the 30th ult. The oration which came with it abounds in just sentiments, handsomely expressed.

The copies of the report, which you had the goodness to send, have come to hand.

Many considerations would make it agreeable to me to attend the meeting of the Board at Boston. I have heretofore found and enjoyed excellent society in that city, and although I should feel the absence of several worthy persons, who have removed to the " city not made with hands," yet others remain whom it would give me pleasure to meet.

Notwithstanding the inducements I had to make frequent visits to New York, I have not been there for four years past. The state of my health, and the regimen it requires, not permitting me to be far or long from home.

It is certainly desirable that those of our fellow-citizens who are friendly to foreign missions should contribute to repair the loss of the mission printing-office at Serampore. It appears from a late paper that measures for that purpose were taking at New York, and there is reason to hope and expect that the aggregate amount of the collections will be considerable.

The mode of remitting it to India is of some importance. To me it appears advisable that all American missionary measures should, as far as circumstances may admit, be connected with the

American Board for Foreign Missions. I therefore think that the money in question should be remitted to India accordingly. If we were at peace with England, I should prefer having it remitted by the Board, to the missionary society there, and through them to India. Mutual confidence and good-will between societies instituted for the same purpose, and actuated by similar motives of benevolence, should be cultivated.

Having for some days past been less well than usual, I find myself constrained to be more concise than I intended when I began this letter.

With sentiments of esteem and regard,

I am, dear sir,

Your obedient servant,

JOHN JAY.

GOUVERNEUR MORRIS TO JAY.

MORRISANIA, 15th February, 1813.

MY DEAR FRIEND:

Last Tuesday evening my wife was delivered of a boy. I communicate that event because I believe it will give you pleasure. Moreover, I wish you to be one of his godfathers. True it is that, according to the usual course, you may not be able to perform the duties of that office ; but, my friend, should you be mingled with the dust, he shall learn, from the history of your life, that a man must be truly pious to be truly great. I do not fix the day, because I wish you to come on in a fortnight or three weeks, when it best suits your convenience. I will then summon the priest and the other sponsors.

Yours truly,

GOUVERNEUR MORRIS.

JAY TO GOUVERNEUR MORRIS.

BEDFORD, 22d February, 1813.

My good Friend:

I thank you for informing me by your letter of the 15th inst. that you had received "an heritage and gift," which doubtless filled your heart with joy and gratitude.

It would give me pleasure to present in person to you and Mrs. Morris my gratulations on the occasion ; but since the winter began I have not been abroad, and this confinement will, as usual, continue until warm weather. I hope Mrs. Morris and the "spes altera" are doing well, and that the emotions they excite are not interrupted by gout or anxiety.

You request me to be one of the godfathers. Baptism is too generally regarded as being little more than a customary ceremony ; and yet the purpose of it, and the *names* used on the occasion, show it to be a solemn procedure. It confers privileges, and imposes obligations of the highest class. Whoever consents to be employed as a shepherd should recollect that, if a lamb be lost by his negligence, he must answer for it to the owner of the flock. Sponsors, however, not unfrequently become such, with as little sense of personal responsibility, as actors on the stage make the engagements, etc., allotted to their parts.

Had I the prospect of residing here many years I should feel no reluctance, for I should find in my heart and mind sufficient inducements to fulfil the duties in question, in case they should eventually be incumbent on me. But as I expect to remove, at a more early period, to a distant country, where I shall not be in a capacity to attend to persons or things here, it appears to me advisable that some proper person not so circumstanced should be selected.

It is an agreeable circumstance that you will probably continue at Morrisania for many years, and have time and health to prepare the young gentleman to make a figure there, as well as at the more valuable habitation and estate which will, in his baptism, be offered to him by his Sovereign.

That you and he may, here and ever, be happy in and with each other, is the fervent wish of

Your friend,

JOHN JAY.

JAY TO THE REV. JOSEPH M'KEAN.

BEDFORD, 14th April, 1813.

REV. SIR :

I received on Saturday last the interesting letter which you did me the favour to write on the 31st ult., together with the two pamphlets which you were so obliging as to send with it.

Marks of respect to the characters of such men as Dr. Elliot, not only tend to console their afflicted relatives, but also to cherish the virtues by which they were distinguished. Unhappily, there is too much reason for the common remark, that obituary commendations by anonymous writers are so frequently misapplied as to be worth very little. The sermon (as was proper) describes the Doctor's character in general terms, but the testimony which it bears to his merit is ample, clear, and decided ; and, considering from whom it comes, leaves no room for doubt or scruple.

As the intended memoir, to contain a more detailed account of Dr. Elliot, is to be published in the next volume of "Historical Collections," and consequently under the auspices of the society, it will be appreciated by that circumstance, and doubtless have also the advantage of being written in a manner worthy of the subject and of such respectable patrons. This will be bestowing merited praise in a handsome manner. Not a few of the name, and I presume of the same family, of Elliot, have in this country laboured faithfully in promoting the best interests of man. Their services will be remembered in heaven, and ought not to be forgotten on earth. I feel for the Doctor's family. Death daily severs many tender ties . . . but not forever.

I thank you very sincerely for your kind offers of service, and with pleasure reciprocate them. They prompt me to request the favour of you to send me the first volume of the new series, as well as the tenth volume, mentioned in my letter to Dr. Elliot.

I am, reverend sir,

Your much obliged and obedient servant,

JOHN JAY.

JAY TO NOAH WEBSTER.

BEDFORD, 31st May, 1813.

SIR :

I received by the last mail your letter of the 19th inst. The circumstances mentioned in it cannot be regarded with indifference by those who wish you well ; and I feel as well as think so.

It is not improbable that doubts prevail respecting the design and tendency of the work you have in hand. The literary productions of Britain and America being interesting to each other, many are of opinion, and I concur in it, that the English language and its orthography should be the same in both countries. Apprehensions have been entertained that your dictionary would tend to impair that sameness ; and those apprehensions may, to a certain degree, have had an unfavourable influence.

The progress of the subscription having been so long suspended, I think it better to enclose what I intended to subscribe, than trouble your agents at New York with it.

If any plan to render your prospects more promising, and in my power to promote, should be adopted, be pleased to communicate it to me.

I am, sir,

Your obedient servant,

JOHN JAY.

NOAH WEBSTER TO JAY.

AMHERST, June 9th, 1813.

SIR :

For your favour of the 31st ult. with the enclosed bill, be pleased to accept my most grateful acknowledgments. The interest you have manifested in my labours, and the liberality accompanying it, are the more acceptable, as they have been unsolicited.

It is not improbable that some ill-founded apprehensions that I might attempt changes of orthography, have had their effect in preventing subscriptions; but there are several other causes.

On the subject of orthography, gentlemen might have been easy, as any considerable changes must prevent the sale and use of a work of this sort, and they might rationally conclude that I would not put myself to an immense trouble and expense, to write a book which would not find purchasers.

My plan is different from anything before attempted. I have examined and collated the radical words in twenty languages, including the seven Asiatic languages, or rather dialects of the Assyrian stock. This will enable me to explain many things in the English language which have hitherto been obscure. Indeed, this research has opened a field entirely new, and it is probable will lead to many important discoveries, not only in the origin and affinity of languages, but in history sacred and profane.

The price of the work cannot be known at present; but if I live to complete it, I shall not only present you a copy, but hold myself answerable to refund the principal of the sum advanced.

With gratitude and respect, I am, sir,

Your obedient servant,

N. WEBSTER.

RUFUS KING TO JAY.

JAMAICA, L. I., June 20, 1814.

DEAR SIR:

It is the wish of our friends in the City, that you should join with them, in the proposed celebration of the overthrow and expulsion of Bonaparte: many considerations, which seem to me of no ordinary importance, induce me to hope that you will unite with us on this occasion. Mr. Morris will deliver an oration; notwithstanding our admiration of his rare talents, and extensive information, I should, I confess, like that you and I should see the discourse before it is pronounced. Cannot this be brought about? With the highest respect and regards,

I am, Dear Sir,
Your obedient and faithful servant,
RUFUS KING.

JAY TO RUFUS KING.

BEDFORD, 23d June, 1814.

DEAR SIR:

I this moment received your obliging letter of the 20th inst. I sincerely rejoice in the events to which you allude, and should be happy to join our friends in the proposed celebration of them.

In the course of the last winter my disorder was unusually mild, but in the spring I was taken with an influenza, succeeded by a distressing cough, which has enfeebled me so much that I cannot as yet ride more than a mile or two at a time without fatigue. The oration will doubtless correspond with the acknowledged talents of the author. The subject certainly has bearings on and toward topics which prudential considerations render delicate, and which it is desirable should be treated accordingly. I presume it will be committed to your consideration, and that, under a joint revision, it will be freed from any ideas or expressions of doubtful expediency which in the haste of composition may have escaped uncorrected.

Circumstanced as I am, I can only thank my friends for thinking of me; and express my regret

· that I cannot be with them on so joyful an occasion. Unless I regain more health and strength than I at present enjoy, I cannot promise myself the satisfaction of seeing my friends anywhere but here ; and here it will always give me pleasure to see them. It cannot be necessary to say that I remember you among them, or that I am, with the best wishes for your health and prosperity,

Dear sir,

Your obedient servant,

JOHN JAY.

WILLIAM JAY TO JAY.

BLOOMINGDALE, August 11, 1814.

MY DEAR FATHER:

We returned this week from Rockaway, and I believe our time there has not been misspent. Augusta's health is certainly improved and her appetite and strength much increased.

.   .   .   .

Some alarm seems to prevail respecting the safety of the City, but I know not how well it is founded.   The Citizens are now engaged in throwing up entrenchments at Brooklyn. There is a great scarcity of money, and stock of all kinds is very low.   The stock of *four* of the Banks,·viz.: the Union, the Manufacturing, the City, and the Bank of America, is even below par and some as low as 94. The Bank of America and the Manufacturing Bank have not declared *any dividend* and therefore instead of giving an interest of 9 per cent. for the last year, they have yielded only $4\frac{1}{2}$. Notwithstanding this state of things and the consequent diminution in the income of great numbers of individuals, both in town

and country, I can see no change in the manner of living,
nor more attention than usual to economy. People seem
to be now living on their capital and to calculate that before
it is exhausted the return of peace will more.than repair any
inroads they may make on it in the interim. I yesterday
saw Peter; he appeared very well but had scarcely time to
speak to me. I heard no news.

Remember Augusta and myself most affectionately to our
dear sisters, and believe me,

Dear Father,

Your very affectionate Son,

WILLIAM JAY.

TIMOTHY PICKERING TO JAY.

CITY OF WASHINGTON, Oct. 22d, 1814.

DEAR SIR:

I have done myself the honour to make up three packets
addressed to you, this day, containing the despatches from
our ministers from Ghent, their instructions, and the statement of the new secretary of the treasury of his plan of
taxes, and his project of a national bank.

While the proposition respecting an Indian boundary was
declared to be a *sine qua non*, the boundary itself admitted
of modification; and as within it, we are called upon to
relinquish only our *right* of *pre-emption* to the *Indians*, who
are *proprietors of the soil*, I see no objection to it. Without
such demand, *good policy* would require such relinquishment
to prevent encroachments on the Indians, and thereby the
renewal of hostilities; and the dispersion of our citizens
over immense regions, defensible only at insupportable
expense, while we have so many millions of acres of good
lands remaining without inhabitants.

I am disposed to believe that with less pride in rulers and
ministers, and with less hatred to Great Britain in both, the

British propositions might have been made the basis of a negotiation which, governed by wisdom and prudence, might have terminated in peace. With very great respect and esteem,

I am, dear sir, your obedient servant,

TIMOTHY PICKERING.

JAY TO TIMOTHY PICKERING.

BEDFORD, 1st November, 1814.

DEAR SIR :

Accept my thanks for your letter of the 22d ult., and for the papers which you were so good as to send ; they arrived by the last mail.

It is to be regretted that passions, unfavourable to mutual good-will, have for years been industriously and unwisely excited both in Great Britain and America. An inveterate delusion has long prevailed in our country. Providence has made it a scourge for our chastisement, and we well deserve it.

Every independent nation has, as such, a rightful and exclusive jurisdiction over the country within its acknowledged boundary lines. For either nation to propose to the other a system of measures for the security and comfort of the Indians dwelling within their contiguous and respective territories, or for other mutual good purposes, can neither be offensive nor improper ; but to *dictate* such propositions, and to tell us that we *must* accede to them as the price of peace, is to assume a language rarely used unless by the victorious to the vanquished.

It is not clear to me that Britain did *then* expect or desire to conclude the war quite so soon. As to her present or future disposition to peace, or how far it has been or may be affected by a settled or by a still fluctuating state of things in Europe, or by calculations of our becoming more united or more divided, cannot now be known. If we should change our rulers, and fill their places with men free from blame, the restoration of peace might doubtless be more easily accomplished. Such a change will come, but not while the prevailing popular delusion continues to deceive and mislead so great a portion of our citizens.

Things being as they are, I think we cannot be too perfectly united in a determination to defend our country, nor be too vigilant in watching and resolutely examining the conduct of the administration in all its departments, candidly and openly giving decided approbation or decided censure, according as it may deserve the one or the other. Report says that in the public expenditures there has been great culpability; it is desirable therefore that they be thoroughly investigated, and that the results be authenticated and published in such a manner as to obviate doubt and disbelief.

I have just read Mr. King's speech; they who complain that it exhibits too little of the *suaviter in modo*, cannot also complain that it exhibits too little of the *fortiter in re.*

With constant esteem and regard, I am, dear sir,

Your obedient servant,

JOHN JAY.

JAY TO JUDGE PETERS.

BEDFORD, 9th January, 1815.

DEAR SIR:

It is a great while since any letters have passed between us; perhaps some of them have miscarried. The season reminds me that I have survived the last year, and that I have left with it a great number who enjoyed more health and strength. Many friendly wishes have, as usual, been reciprocated on this occasion, but it seems to be questionable whether an average proportion of them will be realized. Public adversity, you know, is at variance with individual happiness; and it has not yet become very probable that this will be a happy year to our country. I should rejoice to find myself mistaken, but I cannot be persuaded that general prosperity will be restored while our nation continues to be misled by the delusions which caused and which prolong our calamities. We have not only declared war unwisely, but have also unwisely (though not unwittingly) excited disgust and resentment. How far angry passions will retard the return of peace may be conjectured rather than calculated. We are yet to learn whether the result of the negotiations at Vienna will impede or promote those at Ghent. While the former are pending, I suspect that Britain will not be anxious to obviate delays. To me, personally, these things cannot long be very interesting, but I feel for those whom I shall leave behind me. You are in the way of knowing more about our national affairs than I am, and I sincerely wish that your views of them may be more consoling than mine are.

My health continues to wear away, but I seldom suffer severe pain. Conversation, books, and recollections still enable me, with the blessing of Providence, to amuse confinement, and to glide on placidly towards that ocean to which the stream of time is bearing us all.

Tell me how you do. With constant esteem and regard, I am, dear sir,

Your very humble servant,

JOHN JAY.

JUDGE PETERS TO JAY.

BELMONT, Jan. 19th, 1815.

MY DEAR SIR:

Your very welcome letter of the 9th inst. I received at the moment I was contemplating sending to you our third volume of Agricultural Memoirs, as a small token of remembrance. I shall, by the first opportunity, have it forwarded to you. A few of us endeavour to keep this subject alive amid the din of arms, which are ever hostile to the arts of peace and their attendant blessings. Too much of this effort falls on me ; but yet some relief from surrounding glooms is found in attention to topics which abstract the mind from the vices and follies plentifully scattered throughout our devoted country. Mortification under what *we are*, is at least for the moment suspended, while we contemplate on what we *have been*. It may return with double force, when we consider *what we might have been.*

But it seems that history affords ample proofs, and ours as much as any other, that "this world was made for Cæsar." The enjoyment of liberty is fugacious ; but despotism, under a variety of shapes, is permanent. There is a tendency to it in all human political institutions ; and the people of every country have, from time immemorial, forged their own chains. Our "free and enlightened" citizens are now very busy at the anvil; but whether their work will now be completed, is not for us to decide. Heaven may send us chastisement without ruin, and possibly the former may save us for a time. Delusion is the order of the day. Gordon, in one of his discourses on Tacitus, endeavours to prove that the people, when deceived by *deluders*, are blind and cruel, yet mean well. Too many of our people are blind, yet few cruel; as to their *meaning well*, they take a lamentable mode of showing it.

Your letter contains an epitome of my thoughts on our political situation. Had I *written a book* (and I have no adversary who would think it worth his while to wish that I had), I could not express myself more clearly on the subject. At *our* age we are lookers-on, and see the game better than those who play it. The insight which calm observation and experience afford is, however, of no use to those who deem themselves too wise to need instruction. We must wait events, like passengers in a bark buffeted by storms, and mismanaged by unskilful pilots and mariners. I hope our vessel is yet staunch, and that she will get into port, whatever untoward appearances may predict. It is indeed distressing when *hope* alone is our comforter. But, alas! all I know is far from furnishing light or brilliancy to the threatening and dusky cloud which overhangs our hemisphere.

Our president is not the man we once supposed him. Party antipathies may possibly paint in too sombre colours; but the stories I hear are distressing, particularly to me, who in early times had a sincere personal friendship for him. He would *then* take some strange flights: *one* of them was his joining in the philippic against you, for not consulting the French minister (Vergennes), when the interest of your country forbade the step. But, in general, I thought and acted with him. In this matter, far otherwise; nor have I, in his modern conduct, been in union with his political sentiments on any important subject, although I entertain no personal enmity.

I have a strong impression that we shall, ere long, have peace; but the why and the wherefore I cannot tell, save that there seems nothing really substantial enough in the litigated affairs of the two nations, to continue the business of throat-cutting; and I fancy our enemy is tired of the employment, after following the trade so long.

I am gratified with the account of your travelling on towards the goal we all must arrive at, with a mind tranquil, and a body without pain. Your companions—books and recollections—are consolatory and essential, when all others have lost their relish.

I thank you for your kind inquiries about my health. I have but lately recovered from a most unfortunate accident, having been thrown on the stones of our turnpike from my horse, who took fright and ran away with me. He was a *Kentucky* racer (a quality I did not know), and no doubt took his revenge for his countrymen, by chastising me for my bad politics. I had three trenched gashes in my pericranium; yet I escaped becoming *cracked-brained*, which may be reckoned uncivil, as it is fashionable nowadays, at least among politicans; and it is the ton to be in the fashion. Believe me always

Most affectionately yours,

RICHARD PETERS.

JAY TO REV. DR. MORSE.

BEDFORD, 14th February, 1815.

DEAR SIR:

On the 4th inst. I received by the mail from New York your interesting letter of the 17th ult. I have read the pamphlets communicated to me by Mr.

Grant, and derived from them the only knowledge I have of the transactions noticed in them. It would not be easy to introduce into my mind doubts of your rectitude. My opinion of it has undergone no alterations. You are drawing consolation from a source which always affords it.

As to the work you mention, I am glad you have undertaken it, because it is desirable, and because I expect it will be well performed. It would give me pleasure to afford the aids you request, but the state of my health admits of very little exertion of mind or body. I can neither read nor write much at a time, without bringing on a feverish weariness.

My public life did not commence so early as you supposed. In 1766 I was a clerk in a lawyer's office, and on leaving it was occupied in professional affairs until the year 1774, when I was sent to the first Congress. In 1775 I was also in Congress; in 1776 the Convention of this State detained me with them. In 1778 I was again sent to Congress, and remained there until September, 1779, when I was sent to Europe. In 1784 I returned home.

From this statement, you will perceive that my knowledge of the important events which occurred before the year 1774 cannot be particular.

The difficulty of collecting materials, and of ascertaining their real value, will increase with time. There are very few of the well-informed official men of those days now alive, and the few who remain will in a few years more be gone. To you I need not remark that many things have been written and said which are not correct. The collection of materials (if nothing to perfect it be left undone) will cost much time, trouble, and expense. Some information may be acquired by letters, but much more and much better may be obtained by personal inspections, applications, and interviews.

Valuable materials exist in the office of the Secretary of State, in the public and *private* journals of Congress, and among the papers of the several States, etc.

You know my sentiments respecting history,— *festina lente.* No good history has been, nor can be, produced in haste.

I regret the impediments which deprived me of the pleasure of the visit you intended. I hope some favourable opportunity of making it will yet occur, and that Mrs. Morse may come with you. We will then converse on these topics, and I will readily communicate to you such materials among those I possess as you may deem interesting.

Be so obliging as to assure Mr. and Mrs. Evarts of my best wishes for the health and prosperity of themselves and their family. I am glad their little boy is doing well. May he long continue to do so in every respect.

I am, dear sir,

Yours very sincerely,

JOHN JAY.

JAY TO JUDGE PETERS.

BEDFORD, WESTCHESTER COUNTY,
14th March, 1815.

DEAR SIR:

On reading your interesting letter of the 19th January, I observed with particular pleasure, from the manner and matter of it, that, notwithstanding the winter of life, and snow falling on your head, you endure like an evergreen.

Your impression that "we should, ere long, have peace" has been verified. If I remember right, you had heretofore an impression that Spain, although her case was apparently desperate, would get safe through her danger; and so it came to pass. Events having justified both these impressions or opinions, I wish you may have another, viz., that the peace will terminate the delusion which caused the war. Several considerations incline me to expect that the peace will *diminish* it, and particularly these:

Unless discontents should arise between France and Britain, French influence will not soon be *very* active in America; and, consequently, will not administer much fuel to renew and feed a flame against England. The peace will deprive the delusion of the sustenance it derived from the patronage which the war created.

The abandonment of the *professed* objects of the war, and that without compensation either in fact or expectation—the manifest incapacity and profusion with which the war has been conducted—the attempts to force supplies of men and money by conscription, etc.—and the immense debt incurred and to be paid, without any *value received*,—all tend to withdraw confidence and good-will from our political projectors; nor can the continuance and operation of war-taxes be congenial with the feelings of a people who, if pagans, would dedicate more temples to Plutus than to Minerva.

These, and the like facts and considerations, will doubtless have the most weight with that portion of the community who have been misled, but who really mean well. They will probably have some effect also on the more considerate of the others. As to the position, that "the people always mean well," or, in other words, that they always mean to say and to do what they believe to be right and just,—it may be popular, but it cannot be true. The word *people*, you know, applies to all the individual inhabitants of a country, collectively considered. That portion of them who individually mean well never was, nor until the millennium will be, considerable. We have not heard of any country, in which the great mass of the inhabitants individually and habitually adhere to the dictates of their consciences. We know how well demagogues and pharisaical patriots mean. Having much of the wisdom of this world, and little of that of the other, they will, like their great predecessor Absalom, always mean and act accordingly.

Besides, Providence sometimes chastises nations with physical epidemics, and sometimes (by "choosing their delusions") with moral epidemics, and after a while removes them. This encourages hope; for if we have arrived at or near the *pessimum* of this evil, the *melius* cannot be far distant.

Accept my thanks for the book you were so kind as to send me. I have found some good things in it, and shall doubtless find more. Many of our citizens, who are more than mere farmers, have of late years improved our agriculture. Would not a good American edition of "Columella" be acceptable to them? It gratifies curiosity, by showing the state of agriculture at a remote period; and, on several topics, affords information which will be useful at any period.

I am glad you escaped and recovered so well from the accident you mention. Kentucky racers, both literal and figurative, will, it seems, have their capers. It would be no loss to the public if some of them were at the plough. Seek for "some honest, sober beast, that full softly treads," and will not mar your meditations.

Adieu, my dear sir,

Yours affectionately,

JOHN JAY.

JAY TO REV. JOHN M. MASON, D.D.

BEDFORD, 22d May, 1816.

DEAR SIR:

Accept my thanks for the friendly letter, and for the book [1] which you were so obliging as to send me by my son. I have made some progress in reading it. The *principle* I approve, and am glad it has employed a pen very able to do it justice.

_____

[1] "A Plea for Catholic Communion."

Had all uninspired expositors been content with the simplicity of the gospel, and not been wise above what is written, the Church would probably have suffered less than it has from worldly wisdom and scholastic subtleties.

With the best wishes for the health and prosperity of yourself and family, I am, dear sir,

Your friend,
JOHN JAY.

JAY TO REV. DR. ROMEYN.

BEDFORD, 12th June, 1816.

REV. SIR:

Your letter of the 1st inst., informing me that I had been elected one of the vice-presidents of the American Bible Society, arrived by the last mail.

I rejoice in the institution of that national society, and assure the Board of Managers that I am very sensible of the honour they have done me in thus connecting me with it.

The events and circumstances under which such societies have been established and multiplied, in my opinion, indicate an origin which makes it the duty of all Christians to unite in giving them decided patronage and zealous support.

I have the honour to be, with respect and esteem, Rev. sir,

Your obedient servant,
JOHN JAY.

JAY TO SIR JOHN SINCLAIR.

BEDFORD, WESTCHESTER COUNTY, N. Y.,
8th August, 1816.

DEAR SIR :

I have received the papers which you were so obliging as to send me. Accept my thanks for them. Gratitude is due to those who employ their time and talents in promoting the common welfare. Your exertions to improve agriculture, and render it more productive, are known and acknowledged. The paper on " mildew in wheat," I have sent to New York to be published. The multitude of interesting facts which have been collected during the last twenty years doubtless furnish materials for a comprehensive system of husbandry ; such a work, ably executed, would be useful.

Credit is also due to your endeavours to make known and excite attention to the means which conduce to health and longevity. The proposed edition of the code on these subjects, in one octavo volume, will be better calculated for general use and extensive circulation, than the larger work from which it is to be extracted. I hope it will soon be finished and find its way to this country. It must be an agreeable reflection to you, that you have been " diligent in well-doing."

My health has for years been declining, and my age reminds me that the re-establishment of it is not to be expected. What you have written of the flesh-brush will induce me to use it more frequently. It can do no harm and may do good, and that is no inconsiderable recommendation.

With the best wishes that your health and longevity may be such as to give additional weight to your remarks respecting them,

I am, dear sir,

Your faithful and obedient servant,

JOHN JAY.

JAY TO JOHN MURRAY, JUN.

BEDFORD, 12th October, 1816.

Accept, my good friend, my thanks for your kind letter of the 22d ult., and for the pamphlets enclosed with it. They came to my hands on the 2d inst. The state of my health is such, that I can read or write but little at a time without fatigue; and, therefore, I cannot prudently venture on the task you recommend.

Whether war of *every* description is prohibited by the gospel, is one of those questions on which the excitement of any of the passions can produce no light. An answer to it can result only from careful investigation and fair reasoning.

It appears to me that the gospel not only recognizes the whole moral law, and extends and perfects our knowledge of it, but also enjoins on *all* mankind the observance of it. Being ordained by a legislator of *infinite* wisdom and rectitude, and in whom there is "no variableness," it must be free from imperfection, and therefore never has, nor ever will require amendment or alteration. Hence I conclude that the moral law is exactly the same now that it was before the flood.

That all those wars and fightings are unlawful, which

proceed from culpable desires and designs (or in Scripture language from lusts), on the one side or on the other, is too clear to require proof. As to wars of an opposite description, and many such there have been, I believe they are as lawful to the unoffending party in our days, as they were in the days of Abraham. He waged war against and defeated the five kings. He piously dedicated a tenth of the spoils; and, instead of being blamed, was blessed.

What should we think of a human legislator who should authorize or encourage infractions of his own laws? If wars of every kind and description are prohibited by the moral law, I see no way of reconciling such a prohibition with those parts of Scripture which record institutions, declarations, and interpositions of the Almighty which manifestly evince the contrary. If *every* war is sinful, how did it happen that the *sin* of waging *any* war is not specified among the numerous sins and offences which are mentioned and reproved in both the Testaments?

To collect and arrange the many facts and arguments which relate to this subject would require more time and application than I am able to bestow. The aforegoing are hinted merely to exhibit some of the reasons on which my opinion rests.

It certainly is very desirable that a pacific disposition should prevail among all nations. The most effectual way of producing it is by extending the prevalence and influence of the gospel. *Real* Christians will abstain from violating the rights of others, and therefore will not provoke war.

Almost all nations have peace or war at the will and pleasure of rulers whom they do not elect, and who are not always wise or virtuous. Providence has given to our people the choice of their rulers, and it is the duty as well as the privilege and interest of our Christian nation to select and prefer Christians for their rulers.

The sentiment expressed in the extract from your brother's letter corresponds with his benevolent disposition. He has been "diligent in well-doing," and his works will not cease to receive, as well as deserve, commendation. When you write to him, assure him of my esteem and regard.

I thank you for the kind wishes expressed in the conclusion of your letter. They refer to topics on which I have been accustomed to meditate, and are far more important than any which belong to this transient scene.

With the best wishes for your welfare, in the most enlarged sense,

I remain, your obliged friend,

JOHN JAY.

JAY TO GOUVERNEUR MORRIS.

BEDFORD, 28th October, 1816.

DEAR MORRIS :

Having heard much of your discourse before the New York Historical Society, it gave me pleasure to receive a copy of it, and to find from the direction that I owed it to your friendly attention. It abounds in interesting remarks ; the diction is elevated throughout, perhaps in some instances beyond the proportion which the topics bear to each other. In landscape, we prefer hill and dale to a plain, however ornamented ; and in a field of eloquence it is agreeable to behold sublimities sloping down into Attic simplicity. I doubt the correctness of saying that Franklin averted thunderbolts from *protected* dwellings. In my opinion, the invention of steamboats is a subject on which it is less difficult to say handsome than sublime things. To me it does not appear probable that the sight of them on Asiatic waters can so powerfully affect the feelings of the Genius of Asia, as to impel him to bow with grateful reverence (not gratulation) to the inventive spirit of America ; and that, too, at the very moment when his eye, glancing over the ruins of cities, which for ages had concurred in proclaiming his superiority in the arts, must remind him of his dignity. I make no apology for these hints ; you know what prompts them.

Your strictures on the defects of history, and the causes of them, are well founded. Whether future historians, with all their advantages, will excel their predecessors in accuracy, and caution, and candour, is a point on which my expectations are not sanguine. For my part, I believe there neither is, nor will be, more than *one* history free from error.

Of that history the discourse has availed itself very ingeniously, deducing from it lessons instructive to all, and new to many. I have often wished that the accounts given in it of the primitive ages had been more particular We know but little about them, and our curiosity must remain ungratified while we remain here. I say *here*, because when we join our ancestors, we shall doubtless learn from them all that we may wish to know respecting the affairs and events of their days. In this and other respects I promise myself much satisfaction from their society, and that at a period which cannot be very distant. The term of my lease has expired, and I have no reason to expect that my continuing to hold over will be of more than ordinary duration. It is consoling to reflect that we *tenants* are informed *where* and *how* we may go and settle in perpetuity, and are assured that our possessions and enjoyments there, instead of being precarious and transitory, will be certain and permanent.

That you and I, and those who are near and dear to us, may be enabled to say with the poet, but in a higher and better sense, " omnes metus, strepitumque Acherontis avari subjicit pedibus," is the fervent wish of your affectionate friend,

JOHN JAY.

I hope our little boy advances in strength, and growth of body and mind.

JOHN ADAMS TO JAY.

QUINCY, Jan. 9th, 1818.

DEAR SIR :

Sketches of the Life and Character of Patrick Henry, by William Wirt, of Richmond, Virginia, have been sent to me by Mr. Shaw, of the Athenæum. My family are reading it to me every evening, and though we have not finished it, we have proceeded far enough to excite an earnest desire to know your opinion of it.

There is in section fourth, page 108, a passage which no man now living but yourself can explain. I hope you have read the volume; but as it is possible you may not have seen it, the paragraph is this:

" A petition to the king, an address to the people of Great Britain, and a memorial to the people of British America, were agreed to be drawn. Mr. Lee, Mr. Henry, and others were appointed for the first; Mr. Lee, Mr. Livingston, and Mr. Jay for the two last. The splendour of their *debut* occasioned Mr. Henry to be designated by his committee to draw the petition to the king, with which they were charged, and Mr. Lee was charged with the address to the people of England. The last was first reported. On reading it, great disappointment was expressed in every countenance, and a dead silence ensued for some minutes. At length it was laid on the table for perusal and consideration till the next day; when first one member and then another arose, and paying some faint compliment to the composition, observed that there were still certain considerations not expressed, which should properly find a place in it. The address was therefore committed for amendment; and one prepared by Mr. Jay, and offered by Governor Livingston, was reported and adopted with scarcely an alteration. These facts were stated by a gentleman, to whom they were communicated by Mr. Pendleton and Mr. Harrison, of the Virginia delegation (except that Mr. Harrison erroneously ascribed the draught to Governor Livingston), and to whom they were afterward confirmed by Governor Livingston himself. Mr. Henry's draught of a petition to the king was equally unsuccessful, and was recommitted for amendment. Mr. John Dickinson (the author of the Farmer's Letters) was added to the committee, and a new draught prepared by him was adopted."

This passage is not so luminous as many parts of the book; but as I understand it, I think it is not correct.

There is no man now living who is able perfectly to correct it but yourself; and in my opinion, it is your conscientious duty to do it.

The question, " Who was the draughtsman of the address to the people of England?" however unimportant to the public it may appear at this day, certainly excited a sensation, a fermentation, and a schism in Congress at the time, and serious consequences afterward, which have lasted to this hour, and are not yet spended. I fear, but I do not know, that this animosity was occasioned by indiscretions of R. H. Lee, Mr. Samuel Adams, and some others of the Virginia delegates, by whom Adams was led into error. I never had a doubt that you were the author of that manly and noble address. But as the subject is now brought before the public by Mr. Wirt, and will excite speculation, you, who alone are capable of it, ought to explain it, and, as I know you will, if at all, without favour or affection.

I am, sir, with friendship as of old,

Your most respectful humble servant,

JOHN ADAMS.

JAY TO JOHN ADAMS.

BEDFORD, 31st January, 1818.

DEAR SIR :

I received your letter of the 9th by the mail which arrived here on the 24th inst.

I have not seen Mr. Wirt's book, nor heard of the " passage " in it, of which your letter contains a copy. You think that passage, as you understand it, is not correct, and observe, that as I am the only man remaining alive who can perfectly correct it, in your opinion it is my " conscientious duty to do it."

For your satisfaction, and pursuant to your opinion, I will proceed to give you a plain statement of facts. There are entries in the printed journals of Congress of 1774 which merit attention ; and I think the extracts from that journal, which I shall introduce, afford inferences which militate against some of the incidents mentioned in the passage. That you may compare and examine both with the greater ease to yourself, I will first insert the passage, and then the extracts.

"A petition to the king, an address to the people of Great Britain, and a memorial to the people of British America, were agreed to be drawn. Mr. Lee, Mr. Henry, and others were appointed for the first ; Mr. Lee, Mr. Livingston, and Mr. Jay for the two last. The splendour of their *debut* occasioned Mr. Henry to be designated by his committee to draw the petition to the king, with which they were charged, and Mr. Lee was charged with the address to the people of England. The last was first reported. On reading it, great disappointment was expressed on every countenance, and a dead silence ensued for some minutes. At length it was laid on the table for perusal and consideration till the next day ; when first one member and then another arose, and paying some faint compliment to the composition, observed that there were still certain considerations not expressed which should properly find a place in it. The address was therefore committed for amendment ; and one prepared by Mr. Jay, and offered by Governor Livingston, was reported and adopted with scarcely an alteration. These facts are stated by a gentleman, to whom they were communicated by Mr. Pendleton and Mr. Harrison of the Virginia delegation (except that Mr. Harrison erroneously ascribed the draught to Governor Livingston), and to whom they were afterward confirmed by Governor Livingston himself. Mr. Henry's draft of a petition to the king was equally unsuccessful, and was recommitted for amendment. Mr. John Dickinson (the author of the Farmer's Letters) was added to the committee, and a new draught prepared by him was adopted. "

" *Tuesday, October* 11*th*, 1774.—Resolved unanimously, That a *memorial* be prepared to the people of *British America*, stating to them the necessity of a firm, united, and invariable observation of the measures recommended by the Congress, as they tender the invaluable rights and liberties derived to them from the laws and constitution of their country.

" Also, that an *address* be prepared to the people of Great Britain.

" Ordered, That Mr. Lee, Mr. Livingston, and Mr. Jay be a committee to prepare a draught of the memorial and address."

The committee assigned the *memorial,* which was first in order, and also deemed first in importance, to Mr. Lee. Mr. Livingston, who was my superior both in age and reputation, was desired to prepare the *address.* He declined it, and urged me to take it. I finally consented, and did write it.

" *Tuesday, October* 18*th*, 1774.—The committee appointed to prepare the *address* to the people of Great Britain brought in a draught, which was read and ordered to lie on the table for the perusal of the members, and to be taken into consideration to-morrow.

" *Wednesday, October* 19*th*, 1774.—The Congress resumed the consideration of the address to the people of Great Britain ; and the same being debated by paragraphs, and sundry amendments made, the same was recommitted, *in order that the amendments may be taken in.*"

I was present in Congress, and attended to the proposed amendments. Mr. Lee (one of the committee) moved that the draught should be recommitted for the purpose mentioned in the journal ; and for *that purpose* it was recommitted. The amendments were made the next day, and the draught was returned to Congress the ensuing morning.

"*Friday, October* 21*st*, 1774.—The address to the people of *Great Britain* being brought in, and the amendments directed being made, the same was approved, and is as follows."

Is it probable that the committee found it *necessary* to assign both the *memorial* and the *address* to Mr. Lee, or that he would readily undertake that double task, or that, notwithstanding his other avocations in and out of Congress, he could finish them *both* between the 11th October, when they were ordered, and the 19th, when the draught of the memorial was reported ?

According to the journal, the draught of the address was recommitted, expressly for the purpose and "*in order that the amendments may be taken in.*" Is it probable that the committee did, nevertheless, lay aside that draught and substitute a *new one ?* How could they have rendered such a procedure reconcilable to the feelings of the writer of that draught, or compatible with their recent approbation of it, or consistent with the design and object of the recommitment? Could any of the members have been so negligent of delicacy and propriety, as to propose or concur in such a measure? Could the embarrassments and difficulties attending it have been surmounted between the *Wednesday*, when the address was recommitted, and the ensuing *Friday*, when (*with the amendments taken in*) it was read and approved?

The subsequent occurrences you mention have not escaped my recollection. I was informed, and I believe correctly, that one person in particular of those you specify, had endeavoured, by oblique intimations, to insinuate a suspicion that the address to the people of *Great Britain* was not written by me, but by Governor Livingston. That gentleman repelled the insinuation. He knew and felt what was due to truth, and explicitly declared it.

Those persons are dead and gone. Their design did not succeed, and I have no desire that the memory of it should survive them. As to the address or petition to the king—who wrote the draught that was reported and recommitted—how far it corresponded with the one that was adopted—whether Mr. Dickinson, after he was added to the committee, prepared an entirely new draught, or only co-operated in amending the one then before the committee—are questions which you only, who have survived all the other members of that committee, can answer with certainty.

Considering who were the members of that committee, viz., yourself, Mr. Lee, Mr. Johnson, Mr. Henry, and Mr. Rutledge, I think the idea of a new draught cannot be correct. That Mr. Dickinson did write the subsequent or *second* address or petition to the king, I have no reason to doubt.

To prepare an acceptable draught of the *first* petition, was no easy task. Instructions as to matters to be inserted in it were given to the committee; and some were proposed which occasioned much debate. You may remember that many of the members of that Congress were anxious that *too much* might not be done or said; and, on the other hand, that there were many members who were anxious that *too little* might not be done or said. Hence there arose and prevailed a more than ordinary degree of solicitude and watchfulness, both as to the purport of subject-matter, and to the force and latitude of expressions. And hence also it may have happened, that (except the draught of a letter to the agents in England) every report made to that Congress received amendments of one kind or other, before they approved and adopted it.

Be pleased to present my best respects to Mrs. Adams. It gives me pleasure to reflect, that your friendship for me has from of "old" continued steadfast, and that my estimation of it has constantly animated the attachment with which I have so long been, and am, dear sir,

Your affectionate friend,

JOHN JAY.

JAY TO JOHN MURRAY, JUN.

BEDFORD, 15th April, 1818.

My Good Friend :

In my letter to you of the 16th October last, I hinted that I might perhaps write and send you a few more lines on the question, whether war of every description is forbidden by the gospel.

I will now add some remarks to those which were inserted in my answer to your first letter. In that answer, the lawfulness of war, in certain cases, was inferred from those Divine *positive* institutions which authorized and regulated it. For although those institutions were not dictated by the moral law, yet they cannot be understood to authorize what the moral law forbids.

The moral or natural law was given by the Sovereign of the universe to all mankind; with them it was co-eval, and with them it will be co-existent. Being founded by infinite wisdom and goodness on essential right, which never varies, it can require no amendment or alteration.

Divine positive ordinances and institutions, on the other hand, being founded on expediency, which is not always perpetual or immutable, admit of, and have received, alteration and limitation in sundry instances.

There were several Divine *positive* ordinances and institutions at very early periods. Some of them were of limited obligation, as circumcision ; others of them were of universal obligation, as the Sabbath, marriage, sacrifices, the particular punishment for murder.

The Lord of the *Sabbath* caused the day to be changed. The ordinances of Moses suffered the Israelites to exercise more than the original liberty allowed to marriage, but our Saviour repealed that indulgence. When sacrifices had answered their purpose as types of the great Sacrifice, etc.,they ceased. The punishment for murder has undergone no alteration, either by Moses or by Christ.

I advert to this distinction between the moral law and positive institutions, because it enables us to distinguish the reasonings which apply to the one, from those which apply *only* to the other—ordinances being mutable, but the moral law always the same.

To this you observe, by way of objection, that the law was given by Moses, but that grace and truth came by Jesus Christ; and hence that, even as it relates to the *moral law*, a more *perfect* system is enjoined by the gospel than was required under the law, which admitted of an eye for an eye, and a tooth for a tooth, tolerating a spirit of retaliation. And further, that, if the moral law was the same now that it was before the flood, we must call in question those precepts of the gospel which prohibit some things *allowed* of and practised by the patriarchs.

It is true that the law was given by Moses, not however in his individual or private capacity, but as the agent or instrument, and by the authority of the Almighty. The law demanded exact obedience, and

proclaimed : "Cursed is every one that continueth
not in all things which are written in the book of the
law to do them." The law was inexorable, and by
requiring *perfect* obedience, under a penalty so inevitable and dreadful, operated as a schoolmaster to
bring us to Christ for *mercy*.

Mercy, and grace, and favour did come by Jesus
Christ ; and also that truth which verified the promises and predictions concerning him, and which
exposed and corrected the various errors which had
been imbibed respecting the Supreme Being, his
attributes, laws, and dispensations. Uninspired
commentators have dishonoured the law, by ascribing
to it, in certain cases, a sense and meaning which it
did not authorize, and which our Saviour rejected
and reproved.

The inspired prophets, on the contrary, express
the most exalted ideas of the law. They declare
that the law of the Lord is *perfect ;* that the statutes
of the Lord are *right ;* and that the commandment
of the Lord is *pure ;* that God would *magnify* the
law and make it honourable, etc.

Our Saviour himself assures us that he came not
to destroy the law and the prophets, but to fulfil ;
that whoever shall do and teach the commandments,
shall be called great in the kingdom of heaven ; that
it is easier for heaven and earth to pass, than one
tittle of the law to fail. This certainly amounts to a
full approbation of it. Even after the resurrection of
our Lord, and after the descent of the Holy Spirit,
and after the miraculous conversion of Paul, and after

the direct revelation of the Christian dispensation to him, he pronounced this memorable encomium on the law, viz.: "The law is *holy*, and the commandments *holy*, *just*, and *good*."

It is true that one of the *positive* ordinances of Moses, to which you allude, did ordain retaliation, or, in other words, a tooth for a tooth. But we are to recollect that it was ordained, not as a rule to regulate the conduct of private individuals towards each other, but as a legal penalty or punishment for certain offences. Retaliation is also manifest in the punishment prescribed for murder—life for life. Legal punishments are adjusted and inflicted by the law and magistrate, and not by unauthorized individuals. These and all other positive laws or ordinances established by Divine direction, must of necessity be consistent with the moral law. It certainly was not the design of the law or ordinance in question, to encourage a spirit of personal or private revenge. On the contrary, there are express injunctions in the law of Moses which inculcate a very different spirit; such as these: "Thou shalt not avenge, nor bear any grudge against the children of thy people; but thou shalt love thy neighbour as thyself." "Love the stranger, for ye were strangers in Egypt." "If thou meet thy enemy's ox or his ass going astray, thou shalt surely bring it back to him," etc., etc.

There is reason to believe that Solomon understood the law in its true sense, and we have his opinion as to retaliation of injuries, viz.: "Say not, I will recompense evil; but wait upon the Lord, and He will save thee." Again : " Say not, I will do to him as he hath done to me. I will render to the man according to his work." And again : " If thine enemy be hungry, give him bread to eat ; and if he be thirsty, give him water to drink ; for thou shalt heap coals of fire upon his head, and the Lord shall reward thee."

But a greater than Solomon has removed all doubts on this point. On being asked by a Jewish lawyer, which was the great commandment in the law, our Saviour answered : " Thou shalt love the Lord thy God with all thy heart, and with all thy soul, and with all thy mind. This is the *first* and the great commandment, and the *second* is like unto it : Thou shalt love thy neighbour as thyself. On *these* two commandments hang all the law and the prophets." It is manifest, therefore, that the love of God and the love of man are enjoined by the law ; and as the genuine love of the one comprehends that of the other, the apostle assures us that " Love is the fulfilling of the *law.*"

It is, nevertheless, certain, that erroneous opinions respecting retaliation, and who were to be regarded as *neighbours*, had long prevailed, and that our Saviour blamed and corrected those and many other unfounded doctrines.

That the patriarchs sometimes violated the moral law, is a position not to be disputed. They were men, and subject to the frailties of our fallen nature. But I do not know nor believe, that any of them violated the moral law by the authority or with the approbation of the Almighty. I can find no instance of it in the Bible. Nor do I know of any action done according to the moral law, that is censured or forbidden by the gospel. On the contrary, it appears to me that the gospel strongly enforces the whole moral law, and clears it from the vain traditions and absurd comments which had obscured and misapplied certain parts of it.

As, therefore, Divine ordinances did authorize just war, as those ordinances were necessarily consistent with the moral law, and as the moral law is incorporated in the Christian dispensation, I think it follows that the right to wage *just* and *necessary* war is admitted, and not abolished, by the gospel.

You seem to doubt whether there ever was a *just* war, and that it would puzzle even Solomon to find one.

Had such a doubt been proposed to Solomon, an answer to it would probably have been suggested to him by a very memorable and interesting war which occurred in his day. I allude to the war in which his brother Absalom on the one side, and his father David on the other, were the belligerent parties. That war was caused by, and proceeded from, "the lusts" of Absalom, and was horribly wicked. But the war waged against him by David was not caused by, nor did proceed from, "the lusts" of David, but was right, just, and necessary. Had David submitted to be dethroned by his detestable son, he would, in my opinion, have violated his moral duty and betrayed his official trust.

Although just war is not forbidden by the gospel

in express terms, yet you think an implied prohibition of all war, without exception, is deducible from the answer of our Lord to Pilate, viz.: "If my kingdom were of this world, then would my servants fight," etc.

At the conclusion of the Last Supper, our Lord said to his disciples: "He that hath no sword, let him now sell his garment and buy one." They answered: "Lord, here are two swords." He replied: "It is enough."

It is not to be presumed that our Lord would have ordered swords to be provided, but for some purpose for which a sword was requisite; nor that he would have been satisfied with *two*, if more had been necessary.

Whatever may have been the purposes for which swords were ordered, it is certain that the use of one of those swords soon caused an event which confirmed the subsequent defence of our Lord before Pilate, and also produced other important results. When the officers and their band arrived, with swords and with staves, to take Jesus, they who were about him saw what would follow. "They said unto him: Lord, shall we smite with the sword?" It does not appear that any of the eleven disciples who were with him, except one, made the least attempt to defend him. But Peter, probably inferring from the order for swords, that they were now to be used, proceeded to "smite a servant of the high-priest, and cut off his right ear." Jesus (perhaps, among other reasons, to abate inducements to prosecute Peter for that violent attack) healed the ear.

He ordered Peter to put his sword into its sheath, and gave two reasons for it. The *first* related to himself, and amounted to this, that he would make no opposition, saying : "The cup which my Father hath given me, shall I not drink ?" The *second* related to Peter, viz., they who take the sword, shall perish by the sword ; doubtless meaning that they who take and use a sword, as Peter had just done, without lawful authority, and against lawful authority, incur the penalty and risk of perishing by the sword. This meaning seems to be attached to those words by the occasion and circumstances which prompted them. If understood in their unlimited latitude, they would contradict the experience and testimony of all ages, it being manifest that many military men die peaceably in their beds.

The disciples did believe and expect that Jesus had come to establish a *temporal* kingdom. "They trusted that it had been he which should have redeemed Israel." "They knew not the Scripture, that he must rise again from the dead ; questioning one with another what the rising from the dead should mean." Even after his resurrection, they appear to have entertained the same belief and expectation ; for on the very day he ascended, they asked him : "Lord, wilt thou at *this* time restore the kingdom to Israel ?"

The order for swords, and the declaration that *two* were *enough*, tended to confirm that belief and expectation, and to inspire a confidence that he who had commanded the winds and the waves, and had raised the dead to life, was able, as well as willing, to render the *two* swords sufficient to vanquish his enemies. Could anything less than such a firm belief and confidence have prompted eleven *such* men, and with only two swords among them, to offer to "smite with the sword" the armed band, which, under officers appointed by the Jewish rulers, had come to apprehend their Master?

Great must have been the disappointment and astonishment of the disciples, when Jesus unexpectedly and peaceably submitted to the power and malice of his enemies, directing Peter to sheath his sword, and hinting to him the danger he had incurred by drawing it: amazed and terrified, they forsook him and fled. This catastrophe so surprised and subdued the intrepidity of Peter, that he was no longer "ready to go with his Master to prison and to death."

It seems that perplexity, consternation, and tumultuous feelings overwhelmed his faith and reflection, and that his agitations, receiving fresh excitement from the danger and dread of discovery, which soon after ensued, impelled him with heedless precipitation to deny his Master. This denial proved bitter to Peter, and it taught him and others that spiritual strength can be sustained only by the spiritual bread which cometh down from heaven.

The Jews accused Jesus before Pilate of aspiring to the *temporal* sovereignty of their nation, in violation of the regal rights of Cæsar. Jesus, in his defence, admitted that he was king, but declared that his kingdom was not of *this* world. For the truth of this assertion, he appealed to the peaceable behaviour of his adherents, saying : "*If my kingdom were of this world, then would my servants fight, that I should not be delivered to the Jews, but now is my kingdom not from hence.*"

Pilate, who doubtless well knew what had been the conduct of Jesus, both before and at the time of his apprehension, was satisfied, but the Jews were not. They exclaimed : "If thou let this man go, thou art not Cæsar's friend ; whosoever maketh himself a king, speaketh against Cæsar." "We have no king but Cæsar."

You and I understand the words in question very differently. Is there the least reason to infer from the belief and conduct of the disciples, that they were restrained from fighting by the consideration that their Master's kingdom was *not of this world?* On the contrary, did they not believe and expect that he had come to restore one of the kingdoms of *this* world to Israel ? The fact is, that they were ready and willing to fight. Did they not ask him : "Lord, shall we smite with the sword ?" It was *his* will, therefore, and not *their* will, which restrained them from fighting ; and for that restraint he assigned a very conclusive reason, viz., because his kingdom was not of this world.

To the advancement and support of his *spiritual* sovereignty over his *spiritual* kingdom, soldiers and swords and corporeal exertions were inapplicable and useless. But, on the other hand, soldiers and swords and corporeal exertions are necessary to enable the several temporal rulers of the states and kingdoms of this world to maintain their authority and protect themselves and their people ; and our Saviour expressly declared that *if* his kingdom had been of *this* world, *then* would his servants fight to protect him ; or, in other words, that *then*, and in *that* case, he would not have restrained them from fighting. The lawfulness of such fighting, therefore, instead of being denied, is admitted and confirmed by that declaration.

This exposition coincides with the answer given by John the Baptist (who was " filled with the Holy Ghost ") to the *soldiers* who asked him what they should do, viz.: " Do violence to no man, neither accuse any falsely, and be *content* with your *wages.*" Can these words be rationally understood as meaning that they should receive wages for *nothing ;* or that, when ordered to march against the enemy, they should refuse to proceed ; or that, on meeting the enemy, they should either run away, or passively submit to be captured or slaughtered ? This would be attaching a meaning to his answer very foreign to the sense of the words in which he expressed it.

Had the gospel regarded war as being in every case sinful, it seems strange that the apostle Paul should have been so unguarded as, in teaching the importance of *faith*, to use an argument which clearly proves the lawfulness of war, viz.: " That it was through faith that Gideon, David, and others waxed valiant in fight, and turned to flight the armies of aliens "; thereby confirming the declaration of David, that it was God who had " girded him with strength to battle ; and had taught his hands to war, and his fingers to fight."

The gospel appears to me to consider the servants of Christ as having two capacities or characters, with correspondent duties to sustain and fulfil.

Being subjects of his *spiritual* kingdom, they are bound in that capacity to fight, pursuant to his orders, with *spiritual* weapons, against his and their spiritual enemies.

Being also subjects and partakers in the rights and interests of a temporal or worldly state or kingdom, they are in that capacity bound, whenever lawfully required, to fight with weapons in just and necessary war, against the *worldly* enemies of that state or kingdom.

Another view may be taken of the subject. The depravity which mankind inherited from their first parents, introduced wickedness into the world. That wickedness rendered human government necessary to restrain the violence and injustice resulting from it. To facilitate the establishment and administration of government, the human race became, in the course of Providence, divided into separate and distinct nations. Every nation instituted a government, with authority and power to protect it against domestic and foreign aggressions. Each government provided for the *internal* peace and security of the nation, by laws for punishing their offending subjects. The law of all the nations prescribed the conduct which they were to observe towards each other, and allowed war to be waged by an innocent against an offending nation, when rendered just and necessary by unprovoked, atrocious, and unredressed injuries.

Thus two kinds of justifiable warfare arose : one against domestic malefactors ; the other against foreign aggressors.   The first being regulated by the law of the land ; the second by the law of nations ; and both consistently with the moral law.

As to the *first* species of warfare, in every state or kingdom, the government or executive ruler has, throughout all ages, pursued, and often at the expense of blood, attacked, captured, and subdued murderers, robbers, and other offenders ; by force confining them in chains and in prisons, and by force inflicting on them punishment ; never rendering to them good for evil, for that duty attaches to individuals in their personal or private capacities, but not to rulers or magistrates in their official capacities. This species of war has constantly and universally been deemed just and indispensable.   On this topic the gospel is explicit.   It commands us to obey the higher powers or ruler.   It reminds us that " he beareth not the sword in vain " ; that " he is the minister of God, and a revenger to execute wrath upon him that doeth evil."   Now, if he is not to bear the *sword* in *vain*, it follows that he is to *use* it to execute wrath on evil-doers, and consequently to draw blood and to kill on proper occasions.

As to the *second* species of warfare, it certainly is as reasonable and as right that a nation be secure against injustice, disorder, and rapine from without as from within ; and therefore it is the right and duty of the government or ruler to use force and the sword to protect and maintain the rights of his people against evil-doers of another nation. The reason and necessity of using force and the sword being the same in both cases, the right or the law must be the same also.

We are commanded to render to our government, or to our Cæsar, "the things that are Cæsar's" that is, the things which belong to him, and not the things which do not belong to him. And surely this command cannot be construed to intend or imply that we ought to render to the Cæsar of another nation more than belongs to him.

In case some powerful Cæsar should demand of us to receive and obey a king of his nomination, and unite with him in all his wars, or that he would commence hostilities against us, what answer would it be proper for us to give to such a demand? In my opinion, we ought to refuse, and vigorously defend our independence by arms. To what other expedient could we have recourse? I cannot think that the gospel authorizes or encourages us, on such an occasion, to abstain from resistance, and to expect miracles to deliver us.

A very feeble unprepared nation, on receiving such a demand, might hesitate and find it expedient to adopt the policy intimated in the gospel, viz.: "What king, going to war against another king, sitteth not down first and consulteth whether he be able with ten thousand to meet him that cometh against him with twenty thousand; or else he sendeth an embassage, and desireth conditions of peace"—that is, makes the best bargain he can.

If the United States should unanimously RESOLVE never more to use the sword, would a certified copy of it prove to be an effectual Mediterranean passport? Would it reform the predatory rulers of Africa, or persuade the successive potentates of Europe to observe towards us the conduct of *real* Christians? On the contrary, would it not present new facilities, and consequently produce new excitements, to the gratification of avarice and ambition?

It is true that even just war is attended with evils, and so likewise is the administration of government and of justice; but is that a good reason for abolishing either of them? They are means by which greater evils are averted. Among the various means necessary to obviate or remove, or repress, or to mitigate the various calamities, dangers, and exigencies, to which in this life we are exposed, how few are to be found which do not subject us to troubles, privations, and inconveniences of one kind or other. To prevent the incursion or continuance of evils, we must submit to the use of those means, whether agreeable or otherwise, which reason and experience prescribe.

It is also true, and to be lamented, that war, however just and necessary, sends many persons out of this world who are ill prepared for a better. And so also does the law in all countries. So also does navigation, and other occupations. Are they *therefore* all sinful and forbidden?

However desirable the abolition of all wars may be, yet until the morals and manners of mankind are greatly changed, it will be found impracticable. We are taught that national sins will be punished, and war is one of the punishments. The prophets predict wars at so late a period as the restoration of the Israelites. Who or what can hinder the occurrence of those wars ?

I nevertheless believe, and have perfect faith in the prophecy, that the time will come when " the nations will beat their swords into ploughshares, and their spears into pruning-hooks ; when nation shall not lift up sword against nation, neither shall they learn war any more." But does not this prophecy clearly imply, and give us plainly to understand, that in the *meanwhile*, and *until* the arrival of that blessed period, the nations will not beat their swords into ploughshares, nor their spears into pruning-hooks ; that nation will not forbear to lift up sword against nation, nor cease to learn war?

It may be asked, Are we to do nothing to hasten the arrival of that happy period? Literally, no created being can either accelerate or retard its arrival. It will not arrive sooner nor later than the appointed time.

There certainly is reason to expect, that as great providential events have usually been preceded and introduced by the intervention of providential means to prepare the way for them, so the great event in question will be preceded and introduced in like manner. It is, I think, more than probable, that the unexpected and singular co-operation and the extraordinary zeal and efforts of almost all Christian nations to extend the light and knowledge of the gospel, and to inculcate its doctrines, are among those preparatory means. It is the duty of Christians to promote the prevalence and success of such means, and to look forward with faith and hope to the result of them.

But whatever may be the time or the means adopted by Providence for the abolition of war, I think we may, without presumption, conclude that mankind must be prepared and fitted for the reception, enjoyment, and preservation of universal permanent peace, before they will be blessed with it. Are they as yet fitted for it? Certainly not. Even if it was practicable, would it be wise to disarm the good before "the wicked cease from troubling"? By what other means than arms and military force can unoffending rulers and nations protect their rights against unprovoked aggressions from within and from without? Are there any other means to which they could recur, and on the efficacy of which they could rely? To this question I have not as yet heard, nor seen, a direct and precise answer.

These remarks would have been written and sent sooner had my health been better. Expedition not being requisite, I attended to them only at intervals which allowed and invited me to do so.

We differ in opinion, and, I am persuaded, with equal sincerity.

With real esteem and regard, I remain,

Your friend,

JOHN JAY.

JAY TO RUFUS KING.

BEDFORD, 8th October, 1818.

DEAR SIR:

On Friday last Mrs. Hamilton favoured us with a visit. Speaking of Dr. Mason, she observed that the state of his health not permitting him to write the life of General Hamilton, she had received from him the papers which had been put into his hands for that purpose.

She expressed her desire to have the life written, and remarked, in substance, that she knew of no person who was both so well circumstanced and qualified for it as yourself. I concurred in this opinion, and at her request promised to write to you on the subject. I should have done it by the mail of this week, but was prevented by company. On the proposed work, viewed in any point of light, I can make no observation that would be new to you. I will therefore only suggest that your long and familiar acquaintance and intercourse with the General, and your comprehensive and accurate knowledge of public affairs, and particularly of those in which he was engaged, afford facilities for it which you only possess in so high a degree.

Permit me to add that the work, being biographical, would derive no inconsiderable advantage from the character of the author. I am persuaded that Mrs. Hamilton would consider herself greatly obliged by your undertaking it.

Be pleased to present my compliments to Mrs.

egotistical history, that you may inform me, in return, of the state of your health, which, I fear, has not been so prosperous ; but is really a subject of no small interest with me.

I have continued in my judicial employment more from habit than uninterrupted inclination ; and it is, at times, burthensome, and always ill-requited. I see Congress are about re-modelling the department, and what they will make of it, I do not know (possibly they do not themselves know), nor do I feel much anxiety on the subject. The whole state of things is so different from what we in our day contemplated, that it is more surprising our judicial arrangements, formed in the early stage of our national existence, should have continued so long and so effectively, than that they should now be changed.

My attention to my judicial duty has abstracted me from my private affairs ; which are, however, free from the embarrassments which have overwhelmed many adventurers, who had better have been idle. My *thorough-bass* amusement consists in rural enjoyments, which have been more profitable to others than myself. I have given you a specimen of this kind of enjoyment by directing our fourth volume of Memoirs to be sent to you, and I hope it will arrive safely to your hands. There may not be much instruction, but we have assisted in raising our fellow-citizens to proper views of the real and substantial interests of our country. There is a most gratifying spirit everywhere on this subject, by which the rising generation may profit ; but it is too late in the day for either you or I to enjoy much of its advantages. So we thought, however, in our revolutionary exertions, and yet what a mass of prosperity and happiness have we lived to see accumulated in every quarter of our country ! When I carry my recollections back to my early knowledge of its husbandry, the contrast exhibited by its present improvement (yet but imperfect) fills me with most pleasing sensations.

There is a jealousy in our mother country still apparent of most of the rapid improvements we have arrived at ; and I have strong expectations that those in agriculture will ere long equal, if not exceed all others. I keep up a good understanding with the British agricultural people with whom I come in contact ; but it amuses me to perceive that, although many are liberal, many are otherwise. Some years ago we sent a volume of our Memoirs to Scotland. It was very civilly received ; but several of their leading agricultors took occasion to observe that we were an hundred years behind *them*, and even very unequal to *English* farming. So I left Sawney and John Bull to settle that point. I sent lately an American scythe and cradle, which they had not before seen ; nor was it used in England. They received it graciously ; and I had *civil* thanks from a vice-president of the Board of Agriculture ; but he at the same time let me know that it was a *Flemish* and not an *American* implement. I desired my friend who transmitted the cold civility, to have it labelled " a *Flemish implement* sent to England *by the way of the United States of America !* " There is an awkward instrument in Flanders containing the rudiments of our scythe and cradle, but as unequal to ours as their *ships* to those of our country ; yet ours are *American* ships, and not a little envied and *squinted* at.

I have been lately reading, with great pleasure, the Life of our late distinguished friend Dr. Franklin. Have you read it ? I see he glosses over in a letter to the then secretary for foreign affairs (Livingston) the affair of Vergennes sending his secretary to England, pending our negotiations in the treaty of peace. I think you told me *all about it ;* and I have ever had different impressions from those the Dr. portrays. He says it was merely to ascertain whether or not the British ministry had serious intentions to make an equal, solid, and lasting peace with *us* and our *allies.* I have always believed there was an underplot in the business. I think something of this appears in your journal, which I assisted to read in Congress in 1782 and 3. Much bruit was made then by the French diplomacy, about your signing the preliminaries without previous notice to them; but I always thought you entirely in the right, not only as a security in so important a measure, but to guard against embarrassments, with reason apprehended from the French manœuvres. I voted against an unwarrantable philippic of censure, brought forward in Congress against your conduct, to please the French. I thought then, and do now, that it was a mean compliance. Our friend Madison, who was generally *then* with us, left his friends on that subject, and I never liked him *the better* for it.

I see Congress have rejected the claim of Beaumachi's representatives. All my recollections put them in the right in so doing. True, Silas Deane made an ostensible private contract with B.; but I always was taught to believe him a mere *showman*, and that the supplies were a gift from France, which she could not openly then avow. The unaccounted *money*, about which much noise has been made, I always believed to have been devoted to secret service and douceurs to French agents, whose remunerations could not publicly appear. All or most of the articles went through my hands, or under my observation, when in the war office, and a more complete piece of *fripponerie* never was seen. Very many of the articles were worthless, and among them the brass cannon were old rampart pieces, only valuable for the metal, which was recast in our foundries. All these things, however, appear now as dreams. What is real, and lives longer than these transactions in my memory, is, that I am always, and have been, truly and affectionately yours,

Richard Peters.

JAY TO JUDGE PETERS.

BEDFORD, January 25, 1819.

DEAR SIR:

I have read your letter of the 12th ult. more than once. Mutuality of friendly feelings always affords gratification ; and the kindness which pervades your letter has made its proper impressions.

As you are in the seventy-fifth year of your age, and I in the seventy-fourth of mine, our leases have expired. We are holding over, and others will soon occupy our places. What to do, and where to go, would be perplexing questions, had not our beneficent Lessor offered us better and permanent habitations.

The death of an excellent daughter last spring was an afflicting event, and I feel it. Convinced that her happiness was augmented by it, I had no reason to grieve on *her* account. I derived consolation, as well as resignation, from reflecting that unerring wisdom had directed that dispensation, and that I was still blessed with the surviving children, who (like their sister) had never given me any other uneasiness than what had arisen from their sickness or afflictions.

Considering the times which have passed over us, I am glad you continued in office. Might not reports of some select cases decided in your court be useful ? And would they not be more correctly prepared for the press by yourself than by others ?

In my opinion, you did well to abstain from speculations. I thought so, and did so. It is, I believe, a just and not a new remark, that a proper education and proper habits, with a moderate share of property, form a better provision for a child, than that greater degree of wealth, which not infrequently leads the unexperienced to idleness and its results.

I have looked into the book which you had the goodness to send me, and for which I thank you. I have read the address, and the notices for a young farmer. They will do good. Although unable to attend much to my own agricultural affairs, yet books and conversation on such subjects entertain me. I wish I could give you a good account of my Tunisian sheep, but the dogs have put it out of my power. I regret the loss they caused ; but I regret it less than another loss, which more nearly affects my convenience. I allude to the death of a favourite mare, which I had rode for twenty-three years with great satisfaction. She lately died suddenly and unexpectedly, in the twenty-ninth year of her age. She was the third in succession, which died in *my* service. The grandam was given to me by my father in 1765. That circumstance associated with various others in attaching me to them.

Agricultural societies are multiplying in this State. One has been formed in this county, and I am the *nominal* president ; having only the will and not the ability to render active services. They have prepared a representation to the Legislature respecting agriculture, and the expediency of establishing an agricultural society for the whole State.

The traits of parsimonious and reluctant commendation observable in some of your British letters, give more intelligence than the writers meant to convey. As almost every vagrant leaf we pick up will inform us of the kind of tree which produced it, so these traits discover the feelings which originated them. It is a pity that such feelings should exist; but they are the offspring of human nature, which is not what it should be, nor what it once was. That Britons should reflect on our *former* and *present* state and condition, without regret, without mortification, and without apprehensions of rivalry and perhaps of danger, can hardly be expected. A doubt whether Britannia will always "rule the waves," cannot have a welcome reception in her mind. Our rapid progress in trade, navigation, and the arts cannot correspond with her views and wishes. The strength resulting from our increasing resources and population recommends a kind of policy and a degree of accommodation not congenial with the temper and propensities of such a nation. Superiors seldom see with complacency inferiors rising towards equality, and by *means* which may not improbably carry them beyond it. There is, nevertheless, great worth in Britain.

I have not seen Dr. Franklin's Life. As he concurred in the opinion of Count de Vergennes, that we should proceed to treat for peace with Great Britain without a previous admission of our independence, he may, in his own mind, have acquitted the Count of the motives to which I ascribed his giving us that opinion ; and also have considered his subsequent explanations on that and certain other topics as satisfactory. After my return in 1784, I was informed of the debate in Congress on the proposed resolution which you mention. In my opinion, Mr. Madison voted consistently. I omit explaining this at present, for it cannot be done in a few words. My letter to Congress respecting the negotiation contained a full and correct statement of facts. Many years have since elapsed, but my sentiments relative to the policy adopted by France on that occasion continue unaltered.

But it is time to conclude, and I will do it by thanking you for affording me so agreeable an occasion to assure you of the esteem and regard, with which I continue

Your friend,

JOHN JAY.

JAY TO JOHN MURRAY, JUN.

BEDFORD, 27th February, 1819.

I thank you, my good friend, for the kind letter (without date) which my son lately delivered to me, and for the pamphlets which were enclosed with it.

The observations of your friend (inserted in your letter) are well written. I am pleased with the writer. He reasons with ability, and abstains from declamation. The lawfulness of the invasion and conquest of Canaan, being made by express Divine command, is indubitable. It does not decide the question, whether *any* wars, unless *so commanded*, are permitted by the moral law, and consequently by the gospel. Such wars occurred both before and after the time of Moses, and are recorded in Scripture without reproof. It does not appear that the war of Abraham against the kings was made by *Divine* command, nor that Jacob

was *commanded* to take " out of the hand of the Amorite, with his sword and his bow," the portion which
he gave to Joseph ; nor does it appear that the war of
David against Hanun, and divers other wars, were
so commanded.

That the theocracy admitted of no other wars by
the Israelites but such as were expressly commanded
by the Almighty, is not clear to me.   Had Solomon
been of that opinion, I think he could not with propriety have taught that "by *counsel* thou shalt make
war ; and in a multitude of *counsellors* there is safety.
Every purpose is established by *counsel;* and with
good advice make war."

This, and other topics with which it is connected,
open a wide field for investigation ; but as the state
of my health does not permit me to be more particular, I will only add that, when the arguments in favour
of just and necessary war shall be shown to be fallacious, I shall not only think, but also act accordingly.

The extract from William Penn forms a useful tract ;
and among other reasons, because it declares that " the
Scriptures were given forth by holy men of God in
divers ages, as they were moved by the Holy Spirit."
I observe that this great truth is also inculcated by the
trustees of the African Free School in their address.

I did hope to have found in your letter some
tidings respecting your brother.   When you write
to him, assure him of my esteem and regard ; and be
pleased to accept the like assurance from

Your friend,
JOHN JAY.

JAY TO ELIAS BOUDINOT.

BEDFORD, 17th November, 1819.

DEAR SIR :

I have received the copy of a circular letter which, as chairman of the committee appointed by the late public meeting at Trenton respecting slavery, you were pleased to direct to me on the 5th instant. Little can be added to what has been said and written on the subject of slavery. I concur in the opinion that it ought not to be introduced nor permitted in any of the new States ; and that it ought to be gradually diminished and finally abolished in all of them.

To me the constitutional authority of the Congress to prohibit the migration and importation of slaves into any of the States, does not appear questionable. The first article of the constitution specifies the legislative powers committed to the Congress. The ninth section of that article has these words :

"The *migration* or *importation* of such *persons* as any of the *now existing* States shall think proper to admit, shall not be prohibited by the Congress prior to the year 1808. But a tax or duty may be imposed on such importations, not exceeding ten dollars for each person."

I understand the sense and meaning of this clause to be, that the power of the Congress, although competent to prohibit such migration and importation, was not to be exercised with respect to the *then existing* States (and them only) until the year 1808 ; but that the Congress were at liberty to make such prohibition as to any new State, which might, in the *mean* time, be established, and further, that from and after *that period*, they were authorized to make such prohibition, as to all the States, whether new or old.

It will, I presume, be admitted, that *slaves* were the *persons* intended. The word *slaves* was avoided, probably on account of the existing toleration of slavery, and of its discordancy with the principles of the Revolution ; and from a consciousness of its being repugnant to the following positions in the Declaration of Independence, viz. :

" We hold these truths to be self-evident : that all men are created equal ; that they are endowed by their Creator with certain unalienable rights ; that among them are life, liberty, and the pursuit of happiness."

As to my taking an active part in "organizing a plan of co-operation," the state of my health has long been such as not to admit of it.

Be pleased to assure the committee of my best wishes for their success, and permit me to assure you of the esteem and regard with which I am, dear sir,

Your faithful and obedient servant,

JOHN JAY.

JAY TO DANIEL RAYMOND.

BEDFORD, 21st December, 1819.

SIR :

I received by the last mail the pamphlet on " The Missouri Question," which you did me the favour to send.

The remarks and statements contained in it place

the pernicious influence of slavery on the welfare of our country in conspicuous and impressive points of view.

The obvious dictates both of morality and policy teach us, that our free nation cannot encourage the extension of slavery, nor the multiplication of slaves, without doing violence to their principles, and without depressing their power and prosperity.

It appears to me desirable that your remarks and statements, as well as the excellent arguments of Mr. King, should be widely diffused; they will have a strong tendency to render public opinion on this very important subject correct and settled. Accept my acknowledgments for this mark of attention, and for the inducements which prompted it.

I am, sir,

Your obliged and obedient servant,

JOHN JAY

WILLIAM JAY TO JAY.

TURIN [N. Y.], October, Sunday 8th, 1820.

MY DEAR FATHER:

We left New York in the steamboat on Wednesday afternoon at 4 o'clock, and after a very pleasant passage arrived in Albany at about the same time the next afternoon. We found at the dock a stage for Schenectady and immediately took our seats in it, and had only time to stop at Mrs. Sedgwick's door, to deliver a letter and inquire about the family. Susan and Matilda came to the carriage and shook hands with us; their husbands were both in Vermont. We passed the night at Schenectady and left it the next morning in the stage before sunrise. Our carriage was as comfortable as any private coach. We travelled 65 miles on Friday without being fatigued; the next day we got within eight miles of this place, and this morning we arrived here safely before breakfast.

The children have behaved extremely well, and have given us scarcely any trouble whatever. They have *not once* seemed tired. I am myself very well, and have got rid of every symptom of influenza. I think of leaving this on Saturday for Utica where I propose spending Sunday and Monday the 15th and 16th, after which I shall hasten home as quick as possible.

The facilities for travelling between Turin and Albany have wonderfully increased within a few years. The road for the whole distance with the exception of only *one mile* is turnpike. The Stages between Albany and Utica, 96 miles, are what are now called *Post Coaches*. The driver sits on a box outside of the Carriage; the baggage is put into a boot behind the Carriage, but connected with the body and is perfectly protected from the weather, and the inside of the carriage is well stuffed and cushioned. The fare from Albany to Utica is only $2. This however is owing to competition and cannot last long, as I am assured it does not even defray the necessary expenses. Augusta had the pleasure of finding her sisters and brothers well, as likewise their families.

She desires to be affectionately remembered to you and sisters. Anna and Maria likewise send their love to you and their Aunts. Be so good as to add mine also.

Believe me, my dear Father,

Your very affectionate son,

WILLIAM JAY.

JUDGE PETERS TO JAY.

BELMONT, November 25, 1820.

DEAR SIR:

Every occurrence in which you have shared, or originated, seems by some strange perversion to be misunderstood, or misstated, by the present generation, when some favorite individual, or topic induces the obliquity. Although I give Mr. Adams his full share of merit in the affair of the Compte de Vergennes' maneuvring with the British administration on the subject of our treaty of 1783, yet I have felt indignant that your name should have been omitted in the Massachusetts Conventional account of the matter, and Mr. Adams held out as the principal figure, when you should have been the prominent and leading portrait in the group. I am sure Mr. Vaughan will not justify this statement of the transaction, tho' he is alluded to us confirming it, by one of the speakers in the Massachusetts Convention. His account of it to me was exactly as you stated it in your letter to Congress, which I saw and read at the time of its being the subject of our consideration; when, as I wrote to you, the unjustifiable vote was taken as to the unmerited censure of proceeding without the concurrence of the French ministry, in our adjustment with Great Britain.

In your letter to me, in answer to my relation of what passed at this place in a conversation with Mr. B. Vaughan, a year or more ago, in relation to the affair, and when I told you he confirmed my recollections on the subject, you only refer to your letter to Congress. I think some additional statement of facts should be left, lest the archives of the office of state may suffer the catastrophe which destroyed all the records of transactions in the war office. The truth of history depends on fair and correct relations of the conduct of individuals to whom public transactions were committed. The biography of those individuals is one thing, the national character is another; but both are united in the inquiry on this subject.

Among the pleasures of memory (which has many pains), the recollection of old friendships is one of the most delightful. Among these, my remembrances of your personal regard is one of the most prominent gratifications. Whensoever any thing turns up in which you were concerned, all my sensibilities recur.

I begin to feel some of the infirmities of age; but, in general, am highly favoured with good health. The most extraordinary depression of property is no cordial to landed proprietors; but those who will soon occupy a small portion, and leave their extensive possessions behind them, need not much deplore the "hard times" which have fallen on us. The friends of *peace* have nothing to encourage them, when universal peace brings along with it universal privation, and much distress to individuals. But we have wantoned in prosperity: and cannot bear the check which circumstances have given to our career—*festina lente* must hereafter be our motto. I trust you enjoy as much health as you have heretofore experienced, though I cannot flatter myself that it is perfect. My best wishes constantly attend you; and I beg you to be assured of the sincere regard with which I am always

Affectionately yours,

RICHARD PETERS.

P.S. I have just got home from the drudgery of a long circuit court, and am not the better for the campaign. Washington has begun his return to Mount Vernon, much broken down. He came convalescent; having had a severe attack of an illness which pervaded all the country in his vicinity. He must renew his stamina, or he will not reach the period of life to which you and I have arrived.

JAY TO JUDGE PETERS.

BEDFORD, 26th December, 1820.

I thank you cordially, my good and constant friend, for your letter of the 25th ult. It affords me no little gratification. We grow old, but our hearts retain their warmth.

The perversion and obliquity you notice have not been recent nor unexpected. Men who are ardent in the pursuit of influence and its fruits, and more attentive to the prosecution than to the propriety of their schemes, usually become and remain hostile to those who steadfastly disapprove of their manœuvres. Instead of regulating their hostility by truth and candour, they generally find it convenient to recur to perversion and obliquity.

The conventional statement to which you allude, was doubtless devised and formed in the manner which its projectors deemed to be best accommodated to the objects they had in view. So many years have elapsed since the negotiations at Paris, that only a few individuals among the present members of any of our popular assemblies probably possess ample and accurate knowledge of those negotiations.

On considering your hint of my making some statement of facts relative to them, in addition to my letter to Congress, which you observe may (like the papers of the War Office) be accidentally destroyed, I think that precaution will not be necessary. I have a book in which are entered that and all my other official letters to Congress.

An accurate and well-written history of the United States down to the conclusion of the late war is desirable, but my expectations on that head are not sanguine. Time is daily obscuring and diminishing the materials, and the task becoming more and more difficult. The marks of talent and rectitude which appear in the *Life of Washington* by Judge Marshall, have induced me to regret that he had not commenced such a history and incorporated that life in it. The mass of information he has collected continues to afford facilities for such a work, and it would more than answer the purpose of a new edition of the other. Whoever may undertake it would, in my opinion, do well to give it the advantage of frequent revision and postpone the publication until a period when the events and circumstances related in it had ceased to produce personal and political excitement.

As to President Washington's valedictory address, I can add nothing material to the information contained in my letter to you of the 29th March, 1811. The attention both of Col. Hamilton and myself was, in our consultation on that subject, confined to the paper in which he had incorporated that address with his proposed corrections. We considered whether in this state it required any further amendment, and nothing occurring to render recurrences to the draft itself, as sent by the President, necessary, it was not then read by either of us ; nor by me at any time. An idea that this confidential reference might perhaps be disclosed, did not enter into my mind, and not having the least apprehension of unpleasant consequences, there was nothing to excite my attention to care or precaution respecting them. Whether the President adopted all or only some of the proposed corrections, or added others, are questions which my memory at this late day does not enable me to answer ; nor do I recollect having read the printed address with an eye to these circumstances. I think Mr. Hopkinson will readily perceive that he cannot assign to Col. Hamilton even the credit of amending and correcting that address, without necessarily and unavoidably assigning to him the discredit of a breach of confidence.

I rejoice in your continuing to enjoy good health. I will not say with the Spaniards " may you live a thousand years," for that would postpone greater blessings.

The *name* and the character of Judge *Washington* interest me in his welfare. I hope he will be restored to health. The prevailing disease which attacked him, I suspect, was the same which visited us—influenza ; few families here escaped. I have had it, but not severely ; it has left a cough which still gives me some trouble. Although too feeble to go often beyond the piazza, yet I experience no depression of spirits, nor frequent returns of acute pain.

Here also the distress of the *times* is felt very sensibly. Habits of expense, unproductive speculations and debts injudiciously contracted, press hard both upon debtors and creditors. How long this state of things will continue, or how much good or evil will eventually result from it, cannot now be calculated. They who hope for the best, and prepare for the worst, will doubtless mitigate some of their troubles, and probably obviate the occurrence of some others.

God bless you, my dear sir.
Yours affectionately,
JOHN JAY.

JAY TO GEORGE A. OTIS.

BEDFORD, WESTCHESTER County, N. Y.
13th January, 1821.

SIR :

I have received your letter of the 23d ult. expressing a desire that Botta's *History* and your translation of it may have my approbation ; and also that
I would mention to you the most authentic of the
documents which are before the public relative to
the negotiations at Paris in 1782.

Having, as yet, received and read *only* the *first*
volume of the *History*, I cannot form, and consequently cannot express, an opinion of the *whole* work.

As to the *first* volume, there are in it certain assertions, representations, and suggestions, of which
there are some which I believe to be *erroneous*, and
others which I suspect to be *inaccurate*. Being too
feeble either to write or to read much at a time without fatigue, I forbear to enumerate them. I will,
nevertheless, for your satisfaction, select and notice
one of the most important, viz. : that anterior to the
Revolution there existed in the colonies a desire of
independence.

The following extracts respect this topic, viz.:

Page 10.—" The love of the sovereign and their ancient
country, which the first colonists might have retained in
their new establishments, gradually diminished in the hearts
of their descendants."

Page 11.—" The *greater part* of the colonists had heard
nothing of Great Britian, excepting that it was a distant
kingdom, from which their ancestors had been barbarously
expelled."

Page 12.—" As the means of restraint became almost illusory in the hands of the government, there must have arisen and gradually increased in the minds of the Americans, the hope, and with it the desire, to shake off the yoke of English superiority . . . The colonists supported impatiently the superiority of the British government."

Page 15.—" Such was the state of the English colonies in America; such the *opinions* and *dispositions* of those who inhabited them, *about the middle of the eighteenth century* . . . It was impossible that they should have remained ignorant of what they were capable; and that the progressive development of national pride should not have rendered the British yoke *intolerable*."

Page 33.—" Already those who were the most zealous for liberty, or the most ambitious, had formed, in the secret of their hearts, the resolution to shake off the yoke of England, whenever a favourable occasion should present. This design was encouraged by the *recent* cession of Canada."

Page 199.—" The colonists looked upon it [the Congress of 1774] as a convention of men who, in some mode or other, were to deliver their country from the perils that menaced it. The greater part believed that their ability, &c., would enable them to obtain from the government a removal of the evils that oppressed them, and the re-establishment of the ancient order of things. Some others cherished the belief that they would find means to conduct the American nation to that independence which was the first and most ardent of their aspirations; or rather the sole object of that intense passion which stung and tormented them night and day."

Page 314.—" Both [Putnam and Ward] had declared themselves too openly in favour of independence. The *Congress desired* indeed to procure it, but withal in a propitious time."

Page 388.—" Thus ceased, as we have related, the royal

authority in the different provinces. It was replaced progressively by that of the people; that is, by Congresses or Conventions extraordinary, that were formed in each colony. But this was deemed insufficient by those who *directed* the affairs of America; their real object being *independence*," &c.

Explicit professions and assurances of allegiance and loyalty to the sovereign (especially since the accession of King William), and of affection for the mother country, abound in the journals of the colonial Legislatures, and of the Congresses and Conventions, from early periods to the second petition of Congress in 1775.

If these professions and assurances were sincere, they afford evidence more than sufficient to invalidate the charge of our desiring and aiming at independence.

If, on the other hand, these professions and assurances were factitious and deceptive, they present to the world an unprecedented instance of long-continued, concurrent, and detestable duplicity in the colonies. Our country does not deserve this odious and disgusting imputation. During the course of my life, and until after the second petition of Congress in 1775, I never did hear any American of any class, or of any description, express a wish for the independence of the colonies.

Few Americans had more or better means and opportunities of becoming acquainted with the sentiments and dispositions of the colonists, relative to public affairs than Dr. Franklin. In a letter to his son, dated the 22d March, 1775, he relates a conversation which he had with Lord Chatham in the preceding month of August. His Lordship having mentioned an *opinion* prevailing in England, that America aimed at setting up for herself as an *independent* state, the Doctor thus expressed himself : " I assured him that, having more than once travelled almost from one end of the continent to the other, and kept a great variety of company, eating, drinking, and conversing with them freely, I never had heard in any conversation from any person, drunk or sober, the least expression of a wish for a separation, or a hint that such a thing would be advantageous to America."

It does not appear to me necessary to enlarge further on this subject. It has always been and still is my opinion and belief, that our country was prompted and impelled to independence by *necessity*, and not by *choice*. They who know how we were then circumstanced, know from whence that necessity resulted.

It would, indecd, be extraordinary, if a foreigner, remote (like Mr. Botta) from the best sources of authentic information, should, in writing such a history, commit no mistakes. That gentleman doubtless believed his narrations to be true, but it is not improbable that he sometimes selected his materials with too little apprehension of error, and that some of his informers were too little scrupulous. This remark derives a degree of weight from the following passage in the *History*, viz.: General Montgomery " left a wife, the object of all his tenderness, with *several children*, still *infants*, a spectacle for their country, at once of pity and admiration. The state, from gratitude towards their *father*, distinguished them with every mark of kindness and protection." I have been acquainted with General Montgomery's widow from my youth. The fact is that she never had a child.

In making the translation, attention has doubtless been paid to the rule, that a translator should convey into his translation, with perspicuity and precision, the ideas of his author, and no others, and express them, not literally, but in well-adapted classical language. How far your translation is exactly correct, I am an incompetent judge; for not understanding the language of the original, I cannot examine and compare the translation with it. Of the style and manner of the translation, I think well.

Which are the most *authentic* documents before the public relative to the negotiations at Paris in 1782, is a question which I am not in capacity to answer. Many years have elapsed since I have read any of them, and others have since been published which I have not seen. Without a previous and careful examination of each of them, it would be rash and unfair to give a preference to either.

On receiving your *first* letter, I conjectured that you were of the respectable family of your name in Massachusetts; and that conjecture appears from your last to have been well founded. If, in going from Philadelphia to Boston, you should not find it inconvenient to take the road through this town, you will meet with a welcome reception from

Your obedient servant,
John Jay.

JAY TO JUDGE PETERS.

BEDFORD, 12th March, 1821.

DEAR SIR :

My letter to you of the 26th December last, contained some remarks relative to the perversions and obliquities which you had noticed, and which I observed were neither *recent* nor *unexpected.* In that letter there was not room for explanatory details. Those remarks were therefore concise and general. To supply that deficiency is the design of this letter

These perversions and obliquities began on the receipt of a letter which I wrote to Congress, and of which the following is a copy.

[*Here was inserted the letter of* 20*th September,* 1781, *relative to the instruction to the American commissioners appointed to negotiate the treaty of peace.* See vol. ii., p. 69.]

This letter was written under the influence of indignant feelings, and in some respects with too little of deliberate consideration. The impressions it made on those who had originated and urged the *instruction* mentioned in it may easily be conceived.

That this instruction was more complimentary than wise was afterward evinced by the circumstances which constrained the American commissioners at Paris to disobey it. That disobedience gave additional excitement to the displeasure and to the complaints of the French and their consociates. Nor were they pleased with the implied approbation of

that disobedience, which resulted from my appointment to the office of Secretary for Foreign Affairs,
before my arrival in 1784. From time to time after
my return, I was informed of various incidents which
showed that their malevolence was far from being
dormant.

The presumptuous attempts of the *republican* minister Genet, to facilitate the designs of France at the
hazard of our peace and neutrality, gave occasion to
the measures of President Washington on that subject. Disappointed and irritated by these impediments, Genet and his partisans indulged themselves
in animadversions on the administration and its
advocates, which were neither candid nor decorous.

The treaty with England in 1794, did not accord
with the views and wishes of France, nor with the
views and wishes of sundry individuals among us.
Although the strenuous efforts made to defeat it did
not succeed, yet the feelings and motives which
prompted those efforts continued to operate.

Certain politicians, desirous to give a new direction
to public opinion, finally succeeded in forming a party
for the purpose, and in introducing a policy varying
from that which President Washington and his *friends*
had preferred. Those friends were not regarded with
a friendly eye.

They who censured the precipitate commencement
and the unsuccessful conduct of the late war with
England incurred the resentment of those by whom
these errors were committed.

Among those who had been active Federalists, there

were individuals who, at subsequent periods, were induced to think it *expedient* for them to join the opposing party. They who *thus* pass from one side to the other are apt to mistake cunning for wisdom, and to act accordingly.

These details will suffice to explain the concise remarks in my letter. *Many* more might be added, and I could fill much paper with apposite anecdotes; but I forbear to enlarge on topics which (*mutatis mutandis*) the history of Greece and other countries, as well as observation and experience, have rendered familiar to us both.

In the course of my public life, I have endeavoured to be uniform and independent; having, from the beginning of it in 1774, never asked for an office or a vote, nor declined expressing my sentiments respecting such important public measures as, in my opinion, tended to promote or retard the welfare of our country.

You will, I am persuaded, pardon this egotism, and believe me to be, dear sir,

Your constant and affectionate friend,

JOHN JAY.

JAY TO LINDLEY MURRAY.

BEDFORD, 24th April, 1821.

MY GOOD FRIEND:

It gives me pleasure to learn from my son, that, in a letter lately received by your nephew, you made inquiries respecting me.

We have both experienced afflicting dispensations. Your portion of health has for a long time been diminished ; and I have not had a well day for the last twelve years. You have been deprived of an excellent brother, who was an excellent man ; and I of several relations, and particularly of an amiable and affectionate daughter. It is a comfort to hope and believe that such dispensations answer merciful purposes, and that the time will come when we shall rejoice in having been reminded by adversity, that temporal enjoyments are transient.

The winter having been more cold than common, has confined me to the house during the course of it ; and the weather this spring has not yet been so mild as to admit of my going abroad without risk. Although my old complaint has gradually reduced me to a state of incurable debility, yet I seldom suffer from acute pain, except occasionally from rheumatism. In various respects, I have abundant reason to be thankful.

We have both passed the usual term of human life, or (as the lawyers say) our leases have expired, and we are now holding over. To be thus circumstanced, is not very important to those who expect to remove from their present abodes to better habitations, and to enjoy them in perpetuity. That we may both be, and continue to be, numbered with these, is the sincere desire of

Your affectionate friend,

JOHN JAY.

JAY TO GOVERNOR BROWN.[1]

BEDFORD, 30th April, 1821.

SIR :

I have received, and thank you for, the interesting report of the joint committee of both houses of your Legislature, relative to certain proceedings of the Bank of the United States, which you were so obliging as to send me.

Controversies between the national and a state government, or any of their respective departments, are to be regretted. It is desirable that the one which occasioned this report, should be brought to an amicable and satisfactory termination ; and that the limits which bound the authorities of the national and state governments be well ascertained and observed.

However extensive the constitutional power of a government to impose taxes may be, I think it should not be so exercised as to impede or discourage the lawful and *useful* industry and exertions of individuals. Hence, the prudence of taxing the products of beneficial labour, either mental or manual, appears to be at least questionable.

Whether taxation should extend only to property, or only to income, or to both, are points on which opinions have not been uniform. I am inclined to think, that both should not be taxed. If the first is preferred, then tax the land and stock of a farmer, but not his crops ; tax his milch-cows, but not their milk, nor the butter and cheese made of it, whether the

---

[1] Of Ohio.

same be sent to market or consumed in his family. Tax the real and personal estate of a physician and a lawyer, but not the conjectural and varying profits they derive from the skilful and industrious exercise of their professions, etc., etc. On this and similar subjects, there will be different opinions. Our minds are probably as little alike as our features ; and it is not uncommon for men of unquestionable talents and candour to take opposite sides of the same question ; neither of them being culpable, both are entitled to allowances for the risk of committing mistakes, to which we are all more or less exposed. It is an agreeable circumstance that prosperity attends you ; and permit me to add, that for its continuance and increase, you have the best wishes of, Sir,

Your obliged and obedient servant,

JOHN JAY.

MRS. MARIA BANYER TO JAY.

GENEVA, N. Y., 28th June, 1821.

MY DEAR PAPA,

I hope Sister has received my letter from Utica which informed you of our route so far. On Sunday evening we rode 17 miles to Union thro' a very beautiful Country resembling some of the finest parts of Connecticut, passing thro' some very pretty villages ornamented with shrubbery and flowers ; the land very rich and well cultivated. As my friends had some near relations at Union we stayed there until Monday afternoon when we rode 8 miles to the Canal. We went thro' this part of the Oneida reservation and saw with great pleasure a very pretty Episcopal Church which has been built for the Indians, and regretted we had not gone there the day before. A lady of Utica told me she had never seen a more devout Congregation; they make the responses very well and sing delightfully. Their Clergyman is a man of talents, zealous in the cause and exemplary in his conduct; there yet remains much to be done. It was painful to observe the difference between their farms and those of their neighbours. The land could not be finer than it is, but we did not see more than half a dozen of them at work; great numbers were supinely lying on the ground or sitting at their doors.

Between 4 and 5 we embarked on the Canal in a neat boat about 70 feet long; it was towed by two horses which are exchanged every two miles;—we glided along very pleasantly at the rate of 4 miles an hour. About sun set it was delightful passing thro' woods of a height I had not before seen; we had some mosquitoes and later in the season they will be a great drawback on the comfort of travelling thro' that region. We passed thro' six locks, the first in the night which I saw thro' the window of my berth; it looked as if we were sinking into a large dungeon. We ascended, which was more agreeable. Having travelled 56 miles in this way we left the canal, but as all who love their Country feel an interest in its success, I know you will be pleased to hear that so far it has answered the most sanguine expectations of its friends. There are two passage boats owned by gentlemen in Utica who last year cleared $2,000 from them, altho' the fare including lodging, tea, and breakfast is only 4 cents a mile. The amount of produce carried down is immense.

It seems almost incredible that the Canal can be carried thro'; near Genesee river it must be dug 25 feet deep thro' solid rock for 3 miles. We rode 8 miles to Auburn yesterday where we stayed during the heat of the day; it is a pretty town. The State Prison is a grand building; the ornamental stone is brought from Oswego, and is very handsome, much resembling Newark stone but of a finer grain. How painful it is to reflect on the vice that renders such structures necessary ! Very different feelings were excited on viewing another stone building errecting for a Theological Seminary. May the purifying principles of the blessed Gospel to which we owe this milder system of punishment daily render all punishment less necessary ! We stayed at Auburn during the heat of the warmest day we have had, and in the after-noon and evening had a delightful ride to this place. The approach to Cayuga Lake is very fine ; a noble sheet of water 40 miles long and 4 broad ; we crossed it on a bridge $1\frac{1}{4}$ miles long ; another bridge still nearer the foot of the Lake and the Steam boat enlivened the prospect. We rode several miles on the borders of the Senecca Lake before we entered this town, but it was too dark to see it to advantage. This is indeed a wonderful country, and thro' out the whole of it has marks of great prosperity ; it seems impossible that a Country of the same dimensions can possibly possess greater advantages than the State of New York. . . .

May our Heavenly Father grant you every blessing. Most truly your gratefully affectionate and dutiful daughter,

MARIA BANYER.

PETER A. JAY TO JAY.

NEW YORK, 5 July, 1821.

MY DEAR FATHER,

I received your letter of the 25th ult. too late to answer it by last week's mail, and I have this morning received that of the 3d inst.

I have directed an estimate to be made of the expence of building two houses on Walker Street. There are several reasons both for and against that Measure. I doubt whether such houses as would be most profitable in that situation can be built and completely finished for less than $5000 each, and the rent at present would not exceed $400, so that reckoning a lot at only $1800 the rent would be less than 6 per Cent. on the capital, and that too without considering repairs, which never fail to amount to something every year. On the other hand the value of the adjoining land would certainly be increased and it is not improbable that rents will rise. There is now so much idle capital in the City that upon pledges of stock money can be borrowed at 5 pr. Ct. Stock of all kinds is enormously high; even 5 pr. Ct. Stock sells at 7 pr. Ct. above par, yielding about $4\frac{1}{2}$ pr. Ct. interest. There is generally a fashion in the money market as elsewhere. Some years ago it was the fashion to employ capital in Manufactures; nobody does so now. At present there is a rage for stock, but this I think cannot last long, and I should think it probable that capitalists will begin by and by to purchase land. If this should be the case, then building at present will be advantageous. But unless land or rents or both should rise, it will not be profitable.

We are all well. Our love to Nancy, William, and Augustus. I am, my dear father,

Your very affectionate Son,

PETER AUGUSTUS JAY.

PETER A. JAY TO JAY.

ALBANY, 10 Oct. 1821.

MY DEAR FATHER,

Our prospects here grow more unpleasant. The more violent members of the Convention begin to act more in a body and to gather strength.[1] They have held at least

---

[1] This was the second of the four State Conventions that have been held to revise the Constitution of New York since its adoption in 1777. The Council of Appointment, with which both Governors Clinton and Jay had been at issue, was abolished, and several other objectionable features eliminated. The appointing power was conferred upon the Governor with and by the advice of the

one caucus. Upon the whole there is a good deal of bad feeling, and I should not be surprized if something very violent should be attempted in relation to the judiciary. This will probably depend upon the likelihood of its succeeding, and of this I cannot yet judge. We have had a long and latterly angry contest about the appointment of justices of the peace. The dominant party who gave up the Council of Appointment with great reluctance were anxious to retain the power of appointing these magistrates at Albany, and Mr. V. Beuren proposed a plan for this purpose which he openly urged on party grounds; others very desirous that the minority should not be utterly excluded from office proposed to elect Justices by the people. This enraged the Jacobins exceedingly, who were obliged to argue in contradiction to their own principles and professions. I voted against both plans and both were lost. The contest ended in the adoption of a Scheme by which the power of appointing is lodged in the Supervisors and County Court. The discussion has produced violent animosity between the followers of Mr. V. Beuren and the N. York delegation, and the latter seem to me to be alarmed and to be acting feebly. I heard yesterday from Mary who was well; I hope Nancy has by this time returned in better health than when she left you.

I went a few days ago to the cattle show of this County and was disappointed. I am much inclined to believe that William could show on your farm as fine cattle, and almost as many of them, as were exhibited.

My love to him and sisters.

> I am, my dear father,
> Your affectionate Son
> PETER AUGUSTUS JAY.

Senate. "The direct sovereignty of the people was thus rendered far more effective, and popular government took the place of parliamentary administration."

PETER A. JAY TO JAY.

NEW YORK, 28 Oct., 1821.

MY DEAR FATHER :

I left Albany yesterday, and arrived here this morning, and finding all well shall return to-morrow. The Convention will I hope adjourn in about a week. Since I wrote you last it has been occupied with the Judiciary. The first attack made upon it was a proposition to abolish the Court of Chancery and to vest the equity jurisdiction in the Supreme Court. This was debated two days and part of a third, and was finally rejected by a great majority. They next took up Mr. Munroe's report and rejected it *in toto* without ceremony ; the subject was then referred to a select Committee of which he was chairman. They reported a new plan. Upon the coming in of this report, the Vice President moved a resolution, the effect and avowed object of which was to turn out the present Chancellor and Judges. This was also rejected by 64 votes to 44, after which the second report was voted down with as little respect as the former, and the judiciary department will probably remain nearly as it is at present, except that all the judges of the County Courts (including the first judge) will hold their offices for five years.

The last division shews the strength of the radical party as it is called, who are forming themselves into a distinct section of the Democratic party.

I am, my dear father,
Your very affectionate Son
PETER AUGUSTUS JAY.

PETER A. JAY TO JAY.

NEW YORK, 15 Nov., 1821.

MY DEAR FATHER :

The Convention adjourned on Saturday, and I immediately went on board the Steam boat and arrived here on Sunday Morning. You will see the new Convention in the newspapers. Many of the Democratic members were dissatisfied with it, but did not dare to separate from their party. I think its chief defects are making the right of suffrage universal, rendering the judges of the Supreme Court dependent, and vesting the power of appointment in almost all instances in the Legislature. There seems to be a passion for universal suffrage pervading the Union. There remain only two States in which a qualification in respect of property is retained. When those who possess no property shall be more numerous than those who have it the consequence of this alteration will, I fear, be severely felt.

Mary and the child are doing well; the former has had a cold which has retarded her recovery, but it is now better. I am obliged to you for your kind letters to John. He behaves very well.

The builders are now roofing the new houses in Walker Street. The Lutheran Chuch in that Street is begun, and the foundation nearly done.

> I am, my dear father,
> Your very affectionate Son
> PETER AUGUSTUS JAY.

NOAH WEBSTER TO JAY.

AMHERST, MASS., November, 1821.

SIR:

When I began the compilation of a large Dictionary of the English language, I limited my views chiefly to a correction of such errors as had escaped former compilers, and the supply of such new terms as have sprung from modern improvements in science. But in searching for the originals of English words, I soon found the field of etymology had been imperfectly explored; and one discovery succeeding another, my curiosity was excited to persevere in the pursuit. At length, finding no safe clue to conduct me through the labyrinth, I adopted a new plan of invesgation—that of examining and comparing the primary elements, articulations, or consonants of words in twenty different languages or dialects; the vowels having been found so mutable as to be of no use.

The result of this examination has been the formation of a synopsis of radical words in more than twenty languages, which is complete, or nearly so. This will probably form a quarto, and be an appendix to the dictionary. This has occupied about ten years; but I do not, and I think the world will not regret the delay which this has occasioned; for if I am not deceived, the discoveries proceeding from this investigation will be quite important, and as new in Europe as in America. This synopsis exhibits a vast number of affinities between the languages examined, which have never before been detected. But what I think of more value, this investigation has developed, in a multitude of words, the primary sense of the root, which has not hitherto been known. There is a primary or radical sense of every verb, from which all its significations in customary use are naturally and easily deducible; and from an ignorance of this sense, and the manner in which men have proceeded from the literal to the metaphorical significations, the most learned critics have often been perplexed in determining the particular sense of words. For instance, a Hebrew word signifies to *bless* and to *curse*. With the knowledge of the primary sense, these difficulties vanish.

The languages of which I have made a synopsis, are the Chaldaic, Syriac, Arabic, Samaritan, Hebrew, Ethiopic, Persian, Irish (Hiberno Celtic), Armoric, Anglo Saxon, German, Dutch, Swedish, Danish, Greek, Latin, Italian, Spanish, French, Russian, with the English.

I am now proceeding with the dictionary, and I am engaged in the letter H. Making my past progress the basis of calculation, it must require the constant labour of *four years* to complete the work, even if my health should be continued. For this blessing I rely tranquilly on the goodness and forbearance of that Being, whose favour I desire to seek in the way which he has prescribed, and which I trust I value above any temporal good.

But I did not begin my studies early enough. I am now sixty-three years of age, and after this age, a small portion only of active life remains. If, however, I should not be permitted to finish the work begun, the synopsis will enable some other person to pursue the plan with advantage, so that my labour will not be lost to my country.

I have thought, that after submitting my MSS. to able judges, if they should think the work to have merit enough to command a sale in England, I may visit that country, and attempt to sell the copy there first; and indeed revise the work at Oxford. But on this I am not determined. What course I shall pursue is not certain. I am contented to leave the event to that good Providence which has hitherto supported me.

The evening before your letter arrived, I was conversing respecting you, sir; and I said to my family, that there are few men whom I wish so much to see as Gov. Jay. If our lives should be spared till next summer, I will make an effort to visit you. However this may be, I shall never forget your public services, nor your private friendship for,

Sir, your most obliged and obedient servant,

NOAH WEBSTER.

JAY TO NOAH WEBSTER.

BEDFORD, 3d December, 1821.

SIR :

I have received your letter of the 8th ultimo, and a subsequent one not dated. Your dictionary will doubtless derive utility and reputation from the extensive investigations you mention. The assiduity with which you have for many years persevered, and still persevere, in accomplishing that arduous task, will, I hope, be followed by results, not only beneficial to the public, but also to yourself.

There are gentlemen in this country by whom, I presume, judicious criticisms and friendly offices would be readily afforded. In case a further revision should be undertaken with zeal and good will, at Oxford or Cambridge, and terminate with explicit commendation, it would excite attention both in Britain and America, and produce useful consequences.

To whatever persons the perusal of the manuscripts may be committed, permit me to hint that they should be *very legible.* This remark is suggested by the recollection of an incident which occurred many years since. The author of a large manuscript, written in an indistinct hand, requested a certain gentleman to favour him with his opinion of it. The gentleman, after a while, returned it, with some polite general observations of little importance. It seems he " had neither time nor patience to decipher much of it."

Should circumstances occur to render it highly probable that your attending a revision in England would eventually promote sales in both countries, or ensure a good price for the copy, the expense incurred by it might be more than compensated. As several years are still necessary to *finish* the work, and as occurrences may in the mean time create objections or afford facilities which cannot now be foreseen, the question, what posterior measures would be advisable, may probably be more easily answered at a future day than at present.

Your intention to favour me with a visit next summer gives me pleasure. Whether our lives will be prolonged to that period, depends on that good Providence on which you happily and wisely rely, and whose beneficence I hope you will continue to experience.

I am, sir,

Your friend and obedient servant,

JOHN JAY.

JAY TO REV. S. S. WOODHULL.[1]

BEDFORD, 7th December, 1821.

REV. SIR :

I received by the last mail your obliging letter of the 17th instant, informing me that the board of managers had unanimously elected me to succeed the late worthy president of the American Bible Society. Those gentlemen have thereby done me honour, and I thank them for it.

The circumstances under which the British and Foreign Bible Society arose and extended its benign influence to distant countries, and the subsequent spontaneous formation of numerous similar societies in other nations, are events so singular, and so little to have been expected, as to afford reason to ascribe

---

[1] Secretary of the American Bible Society.

them to a more efficient cause than any of those from which mere human institutions usually result.

They who regard these societies as deriving their origin and success from the Author and Giver of the Gospel, cannot forbear concluding it to be the duty of Christians to promote the purposes for which they have been established ; and that it is particularly incumbent on their officers to be diligent in the business committed to them.

It has long and uniformly been my opinion, that no person should accept of an office or place unless he be both able and willing to do the duties of it. This principle opposes my acceptance of the one in question. My health has been declining for twelve years past ; my excursions from home have long been limited to short distances ; such are my maladies that they often confine me to the house, and at times to my chamber ; combined with the necessary infirmities of age, they allow me no prospect of convalescence.

As President of the society, I should think I ought to be conversant with the proceedings, and not only attend their annual meetings, but also, at least occasionally, partake in the consultations and assist in the transactions of the board of managers. Were I in capacity to do the duties of the office, I should accept it without hesitation. I say without hesitation, because I should then as much doubt my having a right to decline, as I now doubt my having a right to accept it.

From the preceding particulars relative to the state of my health, the gentlemen of the board will perceive that my inability to serve them is greater in degree than they doubtless apprehend. Be pleased, sir, to assure them of my gratitude for the distinction with which they have honoured me, and that opportunities of manifesting it would give me pleasure.

I am, reverend sir,

Your obedient servant,

JOHN JAY.[1]

JAY TO THE EDITOR OF "THE AMERICAN."

BEDFORD, WESTCHESTER COUNTY, N. Y.,
8th January, 1822.

SIR:

On Saturday last I received a printed paper (which I had not before seen), taken from one of the numbers of the *American*, in these words—viz. :

"We state as a historical Fact, that the present "Constitution of this State was actually adopted by "the Convention then Sitting at Kingston on *Sunday*— "and the adjournment from the Saturday to Sunday "was, if we are correctly informed, on motion of John "Jay."

In 1776 my father removed with his family from Rye to Fishkill. On the 17th day of April, 1777, my mother died there. Notice of that afflicting event was immediately sent to me; I thereupon went without delay from Kingston to Fishkill, where I attended my mother's funeral, and where (for obvious reasons) I remained some time with my father and family. The

---

[1] Mr. Jay subsequently accepted the Presidency of the Bible Society on the assurance that active duties would not be expected of him.

Constitution was adopted during my absence from Kingston,—viz.—on the 20th day of that same month of April.

Be pleased to publish this letter in your next paper.

I am, sir,

Your obedient servant,

JOHN JAY.

GEORGE A. OTIS TO JAY.

QUINCY, 19th February, 1822.

SIR:

I did not receive your very kind and very gratifying communication of the 13th January, 1821, until after I had rejoined my family in this place; and consequently, not till after it was too late to profit, in passing homeward, of your very obliging permission to pay you my respects personally; a satisfaction which I regret in proportion to the just sense I have of its value.

Your remarks on the first volume of Botta, confirmed as they were by Presidents Adams and Jefferson, were communicated to the reviewers of my translation of that author, and were by them introduced into their account of the work published in the *North American Review* for July, 1821.

.   .   .   .

With respect to the animadversions which you did me the honor to address to me upon the first volume, and which I took the liberty to communicate to the late Presidents Adams and Jefferson, the former of these gentlemen wrote me as follows:

" I cannot refrain from expressing the pleasure I have received from the reasoning of Mr. Jay upon the passage in Botta, ' that anterior to the Revolution there existed in the colonies a desire of independence.' There is a great ambiguity in this expression.

It is true, there always existed in the colonies a desire of independence of parliament in the articles of internal taxation and internal policy, and a very general, if not an universal opinion, that they were constitutionally entitled to it, and as general a determination, if possible, to maintain and defend it ; but there never existed a desire of independence of the crown, or of general regulations of commerce, for the equal and impartial benefit of all parts of the empire. It is true, there might be times and circumstances in which an individual or a few individuals might entertain and express a wish, that America was independent in all respects ; but these were *'rari* nantes in gurgite vasto.' For example, in 1756–57 and '58, the conduct of the British generals, Shirley, Braddock, Loudon, Webb and Abercrombie, was so absurd, disastrous and destructive, that a very general opinion prevailed that the war was conducted by a mixture of ignorance, treachery and cowardice ; and *some persons* wished we had nothing to do with Great Britain forever. Of this number I distinctly remember, I was myself one, fully believing that we were able to defend ourselves against the French and Indians, without any assistance or embarassments from Great Britain. In '58 and '59 when Amherst and Wolfe had changed the fortune of the war, by a more able and faithful conduct of it, I again rejoiced in the name of Briton, and should have rejoiced in it to this day, had not the king and parliament committed high treason and rebellion against America, as soon as they had conquered Canada and made peace with France. That there existed a general desire of independence of the crown in any part of America before the Revolution, is as far from truth as the zenith is from the nadir. The encroaching disposition of Great Britain, it was early foreseen by many wise men in all the States, would one day attempt to enslave them by an unlimited submission to Parliament, and rule them with a rod of iron. That this attempt would produce resistance on the part of America and an awful struggle, was also foreseen but dreaded and deprecated as the greatest calamity that could befall them. For my own part, there was not a moment during the Revolution when I would not have given everything I possessed for a restoration to the state of things before the contest began, provided we could have had a sufficient security for its continuance," etc., etc.

Mr. Jefferson says in fewer words:

"I confirm, by my belief, Mr. Jay's criticisms on the passages quoted from Botta. I can answer for its truth from this State southwardly, and northwardly I believe to New York, for which State Mr. Jay himself is a competent witness. What, eastward of that, might have been the dispositions towards England before the commencement of hostilities, I know not ; before that I never had heard a whisper of a disposition to separate from Great Britain; and after that, its possibility was contemplated with affliction by all," etc.

With many acknowledgments for the attentions with which you have deigned to honour my undertaking, and the encouraging tone with which you were pleased to cheer me on to its accomplishment, I pray you to be assured of the profound veneration and perfect esteem of, sir,

Your much obliged and most humble servant,

GEORGE ALEXANDER OTIS.

JAY TO EDWARD LIVINGSTON.

BEDFORD, 28th July, 1822.

SIR :

On the 20th inst. I received a copy of your report to the General Assembly of Louisiana, under a cover directed to me. To whom I am indebted for it, does not appear ; the impression of the seal, which is that of your family, leads me to conjecture that you have had the goodness to send it. There are various important remarks and reflections in it which I believe to be just ; and there are others whose weight I cannot venture to estimate, without more thought and investigation than the state of my health admits of

I will, however, take the liberty of suggesting a few hints on two of the topics.

That the government of a State should have authority to appoint "particular days for rendering thanks to God" for any signal blessing, or imploring his assistance "in any public calamity," is certainly proper. But, can any of our governments be rightfully restrained from providing for the observance of the *Sabbath*, which the Sovereign of the universe had instituted, and which our Saviour has assured us "was made for man"?

Again—Can any government be justifiable in exempting murderers from the punishment of death, in opposition to the positive declaration of the Almighty to Noah, and through him to all his posterity, that " whosoever sheddeth man's blood, by man shall his blood be shed"; not, I presume, at the discretion of private individuals, but under the cognizance and by the authority of government?

Accept my thanks for this mark of friendly attention.

I am, sir,
Your obliged and obedient servant,
JOHN JAY.

RICHARD HENRY LEE TO JAY.

LEESBURG, LOUDON COUNTY, VA.,
January 30th, 1823.

JOHN JAY, ESQ.:

From a person unknown to you an apology for an unlicensed intrusion on your attention, is certainly due. The apology is this, that I am engaged in writing a memoir of the life of an American patriot, a fellow labourer in the cause of American Liberty with yourself.

I beg leave to introduce myself to you, as the grandson and namesake of Richard Henry Lee. My ancestor taught his children to admire and esteem Mr. Jay, and, to admire and esteem him has become hereditary in his descendants. This language, venerable Sir, I feel to be that of *real* sentiment with me.

The principal object of this letter is to obtain from you, if you recollect minutely on the subject, a correct account of the part which my grandfather acted in the three leading Committees appointed by the Congress of *1774*. These were the Committees to prepare an address to the King of England, to the people of Great Britain and to the Colonies. From the Journals of Congress, it appears that the Committee for the first address consisted of Messrs. Lee, J. Adams, Johnson, Henry and Rutledge. The two other Committees were at first composed of Messrs. Lee, Livingston and Jay. To the Committee for the address to the King, Mr. Dickenson was afterward added. It is known that you, Sir, were the writer of the address (which was adopted) to the people of Great Britain. It had been understood generally (as Mr. Marshall in his " Life of Washington " states) that Mr. Lee was the writer of the address to the King. But in a late work, the " Life of Patrick Henry," by Mr. Wirt, it is stated that Mr. Dickenson was the writer. Can you, Sir, give me any information as to the real fact—which of the two gentlemen wrote this address? Mr. Lee, yourself and Mr. Cushing (see Journal) were the persons appointed to prepare an address to the people of Quebeck, and letters to the Colonies of St. John, Nova Scotia, Georgia, East and West Florida. Mr. Jay and Mr. Lee constituted the Committee, to prepare a letter to the American agents in London. You will, respected Sir, confer a great favour on me, by giving me such information as you recollect, as to the fact, which of the gentlemen of these committees wrote these addresses and letters—I hope that you will not withold from me the information which will often introduce (it cannot happen too often) the name of Jay, to my readers. I trust that you will not object to my query as to yourself, for I have ventured to make it, to ascertain how far my grandfather acted as a *writer*. It has been insinuated by the biographer of Mr. Henry, that R. H. Lee was an *unsuccessful writer*, and *not a man of business*. Have you any recollection of his participation in the business and labours of the old Congress?

I have a large and most interesting collection of Mss. consisting of the correspondence, &c., &c., of R. H. Lee, and of all the great and celebrated men of America and Europe, during the Revolution, political, diplomatic, and military.

A letter from you, respected Sir, would be received with great gratification and acknowledged with thankfullness.

I am, Sir, with sentiments of profound respect, &c.,

Your obedient servant,

RICHD. HENRY LEE.

P. S. I perceive from the Journals that the 1st Committee appointed by the Congress 1774, was one to state the Rights of America, in what instances they had been violated and the means of restoring peace, &c. This committee was composed of two members from each Colony, yourself and Mr. Duane, on the part of New York; R. H. Lee and Mr. Pendleton on the part of Virginia, &c. See Journal, 10 p., the declaration and resolves p. 27. I should be happy to learn, what part R. H. Lee took in this Committee, to aid me in vindication from the insinuations above stated.

R. H. LEE.

JAY TO RICHARD HENRY LEE.

BEDFORD, WESTCHESTER COUNTY, N. Y.,
12th February, 1823.

SIR :

I received by the last mail your friendly letter of the 30th ult., the principal object of which you observe is to obtain from me, if I recollect *minutely* on the subject, a correct account of the part which your grandfather acted in the *three* leading committees appointed by the Congress of 1774. These were the committees to prepare an address to the King of England, to the People of Great Britain, and to the Colonies. The committee for the *first* address consisted of Messrs. Lee, J. Adams, Johnson, Henry, and Rutledge. To this committee Mr. Dickinson was afterwards added. You further observe, that it had been generally understood that Mr. Lee was the writer of that address, but that it has since been ascribed to Mr. Dickinson.

So many years have elapsed since the Congress of 1774 that my recollection, as to many of the occasional and incidental circumstances which occurred in the course of their proceedings, is not distinct. It appears from the journals of that Congress, that the committee to prepare an address to the *King*, reported a draught of such an address on the 21st October, that after some debate it was *recommitted*, and Mr. J. Dickinson was on that day added to the committee. So soon afterwards as the 24th of October, they again reported, and on the next day, viz., the 25th October, the address they had reported was debated, and after some amendments, approved. By which of the members of the committee it was written, I do not remember to have been informed. To me it appears probable that the same draught which had been recommitted, was with the co-operation of Mr. Dickinson amended, and again reported. That Mr. Dickinson, between the 21st October when he was added to the committee and the 24th October when they for the last time reported, should have proposed to the committee to lay aside their draught, and that he (with their approbation) should have undertaken, and to their satisfaction have finished an entire *new* address, is in my opinion improbable, especially considering his sense of propriety, and the character and abilities of the gentlemen of that committee.

On the 11th October, 1774, the Congress " Resolved unanimously that a memorial be prepared to the people of British America, stating to them the necessity of a firm, united, and invariable observation of the measures recommended by the Congress, as they tender the invaluable rights and liberties derived to them from the laws and constitution of their country "; also " that an address be prepared to the people of Great Britain. " " Ordered that Mr. Lee, Mr. Livingston, and Mr. Jay be a committee to prepare a draught of the memorial and address. It was agreed in the committee that Mr. Lee should prepare a draught of the proposed *Memorial*, which was the first, both in order and importance, and that I should prepare a draught of the proposed address to the people of Great Britain, both of which was done accordingly.

On the 18th October the address to the people of Great Britain was reported to Congress ; on the 19th October it was debated by paragraphs and sundry amendments made, and was recommitted, in order that the amendments might be taken in. On the 21st October it was returned to Congress, and the amendments directed being made, the same was approved. On the 19th October "the committee reported a draught of a *Memorial* to the inhabitants of the British Colonies; on the 21st October Congress resumed the consideration of the memorial, and the same being debated by paragraphs and amended, was approved. I have always believed that this memorial was written by Mr. Lee ; nor have any reasons to doubt it come to my knowledge.

On the same day, viz., 21st October, the Congress " Resolved that an address be prepared to the People of Quebec, and letters to the Colonies of St. Johns, etc. Ordered that Mr. Cushing, Mr. Lee, and Mr. Dickinson be a Committee to prepare the above address and letters." Hence it appears that your idea of my being one of that Committee is not correct. On the 24th October, "the address to the People of Quebec," being brought in, was read, and after some debate, was re-committed. On the 26th October, "the committee, to whom the address to the inhabitants of Quebec was re-committed, reported a draught, which was read, and being debated by paragraphs and amended was approved. " I have often heard it said, and not heard it contradicted, that this address was written by Mr. Dickinson. On the 25th October the Congress " Resolved that the address to the King be inclosed in a letter to the several Colony agents, etc. " and ordered that Mr. Lee and Mr. Jay prepare a letter to the agents. On the 26th October the letter to the agents being brought in by the committee, was read and approved. This letter was written by Mr. Lee.

The committee (mentioned in the postscript to your letter) appointed to state the rights of the Colonies, etc., included a number of gentlemen whose information and talents enabled them to discuss and elucidate those topics very ably; but I cannot particularize how far Mr. Lee, or any other individual of those gentlemen, contributed to the accomplishment of that business. The uninterrupted deputation of Mr. Lee to Congress by his native and important State, during many years of danger and difficulty, and his continued participation in the transaction of affairs of such moment, afford inferences on which much might be said.

Altho' a recent increase of sickness renders occupation irksome to me, yet as a further increase of it might suspend and perhaps prevent my attending to your inquiries, I think it better to answer your letter thus concisely, than to postpone writing. Those inquiries need no apology; the friendly sentiments expressed in your letter merit and have my acknowledgments. Permit me to hint that the Memoirs you

are preparing would derive advantage from delibera-
tion and frequent revision.

With the best wishes for your success and welfare,

I am, sir,

Your obedient servant,

JOHN JAY.

JAY TO GENERAL LAFAYETTE.

BEDFORD, 20th September, 1824.

DEAR SIR:

Had not the state of my health detained me here,
I should immediately after your arrival at New York
have had the gratification of seeing you there.

Your attachment and services to the United States,
and the friendly attentions with which you have
honoured me, are fresh in my memory; and it will
always give me pleasure to manifest the sense which
I entertain of both.

Altho' my son informed me of your kind intention
to favour me with a visit, yet as your numerous and
entertaining engagements may not soon allow you
leisure for it, I cannot longer forbear to assure you in
this way of those sentiments of unceasing esteem and
regard with which I remain,

Dear sir,

Your friend and obedient servant,

JOHN JAY.

P. S.—Be pleased to present my compliments to
your son, whom I shall also be glad to see here.

GENERAL LAFAYETTE TO JAY.

MY DEAR SIR:

MONTICELLO, November 10th, 1824.

As soon as I found myself once more on the happy shore of America, one of my first inquiries was after you, and the Means to greet my old friend. The pleasure to see your Son was great indeed, but I regretted the distance, engagements, and duties which obliged me to postpone the high gratification to meet you after so long an absence. Since that time I have been paying visits, and receiving welcomes where every sort of enjoyments and sights, exceeding my own sanguine expectations, have mingled with the feeling of a lively and profound gratitude. From you, my dear sir, and in the Name of Congress I have been honoured with a benevolent farewell. Now I am going to Washington City, the Constitutional forms having changed, to await the arrival of the Members of the Houses, and be introduced to each of them with my thanks for their kind invitation to this our American Land.

Your letter reached me on my way through a part of the States ; I wish I could produce myself the answer or tell you when I can anticipate a visit to you. But waiting longer would not enable me to know it, at least for some time. I therefore beg you to receive the grateful respects of my Son and the expression of most affectionate sentiments from

Your old revolutionary Companion

And constant friend,

LAFAYETTE.

MRS. BANYER TO JAY.

MY DEAR PAPA,

NEW YORK, 19th April, 1825.

I sincerely thank you for your affectionate favor of the 5th inst.

. . . . . .

Brother saw your friend Judge Benson last week ; he was very well and promised to take tea with us, but did not come. Col. Varick looks as well as when you saw him, though his legs continue to be very much swelled. Col. Troup honoured me with a visit some days since ; it really grieved me to see him greatly altered ; he says his health is much impaired, as well as his hearing which is so bad that he cannot enjoy the pleasures of general conversation, which to a man of his social disposition must be a great privation. Mr. P. Stuyvesant has long wished to dispose of his place and has lately sold it to a Company who are to give him $100,000 for the Mansion house, 200 house lots and the water right, still leaving him a large real estate. The rise in property has been so great that it is supposed Mrs. Ten Broeck's children will divide to the value of $40,000 each. Rensselair is engaged to Miss Nelson, a grand-daughter of the gentleman who married Lady Kitty. Apropos of her, she made many kind enquiries about you and desired me to give her love to you ; her Sister, Lady Mary, is very sick with a severe cold and fever.

The family here are all well : I wish you could see little Peter, you would be delighted with his intelligence, good temper and affectionate disposition ; there cannot be a more promising child. Mr. Rutherford took us yesterday to see Peale's likeness of Genl. Washington, said by many of the General's old friends to be the best ever taken. I should like you to see it. Judge Peters and many others have addressed very flattering letters to Mr. Peale on the subject.

21st. I am very sorry to tell you that Genl. Clarkson is quite ill ; Mary was sent for this morning and has been with him all day. Brother came home this evening and said Dr. Post thought his disease Dropsy in the chest ; he has not been well for some time but yesterday paid a visit to his son on Long Island ; in the night was taken with shortness of breath. I cannot but hope, however, that he will be relieved & that a life so valuable to his family & to the Community may be spared. Please to remember me with great affection to brother William, sisters, and the Children. My health is better than when I last wrote. That a merciful Providence may preserve yours, my dear Father, is the fondest prayer of

Your dutiful and affecte. daughter,

M. BANYER.

COMMITTEE OF THE CORPORATION OF THE CITY OF NEW YORK TO JAY.

NEW YORK, June 22d, 1826.

SIR :

The corporation of this city have resolved to celebrate, with public demonstrations of respect and joy, the ensuing anniversary of American Independence.

The period of time which has elapsed since the declaration of independence, gives to the coming anniversary a peculiar solemnity and interest. To you, sir, this anniversary must return with feelings grateful to a patriot heart. Engaged in the first scenes of the revolution, when the disproportion between the power of the mother country and the means of the then colonies might have appalled even bold and daring minds—yet conscious of your country's rights, and sensible of their importance to its happiness and welfare, you and your compatriots fearlessly periled your fortunes and your honours in the contest. By your firmness and the wisdom of your counsels, you eminently contributed to the glorious and happy issue which has placed our country in a rank with the most favoured nation of the earth.

Amid the festivities of the anniversary, while we remember your worth, your virtue, and your patriotism, it will add to our pleasures to reflect that you have been permitted by Providence to witness the fiftieth return of a day so conspicuous in the annals of freedom, and also to find your beloved country happy as a people, and prosperous as a nation.

While we present to you in behalf of their citizens their congratulations on the return of this anniversary, we beg leave to assure you that your presence at the intended celebration would afford us the highest gratification. And to this we respectfully invite you.

In behalf of the corporation of the city of New York, we are with great consideration,

Your obedient servants.

JAY TO THE COMMITTEE OF THE CORPORATION OF THE CITY OF NEW YORK.

BEDFORD, June 29th, 1826.

GENTLEMEN :

I have received your letter of the 22d inst., informing me that the corporation of the city of New York had resolved to celebrate, with public demonstrations of respect and joy, the ensuing anniversary of American Independence, and inviting me, on behalf of the corporation, to unite with them in their congratulations on the return of this day.

I feel very grateful for the honour done me by this invitation, and request the favour of you to assure the corporation of my gratitude for it, and my regret that the state of my health renders me unable to comply with their kind wishes.

I cannot forbear to embrace the opportunity afforded by the present occasion, to express my earnest hope that the peace, happiness, and prosperity enjoyed by our beloved country, may induce those who direct her national councils to *recommend* a general and public return of praise and thanksgiving to HIM from whose goodness these blessings descend.

The most effectual means of securing the continuance of our civil and religious liberties, is always to remember with reverence and gratitude the source from which they flow.

I beg you to accept my thanks for the obliging manner in which you have been pleased to allude to my public life.

I have the honour, gentlemen, to be

With great respect,

Your obedient servant,

JOHN JAY.

ADDITIONAL PAPERS.

ADDRESSES TO THE AMERICAN BIBLE SOCIETY, BY JOHN JAY.

At the Annual Meeting, May 9, 1822.

Our late worthy and munificent president having, since the last anniversary of the society, been removed to a better state, the board of managers were pleased to elect me to succeed him : and that the state of my health might cease to be an objection, they have also dispensed with my personal attendance. For the honour they have done me by both these marks of attention, it gives me pleasure to express my sincere and grateful acknowledgments. With equal sincerity I assure the society that, although restrained from active services by long-continued maladies and the increasing infirmities of age, my attachment to this institution, and my desire to promote the attainment of its great and important objects, remain undiminished.

Those great and important objects have, on former anniversaries of this and similar societies, been so comprehensively and eloquently elucidated by gentlemen of signal worth and talents, as that it would neither be a necessary nor an easy task to give them additional illustration. So interesting, however, are the various topics which bear a relation to the purposes for which we have associated, that it cannot be useless, nor, on these occasions, unseasonable, to reiterate our attention to some of them.

There is reason to believe that the original, and the subsequent fallen, state of man, his promised redemption from the latter, and the institution of sacrifices having reference to it, were well known to many of every antediluvian generation. That these great truths were known to Noah, appears from the Divine favour he experienced; from his being a preacher of righteousness; and from the time and the description of the sacrifices which he offered. That he carefully and correctly communicated this knowledge to his children, is to be presumed from his character and longevity.

After the astonishing catastrophe at Babel, men naturally divided into different associations, according to their languages; and migrating into various regions, multiplied into distinct nations. Tradition, doubtless, still continued to transmit these great truths from generation to generation; but the diminution of longevity, together with the defects and casualties incident to tradition, gradually rendered it less and less accurate. These important truths thus became, in process of time, disfigured, obscure, and disregarded. Custom and usage continued the practice of sacrifices, but the design of their institution ceased to be remembered. Men "sought out many inventions," and true religion was supplanted by fables and idolatrous rites. Their mythology manifests the inability of *mere* human reason, even when combined with the learning of Egypt, and the philosophy of Greece and Rome, to acquire the knowledge of our actual state and future destiny, and of the conduct proper to be observed in relation to both.

By the merciful interposition of Providence, early provision was made for preserving these great truths from universal oblivion; and for their being ultimately diffused throughout the world. They were communicated to Abraham. He was also favoured with additional information relative to the expected redemption, and with a promise that the Redeemer should be of his family. That family was thenceforth separated and distinguished from others, and on becoming a nation, was placed under theocratic government. To that family and nation, the Divine oracles and revelations were committed; and such of them as Infinite Wisdom deemed proper for the future instruction of every nation, were recorded and carefully preserved. By those revelations, the promise and expectation of redemption were from time to time renewed, and sundry distinctive marks and characteristic circumstances of the Redeemer predicted. The same merciful Providence has also been pleased to cause every material event and occurrence respecting our Redeemer, together with the gospel he proclaimed, and the miracles and predictions to which it gave occasion, to be faithfully recorded and preserved for the information and benefit of all mankind.

All these records are set forth in the Bible which we are distributing; and from them it derives an incalculable degree of importance; for as every man must soon pass through his short term of existence here, into a state of life of endless duration, the knowledge necessary to enable him to prepare for *such* a change cannot be too highly estimated.

The Gospel was no sooner published than it proceeded to triumph over obstacles which its enemies thought insurmountable, and numerous heathen nations rendered joyful "obedience to the faith." Well-known events afterward occurred, which impeded its progress, and even contracted the limits of its sway. Why those events were permitted, and why the conversion of the great residue of the Gentiles was postponed, has not been revealed to us. The Scriptures inform us, that the coming in of the fulness of the Gentiles will not be accomplished while Jerusalem shall continue to be trodden down by them. As a distant future period appears to have been allotted for its accomplishment, so a distant future season was doubtless assigned for its effectual commencement. Although the time appointed for the arrival of that season cannot be foreseen, yet we have reason to presume that its approach, like the approach of most other seasons, will be preceded and denoted by appropriate and significant indications. As the conversion of the Gentiles is doubtless to be effected by the instrumentality of Christian nations, so these will doubtless be previously prepared and qualified for that great work; and their labour in it be facilitated by the removal or mitigation of obstructions and difficulties. The tendency, which certain recent events have to promote *both* these purposes, gives them the aspect of such indications.

Great and multifarious were the calamities inflicted on the nations of Europe by their late extensive war ; a war of longer duration, and in the course of which more blood and tears were shed, more rapacity and desolation committed, more cruelty and perfidy exercised, and more national and individual distress experienced, than in any of those which are recorded in modern history. During the continuance, and on the conclusion of such a war, it was natural to expect, that the pressure of public and personal dangers and necessities would have directed and limited the thoughts, cares, and efforts of rulers and people to their existing exigences ; and to the means necessary to acquire security, to repair waste, and terminate privations.

Yet, strange as it may appear, desires, designs, and exertions of a very different kind, mingled with these urgent temporal cares. The people of Great Britain formed, and have nobly supported their memorable Bible Society. Their example has been followed, not only by the people of this country, but also by nations who had not yet obliterated the vestiges of war and conflagration. At no former period have the people of Europe and America instituted so many associations for diffusing and impressing the knowledge and influence of the Gospel, and for various other charitable and generous purposes, as since

the beginning of the present century. These associations comprehend persons of every class ; and their
exemplary zeal and philanthropy continue to incite
feelings and meditations well calculated to prepare us
all for the great work before mentioned. We have
also lived to see some of the *obstructions* to it removed, and some of its *difficulties* mitigated.

Throughout many generations there have been
professing Christians, who, under the countenance
and authority of their respective governments, treated
the heathen inhabitants of certain countries in Africa
as articles of commerce ; taking and transporting
multitudes of them, like beasts of burden, to distant
regions ; to be sold, and to toil and die in slavery.
During the continuance of such a traffic, with what
consistence, grace, or prospect of success, could such
Christians send missionaries to present the Bible, or
preach the Christian doctrines of brotherly kindness
and charity to the people of those countries ?

So far as respects Great Britain and the United
States, that obstacle has been removed ; and other
Christian nations have partially followed their example. Although similar circumstances expose some of
them to an opposition like that which Great Britain
experienced, it is to be hoped that an overruling
Providence will render it equally unsuccessful. I
allude to the territorial and personal concerns which
prompted the opposition with which the advocates
for the act of abolition had to contend. It will be
recollected that many influential individuals deeply
interested in the slave-trade, together with others

who believed its continuance to be indispensable to the prosperity of the British West India Islands, made strenuous opposition to its abolition, even in the British parliament. Delays were caused by it, but considerations of a higher class than those which excited the opposition finally prevailed, and the parliament abolished that detestable trade. Well-merited honour was thereby reflected on the Legislature ; and particularly on that excellent and celebrated member of it, whose pious zeal and unwearied perseverance were greatly and conspicuously instrumental to the removal of that obstacle. Their example, doubtless, has weight with those other nations who are in a similar predicament, and must tend to encourage them to proceed and act in like manner.

Although an immense heathen population in India was under the dominion, controul, and influence of a Christian nation, yet it was deemed better policy to leave them in blindness than to risk incurring the inconveniences which might result from authorizing or encouraging attempts to relieve them from it. This policy has at length met with the neglect it deserved. The Gospel has been introduced into India, under the auspices of the British government ; and various means are co-operating to advance its progress, and hasten the time when the King of saints will emancipate that people from the domination of the prince of darkness.

The languages of the heathen nations in general being different from those of Christian nations, neither their Bibles could be read, nor their missionaries be understood by the former. To obviate and lessen these difficulties, numerous individuals have been induced to learn those languages; and the Bible has already been translated into many of them. Provision has been made for educating heathen youth, and qualifying them for becoming missionaries. Schools have also been established in heathen countries, and are preparing the rising generation to receive and to diffuse the light of the Gospel.

The mere tendency of these events to promote the coming in of the Gentiles, affords presumptive evidence of their being genuine indications of the approach of the season assigned for it—or, in other words, that they are providential. This evidence becomes more than presumptive, when combined with that which the few following inquiries and remarks bring into view.

Whence has it come to pass that Christian nations, who for ages had regarded the welfare of heathens with indifference, and whose intercourse with them had uniformly been regulated by the results of political, military, and commercial calculations, have recently felt such new and unprecedented concern for the salvation of their souls, and have simultaneously concurred in means and measures for that purpose? Whence has it come to pass that so many individuals, of every profession and occupation, who in the ordinary course of human affairs confine their speculations, resources, and energies to the acquisition of temporal prosperity for themselves and families, have become so ready and solicitous to supply idolatrous strangers in remote regions with the means of obtaining eternal felicity? Who has "opened their hearts to attend" to such things?

It will be acknowledged that worldly wisdom is little conversant with the transcendent affairs of that kingdom which is not of *this* world ; and has neither ability to comprehend, nor inclination to further them. To what adequate cause, therefore, can these extraordinary events be attributed, but to the wisdom that cometh from *above?* If so, these events authorize us to conclude, that the Redeemer is preparing to take possession of the great remainder of his heritage, and is inciting and instructing his servants to act accordingly. The duties which this conclusion proclaims and inculcates, are too evident and well known to require particular enumeration.

Not only Bible societies, but also the various other societies who in different ways are forwarding the great work in question, have abundant reason to rejoice and be thankful for the blessings which have prospered their endeavours. We of this society in particular cannot fail to participate largely in this gratitude and joy ; especially when we reflect on the beneficent and successful exertions of our late meritorious president to establish and support it, on the number of our auxiliaries and members, on the continuance and amount of their contributions, and on the fidelity and prudence with which our affairs have been managed.

Let us therefore persevere steadfastly in distributing the Scriptures far and near, and without note or comment. We are assured that they "are profitable for doctrine, for reproof, for correction, for instruction in righteousness." They comprise the inestimable writings by which the inspired apostles, who were commanded to preach the *Gospel* to *all* people, have transmitted it, through many ages, down to our days. The apostles were opposed in preaching the Gospel, but they nevertheless persisted. We are opposed in dispensing the Scriptures which convey the knowledge of it ; and let us follow their example. An eminent ancient counsellor gave excellent advice to *their* adversaries ; and his reasoning affords salutary admonition to *our* opponents. That advice merits attention, and was concluded in the following memorable words :

" Refrain from these men, and let them alone ; for if this counsel or this work be of men, it will come to naught ; but if it be of God, ye cannot overthrow it ; lest haply ye be found even to fight against God."

At the Annual Meeting, May 8, 1823.

GENTLEMEN :

It gives me pleasure to observe that this anniversary, like the preceding, brings with it tidings which give us occasion for mutual gratulations, and for united thanksgivings to Him whose blessings continue to prosper our proceedings.

These annual meetings naturally remind us of the purposes for which we have associated ; and lead us to reflections highly interesting to those who consider what and where we are, and what and where we are to be.

That all men, throughout all ages, have violated their allegiance to their great Sovereign, is a fact to which experience and revelation bear ample and concurrent testimony. The Divine attributes forbid us to suppose that the Almighty Sovereign of the universe will permit any province of His empire to remain forever in a state of revolt. On the contrary, the sacred Scriptures assure us, that it shall not only be reduced to obedience, but also be so purified and improved as that righteousness and felicity shall dwell and abide in it.

Had it not been the purpose of God, that His will should be done on earth as it is done in Heaven, He would not have commanded us to pray for it. That command implies a prediction and a promise that in due season it shall be accomplished. If therefore the will of God is to be done on earth as it is done in Heaven, it must undoubtedly be known throughout the earth, before it can be done throughout the earth ; and, consequently, He who has decreed that it shall be so done, will provide that it shall be so known.

Our Redeemer having directed that the Gospel should be preached throughout the world, it was preached accordingly ; and being witnessed from on high, " with signs and wonders, and with divers miracles and gifts of the Holy Ghost," it became preponderant, and triumphant, and effulgent. But this state of exaltation, for reasons unknown to us, was suffered to undergo a temporary depression. A subsequent period arrived, when the pure doctrines of the Gospel were so alloyed by admixtures, and obscured by appendages, that its lustre gradually diminished, and like the fine gold mentioned by the prophet, it became dim.

Since the Reformation, artifice and error have been losing their influence on ignorance and credulity, and the Gospel has been resuming its purity. We now see Christians, in different countries, and of different denominations, spontaneously and cordially engaged in conveying the Scriptures, and the knowledge of salvation, to the heathen inhabitants of distant regions. So singular, impressive, and efficient is the impulse which actuates them, that without the least prospect of earthly retribution, they cheerfully submit to such pecuniary contributions, such appropriations of time and industry, and, in many instances, to such hazards and privations, and such derelictions of personal comfort and convenience, as are in direct opposition to the propensities of human nature.

Can such extraordinary and unexampled undertakings possibly belong to that class of enterprises, which we are at liberty to adopt or decline as we please; enterprises which no duty either commands or forbids? This is more than a mere speculative question; and therefore the evidence respecting the character and origin of these undertakings cannot be too carefully examined, and maturely weighed; especially as this evidence is accumulating, and thereby acquiring additional claims to serious attention.

We observe a strange and general alteration in the

feelings of Christians towards the heathen ; and one
still more strange and unprecedented has taken place
in their feelings towards the *Jews ;* feelings very different from those which so many centuries have universally prevailed.   Although, as it were, *sifted* over
all nations, yet, unlike the drops of rain which blend
with the waters on which they fall, these scattered
exiles have constantly remained in a state of separation from the people among whom they were dispersed ; obstinately adhering to their peculiarities,
and refusing to coalesce with them.   By thus fulfilling
the prophecies, every Jew is a living witness to their
truth.

The same prophecies declare, that a time will come
when all the twelve tribes shall be restored to their
country, and be a praise in the earth : but the precise
time is not specified.   By declaring that "blindness
in part hath happened unto Israel, *until* the fulness
of the Gentiles be come in, and that Jerusalem shall
be trodden down of the Gentiles *until* the times of
the Gentiles be fulfilled," they lead us to conclude,
that their blindness will not be sooner removed, and
therefore that their conversion is not to be sooner
expected.   Individual Jews have, from time to time,
been relieved from their blindness, and become Christians ; and there are expressions in the Scriptures,
which favour the prevailing opinion, that the conversion of a large portion, and perhaps of the whole
tribe of Judah, may precede that of the other tribes.
They are now experiencing less oppression, less contempt, and more compassion than formerly.   Their

obduracy is softening, and their prejudices abating. These changes have the appearance of incipient preparatives for their conversion.

Besides these recent changes in favour of the heathen and the Jews, another has taken place in the disposition and feelings of our people towards the many savage nations who still remain within our limits. The policy formerly observed towards them, together with our rapid population, increased their necessities, but not our endeavours to alleviate them. This indifference has latterly been yielding to a general sympathy for their wretchedness, and to a desire to ameliorate their condition. For this laudable purpose, our government has wisely and virtuously adopted measures for their welfare; and benevolent societies and pious individuals are using means to introduce among them the benefits of civilization and Christianity.

Nor are these the only events and changes which are facilitating the distribution, and extending the knowledge of the Scriptures. For a long course of years, many European nations were induced to regard toleration as pernicious, and to believe that the people had no right to think and judge for themselves respecting religious tenets and modes of worship. Hence it was deemed advisable to prohibit their reading the Bible, and to grant that privilege only to persons of a certain description. Intolerance is passing away, and in France, where it formerly prevailed, Bible Societies have been established by permission of the government, and are proceeding prosperously, under the auspices of men high in rank, in character, and in station.

From the nature, the tendency, and the results of these recent and singular changes, events, and institutions ; from their coincidence, and admirable adjustment, as means for making known the Holy Scriptures, and inculcating the will of their Divine and merciful Author, throughout the world ; and from the devotedness with which they are carrying into operation, there is reason to conclude that they have been produced by Him in whose hands are the hearts of all men.

If so, we are engaged in His service ; and that consideration forbids us to permit our ardour or exertions to be relaxed or discouraged by attempts to depreciate our motives, to impede or discredit our proceedings, or to diminish our temporal resources. The Scriptures represent Christians as being engaged in a spiritual warfare, and, therefore, both in their associated and individual capacities, they are to expect and prepare for opposition. On the various inducements which prompt this opposition, much might be said ; though very little, if any thing, that would be new. The present occasion admits only of general and brief remarks, and not of particular and protracted disquisitions.

Whatever may be the characters, the prejudices, the views, or the arts of our opponents, we have only to be faithful to our Great Leader. They who march under the banners of EMMANUEL have God with them ; and consequently have nothing to fear.

At the Annual Meeting, May 13, 1824.

GENTLEMEN :

We have the satisfaction of again observing, that by the blessing of Providence on the zeal of our fellow-citizens, and on the fidelity, diligence, and prudence with which our affairs are conducted, they continue in a state of progressive improvement. The pleasure we derive from it is not a little increased by the consideration that we are transmitting essential benefits to multitudes in various regions, and that the value and important consequences of these benefits extend and will endure beyond the limits of time. By so doing, we render obedience to the commandment by which He who " made of one blood all nations of men," and established a fraternal relation between the individuals of the human race, hath made it their duty to love and be kind to one another.

We know that a great proportion of mankind are ignorant of the revealed will of God, and that they have strong claims to the sympathy and compassion which we, who are favoured with it, feel and are manifesting for them. To the most sagacious among the heathen it must appear wonderful and inexplicable that such a vicious, suffering being as man should have proceeded in such a condition from the hands of his Creator. Having obscure and confused ideas of a future state, and unable to ascertain how far justice may yield to mercy or mercy to justice, they live and die (as our heathen ancestors did) involved in darkness and perplexities.

By conveying the Bible to people thus circumstanced we certainly do them a most interesting act of kindness. We thereby enable them to learn, that man was originally created and placed in a state of happiness, but, becoming disobedient, was subjected to the degradation and evils which he and his posterity have since experienced. The Bible will also inform them, that our gracious Creator has provided for us a Redeemer, in whom all the nations of the earth should be blessed—that this Redeemer has made atonement " for the sins of the whole world," and thereby reconciling the Divine justice with the Divine mercy, has opened a way for our redemption and salvation ; and that these inestimable benefits are of the free gift and grace of God, not of our deserving, nor in our power to deserve. The Bible will also animate them with many explicit and consoling assurances of the Divine mercy to our fallen race, and with repeated invitations to accept the offers of pardon and reconciliation. The truth of these facts and the sincerity of these assurances being unquestionable, they cannot fail to promote the happiness of those by whom they are gratefully received, and of those by whom they are benevolently communicated.

We have also the satisfaction of observing that the condition of the Church continues to improve. When at certain periods subsequent to the Reformation, discordant opinions on ecclesiastical subjects began to prevail, they produced disputes and asperities which prompted those who embraced the same peculiar opinions to form themselves into distinct associations or sects. Those sects not only permitted Christian fraternity with each other to be impaired by coldness, reserve, and distrust, but also, on the occurrence of certain occasions, proceeded to alternate and culpable acts of oppression. Even their endeavours to increase the number of Christians were often too intimately connected with a desire to increase the number of their adherents; and hence they became more solicitous to repress competition than to encourage reciprocal respect and good-will.

These prejudices, however, have gradually been giving way to more laudable feelings. By the progress of civilization and useful knowledge many individuals became better qualified to distinguish truth from error, and the diffusion of their reasonings among the people enabled them to judge and to act with less risk of committing mistakes. Since the rights of man and the just limits of authority in Church and State have been more generally and clearly understood, the Church has been less disturbed by that zeal which " is not according to knowledge "; and liberal sentiments and tolerant principles are constantly enlarging the sphere of their influence.

To the advantages which the Church has derived from the improved state of society, may be added those which are resulting from the institution of Bible societies. With whatever degree of tenacity any of the sects may adhere to their respective peculiarities, they all concur in opinion respecting the Bible, and the propriety of extensively distributing it without note or comment. They therefore readily become members · of Bible societies, and in that capacity freely co-operate. Their frequent meetings and consultations produce an intercourse which affords them numerous opportunities of forming just estimates of one another, and of perceiving that prepossessions are not always well founded. This intercourse is rendered the more efficient by the great and increasing number of clerical members from dissimilar denominations. Convinced by observation and experience that persons of great worth and piety are attached to sects different from their own, the duties of their vocation, and their respectable characters, naturally incline them to recommend and encourage Christian friendliness.

It is well known, that both cathedrals and meeting-houses have heretofore exhibited individuals who have been universally and justly celebrated as real and useful Christians ; and it is also well known, that at present not a few, under similar circumstances and of similar characters, deserve the like esteem and commendation. As *real* Christians are made so by Him without whom we "can do nothing," it is equally certain that He receives them into His family, and that in *His* family mutual love and uninterrupted concord never cease to prevail. There is no reason to believe or suppose that this family will be divided into separate classes, and that separate apartments in the mansions of bliss will be allotted to them according to the different sects from which they had proceeded.

These truths and considerations direct our attention to the *new* commandment of our Saviour, that his disciples " do love one another " : although an anterior commandment required, that, " as we had opportunity " we should " do good unto all men " ; yet this *new* one makes it our duty to do so " especially to the household of faith." In the early ages of the Church, Christians were highly distinguished by their obedience to it ; and it is to be regretted that the conduct of too many of their successors has in this respect been less worthy of imitation.

Our days are becoming more and more favoured and distinguished by new and unexpected accessions of strength to the cause of Christianity. A zeal unknown to many preceding ages has recently pervaded almost every Christian country, and occasioned the establishment of institutions well calculated to diffuse the knowledge and impress the precepts of the Gospel both at home and abroad. The number and diversity of these institutions, their concurrent tendency to promote these purposes, and the multitudes who are cordially giving them aid and support, are so extraordinary, and so little analogous to the dictates of human propensities and passions, that no adequate cause can be assigned for them but the goodness, wisdom, and will of HIM who made and governs the world.

We have reason to rejoice that such institutions have been so greatly multiplied and cherished in the United States; especially as a kind Providence has blessed us, not only with peace and plenty, but also with the full and secure enjoyment of our civil and religious rights and privileges. Let us, therefore, persevere in our endeavours to promote the operation of these institutions, and to accelerate the attainment of their objects. Their unexampled rise, progress, and success in giving light to the heathen, and in rendering Christians more and more " obedient to the faith," apprise us that the great Captain of our salvation is going forth, " conquering and to conquer," and is directing and employing these means and measures for that important purpose. They, therefore, who enlist in His service, have the highest encouragement to fulfil the duties assigned to their respective stations ; for most certain it is, that those of His followers who steadfastly and vigorously contribute to the furtherance and completion of His conquests, will also participate in the transcendent glories and blessings of His triumph.

At the Annual Meeting, May 12, 1825.

Gentlemen :

You have the satisfaction of perceiving, from the report of the board of managers, that the prosperous and promising state of our affairs continues to evince the laudable and beneficial manner in which they have been constantly conducted.

We have to regret that the pleasing reflections and anticipations suggested by these auspicious circumstances are mingled with the sorrow which the recent death of our late worthy and beloved Vice-president has caused, and widely diffused. Our feelings are the more affected by it, as the benefits we have derived from his meritorious and incessant attention to all our concerns have constantly excited both our admiration and our gratitude.

As the course of his life was uniformly under the direction of true religion and genuine philanthropy, it forbids us to doubt of his being in a state of bliss, and associated with "the spirits of just men made perfect." Notwithstanding this consoling consideration, his departure will not cease to be lamented by this society, nor by those of his other fellow-citizens on whom his patriotic services, his exemplary conduct, and his disinterested benevolence have made correspondent impressions.

But the loss we have sustained by this afflicting event should not divert our thoughts from subjects which bear a relation to the design of our institution, and consequently to the purpose for which we annually assemble.

It may not therefore be unseasonable to remark, that the great objects of the Bible, and the distribution of it, *without note or comment*, suggest sundry considerations which have claims to attention.

Christians know that man was destined for two worlds—the one of transient, and the other of perpetual duration ; and that his welfare in both depends on his acceptance and use of the means for obtaining it, which his merciful Creator has for that purpose appointed and ordained. Of these inestimable and unmerited blessings the greater proportion of the human race are yet to be informed ; and, to that end, we are communicating the same to them exactly in that state in which, by the direction and inspiration of their Divine Author, they were specified and recorded in the Bible, which we are distributing without note or comment.

As these gracious dispensations provide for our consolation under the troubles incident to a state of probation in this life, and for our perfect and endless felicity in the next, no communications can be of higher or more general interest. Wherever these dispensations become known and observed, they not only prepare men for a better world, but also diminish the number and pressure of those sufferings which the corrupt propensities and vicious passions of men prompt them to inflict on each other; and which sufferings are of greater frequency and amount than those which result from other causes.

Time and experience will decide whether the distribution of the Bible, without note or comment, will have any, and what effect, on the progress of the Gospel. Hitherto nothing unfavourable to this course of proceeding has occurred; and the expedience of it continues to derive a strong argument from its tendency to decrease the inconveniences which usually attend the circulation of discordant comments. Whenever any questionable opinions relative to any Scripture doctrine meet with zealous advocates, and with zealous opponents, they seldom fail to excite the passions as well as the mental exertions of the disputants. Controversies like these are not always conducted with moderation and delicacy, nor have they been uniformly consistent with candour and charity. On the contrary, the ardour with which the parties contend for victory frequently generates prejudices; and insensibly renders them more anxious to reconcile the Scriptures to their reasonings, than their reasonings to the Scriptures. The doubts and perplexities thereby disseminated are not favourable to those whose faith is not yet steadfast, nor to those who from temperament or imbecility are liable to such impressions.

These remarks, however, are far from being applicable to those excellent and instructive comments which have been written by authors of eminent talent, piety, and prudence; and which have been received with general and well-merited approbation.

It is to be regretted that comments of a very different character and description have caused errors to germinate and take root in Christian countries. Some of these were fabricated by individuals, who, finding that they could not carry their favourite propensities and habits with them through the " narrow way" prescribed by the Gospel, endeavoured to discredit Christianity by objections which exhibit stronger marks of disingenuous, than of correct and candid reasoning. By artfully and diligently encouraging defection from Scripture, and from Scripture doctrines, they gradually introduced and spread that contempt for both, which in the last century was publicly displayed in impious acts of profaneness, and in dreadful deeds of ferocity. These atrocities repressed the career of infidelity, and infidels thereupon became less assuming, but not less adverse.

Even among professing Christians, and of distinct denominations, there are not a few of distinguished attainments and stations who have sedulously endeavoured so to interpret and paraphrase certain passages in the Bible, as to render them congruous with peculiar opinions, and auxiliary to particular purposes.

Certain other commentators, doubtless from a sincere desire to increase Christian knowledge by luminous expositions of abstruse subjects, have attempted to penetrate into the recesses of profound mysteries, and to dispel their obscurity by the light of reason. It seems they did not recollect that *no man can explain what no man can understand.* Those mysteries were revealed to our faith, to be believed on the credit of Divine testimony; and were not addressed to our mental abilities for explication. Numerous objects which include mysteries daily occur to our senses. We are convinced of their existence and reality, but of the means and processes by which they become what they are, and operate as they do, we all continue ignorant. Hence it may rationally be concluded, that the mysteries of the *spiritual* world are still farther remote from the limited sphere of human perspicacity.

Among the biblical critics, there are some who have incautiously intermingled their learned and judicious investigations with enigmatical subtleties and hypothetical speculations, which tend more to engender doubts and disputes than to produce real edification.

Additional animadversions on this subject would

be superfluous ; nor can it be necessary to examine, whether an indiscriminate circulation of comments would merit or meet with general approbation. They who think it advisible that comments should accompany the Bible, doubtless prefer and intend what in their opinion would be a judicious, limited, and exclusive selection of them. It is well known that, composed as this and other Bible societies are, such a selection could not be formed by them with requisite unanimity. They therefore wisely declined disturbing their union by attempting it, and very prudently concluded to distribute the Bible without any other comments than those which result from the illustrations which different parts of it afford to each other. Of this no individuals have reason to complain, especially as they are perfectly at liberty to circulate their favourite authors as copiously and extensively as they desire or think proper.

Our Redeemer commanded his apostles to preach the Gospel to every creature : to that end it was necessary that they should be enabled to understand and to preach it correctly, and to demonstrate its Divine origin and institution by incontestible proofs. The Old Testament, which contained the promises and prophecies respecting the Messiah, was finished at a period antecedent to the coming of our Saviour, and therefore afforded no information nor proof of his advent and subsequent proceedings. To qualify the apostles for their important task, they were blessed with the direction and guidance of the Holy Spirit, and by him were enabled to preach the Gospel with concordant accuracy, and in divers languages : they were also endued with power to prove the truth of their doctrine, and of their authority to preach it, by wonderful and supernatural signs and miracles.

A merciful Providence also provided that some of these inspired men should commit to writing such accounts of the Gospel, and of their acts and proceedings in preaching it, as would constitute and establish a *standard* whereby future preachers and generations might ascertain what they ought to believe and to do ; and be thereby secured against the danger of being misled by the mistakes and corruptions incident to tradition. The Bible contains these writings, and exhibits such a connected series of the Divine revelations and dispensations respecting the present and future state of mankind, and so amply attested by internal and external evidence, that we have no reason to desire or expect that further miracles will be wrought to confirm the belief and confidence which they invite and require.

On viewing the Bible in this light, it appears that an extensive and increasing distribution of it has a direct tendency to facilitate the progress of the Gospel throughout the world. That it will proceed, and in due time be accomplished, there can be no doubt ; let us therefore continue to promote it with unabated zeal, and in full assurance that the omnipotent Author and Protector of the Gospel will not suffer his gracious purposes to be frustrated by the arts and devices, either of malignant " principalities and powers," or of " spiritual wickedness in high places."

JAY TO THE CORPORATION OF TRINITY CHURCH.[1]

. . . .

Permit us now to request your attention to a subject of more importance : it affects us all. You will recollect that Mr. Streebeck, in his letter respecting our call, mentioned his expectation of being *inducted*, according to the forms of what is called "the office of Induction."

At that time we knew so little of that paper as to be unable to say anything decided to him about it ; we afterward procured and considered it. To us it appeared to be liable to objections so manifest and so insuperable, as that we never could consent to have a minister inducted into our Church in that way.

That office of induction ought not, in our opinion, to be permitted to glide silently into operation, and acquire claims to obedience from successive instances of unguarded acquiescence. Whether that instrument is with or without precedent in the Christian Church, or by whom or for what purposes it was de-

---

[1] "Mr. Jay, finding on his removal to Bedford no Episcopal church in the vicinity, constantly attended the one belonging to the Presbyterians ; nor did he scruple to unite with his fellow-Christians of that persuasion in commemorating the passion of their common Lord. His catholicism, however, did not diminish his attachment to his own denomination. He was instrumental in erecting an Episcopal church in Bedford, and was, during the rest of his life, a generous benefactor to it, and, by his will, left a liberal annuity to its pastor. His reluctance to hold any office led him to decline a seat in the vestry of this church, but his advice and aid were frequently asked and cheerfully given. Some matters of business requiring a communication to the vestry of Trinity church, in the city of New York, he was requested to prepare it ; and he took the opportunity of addressing to that powerful and influential corporation some remarks on topics which he regarded as deeply interesting to the Church at large. The draught was cordially approved and adopted by the Bedford church.'
—Jay's "Life of Jay," Vol. I., p. 434.

vised, are questions on which we make no remarks. Amid the prayers and piety by which it is decorated, are to be found unconstitutional assumptions of power, accompanied with a degree of parade and pageantry which, however conducive to other objects, have no natural connection with the mere business of induction. We believe that episcopacy was of apostolic institution, but we do not believe in the various high-church doctrines and prerogatives which art and ambition, triumphing over credulity and weakness, have annexed to it.

By the office of induction, the bishop is to give a formal commission, under his episcopal seal and signature, to the minister whom the corporation had called and engaged to be their rector; giving and granting to him the bishop's license and *authority* to perform the office of a priest of that parish.

We believe that every Episcopalian priest, ordained according to the rules of our Church, has, in virtue of that ordination, good right and authority to preach the Gospel and perform divine service in any parish; but we admit the propriety of being restrained by the bishop from calling and settling any other than an Episcopalian minister so ordained and of fair character. We therefore think it fit that the bishop's approbation on these two points should precede a call. We believe that we have a right to contract with and employ any such minister to be our rector; and that such contract is the only valid and proper commission which he can have to be our particular minister or rector.

We believe that both we and such minister have good right to make such a contract; that when made it is a civil contract; and that the convention have no authority to divest either priest or laymen of their right to make it.

By the office of induction and the commission directed by it, the *bishop* does induct the minister into the parish, and does ordain that he shall claim and enjoy all the accustomed temporalities appertaining to his cure.

We believe that the induction of a priest into a parish is neither more nor less than giving him the key of the church, and putting him in possession of such houses, tenements, and lands as he is entitled, by his contract with the corporation, to occupy and enjoy. This is a business which can lawfully be done only by the proprietors, nor can we perceive the least shadow of right in the bishop or in any other person to meddle with it.

As the bishop has no title to, nor care of, nor any business with, the temporalities of any church, we reject with decision every order or ordinance of his respecting the property of our corporation; we think it highly improper that he should attempt to meddle with our estate, or presume to order any person whatever to claim and enjoy all or any part of it. As to the pretence that he does it because they who serve at the altar should live of the things of the altar; or in other words, that we ought to maintain our minister, it is too frivolous to be even plausible. As the Lord and Giver of all property had already made an ordinance on this subject, another ordinance of the like import by the bishop was, to say the least, unnecessary. In this case his admonitions would be more proper than his orders. Besides, the bishop must know, and does know, that whatever relates to the support of the minister is always settled and fixed by a contract between him and his congregation before his induction as their rector. And therefore it can neither be very necessary nor very decorous for the bishop to ordain that the minister shall claim and enjoy what the corporation had previously promised and engaged that he should have and enjoy.

By the same instrument the bishop further ordains that the said minister shall claim and enjoy the said temporalities, *not for any prescribed or limited time*, but until he shall be separated from the congregation by *episcopal authority.*

In cases where the contract with the minister is clearly expressed and well understood to be for a limited time, can the bishop, with any appearance of probity or propriety, ordain that the minister shall, after the expiration of that time, still continue to claim and enjoy the temporalities without a new contract? Or is it the object and design of this same office of induction, to divest us of the important right which we have by the laws of God and of our country, to make civil and lawful contracts of *limited duration* with any person for his services, whether priest or layman? We fear this design is in operation, for we understand that every priest who shall make such a contract is to be excluded from a seat in the Convention.

We for our parts are far from being prepared to admit the validity and power of any canon to divest us of this right, or to punish or disfranchise a priest for exercising it. We know of nothing in the Gospel which forbids such contracts. To insist that we shall take a priest for better or for worse, and to keep him and to pay him whether he proves worthy or unworthy, faithful or unfaithful, whether we like him or whether we do not like him, is really demanding more than ought either to be demanded or to be complied with. It is said that the bishop may afford relief. It is true that he may; but it is also true that he may not.

As to the bishop's being the arbiter and judge of disputes between a congregation and their rector, we observe, that all such of their disputes as turn on questions of a civil nature belong to the jurisdiction of the courts of law; and that no canon can either deprive those courts of that jurisdiction, nor divest any freeman of his right to have those disputes determined by the laws and by a jury of the country; and consequently, that no canon can or ought to constitute the bishop to be the arbiter or judge of them. But where the disputes turn on points of doctrine, we admit the fitness of their being decided by the bishop, so far as to settle the dispute; but not in all cases so far as to settle the doctrine; for there has been a time when, if the people had continued to believe and adhere to all the decisions and doctrines of their bishops, we should not have heard of, nor have been blessed with the reformed Protestant religion.

We cannot consider it as being altogether consistent with decorum, that the office of induction should order the senior warden, who is the first officer of the corporation, to stand at an appointed place, on the day of induction, during Divine service, holding the keys of the church in his hand in open view, as a mere pageant. We cannot approve of his being directed then to deliver the keys to the new incumbent, as a *token* that the parish did *acknowledge* him to be, what they had already made him to be, *their rector.* We can as little approve of what the new incumbent is thereupon to say to the senior warden, viz., " I receive these keys as pledges of the bishop's *episcopal induction,* and of your *recognition.*"

Recognition of what? That they, the church-wardens, vestry, and congregation, are all ciphers in the business. It is not easy to observe and examine these things without feeling some degree of indignation. We cannot dismiss the office of induction without expressing our disapprobation of introducing an opinion on a disputed point into one of the prayers directed to be used on the day of induction ; it is this :

" O holy Jesus, who has purchased to thyself an universal church, and has promised to be with the ministers of *apostolic succession* to the end of the world."

This is not the promise literally, but the promise

paraphrased and expounded. The promise of our Saviour is, " And lo, I am with you alway, even unto the end of the world."

As the apostles were all to die in a few years, this promise could not be understood as limited to them personally, but as extending to a certain description of persons throughout all ages of the world. To what description of persons does the promise extend ? is the question. To this question, they who made the above paraphrase answer, that it intends and extends to " *the ministers of apostolic succession.*" If it be asked, whether the ministers of the Calvinistic and of certain other churches are of apostolic succession, it is answered by all our bishops and clergy that they are not. It follows, therefore, of necessary consequence, that our bishops and clergy, and their congregation, when they offer up their prayer to Almighty God, must offer it with the meaning and understanding that the gracious promise mentioned in it is confined to Episcopalian ministers, and therefore excludes the ministers of all other denominations of Christians.

Who is there among us that can be prepared to declare, in solemn prayer, and in such positive and unqualified terms, that none but Episcopalian ministers have any part or lot in this important promise ? Who is there that can be certain that the apostles, as to that promise, were not considered as the representatives of all who should become sincere and pious converts to, and believers in, the doctrines which they were sent to publish and to teach ? What good reason can be assigned for our being called upon by the office of induction to adopt thus solemnly in prayer a doubtful exposition and construction of the promise ; for doubtful it most certainly is, having from the reformation to this day been a subject of controversy and dispute between the ablest and best Christian divines.   Great, indeed, must be the confidence and hardihood of those advocates for this construction of the promise who can, without hesitation, deny that our blessed Redeemer was with those non-episcopalian ministers and congregations amounting to several hundred thousands, who for his sake endured all the varieties and rigours of persecution.   If the great Captain of our Salvation was not with them, how and by whom were they enabled to meet and sustain such trials so firmly, to resist the adversary so resolutely, and to fight the good fight of faith so triumphantly ?

It may not be unworthy of remark, that as a prophecy is best understood from its completion, so the manner in which a Divine promise is performed, affords the best exposition of its true and original meaning.

Lastly.   Let it be remembered, and corporations should recollect their charters, that in the year 1795 the Protestant-Episcopal church in this State did apply for and did obtain an act of the Legislature in this State, passed the seventeenth day of March in that year, which contains the following clause :

"And be it further enacted, that the churchwardens and vestry for the time being, shall be, and hereby are vested with full power to call and induct a rector to the church, when and so often as there shall be a vacancy therein."

We submit to your consideration whether measures should not be taken to do away the office of induction ; and if there must be such a thing introduced into the church, that it may be such a one as will leave both clergy and laity in quiet possession of their respective rights.

It is with sincere regret and reluctance that we find ourselves urged, by obvious considerations, to proceed to remarks on another interesting topic, which cannot be agreeable to many whose affections and good-will we are solicitous to cultivate by every becoming mark of respect. We know how much the welfare of our infant church depends on their friendly disposition towards us, and it certainly is as little our inclination as it is our interest to incur their displeasure. But painful as it may be, we must maintain our right, even at the risk of losing their good-will.

For a considerable time past, we have observed a variety of circumstances connected with church affairs which, on being combined and compared one with the other, justify inferences which, in our opinion, are exceedingly interesting, not only to the rights of the laity, but also to our churches in general, and to yours in particular. We allude to the gradual introduction and industrious propagation of high church doctrines. Of late years, they have frequently been seen lifting up their heads and appearing in places where their presence was neither necessary nor expected. There never was a time when those doctrines promoted peace on earth or good-will among men. Originating under the auspices and in the days of darkness and despotism, they patronized darkness and despotism down to the Reformation. Ever encroaching on the rights of governments and people, they have constantly found it convenient to incorporate, as far as possible, the claims of the clergy with the principles and practice of religion ; and their advocates have not ceased to preach for Christian doctrines the commandments and devices of men.

To you it cannot be necessary to observe, that high church doctrines are not accommodated to the state of society, nor to the tolerant principles, nor to the ardent love of liberty which prevail in our country. It is well known that our church was formed after the Revolution with an eye to what was then believed to be the truth and simplicity of the Gospel ; and there appears to be some reason to regret that the motives which then governed have since been less operative.

We know that our obscure and unimportant corporation can do but little. Providence has placed you under different circumstances. You have stronger inducements to watchfulness, more means to do good, and more power to avert evil.

Permit us to hope that the subjects of this letter will engage your serious consideration. Whatever may be the result, we shall have the satisfaction of reflecting that we have done our duty, in thus explicitly protesting against measures and proceedings which, if persevered in, must and will, sooner or later, materially affect the tranquillity and welfare of the Church.

EXTRACTS FROM THE WILL OF JOHN JAY.

I, John Jay, of Bedford, in the county of West-chester, and State of New York, being sensible of the importance and duty of so ordering my affairs as to be prepared for death, do make and declare my last will and testament in manner and form following, viz.:— Unto HIM who is the author and giver of all good, I render sincere and humble thanks for his manifold and unmerited blessings, and especially for our redemption and salvation by his beloved Son. He has been pleased to bless me with excellent parents, with a virtuous wife, and with worthy children. His protection has accompanied me through many event-ful years, faithfully employed in the service of my country ; and his providence has not only conducted me to this tranquil situation, but also given me abun-dant reason to be contented and thankful. Blessed be his holy name. While my children lament my departure, let them recollect that in doing them good, I was only the agent of their Heavenly Father, and that he never withdraws his care and consolations from those who diligently seek him.

I would have my funeral decent, but not ostenta-tious. No scarfs—no rings. Instead thereof, I give two hundred dollars to any one poor deserving widow or orphan of this town, whom my children shall select.

·   ·   ·   ·   ·   ·   ·

I appoint all my children, and the survivors or survivor of them, executors of this my last will and testament. I wish that the disposition which I have therein made of my property, may meet with their approbation, and the more so, as their conduct relative to it has always been perfectly proper, reserved, and delicate. I cannot conclude this interesting act, without expressing the satisfaction I have constantly derived from their virtuous and amiable behavior. I thank them for having largely contributed to my happiness by their affectionate attachment and attention to me, and to each other. To the Almighty and Beneficent Father of us all, to his kind providence, guidance, and blessing, I leave and commend them.[1]

ACTION OF THE NEW YORK BAR ON THE DEATH OF JOHN JAY.

CITY HALL, NEW YORK, Tuesday, May 19, 1829,
Five O'clock, P. M.

The Bar of the State of New York, now attending the sitting of the Supreme Court, met pursuant to their adjournment, D. B. Ogden, Chairman; John Sudam, Secretary. James Tallmadge, Esq., Chairman of the Committee

---

[1] Mr. Jay died at his residence at Bedford, Westchester County, New York, May 17, 1829, in the eighty-fourth year of his age.

appointed this morning, reported the following Preamble and Resolutions, which were unanimously adopted.

The Committee respectfully report:

That the recent decease of the late venerable JOHN JAY is the cause of deep grief, and the present engrossing subject of private and public feeling.

John Jay was a native of our State; and a member of this Bar. The events of the American Revolution called him early into public life. His inherent love of political and virtuous liberty made him an early and active agent in laying the foundations of this nation, of which he soon became one of the brightest, and continued one of its fairest pillars. In 1777 he was appointed the first Chief Justice of this State, under the Constitution which he had eminently contributed to frame, and most of which was drafted by his pen. He was a member of the first Congress of the United States, and bore a conspicuous part in all its important duties, and presided for some time over the deliberations of that body. The exigencies of this nation required and commanded his great talents, discretion, firmness and skill, in various interesting and important duties during the Revolutionary struggle. At times as Chairman of the Committee of Public Safety he secured the domestic tranquillity, and at other times he was employed in important foreign missions and diplomatic trusts. He bore a prominent part in the negotiations for our Independence as a nation, and the ultimate treaty of peace. He continued to represent his country at foreign Courts for a number of years. He was, shortly after his return, called to preside as Chief Justice of the Supreme Court of the United States, which place he afterwards left to accept the Executive Chair of the State of New York. When he had performed that last and highest duty to his native State, he declined all further judicial or political employment, and retired to the calm shade of domestic retreat, where the evening of his days was spent in social and benevolent intercourse, and in the signal observance of that religion which had been the bright beam of the morning and the evening of his life, the rights and toleration of which he had secured to this people in one of the most important articles of our Constitution.

There is no place more fit, and no persons are more willing to express their sincere feelings on this occasion than this Bar, where the talents and acquirements of the deceased were so early and so often displayed.—Therefore,

Resolved, That the members of this Bar are impressed with deep grief upon the decease of their illustrious brother, John Jay. They find, however, a consolation in the reflection that his conduct through a long and useful life, has given a lustre to our profession and to this Bar, and that while his character for private virtues and public worth has justly endeared him to the nation, his patriotism, his great talents as a statesman, and his great acquirements as a jurist, his eminent piety as a Christian, and probity as a man, all unite to present him to the public as an example whose radiance points to the attainment of excellence.

Resolved, That in respect for the character of the deceased, the members of this Bar will wear crape during the period of thirty days.

Resolved, That the Chairman and Secretary are desired to transmit a copy of the proceedings of this meeting to the family of the deceased.

Resolved, That the proceedings be signed by the Chairman and Secretary, and published in the different newspapers of this city.

D. B. OGDEN, Chairman.

JOHN SUDAM, *Secretary.*

INDEX.

END OF VOLUME IV.